Financial reforms, stabilization and development in 21st-century Turkey

Haluk Haksal

Vernon Series in Economic Development

VERNON PRESS

www.vernonpress.com

In the Americas:
Vernon Press
1000 N West Street,
Suite 1200, Wilmington,
Delaware 19801
United States

In the rest of the world:
Vernon Press
C/Sancti Espiritu 17,
Malaga, 29006
Spain

Cover illustrations by Natalie Scott, reprinted with permission.
www.nataliescott.co.uk.

Vernon Series in Economic Development

Library of Congress Control Number: 2016959065

ISBN: 978-1-62273-168-8

Preface

This book provides insights on different phases a developing country has had to experience over decades while attempting to achieve economic development. The basic message is simple: Policy makers should not strive to achieve price stability at any cost, as stability in product markets does not necessarily mean that this would automatically be translated into economic development. As the title suggests, my aim is to discuss the impact of financial reforms on stability and development in Turkey. The Turkish Central Bank is placed at the center of the analysis as monetary policies have a significant impact both on stability and development.

It was the late 1990s. There was an ongoing widespread privatization process in Turkey. I was discussing with a senior from my circle who was commenting as follow: "You see, the government privatizes this sugar factory because it's in deficit, although it provides employment to so many people!!".

This view inspired me in writing the book as apparently it promoted the development in the country because it was against laying off of employees. However, we have to question how the wages of employees were to be funded, in case a state-owned enterprise was in deficit. What happens if a central bank prints more money than the GDP of an economy to fund, among others, deficits in the economy? Would this approach not create more inflationary pressure?

As one logs onto the Turkish Central Bank's website, after the reforms in central banking were undertaken in the early 2000s, the first sentence that appears on the screen is:

"The primary objective of the Bank is to achieve and maintain price stability".

This approach is understandable as Turkey had suffered from high inflation from the early 1970s to early 2000s, which has undoubtedly had a negative impact on economic development! While I point out in the book that the reform process on central bank independence launched in 2001 has been crucially important for price stability, I also emphasize the need for cooperation with government institutions to target unemployment rates, which would undermine its independence to some degree. At the end of the book, the reader will make his own opinion whether the monetary policy should exclusively focus on price stability, as it is highlighted on the Turkish Central Bank's website, or this should be one of its main objectives together with other objectives targeting development, for instance, monitoring also unemployment rates. In fact, there should be a path to be followed in between the two axes, i.e., decreasing unemployment levels without provoking price instability or targeting both price stability and the creation of employment. This study aims to provide a perspective on the need for such an approach.

The book has its origins from my Ph.D. studies at the University of Geneva. Therefore, the audience primarily is researchers, experts, economists, undergraduate and masters' students. Nevertheless, also non-specialists in the field, who have an interest in international economics and politics can only skip the technical parts and increase their understanding of this emerging economy, as the whole book is expressed in a simple language. While monetary policies followed over time are placed at the center of the study, the political processes within which the country was involved provide a historical perspective to readers who would like to learn more about the dynamics of Turkish politics. The time frame I examined goes mainly from 1980 to 2010, with some flashbacks to earlier times when appropriate. This also means that the book is not about an economic analysis of recent period as it mainly examines the monetary policies and its consequences in the time frame considered.

Despite the highly autonomous nature of researching, this book could not have been completed without the assistance, support and cooperation of innumerable people. This is a work of long years, enriched with discussions held with experts in different fields. I will not be able to mention everyone because of the limited space I have here. I am thankful to Sevket Pamuk, professor from Bogazici University and Yilmaz Akyuz, former director of the Division on Globalization and Development Strategies at the United Nations Conference on Trade and Development (UNCTAD), for their precious comments and suggestions both during the research and the revision processes in the last years. I would like to express my gratitude to my thesis director Victoria Curzon-Price, professor from the University of Geneva, who has shared her immense knowledge with me. Special thanks go to the members of my "Jury de thèse", Céline Carrère and Jonas Pontusson, professors from University of Geneva, Mehmet Arda, a former UNCTAD staff and professor from the University of Galatasaray and also Zuhayr Mikdashi professor from the University of Lausanne, for their availability and valuable suggestions, which enriched the overall content of the study. I am also thankful to Ahmet Faruk Aysan, Burak Saltoglu, and Mine Eder, professors from Bogazici University and Fatih Ozatay and Izak Atiyas, professors at TOBB and Sabanci University, respectively, for their comments and suggestions. I would like to thank Kevin Korner, a Deutsche Bank Research expert in "Global Risk Analysis" and Dominique O'Kane, a former Lehman Brothers expert in "Fixed Income Quantitative Credit Research" for their contribution as practitioners to the section on CDS related issues. I am also thankful to Botan Berker, the former general manager of Fitch Ratings Turkey, for the interview, which allowed me to include real life experiences regarding credit rating practices and country experiences.

I am thankful to several government officials and staff of various international organizations and private and public corporations for the discussions we held. It was meaningful and exciting for me to interview John Williamson, author of the "Washington Consensus", at the November 2009 UNCTAD International Debt Conference. I also interviewed Mikhail Kasyanov, former Russian Prime Minister, whom I had the opportunity to ask a few questions on the 1998 Russian debt crisis. I would like to thank a wide range of experts including Deniz Igan, economist at the IMF Research Department, Sahin Yavuz, senior expert in Turkish Competition Agency, Murat Topkaya and Serdar Erkilic (Turkish Central Bank Research Department), Hakan Tokac (Turkish Undersecretariat of Treasury) and many others that I cannot mention here.

I owe special thanks to my beloved Aynur Akkaya for her warm support since the beginning of the study. She believed in me and encouraged me through every difficulty that the different phases of this huge work implied. Finally, love to all my family, friends, and colleagues for their kind support.

Haluk Haksal

August 2016, at my garden in Lausanne

Table of Contents

List of figures

List of tables

List of abbreviations

ACFM	Asset Class Factor Model
AKP	Justice and Development Party
AP	Justice Party
ANAP	Motherland Party
BIST	Borsa Istanbul
BRSA	Banking Regulation and Supervision Agency
C	Consumption
CA	Current Account Balance
CAP	Common Agricultural Policy
CAPM	Capital Asset Pricing Model
CAR	Capital Adequacy Ratio
CB	Central Bank
CBI	Central Bank Independence
CBT	Central Bank of Turkey
CBRT	Central Bank of the Republic of Turkey
CDS	Credit Default Swap
CEFTA	Central European Free Trade Agreement
CGE	Computable General Equilibrium
CHP	Republican People's Party
CORS-TR	Continuously Operating Reference Stations
CMB	Capital Market Board
CPI	Consumer Price Index
DP	Democratic Party
DYP	True Path Party

EBRD	European Bank of Reconstruction and Development
ECTA	European Competitive Telecommunication Association
EEC	European Economic Community
EFTA	European Free Trade Agreement
EMS	European Monetary System
ERM	Exchange Rate Mechanism
ESA-95	European System of Accounts 1995
EU	European Union
FDI	Foreign Direct Investment
FGMs	First Generation Models
FIAS	Foreign Investment Advisory Service
FSF	Financial Stability Forum
FTA	Free Trade Agreement
FX	Foreign Exchange
G	Government Spending
GDFI	General Directorate for Foreign Investment
GDP	Gross Domestic Product
GNAT	Grand National Assembly of Turkey
GNP	Gross National Product
GS SCAD	Goldman Sachs Sustainability of Current Account Deficits Model
GSP	Generalized System of Preferences
HLIs	Highly Leveraged Institutions
I	Investment
IIPRs	Industrial and Intellectual Property Rights
ILO	International Labor Organization
INSPIRE	Infrastructure for Spatial Information in the European Community

IPU	Inter Parliamentary Union
IRA	Independent Regulatory Agency
ISDA	International Swaps and Derivatives Association
ISI	Import Substitution Industrialization
LDCs	Least Developed Countries
LTCM	Long Term Capital Management
MAGNET	Modular Agricultural GeNeral Equilibrium Tool
MC	Marginal Cost
M-F Model	Mundell-Fleming Model
MFN	Most Favored Nation
MiFID	Markets in Financial Instruments Directive
NDA	Net Domestic Asset
NFI	Net Factor Income
NPLs	Non-Performing Loans
NPAA	National Program for the Adoption of the *Acquis*
NRAs	National Regulatory Authorities
NX	Net Exports
OYAK	Armed Forces Mutual Assistance Foundation, in Turkish
PBCs	Political Business Cycles
PDV	Present Discounted Value
PPA	Public Procurement Agency
PPP	Purchasing Power Parity
PSBR	Public Sector Borrowing Requirement
PWC	Price Waterhouse Coopers
REER	Real Effective Exchange Rate
RP	Welfare Party

ROR	Rate of Return
S	Savings
SAA	Stabilization and Association Agreement
SDIF	Savings Deposit Insurance Fund
SGMs	Second Generation Models
SHP	Social Democrat People's Party
SIMSDI	Survey of Implementation of Methodological Standards for Direct Investment
SIPRI	Stockholm International Peace Research Institute
SODEP	Social Democracy Party
SOE	State Owned Enterprise
SPO	State Planning Organization
T	Taxes
TGMs	Third Generation Models
TL	Turkish Lira
TFEU	Treaty on the Functioning of the European Union
TOKI	Governmental Mass Housing Administration
TOR	Turnover Rate of (Central Bank) Governors
TSF	Turkish Sugar Factories
TURKSTAT/TUIK	Turkish Statistical Institute
TURKDEX	Turkish Derivatives Exchange
TUSIAD	Turkish Industry and Business Association
UIP	Uncovered Interest Parity
UN	United Nations
UNCTAD	United Nations Conference on Trade and Development

Y	Domestic Income or Gross Domestic Product
YOIKK	Coordination Council for the Improvement of the Investment Climate,
WIPO	World Intellectual Property Organization
WPI	Wholesale Price Index

Chapter 1

Introduction-hypotheses and research questions

"Ta Panta Rhei": No man ever steps in the same river twice, for it's not the same river and he's not the same man.

Heraklitus of Ephesus (544 B.C. - 483 B.C.)

Introduction

Turkey is a developing country that in the 1930s chose state control in the hope to realize strong economic growth. While state-led economic development model initially allowed a positive trend, it did not work in the long-term. However, dismantling state presence in the economy during the 1980s even worsened the situation, leading to serious financial crashes in the following years. Then, Turkey moved to reforming financial markets and it seems that something changed by the mid-2000s putting an end to persistent economic instability though there are still serious concerns regarding economic development by the eve of 2020s.

This book tells this exciting story!

1.1. Background to the research

I have chosen this topic in order to shed light on the dynamics behind the transition process from a state-led to a market-based economy, inspired to a considerable extent by the objective of gaining full membership of the European Union (EU). The integration process has involved unprecedented challenges as well as providing important economic and political insights. My objective is to focus in particular on the degree of Turkey's convergence to EU regulatory standards and to examine the impact of financial reforms from 1980 to 2010 on stability and development in Turkey.

This topic interests me because it offers an excellent opportunity to investigate several key factors behind a sound development policy. The book not only explores the complex relationship between economic instability and structural reforms in an emerging economy, but it also investigates why the international development policies proposed to developing countries have not always been successful.

1.2. Research problem - hypotheses - research questions

The role that governments play in devising economic reforms is the first factor, which needs to be examined. Turkey has traditionally pursued an inward-looking strategy through planned development programs where the state held a dominant position through public ownership. At the same time, its major goal has been to place itself within the Western world, which has always been identified with a functioning market economy[1]. For many years the pursuit of these inconsistent objectives was resolved in favor of State planning. However, aiming for full membership of the EU necessarily implied shifting the balance in favor of markets. Nowhere was this radical change more dramatic than in financial markets. How can a developing country with a state regulated and underdeveloped financial sector adopt a financial regulatory system designed for a highly sophisticated free-market financial system? What problems are likely to be encountered? This context leads me to investigate how culturally appropriate a de-politicized financial framework is for Turkey and how the deregulation of financial markets needs to be managed in an emerging market economy like Turkey's.

Having identified the **research problem**, I can now formulate my principal **research questions and hypotheses:**

- Do deregulation of financial markets and elimination of exchange controls on capital movements create conditions for stable growth?

[1] Throughout the book we identify the term "functioning" market economy as defined by the Copenhagen criteria introduced in section 1.6 below "The EU Requirements - Copenhagen Criteria".

- What is the role of institutions, culture, and tradition? What is the appropriate regulatory framework for an emerging market economy like Turkey?

Finally, subsidiary questions, which rose during my investigations included:

- What is the role of monetary stability and the attitude of the central bank? How do central bank policies affect the vulnerability of an economy? Is its independence important?

- Was the "institutional migration" successful? If not, why was it not? Is it possible that "import" of Western pro-market formal institutions, i.e., an independent central bank or free financial markets, was not compatible with Turkish traditions and caused chaos rather than successful transition? Or perhaps it did go rather well?

To conclude, the Republic of Turkey has a long history of importing Western institutions since its foundation in 1923 by Kemal Ataturk[2]. When import substitution industrialization (ISI) policy and State Owned Enterprises (SOEs) were the Western recommendation for economic development that is what Turkey did. When it was the period of the "Washington Consensus", Turkey followed. When it was the EU guidelines, again Turkey considered them as a blueprint. Finally, what has Turkey obtained from all these policy imports? After several decades of unstable macroeconomic conditions and problems, Turkey in the early 2010s was, under certain aspects, one of the most successful emerging economies in the world. It even out-performed many advanced EU economies in its public debt/GDP ratio in the second half of the 2000s. This perspective leads me to explain in the next section the context of the study.

1.3. Context of the study

Towards the end of the 1970s, several countries began a radical change in how to run their economies. In China, Deng Xiao Ping began turning China away from central planning towards decentralized markets. In the U.K., Margaret Thatcher began doing the same, while Ronald Reagan and Mikhail Gorbachev followed shortly after. The winds of change had begun to blow. Turkey, along with many other countries in Latin America and South East Asia, was also caught up in this movement. Unlike other developing economies, however,

---

[2] See Annex 1 for a chronological overview

Turkey had the added incentive that its aim was to join the EU (at that time). Not only were ideas changing, the incentive to apply them was pressing. This is a story of new ideas in economic development migrating around the world, applied with greater or lesser success depending on the country. It is a story of crises and the lessons to be learned from them. It is a story of how institutions developed in one part of the world become adopted and adapted in other parts of the world, each time with tensions, difficulties, crises. It is an on-going story of global intercultural institutional migration, of gradually sorting out best practices, adopting norms and standards, not in a forced top-down manner, but in a gradual, decentralized process of trial and error. This book tells the story and analyses the role that Turkey has played in this process from 1980 onwards (with some flashbacks to earlier times when appropriate) with special reference to the deregulation of its financial markets. One reason for concentrating on this area is because, in country after country, the transition process from state-planning to a market-based economy resulted in dramatic financial crises. Can we learn from these crises? Can the integration of an emerging economy into the global market become smoother? And in Turkey's case, what role did the EU play?

I shall give particular consideration to two essential anchors which have served as benchmarks in the adaptation of Turkey's financial market regulations to international standards: The "Washington Consensus" principles, an international development policy based on agreement among, principally, the IMF and the World Bank[3] and the "Acquis Communautaire", the legal and institutional framework by which the EU defines its requirements[4]. Turkey's structural changes in its financial markets were launched in 1980 in line with the "Washington Consensus" principles, at a time when deregulation of financial markets was broadly associated with economic growth.

This process coincided with Turkey's political will to advance the European Community integration program by introducing structural reforms. Turkey applied for a full membership in 1987 and the deregulation process reached its pinnacle two years later, in 1989, with the full liberalization of the capital account. However, shortcomings emerged due to the lack of an adequate institutional framework culminating in a financial crisis in 1994, a severe shock to the economy. Adoption of the Customs Union with the EU in the aftermath

---

[3] A detailed examination of the "Washington Consensus" principles is provided in Section 2.1

[4] Commission of the European Communities (2001), p. 46

of the 1994 crisis was not only one of the objectives envisioned by the 1963 Association Agreement but also represented a further step towards integration with the EU[5]. The Luxembourg European Council meeting in December 1997 proposed a strategy to promote Turkey's accession and identified adoption of the "Acquis Communautaire" as a key element for convergence[6]. The European Commission adopted a communication in March 1998 on a "European Strategy" for Turkey, incorporating the initial operational proposals of the Luxembourg strategy. In December 1999, the Helsinki European Council granted Turkey the status of candidate country. Despite this promising progress, the economy experienced the most severe financial crisis of its history a little over a year later in February 2001. Nonetheless, accession negotiations started in October 2005.

The impression given by this sequence of events is that of a country with a great political will to adopt huge economic reforms at break-neck speed, somehow even using the inevitable accompanying crises to continue forcing the economy to bend to the political will of the nation.

1.4. Justification of research and Methodology

My study explores the case of a country in a unique position with several contradictory features. Turkey, a candidate country to the EU, is at the same time an emerging economy. Traditional state-led development plans were in conflict with the functioning market economy philosophy of the EU. Moreover, while several reforms undertaken during the 1920s and 1930s showed that Turkey aimed to become part of the secular Western world, it also presents an Oriental and Mediterranean style as a historical heritage. In fact, the Turkish Republic founded in 1923 as a national secular state is composed of many religious and ethnic groups, the Muslim-Turkish group representing a clear majority (more than 90 percent). These cultural and historical differences make the whole process more complex.

These contradictory features have created particular challenges for policy makers both in the EU and Turkey. Given that influential political figures in

---

[5] Customs Union entered into force in January 1996.

[6] Commission of the European Communities (1999), p. 30

positions of power, risk being removed in a competitive environment, the process of adopting modern rules and regulations also represents a major political challenge. Financial market regulatory reforms are no different and can, therefore, be considered as a Litmus test for the application of the rest of the "Acquis Communautaire".

Most of the research on transition economies have a tendency to associate increased growth and prosperity with price stability. However, there is little research on how the unstable, volatile and inflationary environment can also result in rapid growth. Perhaps the occasional crisis is the price to be paid for unusually rapid growth? Does it matter the way growth is financed? I examine the Turkish case in order to find the causes and learn the lessons, which can become useful guidelines for other developing countries opening their economy to global markets.

A further justification for this study is its relatively uncommon qualitative methodology and emphasis on institutions in a field more accustomed to quantitative research. The book topic allows me to explore what a quantitative analysis cannot explain. I investigate, for instance, the following question: Why did some emerging economies, including Turkey that introduced stabilization programs successfully, achieve high GDP and low CPI levels but have nonetheless been unable to avoid financial crises? In this context, a quantitative methodology working on time series of GDP or CPI data does not suggest an answer. Moreover, I observe the particular context in a specific country, which allows me to explore the impact of diverging cultural, traditional and historical factors and introduce them into the analysis. Therefore, to test out the initial hypotheses I use a qualitative methodology. I show that a weak institutional and regulatory framework was a major reason behind unstable conditions and crises. Thus, my approach is based on the analysis of relations and not on analysis of correlations as in a quantitative methodology.

I used official statistical data and documents from both Turkish government authorities and the EU, International Financial Statistics from the IMF, Datastream and Reuters' data from Universities of Geneva and Lausanne. The methods I used are observations and interviews held with experts in different areas including personal interviews and telephone and e-mail contact. These constituted the most appropriate methods for my research topic.

My findings demonstrate the impact of specific changes in the institutional and regulatory framework on the macro-financial risk profile of Turkey. This provides insight into why some measure of economic success was finally achieved. To prove my results, I use a variety of data. For instance, I make a comparison between macro data and assignments from a major credit ratings agency (Fitch Ratings). Then, I compare these results with Credit Default Swap

(CDS) spreads. Finally, I confirm my findings with Foreign Direct Investment (FDI) flows, which are also an independent measure of how external observers view the Turkish experiment. All these data on Turkey are compared with data from a sample of EU economies, which gives me the possibility to place Turkey in a comparative perspective.

Consequently, I enumerate the contributions of my study to the ongoing debate as follows: First, it approaches the development problem from the angle of the institutional and regulatory framework, thereby exploring factors that would be lost in a quantitative approach. Secondly, it identifies reasons for the chronic instability of the Turkish economy as well as factors behind some undeniable economic successes. Nevertheless, while an increased GDP and reduced CPI levels are important, my analysis shows that this needs to be achieved together with reforms introducing an adequate de-politicized regulatory framework. In the absence of the latter, the likelihood of a crisis will be higher, which in turn would cause a high level of inflation and low or negative growth, together with a severe shock that will hit the economy. Thus, the study illustrates basic elements behind a stable, and not volatile, growth. Finally, a book-length study examining the reforms Turkey undertook in the financial area in this period does not exist, which enhances its originality and contributes to the literature.

To note that the concept of economic development is different than economic growth though these have been used interchangeably in literature[7]. Growth refers to the market value of final goods and services produced in an economy in a year, typically measured by gross domestic product (GDP). An increase in per-capita GDP is a characteristic of economic growth. Nevertheless, it does not necessarily lead to an improvement in living standards of people if growth is not evenly distributed. Development is a broader concept than growth as it consists of the removal of different types of obstacles that leave people with fewer opportunities of exercising their preferences and it thus aims to enable individuals to make effective choices by increasing their capabilities[8]. While growth may be seen as a necessary condition for development, high GDP growth does not necessarily contribute to development. Poor countries are also less developed but for instance, some of the oil-rich countries with high per capita GDP present difficulties in different areas of development. In case the growth is low or unstable, governments will be obliged to cut public expenditures including education, healthcare, and

[7] Grabowski, R., Self, S. and Shields, M.P. (2015), pp, 5, 7, 9

[8] Chandler, D. (2012), pp. 115, 116, Amartya (1999), pp. 11-19

social welfare. Thus, economic growth must occur first and only then policy makers can direct these resources to promote development[9].

There is no a universal framework to measure the degree of development, as different individuals in different socioeconomic contexts may have different development priorities. Therefore, a variety of variables and indexes are used as a proxy for measuring development, i.e., a measure of health (life expectancy, infant mortality, immunization rates), education (youth or adult literacy rate, enrollment rates, average years of education) or other economic conditions (unemployment rate, inequality of income distribution, child labor, poverty rate, women's literacy and employment rates etc.).

This study is on the impact of EU-inspired financial market regulations on stabilization in Turkey and on emerging problems. In addition, I will also question in chapter 5 whether stable circumstances achieved thanks to the adoption of these international development policies contributed to development. I will have a look at one of the economic conditions above, the unemployment rate, to have an idea about the size of this social phenomenon over time. I will then suggest in Chapter 6 for further research the use of other development proxies from inequality of income distribution and women's literacy and employment rates to life expectancy and infant mortality and others, to examine the degree of development in Turkey.

Finally, the book also shows that while "institutional migration" is common and emerging markets around the world frequently adopt institutional features from elsewhere, local differences and inconsistent policies can often lead to unexpected results.

1.5. Outline of the book

Throughout this study, the European Commission's regular reports, the European Council's decisions and the Treaty on the Functioning of the European Union (TFEU) have been the main source of "EU requirements", while Annex 1 provides information also regarding the different stages of relations between Turkey and the "Community". The book is composed of six chapters:

---

[9] O'Hearn, D. (2009), p. 1

Chapter 1 is the introduction, which lays the foundations for the book. Chapter 2 examines the Washington Consensus principles-led deregulation process in Turkey. Section 2.1 describes the "Washington Consensus" principles, which were closely followed during the deregulation process in several emerging economies, including Turkey. I examine the case of Thailand as a proxy and observe that the absence of an adequate institutional and regulatory framework was one of the root causes of the 1997 East Asian currency crisis, which resulted from an unsustainable asset bubble. Section 2.2 focuses on the deregulation process of Turkish financial markets and analyzes problems arising from the adaptation of the "Washington Consensus" principles and of the EU "acquis" into national legislation. It questions factors behind financial instability and investigates the role of the State through a survey of previous studies in literature. Section 2.2.1 covers the period from 1980 to 1988, during which policy makers introduced the "Washington Consensus" principles, and examines the Turkish Central Bank's monetary policy through an analysis of its balance sheet.

Chapter 3 examines the impact of international development policies on the Turkish economy with an emphasis on the dynamics behind the problems that can potentially arise with their implementation. In section 3.1, I overview business cycle theory and introduce the Mundell-Fleming framework. While the former emphasizes the role of interest rates and provides insight on the dynamics of boom-bust cycles in the first half of the 20th century, the latter makes evident the impact of the exchange rate regime chosen on the effectiveness of central bank policies. In section 3.2, I examine "currency crisis models". While "first generation models" are an extension of the Mundell-Fleming model, I use the latter to explain the 1994 financial crisis, whereas I use the "second generation models" and the "third generation models" to explain the 2001 Turkish currency crisis. Thus, sections 3.1 and 3.2 provide us with a theoretical perspective on problems that can arise in emerging markets integrating into global markets. In section 3.2.3.1, I explain the main features of hedge funds which can, in certain circumstances, lead to destabilizing short-term portfolio investment in emerging economies. Section 3.3 examines how the Turkish financial markets collapsed in 1994 and 2001. Section 3.3.1 covers the period from 1989 to the 1994 financial crisis and considers problems that appeared in adopting international standards. Section 3.3.2 analyzes the period from 1995 to 2002. It discusses the implications of realizing the Customs Union with the EU, a milestone in the process for full membership. Then, an analysis of the banking sector's fragile structure in the same section leads to a detailed analysis of dynamics behind the 2001 currency crisis.

Chapter 4 examines institutional transformation from 1999 to 2002. Section 4.1 focuses on adoption of the EU-inspired regulations in reforming the Turkish

Central Bank and the creation of independent supervisory institutions. Section 4.1.1 starts with a review of EU requirements on monetary policy. Then, section 4.1.2 introduces a theoretical discussion aiming to define central bank independence. Section 4.1.3 examines how the Turkish Central Bank gained its independence and section 4.1.4 focuses on the creation of independent regulatory agencies. Section 4.2 examines political efforts to adopt the EU-inspired standards on privatizations, FDI and property rights over time. Sections 4.2.1 and 4.2.2 present improvements in the privatization process and FDI flows as evidence of the effect of adoption of EU-inspired institutional and regulatory changes. In addition, these sections aim to demonstrate the impact of improved institutional climate on country risk perceptions. Section 4.2.3 overviews the property rights situation in Turkey.

Chapter 5 examines the impact of EU-inspired regulatory reforms on Turkey's macro-financial risk profile. It uses market-based metrics to measure the degree of success of these reforms. Sections 5.1 and 5.2 examine two major market indicators of risk exposure, namely credit ratings assignments and CDS spreads. Thus, this section not only shows the improvements in Turkey's macro-financial risk profile after the completion of reforms but also compares Turkey with a sample of EU countries in terms of risk and expected return. Section 5.3 addresses certain outcomes that diverged from expectations in adopting the EU standards.

Finally, Chapter 6 draws our findings together, discusses the impact of adopting international standards, through a process of trial and error, on overall growth and unemployment in Turkey.

1.6. Scope of the book

While the book outline above highlights major topics covered in this study, I would like to make evident its scope as its basic structure includes also non-economic, i.e., political aspects, due to its interdisciplinary nature. This study aims to investigate the impact of financial market regulatory reforms introduced in Turkey during the 2000s, which boils down to the question of **regulatory and institutional quality**.

The state shapes the economic life of a country in a variety of ways[10] and its performance interacts with the quality of institutions. Nevertheless, it is

---

[10] La Porta, R. et al. (1998), p. 6

difficult to define the concept of regulatory quality as it will depend on preferences of different agents. While international institutions like the World Bank and OECD would associate the purpose of "good" regulation with the achievement of sustainable economic growth, poverty reduction, and better governance, a politician in the office can associate it with regulations that would increase, among others, his popularity[11]. On the other hand, a social scientist would define institutional quality according to how economic and socio-political considerations are balanced within his preference function[12].

Empirical overview to institutional quality

Most empirical measures of institutional quality identify it with non-interventionist economic policies, protection of property rights, the rule of law, bureaucratic "red tapes", the quality of the judiciary and the level of corruption[13]. Different authors use different proxies leading them to a variety of results. La Porta et al. (1998) measured institutional quality using proxies for interventionism, quality of bureaucracy, government size and political freedom. Ades and di Tella (1999) and Treisman (1998) focused on rent-seeking opportunities and corruption in the absence of competition. Bliss and Di Tella (1997) investigated whether competition reduces the level of corruption. Treisman (1998) also investigated causes of corruption discussing a variety of potential factors ranging from cultural and institutional traditions to historical legacy[14]. Rajan and Zingales (2000) focused on historical case studies and argued that competition reduces rents and consequently improves the quality of institutions. Cadot (1987) built a model of corruption in the context of game theory and investigated incentive structure behind bureaucratic procedures. Straub (2000) argued that the extent of corruption was a function of the size of SOEs, the degree of protectionism, the level of price controls and the number of regulations, among others. Islam and Montenegro (2002) found that trade openness is positively associated with institutional quality in addition to freedom of the press and checks and balances in the political system. They explained that more open economies tended to have "better institutions"[15] because in a more competitive context, economic agents with poor institutions

[11] World Bank (2010), p. 3

[12] Ibid

[13] World Bank (2010), p. 7, Knack and Keefer (1995), pp. 1, 2, North, D. (1981), p. 19

[14] Treisman (1998), p. 46

[15] Islam and Montenegro (2002), p. 3

would have incentives to change them for better ones. Moreover, rent-seeking and corruption would become harder when there is competition among agents. Finally, agents in open economies learn from practices in other economies leading to an improvement in institutional quality, for example, domestic and foreign businesses can lobby for better regulation in the banking sector. All these factors can contribute to a rapid evolution of institutional quality in open economies[16].

To note that measuring regulatory quality is not an easy task as it will depend on proxies selected. Let us overview the approach of an international institution in measuring regulatory quality.

The OECD approach in measuring regulatory quality

The OECD has developed indicators, through a series of surveys, to analyze the regulatory practices of OECD countries over time. These range from regulations promoting transparency and stimulating competition to those eliminating unnecessary regulatory barriers to trade and investment[17]. These proxies for "good" regulations aim to measure whether the countries' regulatory systems meet the quality standards that reflect the best practices. By the year 2005, 26 of the 30 OECD countries promoted regulatory reforms and 21 of them had introduced policies expressing explicit principles of "good" regulation[18]. The successful design and implementation of a new regulatory framework depend also on the adequate set of institutions to introduce and maintain regulatory quality. Independent regulatory agencies are an example of specific institutions serving this purpose[19]. On the other hand, quality assurance over time requires the use of a variety of tools ranging from consultation with businesses and the public to regulatory impact analysis[20], the latter aiming to identify and monitor whether the expected results of regulatory proposals are achieved. The most important contribution of the OECD regulatory impact analysis is not the precision of calculations but understanding the real-world impact of new regulations, i.e., whether regulations achieve the policy objectives at the lowest

---

[16] Islam and Montenegro (2002), p. 4

[17] For a detailed expositions of OECD Indicators of Regulatory Management Systems by the year 2005, see OECD (2008a), p. 2

[18] OECD (2008a), p. 3

[19] OECD (2008a), p. 3

[20] Ibid., p. 4

total cost[21]. By 2005, all OECD member countries had carried out some form of regulatory impact analysis, aiming to select "good" regulations in their specific contexts[22].

To note that, while the importance of institutions is widely accepted, there is no theoretical framework to identify which institutions, in what combinations are the most important ones for economic development[23]. Major reasons behind this are, in addition to measurement difficulties, the historical, cultural and social divergences among countries.

Historical and cultural divergences in the Turkish context

Considering country-specific conditions, the historical background I introduce in chapters 2, 3 and 4 provides a larger perspective on what the Turkish Republic inherited from the Ottoman Empire and the development approach since its foundation in 1923. The Ottoman sultans had absolute power through near complete control over the military and the bureaucracy[24]. While the Empire had traditionally maintained lands under state ownership and had intervened in economic management when necessary, the Republic of Turkey promoted and respected private property rights[25]. However, state intervention in economy occurred in a variety of forms and lasted until the adoption of the Washington Consensus principles in 1980. This began the initial phase of non-interventionist economic policies and made evident the need for unfamiliar market compatible institutions. This book aims to show that while the Washington Consensus prescriptions were necessary, they were, at the same time, not sufficient as Turkey needed an "adequate" institutional and regulatory framework, especially in its financial markets. To explain what I mean by the term "adequate" in the Turkish context let us first introduce the EU membership requirements[26].

---

[21] OECD (2008b), pp. 3, 4

[22] OECD (2008a), p. 6

[23] Payne, M. and Losada, C. (1999), p. 4

[24] La Porta, R. et al. (1998), p. 11

[25] Section 4.2.3.1

[26] I use the terms « adequate » and « appropriate » interchangeably throughout the book.

The EU requirements - Copenhagen Criteria

The European Council identified in 1993 the economic and political requirements (Copenhagen criteria) that the candidate countries need to fulfill for full membership. These are[27]:

1. the political criteria**:** stability of institutions guaranteeing democracy, the rule of law, human rights, and respect for and protection of minorities;
2. the economic criteria: the existence of a functioning market economy as well as the capacity to cope with competitive pressures and market forces within the Union;
3. the institutional criteria: the ability to take on the obligations of membership including adherence to the aims of political, economic and monetary union. It includes the whole range of policies and measures that constitute the Acquis Communautaire that candidate countries must adopt, implement and enforce. This requires the administrative capacity to transpose European Community legislation into national law, to implement it and to effectively enforce it through appropriate administrative and judicial structures.

   [....]

Regarding the economic criteria, the European Commission defined a series of sub-criteria:

1. Being **a functioning market** economy requires:
   - the existence of a broad consensus about essentials of economic policy;
   - macroeconomic stability (including price stability, sustainable public finances, and external accounts);
   - a free interplay of market forces (including liberalized process and trade);
   - free market entry and exit (including issues of establishment/bankruptcies of firms);
   - an adequate legal system (including a system of property rights, enforceability of laws/contracts) and a sufficiently developed financial sector.

---

[27] European Commission, official website

2. Being **competitive** in the EU requires:
   - the existence of a functioning market economy;
   - sufficient human and physical capital (including education, research, and infrastructure);
   - adequate sectoral and enterprise structures (including issues of enterprise restructuring, sectoral shift, role of small and medium-sized enterprises);
   - limited state influence on competitiveness (including issues of trade policy, competition policy, state aids, support for small and medium-sized enterprises);
   - sufficient trade and investment integration with the EU.

In addition, it argued that[28]:

"The progress of candidate countries in meeting economic accession criteria is assessed annually by the Commission in its progress reports on each candidate country."

I examine in particular the first two conditions of the Copenhagen criteria, for a functioning market economy, namely:

- the existence of a broad consensus about essentials of economic policy;
- and macroeconomic stability (including price stability, sustainable public finances, and external accounts).

This is the reason why this study mainly examined the way the EU requirements on central banking were adapted to Turkey. I also focus on other Copenhagen economic criteria when these had a complementary function in telling the story, i.e., meeting the EU requirements in areas ranging from competition and state aids to industrial and intellectual property rights, and property rights themselves.

In the light of the literature on institutions, the approach of the OECD on measuring regulatory quality and the Copenhagen criteria introduced above, I can now make clear what I mean by an "adequate" institutional and regulatory framework in Turkish financial markets.

---

[28] European Commission, official website

What do I mean by an "adequate" institutional and regulatory framework in my study?

I start with the Copenhagen criteria for a functioning market economy. Turkish economic policies were traditionally politically managed until 1980, while it experienced macroeconomic instability from the early 1970s to 2000s. The definition of "functioning" market economy in Copenhagen criteria above leads me to state that Turkey lacked a crucially important institution for macroeconomic stabilization that is an independent lender of last resort: the Central Bank. Its independence is essential to combat crony capitalism and the constant politicization of economic affairs, without which it cannot achieve a stable macroeconomic monetary environment. These ends must correspond to a broad consensus about essentials of economic policy. This is the reason why the study focused on the Turkish Central Bank. In addition, the creation of an independent regulatory agency in the banking sector fulfilled another basic need in the Turkish economy, namely to de-politicize the interaction between the central bank and the banking sector. This was crucially important for stability in financial markets leading to a functioning market economy. Moreover, the other Copenhagen criteria allowed me to investigate the dynamics of the Turkish economy over several decades and to shed light on its historical and cultural features. Although these are not directly related to the Turkish financial markets, it is important to have a broad view of historical and cultural heritage in addition to political trends in order to increase our understanding of specific conditions and features of the Turkish economy. Thus:

- I examine the way "free interplay of market forces and free market entry and exit" were introduced in Turkey by investigating aspects ranging from the Customs Union with the EU to the FDI policy, privatizations and state aids, all requiring regulatory reforms;
- I discuss the evolution of the "legal system of property rights" over decades to investigate which reforms Turkey envisaged to introduce, in an attempt to get closer to EU standards;
- I emphasize the importance of the creation of an independent regulatory agency aiming to assure competition in Turkish markets: The Turkish Competition Agency.

To note that both the Washington Consensus principles and the Copenhagen criteria broadly promote private initiative. Nevertheless, while the Washington Consensus served only to dismantle state presence in the economy, the EU requirements contributed to macroeconomic and financial stability through the creation of an "adequate" institutional and regulatory framework. Thus, I identify the term "adequate" in the Turkish context with institutions that allow both a functioning market economy and the appearance of competitive forces in markets. More specifically, the creation of an independent supervisory institution on competition in 1997, another in the banking sector in 2000 and introducing regulatory reforms in 2001 allowing the Central Bank to become an independent institution, correspond to an "adequate" institutional and regulatory framework in the context of this study. One of the proxies allowing me to measure whether Turkey adopted an "adequate" institutional and regulatory framework in the banking sector is the following: It gained, by the mid-2000s, its intermediation function between the financial sector and the real economy, as during previous decades, banks used to make profit mainly through speculative operations, i.e., the interest rate carry trades (see Chapter 3).

On the other hand, the book attempts also to make evident the problems related to the adoption of the inflation targeting framework. It allows me to question whether this policy could be the "adequate" one also in promoting development in Turkey over time, as high and persistent unemployment rates during the 2010s have signaled the need for policies capable also for the creation of employment. To note that Turkey adopted the inflation-targeting monetary policy and the central bank independence as the global best practice in April 2001 and the CBRT's mandate is defined as follows: "The primary objective of the Bank is to achieve and maintain price stability."

Throughout the book, the reader will question and make his own opinion whether the CBRT should have a unique mandate as defined above or broader mandates, including the development-oriented ones. We will observe that the inflation-targeting monetary policy has allowed a relative price stability in the general price level in the Turkish case, without nevertheless having a significant impact on the real aspects of the economy.

1.7. Definition: an additional 11th principle to the "Washington Consensus"

During my examination of financial market regulatory framework changes, I present the two major anchors that Turkey followed in opening its economy to global markets: The "Washington Consensus" principles and the EU "Acquis Communautaire". During the 1980s, Turkey implemented all "Washington Consensus" prescriptions except the last one, on the protection of property rights. A politicized state based economic management, together with a weak regulatory framework, impeded the achievement of the two major goals of financial market reform: The creation of competitive forces and the attainment of a functioning market economy. In chapters 2 and 3, I show that during the two decades of deregulation of financial markets from the early 1980s to the early 2000s, Turkey suffered from highly unstable macroeconomic circumstances. I identify the reason behind instability as being the absence of a de-politicized institutional framework. Thus, I propose an additional **11th principle to the "Washington Consensus"** which I define as follows:

> "A de-politicized institutional and regulatory framework through which the state presence assures the respect of the rule of law and protects property rights. In this framework, while the presence of state is essential, it is needed to be present through supervisory regulatory agencies far from political influence, assuring formation of competitive forces in markets aiming thus to promote and reinforce private sector-led development."

We will observe in Chapter 5 the impact of our 11th element of "Washington Consensus" on the Turkish economy.

1.8. Delimitations of scope and assumptions

I identified my research problem as how culturally appropriate a de-politicized institutional framework for re-conceptualizing economic management in Turkey might be. Thus, my book is a case study on a specific country adopting a Western-style pro-market regulatory framework. I investigate whether this "institutional migration", in terms of Douglass North, has been successful. Douglass North emphasized the role of informal constraints such as culture, habits, and codes of conduct specific to single cases which cannot be changed by the will of governments[29]. While "import" of Western pro-market formal institutions (like an independent central bank or free financial markets) may be possible, I investigate whether these formal rules are compatible with Turkish "informal constraints". While I will explore these issues further throughout the book, I cannot state that another emerging market economy adopting pro-Western market rules will face the same degree of difficulty as Turkey. For instance, I will demonstrate that in Turkey historically, public ownership created inefficiencies and persistent fiscal deficits, while the Central Bank functioned as a state agency to meet government deficits by creating high-powered money. Attempts to make the Central Bank independent provided incentives to the banking sector to purchase government securities. While I will examine these aspects in detail during the book, here I want to emphasize that these problems reflect specific circumstances related to the Turkish case. In Turkey, de-politicized regulatory reforms were introduced two decades after the initiation of the deregulation process. Would such a delay also be the case in other emerging economies? Differences between countries will depend in part on government relations with interest groups whose power will fluctuate according to changes in the fortunes of political parties. In the 1990s, Turkey experienced political scandals related to bank defaults and organized crime. Would this be the case in another country and cause a delay in achievement of reforms?

Therefore, while I will draw conclusions based on the importance of the institutional and regulatory framework as part of a sound development policy, I will assume that country-specific conditions will still, to a certain extent, influence the outcome.

---

[29] North, D.C., (1994), pp. 360-366

EU "requirement" versus EU "inspired" rules

I associate the term EU "requirements" with the EU Commission's Progress Reports on Turkey and the "Acquis Communautaire", which involve an obligation for a candidate country. Nevertheless, this study focuses on the way the EU requirements are adapted to the Turkish environment, which can potentially give an outcome diverging from the expected one. The following example aims to make clear this aspect: State aids have always been an important obstacle in achieving a functioning market economy in Turkey. An independent regulatory agency on state aid is an EU requirement, as frequently emphasized in the EU Commission's Progress Reports on Turkey during the 2000s. To note that the Turkish government finally created the State Aids Supervisory and Regulatory Agency in 2010[30]. Nevertheless, it was established under the auspices of a ministerial department, far from the spirit of the EU requirements on this subject. Therefore, in the context of this study I call an "EU-inspired" institution or rule, the adapted version of the original EU "requirements" to local conditions. This implies that the adapted version in Turkey can potentially either correspond to EU "requirements" or diverge from the latter to different degrees. To test this divergence can be subject to further research in the years ahead.

1.9. Conclusion

This chapter laid the foundations for the book. It introduced the research problem, research questions and hypotheses. It went on to explain the purpose, justify the research, describe the methodology and emphasize its contributions to the field. It then outlined the study, explained the scope and gave the limitations. On these foundations, I initiate the book with the "Washington Consensus" principles in Chapter 2.

---

[30] Section 4.1.4, discussion points 2 and 3

Chapter 2

Deregulation Process and Macroeconomic Stability

Introduction

The Chapter 1 identified the research issues, hypotheses and outlined the book. This chapter aims to investigate the first research question of the study:

> "Do deregulation of financial markets and elimination of exchange controls on capital movements create conditions for stable growth?"

Section 2.1 is organized around four major topics: an overview of the "Washington Consensus", its implementation in Thailand, major critics of the "Washington Consensus" and my view on these prescriptions. Section 2.2 is on the implementation of these prescriptions in Turkey. It starts with a historical background on the Turkish economy. Then, it attempts to define financial stability and questions what kind of institutions Turkey would need to achieve stability in its financial markets. Finally, it examines the way the "Washington Consensus" principles were introduced in Turkey as well as the Turkish Central Bank's balance sheet and its monetary policy from 1980 to 1988.

2.1. Washington Consensus

John Williamson, economics professor, advisor to the IMF from 1972 to 1974 and author of numerous studies on international monetary and development issues, coined the term "Washington Consensus" in 1989, to designate a list of policy instruments for Latin American countries that became a blueprint for international development policy. The list represented a new agreed-upon structure[31] for investment, capital, and productivity as a sound development policy alternative to state intervention[32]. The "Washington Consensus" identified an excessive state involvement as the main cause of weak economic progress and proposed private sector-led development as a solution. Reducing the size of large public sectors in favor of private initiative was expected to lead to a more efficient allocation of resources. The economic policies suggested as remedies to underdevelopment were prudent macroeconomic policies in an outward-oriented economy and free market dynamics[33]. This new, bottom-up approach was to be introduced through the following instruments:

1. Fiscal discipline:

   John Williamson pointed out that despite diverging interpretations of fiscal discipline[34] there was a very broad agreement that large and persistent fiscal deficits were a major source of macroeconomic instability in the form of unstable prices, payment deficits, and capital flight. Unless the deficit was used to finance productive infrastructure investment, it was a sign of policy failure to match public expenditures with public revenues[35];

2. Reordering public expenditures:

   The spirit behind this point was to reduce public expenditure in politically sensitive areas that receive more resources than returns, i.e., reducing subsidies[36]. Moreover, this point proposed also redirecting expenditures towards primary health, education, and public infrastructure investment in an attempt to improve resource allocation and income distribution[37];

---

[31] This was a broad agreement among the United States' government, the Federal Reserve, International Financial Institutions (IFIs) and academia (Williamson, J. (1990), p. 1).

[32] Ibid., p. 1

[33] Ibid., p. 11

[34] One view advanced that fiscal discipline does not necessarily imply a balanced budget, but rather a stable debt/GDP ratio. Similarly, another view considered that short-term deviations from a balanced budget were acceptable as long as they were cancelled out over the entire business cycle. Another issue open to debate was the term "primary deficit", which excludes interest payments on public debt, emphasizing only expenditures that were in principle directly controllable by the authorities and reducing significance of the cost of debt service (Williamson, J. (1990), p. 2).

[35] Ibid., p. 3

[36] Ibid., p. 4

[37] Ibid., p. 5

3. Tax reform:

Although views diverged on this point and represented varying degrees of aversion to tax increases, the broad agreement was to propose tax increases only as an inferior alternative to expenditure cuts;

4. Interest rate liberalization:

The "Washington Consensus" agreed that two main principles should guide the level of interest rates. First, interest rates needed to be market-determined to avoid misallocation of resources. Second, positive real interest rates were necessary to discourage capital flight, to encourage savings and to make capital accumulation more likely. John Williamson underlined that it could be difficult to achieve and maintain positive and moderate market determined interest rates over time, in particular when the latter diverged considerably from international benchmark rates;

5. Maintaining a competitive exchange rate:

According to "Washington Consensus" while market forces were considered major drivers behind the exchange rates, they needed to be, at the same time, consistent with macroeconomic objectives. Thus, in the case of a developing country, the real exchange rate needed to be sufficiently competitive to maximize GDP growth while maintaining, at the same time, a sustainable current account deficit. In addition, such exchange rate level needed also to be stable over time as private-sector confidence is determinant in attracting further investment in potential export industries. A competitive real exchange rate implicitly assumed an "outward oriented" policy rather than import substitution. John Williamson, unlike several economists who supported either firmly fixed or freely floating regimes, favored[38] a "fixed but flexible" approach[39];

6. Trade Policy:

According to "Washington Consensus", import liberalization was another element of an "outward oriented" economic policy. The ability to import intermediate products at competitive prices had a positive impact on exports, contrary to protectionist policies which avoided foreign competition and thus created costly distortions with a negative impact on exports. There were

---

[38] Williamson, J. (2000), p. 253

[39] The so called "intermediate regime" or "soft pegs" (see Table 3.3, at the end of section 3.3.1). I will analyze this aspect under the Mundell-Fleming framework, in section 3.3.2.3 "discussion" points "7" and "8".

diverging views on two aspects: The first concerned new industries which could merit a substantial but strictly temporary protection. The second related to timing: Step by step or rapid liberalization;

7. Liberalization of inward FDI:

The "Washington Consensus" disapproved restrictions on inward FDI arguing that this type of investment can provide needed capital and know-how and be useful in reducing borrowing requirements of the economy and thus can potentially replace part of the international public debt[40];

8. Privatization:

According to "Washington Consensus", advantages of privatization ranged from its positive impact on government budget to increased efficiency. The sale of the SOEs was to provide the government with cash revenue in the short-term. Additionally, the fact that government will not need to provide any future financial support alleviated budgetary liabilities in the long-term. However, the main rationale behind privatization lay in disciplines and incentives for efficiency provided by the private sector when compared with SOEs. According to "Washington Consensus", market risk faced by private enterprises motivated their managers to consider problems seriously, whereas the subsidies that kept state enterprises from defaulting reduced the incentive for efficiency in the public sector;

9. Deregulation:

The process of deregulation was initiated in the United States by the Carter administration in the late 1970s and was carried forward during the Reagan administration during the 1980s and by Deng Xiao Ping in China in the same period of the "Washington Consensus". The success of these policies within the United States and elsewhere led to assume that similar benefits could also be obtained in the developing world. Several Latin American countries were highly regulated at that time, with the regulatory framework covering price controls, import barriers, restrictions on foreign investment inflows and profit outflows, high corporate income taxes and arbitrary credit allocation. Besides the negative effects of the regulation itself, low salaries received by regulators created the potential for corruption. The consequent distortions in productive activity, i.e., politicized decision making, was a major factor in uncertainty;

10. Property rights:

---

[40] Williamson, J. (1990), p. 8

Finally, the "Washington Consensus" proposed the protection of property rights, which were not secure in Latin American countries.

In an interview made for this study, John Williamson stated that the "Washington Consensus" was not intended to accelerate private capital flows[41]. This is, however, exactly what happened. The first impact of these prescriptions in many developing countries, including Turkey, was increased private capital flows serving in most of the cases to finance fiscal deficits. While it was also possible to observe high growth rates in the initial phase, misbehavior by the sovereign debtors or by the creditors could destabilize the whole economy at a later date, making credit less readily available and at a higher cost[42]. Several developing and transition countries following the prescriptions described above experienced severe crises in the 1990s and 2000s, i.e., the 1994 Turkish currency crisis, the 1997 East Asian currency crisis, the 1998 Russian debt crisis, the crisis in Argentina in 2000 and the most severe currency crisis that Turkey had experienced in its history, in 2001. While I will start to analyze the Turkish case in section 2.2, let us now first have a look at macro trends during the 1990s in Thailand, the country where the 1997 East Asian currency crisis was triggered before rapidly spreading other economies in the region[43]. It is important to note that the crisis occurred after several decades of continuous growth and strong trade performance. During the three decades preceding the crisis, per capita income levels increased fourfold in Malaysia, fivefold in Thailand and tenfold in Korea[44]. The "Washington Consensus" prescriptions produced a prolonged boom phase, which later resulted in a severe bust. Thus, this overview will give us the possibility to reflect on the dynamics of a deregulated emerging economy, which at the same time remained unable to introduce the "needed" institutional and regulatory reforms. We will discover in Chapter 3 that the Turkish crises of 1994 and 2001 occurred following similar cycles of boom and bust.

---

[41] Personal interview held during the 7th UNCTAD Debt Management Conference held on 11 November 2009, at the Palais des Nations, in Geneva.

[42] Buchheit, L.C. and Gulati, G.M. (2009), p. iii

[43] Stiglitz, J. (1999), p. 95

[44] Fisher, S. (1998), p. 167

2.1.1. The impact of the "Washington Consensus" principles in an emerging market: Thailand during the 1990s

In Thailand, annual growth rates averaged 3.95, 5.82 and 5.22 percent during the periods 1970-1980, 1980-1990 and 1990-1997 respectively[45]. Let us overview the last period, as the restrictions on capital flows were reduced in 1990 in line with the IMF conditionality and commercial banks were allowed to have larger foreign currency risk exposures[46]. In 1993, the capital account was further liberalized by giving the possibility of tax advantages for borrowing in foreign exchange from abroad[47]. The result was a substantial increase in banks' short-term debt in a few years (Table 2.1, col. 11). As the local currency was pegged to the USD, the low offshore interest rates offered carry trade opportunities[48]. Table 2.1 illustrates some key economic indicators in Thailand from 1988 to 1998. Note that in the years prior to the crisis, i.e., from 1993 to 1996, an appreciating currency, an increasing current account deficit and dependence on short-term external debt (Table 2.1, columns 7, 8 and 11, respectively) showed that the economy was vulnerable to a sudden capital reversal. In keeping with the predictions of these indicators, despite high growth, low inflation and a balanced budget, the 1997 currency crisis became unavoidable. To note, in the aftermath of the crisis, a depreciating real exchange rate (col. 7) and the consequent dramatic improvement in current account balance (col. 8). On the other hand, the worsening budget balance was significant. The Thai financial crisis revealed two flaws in the "Washington Consensus":

1. Sustainability of real currency appreciation (col. 7) and current account deficits (col. 8) and;
2. The relationship between the public sector deficit (col. 9) and the banking sector FX liabilities (columns 10 and 11), in presence of bailout guarantees.

---

[45] Kawai, H. and Urata, S. (2003), p. 59

[46] Thailand accepted Article VIII of the IMF, i.e., capital account convertibility, in 1990 (Vanichvatana, S. (2007), p. 44).

[47] Ibid.

[48] The basic mechanics of a carry trade is explained in section 5.3.

Table 2.1: Thailand macro data 1988-1998, an unfolding crisis

	(1) GDP	(2) CPI	(3) CPI %	(4) Int. rates	(5) Debt/ GDP	(6) Res./ debt	(7) REER	(8) CA/ GDP	(9) Bud./ GDP	(10) Banks' l. t. d.	(11) Banks' s. t. d.
1988	13.3	48.1	3.9	8.7	40.7	149.8	-	-2.4	1.9	266	2'218
1989	12.2	50.7	5.3	10.6	37.1	176.6	-	-3.3	3.2	326	2'832
1990	11.2	53.7	5.9	12.9	40.1	137.0	-	-8.3	4.7	286	3'947
1991	8.6	56.8	5.7	11.2	44.4	119.7	97.8	-7.5	4.9	338	4'139
1992	8.1	59.1	4.1	6.9	44.3	112.0	96.3	-5.4	3.0	731	5'532
1993	8.3	61.1	3.4	6.5	46.7	112.4	97.1	-4.8	2.2	2'648	10'371
1994	9.0	64.2	5.0	7.3	51.1	103.8	100.0	-5.4	1.9	6'420	21'556
1995	9.2	67.9	5.7	11.0	69.1	70.7	98.6	-7.8	2.8	8'242	33'697
1996	5.9	71.8	5.9	9.2	65.9	81.1	102.9	-7.9	2.3	13'011	28'858
1997	-1.4	75.9	5.6	15.7	64.8	70.4	94.1	-2.0	-1,9	14'818	24'403
1998	-10.5	82.0	8.0	13.0	69.9	103.9	81.9	12.7	-2.4	10'885	17'437

Sources: IMF/International Financial Statistics and Bank of Thailand official website

Notes to Table 2.1

1. Constant GDP at 1988 constant prices, annual percentage change;
2. Consumer Price Index, 2007=100;
3. Consumer Price Index, annual percentage change;
4. Money market rates taken as proxy;
5. Debt is Gross External Debt[49] composed of the debt of general government, monetary authorities, banks and other sectors, the latter including private sector and state-owned enterprises;
6. "Res." stands for international reserves and "debt" stands for short-term liabilities of Gross External Debt defined in (5);
7. Monthly Real Effective Exchange Rate values provided by the Bank of Thailand website and own calculations (transformed in annual average values); For the crisis year 1997, to note that although the annual average value is 94.1, the average of the first six months prior the crisis was 106.2, signaling that the currency was overvalued.
8. Current Account deficit/GDP ratio, in percentage;
9. Annual budget balance values/GDP ratio, in percentage;
10. Banking sector long-term foreign liabilities, in million USD;
11. Banking sector short-term foreign liabilities, in million USD.

---

[49] The IMF defines the Gross External Debt as the outstanding amount, at any given time, of those actual current and non-contingent liabilities that require payment(s) of principal and/or interest by the debtor at some point(s) in the future and that are owed to non-residents by residents of an economy (IMF (2003), p. 7).

1. Sustainability of real currency appreciation and of current account deficit[50]:

Thailand's current account deficit grew because of accumulated domestic inflation, an appreciating currency, and enthusiastic foreign borrowing/lending. Suddenly, international financial markets took fright and capital flows dried up. Why?

Although there is a lack of consensus on the threshold level of the current account deficit/GDP ratio, most researchers agree that it is an important indicator. Dornbusch (2001) sets the sustainable level of real appreciation[51] at 25 percent or more, leading to a current account deficit exceeding 4 percent of GDP. Milesi-Ferretti, G.M. and Razin, A. (1996) in a similar study investigate whether a current account deficit of 5 percent of GDP could be sustainable for three to four years. They conclude that this alone is not a sufficient indicator of sustainability, arguing the importance of the exchange rate policy and structural factors such as the degree of openness, the health of the financial system and the levels of domestic saving and investment[52]. They further advance that rapidly growing countries can sustain persistent current account deficits without increasing their external indebtedness relative to GDP[53]. Calvo G.M. and Vegh, G.A. (1998) develop a similar approach and argue that capital markets are reluctant to keep lending to LDCs presenting current account

---

[50] To avoid confusion a brief overview on definition of "sustainability" will be useful. Let us start with "solvency", which is defined in relation to an economy's present-value budget constrain. An economy is said to be solvent if the present discounted value (PDV) of future trade surpluses is equal to current external indebtedness. In the case of public finances, solvency is associated with the present discounted value of future budget surpluses clearing the current public debt (Milesi-Ferretti, G.M. and Razin, A. (1996), p. 4). By contrast, "sustainability" implies that the continuation of current policy stance into the indefinite future does not violate solvency (in this case budget) constraints. Defining sustainability in relation to solvency is simpler for budget imbalances since it can be associated, to some degree, with direct policy decisions on taxation and government expenditure, whereas defining it in relation with current account imbalances is more complex because it reflects interactions among the savings and investment decisions of government and domestic private agents as well as the lending decisions of foreign investors. Although government decisions may be taken as given over a certain period of time, private agents' decisions may not, depending among other things on their portfolio preferences in relation with their perception of changing risk exposures. Moreover, the exchange rate depends on the future evolution of policy variables, as do all the other variables under consideration.

[51] Dornbusch, R. (2001), pp. 3, 4

[52] Milesi-Ferretti, G.M. and Razin, A. (1996), p. 65

[53] Ibid., p. 22

deficit higher than 80 percent of GDP growth[54]. Figure 2.1 compares current account deficit in Thailand and the Calvo and Vegh threshold corresponding to 80 percent of GDP growth, during the 1990s. To note that the CA/GDP violated the Calvo and Vegh threshold from 1995 until the 1997 crisis.

Fig. 2.1: Thailand – Current Account balance and Calvo and Vegh threshold, in percentage

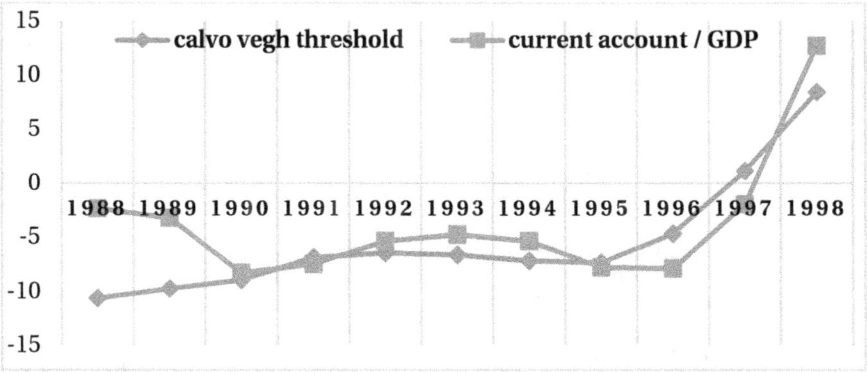

Source: Table 2.1 and own calculations

Let me now overview another approach investigating the sustainability of current account deficits, which seems more realistic as it stands on a dynamic framework. Private sector analysts interested in investigating emerging economies' risk exposure have used intensively the Goldman Sachs model (GS SCAD sustainability of current account deficits model) developed in 1997[55]. Deutsche Bank developed a similar model of current account sustainability in 2000. In most of the models of this type, the dynamics behind sustainability of current account deficit is based on the following scheme:

Solvency implies that the ratio of net international demand for a country's liabilities matches foreigners' net demand for these claims on future income flows[56]. According to standard portfolio theory, let us write the net international demand for a country's liabilities as follows[57]:

---

[54] Calvo, G.A. and Vegh, C.A. (1999), p. 52

[55] Edwards, S. (2002), p. 515

[56] Edwards, S. (2000), p. 15

[57] Ibid.

$$\delta_j = \alpha_j(\Omega - \Omega_J) - (1 - \alpha_{JJ})\Omega_J$$

where, α_J is the percentage of the world's wealth (Ω) that international investors are willing to hold in the form of country *j*'s assets, Ω_j is country *j*'s wealth and α_{jj} is country's *j* asset allocation on its own assets.

The asset allocation shares α_j and α_{jj} depend on expected return and perceived risk by investors[58].

Let us assume that:

country *j's* wealth is a multiple λ of its GDP;

country *j's* wealth is a fraction β_j of world's wealth.

We can write the international net demand for country *j*'s assets as[59]:

$$\delta_j = \lfloor \alpha_j \theta_j - (1 - \alpha_{jj}) \rfloor \lambda_{jj} GDP_j$$

where,

$$\theta_J = \frac{(1-\beta)}{\beta}$$

If we denote $\lfloor \alpha_j \theta_j - (1 - \alpha_{jj}) \rfloor \lambda_{jj} = \psi_j$, then,

$$\delta_j = \psi_j * GDP$$

which means that, in the long-term, the net international demand for country *j*'s assets can be expressed as a proportion ψ_j of the country's GDP[60].

---

[58] Edwards, S. (2000), p. 15

[59] Ibid.

[60] Ibid.

In this context, the important aspect to note is when $\lfloor \alpha_j \theta_j - (1-\alpha_{jj}) \rfloor < 0$, which means that domestic residents' demand for foreign liabilities exceeds foreigners' demand for the country's liabilities[61]. Under these circumstances, the country will need a new source of foreign exchange to maintain a stable net external liabilities/GDP ratio.

Though it will never be possible to have sufficient data to put actual figures to these expressions, this framework shows that sustainability of current account balances varies across countries and depends not only on the growth rate as considered by Calvo and Vegh, but also on variables that over time affect portfolio decisions of international and domestic investors[62]. To note that international investors' perception of risk became a determinant factor in Thailand's case, given that a persistent current account deficit requires persistent capital inflows to finance it. I will discuss in Chapter 5, the Credit Default Swaps (CDSs), which instantaneously provide information about the perception of default risk of international investors, and by extension, the solvency of an economy.

2. The relationship between the public sector deficit and foreign liabilities of the banking sector, in presence of bailout guarantees

Another flaw in the "Washington Consensus" prescriptions lay in the relationship between budget balance and banking sector foreign liabilities. With the liberalization process in Thailand during the early 1990s, capital inflows created asset bubbles in stocks, land, and property[63]. Short-term, low-cost foreign borrowing was used to fund long-term real estate projects[64]. Overpriced properties were also used as collateral for loans, which became increasingly non-performing[65]. While the financial sector credit to GDP ratio rose from 83 percent in 1990 to 147 percent in 1996, the debt to equity ratio of corporations increased from 160 percent in 1988 to 230 percent in 1996[66]. Thus, although inflation was low, asset bubbles increased the overall risk of the

---

61 Edwards, S. (2000), p.16

62 Ibid.

63 Vanichvatana, S. (2007), p. 44

64 Ibid.

65 Ibid.

66 Berben, R. P., Berk, J. M., Nitithanprapas, E., Sangsuphan, K., Puapan, P, Sodsriwiboon, P. (2002), p. 37

economy. Unhedged foreign exchange positions were increasingly translated into credit risk exposure[67]. Moreover, implicit government guarantees created moral hazard by encouraging excessively risky lending. The logic of bankers was "if the loan is repaid I make money; if the borrower defaults the taxpayer loses"[68]. Under these circumstances, implicit bailout guarantees by the government became a major cause triggering a crisis[69]. Why? This phenomenon is important in illustrating one of the failures of the "Washington Consensus". From Figure 2.2, we observe that Thailand had a budget surplus until the crisis year 1997. Thus, one could state that it was in line with "Washington Consensus" scheme. However, forward-looking investors in global markets also looked at future government expenditures[70]. The increasing short-term liabilities of the banking system caused international investors to take into consideration the size of future budget deficits in relation with the likelihood of realization of contingent liabilities[71] (Fig. 2.3). In fact, the future deficit depended on the increasing risk exposure of banks. In such circumstances, the optimal strategy for rational investors was to divest as soon as information about prospective deficit arrived[72]. In other words, investors discounted the expected future deficit without waiting for the banking system to fail and excessive money creation to bail them out. Thus, the speculative attack started as soon as investors perceived that the banking sector deficit was unsustainable and the assets backing the bank debt looked shaky[73].

The Asian crisis showed that global investors are able to discover "hidden" deficits in a dynamic setting. Their perception of risk and expected returns in association with institutional weaknesses can trigger a crisis. It follows that a static approach based on standard macroeconomic indicators is not sufficient to predict a crisis and that close attention must be paid to local institutional factors.

---

67 Dollar, D. and Driemeier, M. H. (2000), p. 5

68 Burnside, C., Eichenbaum, M. and S. Rebelo (2001), p. 1155

69 Ibid.

70 Ibid., p. 1191

71 because of implicit government bailout guarantees to the failing banking system

72 Burnside, C., Eichenbaum, M. and S. Rebelo (2001), p. 1158

73 Ibid., p. 1191

Fig. 2.2: Thailand - Budget Balance/GDP ratio, in percentage

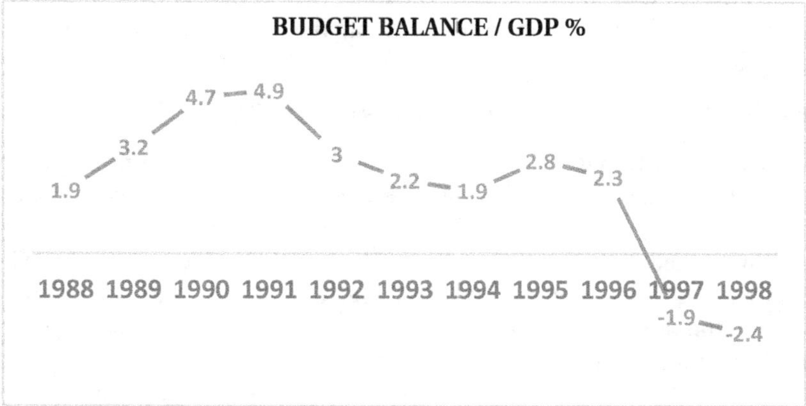

Source: Bank of Thailand, official website

Fig. 2.3: Banking sector foreign liabilities, in million USD

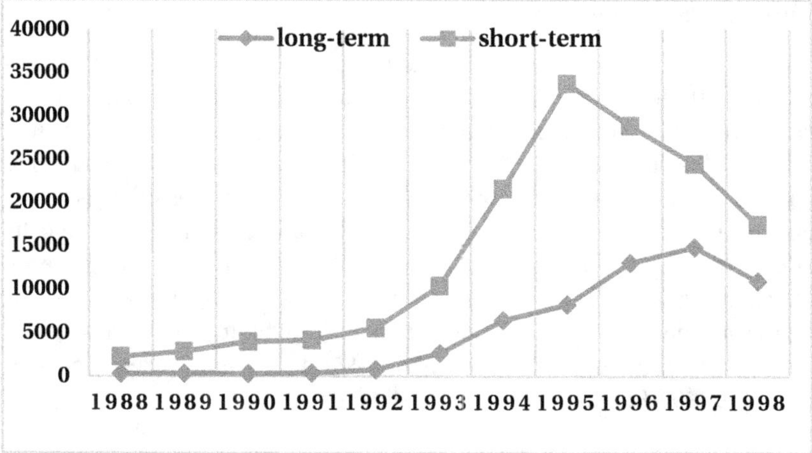

Source: Bank of Thailand, official website

Critics of "Washington Consensus" principles

In the aftermath of the 1997 East Asian currency crisis, many economists criticized the "Washington Consensus" and offered various solutions. Joseph Stiglitz made the following points:

- **Dynamics behind factors making markets work well**

The "Washington Consensus" associated good economic performance with liberalized trade, macroeconomic stability, and low inflation. Enhanced private market involvement should have allocated resources efficiently and accelerated growth. Undoubtedly, these were necessary factors for markets to work well. Without them for example, high and volatile inflation would create uncertainty and increase the risk exposure of the overall economy. However, Joseph Stiglitz advanced that policies laid out by "Washington Consensus" were not complete and that macro stability, trade liberalization and low inflation were not sufficient to make markets work. Striving to further reduce an already low inflation rate was not likely to contribute to the overall growth. Complementary measures were required to ensure sound financial regulation, competition policy, human capital formation and policies to facilitate the transfer of technology and to encourage transparency[74];

- **Confusion between means and ends[75]**

Joseph Stiglitz pointed out that there was confusion between means (privatization, trade liberalization and a nominal increase in GDP) and ends (a more sustainable, equitable and democratic growth which would bring about a general increase in well-being)[76]. Joseph Stiglitz further advanced that, attempts to initiate rapid deregulation ignored the very sensitive issue of sequencing. For example, in the process of liberalization Thailand lifted its previous restrictions on bank lending to real estate without establishing a more sophisticated regulatory regime. Together with other factors, the result of this oversight was the large-scale misallocation of capital to fuel a real estate bubble, which was an important cause of the 1997-East-Asian currency crisis[77]. Regarding the 1998-Russian debt crisis he stated[78]:

---

[74] Stiglitz, J. (1999), p. 99

[75] Stiglitz, J. (2002), p. 32

[76] Stiglitz, J. (2004), p. 11

[77] Stiglitz, J. (1998b), p. 14

[78] Stiglitz, J. (2002), p. 57

> "A rapid privatization, no matter how done, was led in the naïve belief that once control over property was given out, a rule of law would emerge."

Joseph Stiglitz further added that the neglect of the institutional framework necessary to support effective markets served to intensify distortions rather than eliminate them and that ultimate development objectives were compromised as a result. According to him, the basic problem underlying the economic theory of the "Washington Consensus" was the fact that it did not take dynamics of economic development and transition into account. Although it described the target it was not able to provide the way to get there[79].

- **Need for competition**

Joseph Stiglitz argued that the "Washington Consensus" was applied to financial systems dominated by SOEs and public ownership in which competition was limited, whereas what was needed was to promote competition[80]. Joseph Stiglitz explained as follows his alternative development strategy[81]:

> "Development represents a transformation of society, a movement from traditional relations, traditional ways of thinking, traditional ways of dealing with health and education, traditional methods of production, to more "modern" ways. For instance, a characteristic of traditional societies is the acceptance of the world as it is; the modern perspective recognizes change, it recognizes that we, as individuals and societies, can take actions that, for instance, reduce infant mortality, extend lifespans, and increase productivity. Key to these changes is the movement to "scientific" ways of thinking, identifying critical variables that affect outcomes, attempting to make inferences based on

---

[79] Stiglitz, J. (2002), p. 2

[80] Stiglitz, J. (1998b), p. 15

[81] Stiglitz, J. (1998a), pp. 3, 25

> available data, recognizing what we know and what we do not know.
>
> [....]
>
> Change is not an end in itself, but a means to other objectives. The changes that are associated with development provide individuals and societies more control over their destiny. Development enriches the lives of individuals by widening their horizons and reducing their sense of isolation. It reduces the afflictions brought on by disease and poverty, not only increasing lifespans but improving the vitality of life. Given this definition of development, it is clear that a development strategy must be aimed at facilitating the transformation of society, in identifying the barriers to, as well as potential catalysts for, change.
>
> [....]
>
> The state has an important role to play in appropriate regulation, social protection, and welfare. The choice should not be whether the state should be involved but how it gets involved. Thus, the central question should not be the size of the government but the activities and methods of the government.
>
> [....]
>
> We should not see the state and markets as substitutes. The government should see itself as a complement to markets, undertaking those actions that make markets fulfil their functions better."

As we see, Stiglitz made many broad and sweeping criticisms of the "Washington Consensus" emphasizing market imperfections and utilizing more variables in a wider scope[82]. It is probably fair to say that he sees a broad mandate for the state in the areas of regulation, social protection, and social

---

[82] Fine, B. (1998), p. 3

welfare. Other authors, as we shall see, put more emphasis on institutions and property rights[83]. For example, another well-known economist, Dani Rodrik, argued that the "Washington Consensus" principles did not produce expected results because of an inadequate institutional framework[84]. Trade liberalization will not work if capital markets do not allocate financial resources to expanding sectors, if customs officials are corrupt or if labor markets do not work properly and so on. In this regard, property rights and rule of law play an important role[85]. The evolution of property rights and their effect on investment are central issues in the political economy of development. In this context, the state plays an important role in protecting property rights and in providing the preconditions necessary for economic growth. Rodrik[86] advanced that while the original version of "Washington Consensus" included property rights, in practice it put the accent mainly on the importance of macroeconomic market fundamentals and inflation targeting policy, and the role of institutions was largely ignored. Thus, Rodrik argued that in addition to the ten points in the original text, the "augmented Washington Consensus" should cover the following items, emphasizing primacy of institutions: corporate governance; anti-corruption; flexible labor markets; World Trade Organization (WTO) agreements; financial codes and standards; gradual capital account opening; non-intermediate exchange rate regimes[87]; independent central banks/inflation targeting; social safety nets and targeted poverty reduction. Rodrik further argued that countries with better institutions and more secure property rights are more likely to invest in physical and human capital and thereby achieve a greater level of income[88]. Several studies support these hypotheses. Knack and Keefer (1995) test and confirm a positive impact of property rights on investment and growth. Hall and Jones (1998) find that the quality of institutions, typically measured using survey-based perceptions of the rule of law[89], has an impact on output per worker. Johnson, McMillan and

---

[83] De Soto, H. (1989), p. 159

[84] Rodrik, D. (2006), pp. 977, 978

[85] Rodrik, D., Subramanian, A. and Trebbi, F. (2002), p. 1

[86] Ibid., pp. 1-3 and Rodrik, D. (2006), pp. 3, 4

[87] According to Rodrik, intermediate exchange rate regimes, i.e., soft pegs, can increase probability of crises if at the same time capital account is open to global markets, because central bank intervention may be inappropriate and/or politicized. I recall that John Williamson was in favor of such hybrid regimes (see section 2.1, point 5).

[88] Acemoglu, D., Johnson, S. and Robinson, J. A. (2001), p. 1369

[89] Rigobon, R. and Rodrik, D. (2004), p. 1

Woodruff (2002), surveying private manufacturing firms in May-June 1997 in Russia and Ukraine and from September to December 1997 in Poland, Slovakia, and Romania, found that weak property rights discourage firms from reinvesting their profits. Acemoglu, Johnson, and Robinson (2001) investigate from a historical perspective why some countries grew rich and others remained poor. They conclude that improving institutions provide substantial economic gains[90]. Easterly and Levine (2002) show that macroeconomic policies like trade openness, inflation, and real exchange rates do not present an independent effect on the long-term economic performance, whereas institutional quality does[91].

Douglass North defines institutions as humanly devised constraints that structure human interaction[92]. They are made up of formal constraints (i.e., rules, laws, constitutions) and informal constraints (i.e., norms of behavior, conventions, codes of conduct) and both have an impact on economic performance. Together they define the incentive structure of economies. While the rules may be changed instantly through a prompt political decision, the informal norms usually change only gradually[93]. Since it is the norms that

---

[90] Acemoglu, D., Johnson, S. and Robinson, J.A. (2001), p. 1395

[91] Easterly and Levine (2002), pp. 31-33

[92] North, D.C., (1994), p. 360

[93] I would like to introduce here Olivier Williamson's classification, which considers four levels of social analysis in explaining the New Institutional Economics. Informal constraints (norms, customs, traditions as well as religion) are located at the first level, where institutions change very slowly, in centuries or millennia. The second level is the institutional environment, where formal rules (constitutions, laws, property rights) are introduced. Thus, this level includes the executive, legislative, judicial as well as bureaucratic functions of government. Major changes in the rules occur in the order of decades or centuries. If we consider this level as the rules of the game (i.e., property), the next level deals with the play of the game (i.e., contract). In fact, institutions of governance, i.e., markets and firms, are located in the third level, concerning a period in the order of a year to a decade. Finally, the fourth level concerns the neoclassical analysis, where the firm is typically described as a production function and adjustments to prices and output occur continuously, where agency theory deals with efficient incentive alignment (Williamson, O.E. (2000), pp. 596-601; Williamson, O.E. (1998), pp. 25-29).

provide "legitimacy" to a given set of rules, a sudden change can virtually never provide the expected results in the short-term[94]. Thus, performance will likely be different than anticipated. Moreover, economies that adopt the formal rules of another economy will have very different performance characteristics than the first economy given differences in different informal norms and enforcement. The implication is that transferring the formal political and economic rules of successful Western market economies to third-world and Eastern European economies is not sufficient for good economic performance.

Thus, "improving" the institutional framework in emerging markets seems a complicated issue. Hernando de Soto argued that since the nineteenth century many developing countries have copied the laws of the advanced nations in order to give their citizens the institutional framework to produce wealth, but it did not give the expected results[95]. While cultural differences can play a role, Hernando de Soto argued that the reasons behind these failures have gone beyond cultural and genetic heritage because it is possible to observe similar problems in transition economies belonging to different cultures. For instance, both in Latin America and Russia, increasing inequalities, underground economies, organized crime, political instability and capital flight have become common problems that impede wealth creation and lead to chronic unstable

---

In the context of this book, the first level in Turkey initiated with the SOEs-led development models by the end of the 1920s. Informal constraints formed were passed down inter-generationally as customs and traditions providing the continuity that I can call culture. We will observe during the book how difficult it was to shake off seventy years of statist development policies and crony capitalism. It will be evident the persistent presence of the traditional "state will come to our help" philosophy, which was strongly associated with the Turkish economic culture. The typical example in this regard is the way the Turkish Central Bank operated since its creation in 1930. While it was traditionally politically managed since the beginning, its independent status from 2001 onwards aimed to put an end to these informal constraints. I pointed out in section 5.3 "Concluding remarks" that in 2006 the Central Bank had to intervene as it was difficult to change the expectations of market players, which appeared as unwritten customs or norms. At the same time, the increasing volume in the Turkish derivatives market in that period means that the use of risk management tools increased over time, leading to a gradual change of customs. Since the Turkish Central Bank was created in 1930 and the analysis considers the period until 2010, the time frame for this first level, in the context of this book, is less than one century.

Some examples regarding the next levels are: Laws on property rights examined in chapter 4 are located in the second level described above. Privatizations, examined in the same chapter, need to be considered with reference to both the rules of the game and the play of the game, thus the second and the third levels. Whereas, incentive mechanisms and agency theory corresponding to the fourth level, are examined in Annex 4.

[94] North, D.C. (1994), p. 366

[95] De Soto, H. (2000), p. 11

circumstances[96]. It is not surprising to note that this sort of problem was encountered also in Turkey in the 1980s and 1990s. Hernando de Soto identified the root cause of the problem in a weak legal basis in protecting property rights[97]. In fact, sophisticated and enforceable property rights have led advanced nations to create and maintain capital. It is worth to note that property rights may relate not only to houses, cars or machinery but also to rental agreements, foreign currency certificates and their free convertibility and all sort of credits[98]. Consequently, property rights can be lost not only through confiscation or expropriation but also simply through regulations that, for instance, freeze savings or introduce measures against speculation. Thus, property rights are both real and personal[99] and provide to their holders the inalienable and exclusive entitlement to them, i.e., the power to dispose of them freely or to use them to the exclusion of all others[100]. A legal framework to secure property rights encourages holders to invest in their property because of certainty that the property will not be usurped. The true purpose of property rights, thus, is not to benefit the individuals holding these rights, but to give them the incentive to increase the value of their assets by investing or innovating, which would have beneficial results for the whole society[101]. An efficient state facilitates the ways in which property rights are transferred and organized between private individuals[102]. The following quote on "deregulation" from Hernando De Soto provides further insight on the institutions conducive to economic development:

> "Deregulation involves depoliticizing the economy in order to protect the state from the manipulation of redistributive combines and the economy from politicians, just as the church

96 Ibid., p. 8

97 Ibid., p. 10

98 De Soto, H. (1989), p. 159

99 While "real rights" are in relation to things, through ownership, possession or usufruct, "personal rights" are in relation to other people through contracts (De Soto, H. (1989), p. 159).

100 Ibid.

101 Ibid., p. 160

102 Ibid., p. 163

was separated from the state[103]. Although all economic, religious and political systems are interdependent and make up a country's social order, each must have a large measure of autonomy so that none lives at the expense of the others. The economic sphere needs to be freed from the grip of political power brokers and from the influence of arbitrary lawmaking and parasitic interests. The political sphere, for its part, must be made independent of the economic power structure. Its efficiency and strength must be increased by limiting it to administrating a manageable number of problems.

[....]

Deregulation would mean freeing public resources so that the state could use them to ensure that strict, efficient rules of the game were imposed[104].

[....]

The state must bring an efficient system of justice within the reach of the entire population. Instead of controlling the economy primarily by regulations, the state should do so, after the event if necessary, through the judiciary. The state would thus be concerned less with administrating resources and more with administrating justice to ensure that laws are respected.

[....]

An interventionist state requires a bureaucracy, inspectors, penpushers, economists, accountants and other officials who are not as necessary when the law is simpler to apply because the judicial system functions when there are litigants, who are

---

103 Ibid., p. 249

104 De Soto, H. (1989), p. 250

relatively few in number and not when unmanageable masses of citizens are involved.

[....]

It is perfectly valid to want a state's many functions to include redistribution. The crucial thing is that resources be redistributed to the needy in ways which do not discourage production, labor, and saving. If redistribution remains a pretext to go on damaging property rights or for undermining the security of contracts we will remain underdeveloped[105]. Redistribution should, therefore, take forms which do not distort economic incentives, as does the transfer of money through taxation. The aim of deregulation is the same as mercantilists claim to pursue, including land, labor, credit, education, transport, safety and assistance to those who have the least[106]. The difference lies in the fact that a deregulated state achieves these objectives by facilitating and controlling the functioning of the market, not by replacing it. In short, all of us need to be governed by just, efficient laws instead of by the arbitrary authority of the state."

Is the "Washington Consensus" framework incomplete?

The sharp policy change in Turkey in the early 1980s was a response to persistent budget deficits, the result of a statist approach where politicized management of the economy led to chronic macro instability, which continued for two more decades at varying degrees, culminating with the 2001 financial crisis. Finally, in the aftermath of this crisis, policy makers achieved relatively stable macro circumstances in a few years. How was this positive change achieved in such a short time, while for two decades after the initiation of the deregulation process in 1980, unstable macro conditions had led to two major crises? What was the new ingredient in economic policy making? I argue that

105 De Soto, H. (1989), p. 251

106 Ibid., p. 252

while introducing the "Washington Consensus" principles was a well-intentioned attempt to leave behind an inefficient statist regime, it was nevertheless insufficient to complete a transition to a "functioning" market economy. Rodrik criticized the "Washington Consensus" emphasizing the role of institutions, proposing several additional points to the ten "Washington Consensus" prescriptions, while de Soto provided insight on the relationship between the respect of property rights and development.

My analysis is based both on Douglass North's approach, where I identify his "informal rules" with cultural specificities in Turkey and Dani Rodrik's suggestions including additional points with emphasis on institutional reforms. Moreover, Hernando de Soto's approach on property rights provides an often over-looked element needed in a transition economy. He defines the state as the entity charged with implementing the rule of law among private agents through an effective judicial system, where the absence of enforceable property rights constitutes an obstacle for development. I will, through the book, examine under this optic the way the Turkish state was involved in economic decision making in the pre-1980 period. Rapid Turkish growth rates from the 1980s to the 2000s will show that adopting the "Washington Consensus" principles was quite successful at the cost of its volatility, which was a destabilizing factor leading to unexpected crises. But would we give up the rapid growth in order to avoid the financial crises? Of course not! We need to find the causes and learn the lessons. There is room for some regulatory innovation here and perhaps Turkey could show the way. While these risky circumstances led to two financial crises, a detailed analysis from 1980 to 2010 shows the positive impact of a de-politicized institutional framework after 2002. Thus, inspired by the approaches of Douglass North, Dani Rodrik, and Hernando de Soto, I will show that introducing a de-politicized institutional framework is a necessary tool in development policy.

In addition, I briefly introduce here my view on two "Washington Consensus" principles, those on interest and exchange rates.

- **Market-determined interest rates**: The "Washington Consensus" required that interest rates needed to be market-determined to avoid misallocation of resources, and that real interest rates needed to be positive, discouraging capital flight. The Turkish case will show that under unstable macro circumstances, foreign investors will continue to keep their investment only at higher real interest rates, with the consequent negative impact on budget deficit and increase in sovereign default risk. However, I will show through the Turkish case that the completion of EU-inspired regulatory and institutional reforms led to lower real interest rates, though they are still quite high in Turkey compared with countries of similar economic development levels. This also means that foreign and domestic investors have incentives to invest in Turkey when stable circumstances provide the opportunity to make gains not from speculative capital movements but from stable growth. In other words, we will observe that, once a de-politicized institutional framework eliminates uncertainty, and prevents wasting resources, the economy will not need high real interest rates to avoid capital flight. Investors' expectations will be to gain from investing in production which will further foster overall welfare;

- **Competitive exchange rates**: While the concept of competitiveness can change from one economy to another, depending also on trading partners, I argue that it is a difficult task to maintain, broadly, a competitive exchange rate in emerging markets where capital inflows tend to appreciate the local currency and lead to current account imbalances. The Turkish case will show that a growing current account deficit has been a major risk factor after the completion of regulatory and institutional reforms[107]. To note that, in line with my analysis on sustainability of real currency appreciation and current account deficit in Thailand, although it will never be possible to find the exact data in computing the values in section 2.1.1[108], these equations provide insight on the dynamics behind current account deficit sustainability, i.e., dependence on investors' portfolio preferences, which will in turn depend, in the Turkish case, not only on improvements in the institutional framework but also on a wide range of political factors, for instance, on the advancement of the EU membership process. To note also that by competitive exchange rates the Washington Consensus was referring to artificially unsustainable overvalued currencies in Latin America, while in fact Thailand, Turkey, and others have suffered from market-driven overvaluations (rather like Switzerland).

To conclude, both interest rates and exchange rates are major risk factors in an economy open to global markets. However, volatile rates can attract only short-term capital flows leading to boom and bust cycles. We will see the impact of institutional improvements on both interest and exchange rates, which in turn became an additional factor attracting long-term FDI to Turkey, leading to stable growth. Finally, we will also observe that an improved institutional framework, together with the privatization of inefficient SOEs and the achievement of lower real interest rates made fiscal discipline in Turkey since 2002 possible.

---

107 See section 5.3

108 See equations related to models on sustainability of current account deficits.

Consequently, I will suggest adding an 11th point to the "Washington Consensus": **Regulatory and institutional reforms leading to a de-politicized framework where priority is given to respect of the rule of law and protection of property rights.** My analysis will also show that the lacking aspect in the "Washington Consensus" was a de-politicized economic management, promoting a supervisory framework separating the state from direct involvement in the economy.

Let me examine in the next section implementation of the "Washington Consensus" principles in Turkey. I start with an overview of historical aspects, which will shed light on dynamics behind the Turkish economy over the past decades.

2.2. First Phase from 1980 to 1988: Introducing the "Washington Consensus" principles

Historical background on the Turkish economy

In this section, I examine financial market developments during the transition period from 1980 onwards. However, let us first have an overview of the pre-1980 period to show the structure of the economy before the transition[109].

The Turkish Republic was founded in 1923 and several factors, from a huge debt inherited from the Ottoman Empire to the Great Depression of 1929, revealed the lack of capital and also entrepreneurial skills in the private sector[110]. The debate had gone beyond diverging views on whether state involvement or private initiative was preferable. Consequently, development through public investment appeared as the only route available[111]. Also, admiration for rapid state-directed industrial development in the Soviet Union

[109] I return to this period also in Chapter 4, section 4.2.3, when I examine the respect of property rights in Turkey before 1980.

[110] Dogruel, F. and Dogruel, A.S. (2011), p. 6

[111] Ibid.

led to Turkey's five-year development plans[112]. Thus, economic nationalism was institutionalized in the early 1930s and was pursued through the creation of numerous SOEs, leading to public investments in manufacturing, energy and mining sectors, which were expanded to many others[113] (from sugar, tobacco, airline, maritime and ports to post, telegraph, telephone, and transports[114]). A powerful state bureaucracy used economic resources to restructure the society and the economy[115]. State-business interactions became the norm over the decades.

A multi-party democratic period was initiated in the aftermath of World War II and allowed Adnan Menderes, leader of the Democratic Party, to form a government in 1950, giving priority to private initiative[116]. However, this was based more on distributing favors to businessmen than on free market competition[117]. This first attempt in Turkish history to introduce private sector-led development was no more than "crony capitalism": it terminated with the 1960 military intervention[118], which institutionalized the state presence even more solidly through the creation of the State Planning Organization and the pursuit of a strict import substitution industrialization policy[119]. Two major interest groups appeared in this restricted environment, i.e., the military establishment and influential family business groups:

1. The armed forces' pension fund: The military government established the OYAK[120] in 1961 as a pension fund to provide retirement benefits for military officers. Though OYAK management claimed never to have

---

[112] Patton, M. J. (1999), p. 50

[113] Guran, M.C. (2011), p. 26

[114] Railways since 1920s (Atalay, B. (2002), pp. 34-36)

[115] Karadag, R. (2010), p. 12

[116] Unay, S. (2006), p. 90

[117] Karadag, R. (2010), p. 12

[118] See Annex 3 for a brief chronological account of the governments formed from the 1960 military rule onwards.

[119] Karadag, R. (2010), pp. 12, 13

[120] OYAK is composed of the initials of Armed Forces Mutual Assistance Foundation, in Turkish.

received aid from the state, it always benefited from tax exemptions[121]. While its tax advantages have been accorded to its core activities as a pension fund and do not extend to the numerous companies that it invests in, I can argue that as a player in the private sector with a privileged treatment, OYAK's special status contradicted the EU-inspired competitive market rules. In addition, OYAK benefited from legal protection enjoyed only by public officers[122].

2. An intensive import substitution industrialization policy during the 1960s and the 1970s made import licenses for investment goods and raw materials a crucial resource for private initiative, granted to a few family business groups in close relationship with politicians and the military[123].

Governments during the following two decades both expanded the activities of existing SOEs and created new ones, including the milk industry (1963), petrochemicals (1965), electronics and tea during the 1970s[124]. However, this vast state-owned sector became progressively technologically backward and a source of growing inefficiencies over the following decades. Patronage fostered inefficient allocation of resources on both micro and macro levels, weighing heavily on the cost structure of overall production. Over-employment of unskilled labor in SOEs, which had become a way to hide unemployment without considering the specific knowledge that the occupations required, also led to mistakes. Nevertheless, the problem was not only lack of skills and knowledge. Arbitrary pricing methods for SOE products maintained average prices lower than their cost, further fostering deficits. Moreover, the overloaded state apparatus maintained unnecessary administrative procedures, creating conditions for corruption[125]. To summarize, the initially temporary state interventionism of the 1930s as a substitute for the absence of private initiative

---

[121]Article 35 (OYAK Law) stated that the exemptions of the Foundation included foundations tax, income and inheritance tax, stamp duty, income tax (on dues collected from the permanent and temporary members) and expenditure tax (Demir, F. (2005), p. 678).

[122] Article 37 (OYAK Law) stated that the entire property as well as the revenues of and credits to the foundation will enjoy the same rights and privileges as State property. Offences against them will be subject to the same legal action as offences against State property (Demir, F. (2005), p. 678).

[123] Karadag, R. (2010), p. 13

[124] Aksoy, A.S. (1994), p. 5

[125] For a detailed exposition of costs of administrative barriers, see section 4.2.2.1.

was transformed into permanent institutional structures during the 1960s and 1970s[126].

Table 2.2 shows that on average 62.4 percent of the public sector borrowing requirements (PSBRs) from 1975 to 1980 were due to SOE losses. This means that state interventionist policies not only failed to lead to capital accumulation, but they even became a root cause of economic instability. How were these deficits covered? The Turkish Central Bank was traditionally politically managed. One can easily observe that SOE losses led to excessive money creation. This is a central theme in our book, as the Central Bank's independence is a crucially important aspect of a functioning market economy and an important element in EU requirements.

Table 2.2: Contribution of SOEs' losses to PSBR, from 1975 to 1980, in percentage

Years	SOEs' budget deficit/GDP	PSBR/GDP	SOEs' budget deficit/PSBR
1975	5.2	6.1	85.2
1976	7.1	8.7	81.6
1977	5.0	10.4	48.1
1978	2.0	4.1	48.8
1979	5.2	9.4	55.3
1980	5.8	10.5	55.2
1975-80	5.1	8.2	62.4

Source: Guran, M.C. (2011), p. 31; The last line represents the annual average from 1975 to 1980.

While I will examine the Turkish Central Bank's balance sheet and monetary policies during the 1980s in section 2.2.1.1, I emphasize here that the balance-of-payments crisis in the late 1970s became unavoidable. Macroeconomic instability together with short-lived coalition governments fostered social turbulence. Civilian political leaders were committed to introducing policies to achieve economic stability. To this end, Suleyman Demirel's government had the courage to adopt and apply unpopular measures, launching the "Washington Consensus" process on 24 January 1980. This led to a military rule, which governed for two years from 1980 to 1982. The military applied the IMF program, contrary to the 1960 military government, which had increased state presence in the economy, though Turkey regularly signed IMF Stand-by agreements during the 1960s (Table 2.4). We further note that while the generals withdrew in 1983, all previous political parties were suppressed and their leaders were banned from politics.

---

126 Guran, M.C. (2011), p. 30

This allowed Turgut Ozal to come to power[127] and complete the unpopular "Washington Consensus" reforms.

Turkey encountered many difficulties during this long transition period and experienced two major financial crises in 1994 and 2001. What were the elements behind these crises? Were they due to an institutional error? What was the status of financial regulation, competition policy, and transparency in Turkey? Was the pre-existing institutional framework capable of fostering the transition to a functioning market economy or did it first have to change?

I start with some definitions of financial (in) stability and financial markets.

Defining financial (in) stability

I seek to approach this topic through a review of literature. Mishkin (1999) states:

> "Financial instability occurs when shocks to the financial system interfere with information flows so that the financial system can no longer do its job of channeling funds to those with productive investment opportunities"[128].

127 Turgut Ozal was born in 1927, in Malatya, a city in South-eastern Turkey, to a conservative and religious family with modest means (Onis, Z. (2004), p. 4). His father was an "imam" (religious teacher). He graduated in 1950 from the Istanbul Technical University (ITU) with a degree in electrical engineering. He worked as a public sector employee in the Electrical Power Survey Administration. In 1952, he studied economics and engineering in the U.S. (Reich, B. (1990), p. 395). The following year he returned to Turkey and participated in several hydraulic power and electrification projects. After the 1960 military intervention, he joined a group of technocrats and social scientists in setting up the State Planning Organization (SPO). Suleyman Demirel (leader of the center-right party AP from 1962 to 1980) was a few years his senior at the ITU. During the early 1960s Turgut Ozal joined the AP and had the position of technical advisor to Suleyman Demirel, who became Prime Minister following the general elections of 1965. Ozal became Under-Secretary of the SPO in 1967. As the 1971 military intervention outlawed Prime Minister Suleyman Demirel, Turgut Ozal went to Washington D.C. where he worked for the World Bank for two years (Reich, B. (1990), p. 396). From 1973 to 1979 he held top level managerial positions in the private sector in Istanbul. Turgut Ozal became a major political figure from 1983 to 1993, both as prime minister and president of Turkey.

128 Mishkin, F.S. (1999), p. 7

This definition stresses the intermediation role of the financial system in providing credit to the real sector. Mishkin advances the idea that[129]:

> "Financial intermediaries and particularly banks have a very important role in financial markets since they are well suited to engage in information-producing activities that facilitate productive investment for the economy. Thus, a decline in the ability of these institutions to engage in financial intermediation and to make loans will lead directly to a decline in investment and aggregate economic activity.
>
> [....]
>
> Increasing asymmetric information problems will lead to financial instability."

According to Davis (2003), financial instability and systemic risk are characterized by "heightened risk of a financial crisis" and what he describes as "a major collapse of the financial system, entailing inability to provide payments or to allocate credit to productive investment opportunities". He further states that financial crises have a major impact on general economic activity and associates achieving financial stability with the management of systemic risk. The latter manifests itself in the event of failure of market liquidity, the breakdown of market infrastructure and solvency problems within financial institutions. This definition emphasizes the role of the financial system in supporting the real sector and the likelihood of insolvency due to systemic risk exposure[130].

Schinasi (2004) provides the following definition of financial stability[131]:

> "A financial system is a range of stability whenever it is capable of facilitating (rather than impeding) the performance of an economy and of dissipating financial imbalances that arise

[129] Ibid., p. 8

[130] Davis, E. (2003), p. 2

[131] Schinasi, G. J. (2004), p. 8

> endogenously or as a result of significant adverse and unanticipated events."

His first term, "range of stability", views financial stability along a continuum rather than as a static condition. He further states[132]:

> "The concept of continuum is relevant because finance involves uncertainty, is dynamic (meaning both inter-temporal and innovative) and is composed of many interlinked and evolutionary elements (infrastructures, institutions, markets). Accordingly, financial stability is expectation based, dynamic and dependent on many parts of the system working reasonably well. What might represent stability at one point in time might be more stable or less stable at some other time, depending on other aspects of the economic system, such as technological, political and social developments."

Schinasi uses the second term "facilitating the performance of an economy" with the intended meaning that finance contributes to the efficient allocation of real resources, the rate of growth output, the process of saving, investment and wealth creation[133].

Several central banks have adopted specific definitions coherent with their objective of safeguarding financial stability[134]. The former Governor of Turkish Central Bank Durmus Yilmaz, during a speech at the OECD World Forum held in 2007 in Istanbul, explained "Financial Stability" from the Turkish perspective as follows[135]:

> "If we consider the last two decades of the Turkish economy, we can say that Turkey learned its lesson very well by actually going

---

[132] Ibid., p. 7

[133] Schinasi, G. J. (2004), p. 9

[134] For a survey of a sample of central bank definitions of financial stability, see Alawode, A., and Al Sadek, M. (2008), pp. 11-13

[135] Central Bank of the Republic of Turkey (2007), p. 4

> through several crises and economic downturns. Thus, we now are aware of how important it is to have a sound financial system, which is resilient to potential shocks. The distortions in the banking sector and weak institutional structure of the financial system led to important systemic risks in the Turkish economy making it impossible for the economy to survive without financial sector reforms taking place. Therefore, the restructuring program for the financial sector was launched with the goal of eliminating the distortions in the financial sector, improving its intermediary function and thus enhancing its competitiveness by international standards.
>
> [....]
>
> Today, we have a stronger banking sector, which forms the basis of macroeconomic stability, as well."

What kind of institutional arrangements are needed to generate financial stability?

One of the things we have learned from many episodes of financial instability is the need for independent regulatory agencies in the shape of, for instance, an independent central bank. Too many financial crises are due to excessive money creation by a central bank taking its orders directly from its government. The Bank of England, for example, became independent only in 1979, the Bank of France in 1994. This is a new development, but it has spread far and wide because it is an essential element in fighting inflation and avoiding financial crises.

On the other hand, it is a difficult step, politically speaking. After all, how convenient it is, as a government, to always be able to order the central bank to create cash whenever it is needed! Giving up this sovereign right is indeed painful. But most countries have taken this step because the public demands price stability. To achieve legitimacy in the eyes of the public, central bank must not only be independent from government, it must also be seen to act fairly towards all banks and business entities. It must be independent from the banks it supervises. It must earn the respect of the government, the banks, and the public because financial markets are so important for the whole economy.

Regulation and supervision must be done in an independent and transparent manner, otherwise, financial mismanagement develops. This is what experience has taught us.

But why would governments transfer power to such independent agents? Two categories of reasons are advanced: "functional" and "non-functional"[136]. The logic behind the "functional" approach is based on the "principal-agent" theory. "Principals" delegate some of their powers to agents[137], in this case, elected officials delegate to the Independent Regulatory Agencies (IRAs). Such transfers of power involve both costs and benefits for the delegating party. Delegation is in the interest of the principal because benefits are expected to be higher than the "agency costs"[138]. Thatcher and Sweet (2002) argue that principals prefer to delegate some power to agents for the following reasons[139]:

- credible commitments: agents are expected to work in such a fashion as to enhance the credibility of promises made by principals;
- information asymmetries: agents are expected to develop expertise in technical areas of governance;
- efficiency of rule-making: agents are expected to respond to specific problems, while principals set the more general terms of policy;
- unpopular decisions: principals avoid taking blame in the event of regulatory failures or other unpopular outcomes.

I would argue that legitimacy and increased transparency are features which should be added to the "principal-agent" theory. It presents, however, other relatively weak aspects as, for instance, "principals" tend to choose agents that are as similar to them as possible in terms of preferences[140]. "Principals" are also tempted to control the behavior of agents. In the case of independent regulatory agencies, "agents" do not necessarily share the views of their political "principals", having been intended to be independent from political influence. From the principals' point of view here, the idea of delegation is based on the need to increase the credibility of policy commitments[141].

[136] Thatcher, M. and Sweet, A. S. (2002), pp. 3, 4, 12, 13

[137] Ibid., p. 3

[138] Thatcher, M. and Sweet, A. S. (2002), pp. 3,4

[139] Ibid., p. 4

[140] Gilardi, F. (2008), p. 28

[141] Gilardi, F. (2008), p. 29

Independent regulatory agencies generally are fixed on long-term goals when compared with governments, and as a result, IRAs would not be exposed to the sharp changes following elections, even if new governments have different perspectives.

On the other hand, the "non-functional" or evolutionary approach takes a different view. Thatcher argues that "Policy Learning and Institutional Isomorphism" (or transfer of institutions) have better explanatory power in many cases[142]. Societies adapt and change by learning and imitating each other. In the EU, the spread of common institutions and regulations was accelerated by the desire to harmonize competitive conditions throughout the Single Market. This is what Thatcher and Sweet[143] define as Coercive Isomorphism or "the diffusion of institutional forms and practices through legal obligation backed up by monitoring and enforcement mechanisms". European integration offers many examples of these "isomorphic" processes, and in particular, the Maastricht Treaty imposed independent central banks on all member states in 1992[144]. Both interpretations of the spread of independent regulatory agencies offer useful tools of analysis for understanding this phenomenon.

I end this section with a quote from Majone (1994), who provides this perspective on regulation replacing state planning in the transition to a functioning market economy[145]:

> "Deregulation and privatization have created the conditions for the rise of the regulatory state, to replace the dirigiste state of the past. Reliance on regulation –rather than public ownership, planning or centralized administration– characterizes the methods of the regulatory state."

The next section will show that financial market reforms in Turkey during the 1980s were not accompanied by an independent regulator. This lack became evident as time went by.

---

142 Thatcher, M. and Sweet, A. S. (2002), p. 12; See also DiMaggio, P. and Powell, W. (1991), pp. 65-73

143 Thatcher, M. and Sweet, A.S. (2002), p. 12

144 Ibid., p. 13

145 Majone, G. (1994), p. 77

Political and economic circumstances that made reforms possible

As we observed in the beginning of this section, the Turkish economy has been, until 1980, highly regulated and state-dominated. Its major feature was import substitution industrialization policy, which protected the economy from competition in international markets. The balance-of- payments crisis that beleaguered the state in the late 1970s was brought about by economic instability, which together with political violence and deadly street demonstrations, generated social turbulence. The center-right party AP leader Suleyman Demirel formed a minority government in November 1979 and appointed Turgut Ozal, his former technical advisor to an economic policymaking post. The government introduced, with the assistance of the IMF, a stabilization program on 24 January 1980[146]. While the reform program was formally introduced on this date, it was effectively made possible after the military intervention on 12 September 1980[147], which supported these unpopular measures[148]. The generals appointed Turgut Ozal as state minister in charge of the economy[149].

To note that the inflation rate fell from 116 percent per annum in 1980 to 27 percent per annum in only a couple of years (Table 2.3) thanks to the "Washington Consensus"-inspired policies. This was seen as the initial phase of a success story and allowed Turgut Ozal to win the November 1983 general elections[150]. He went on to become the leading political figure of the whole 1980s.

Let me now overview, in the next section, the initial phase of the deregulation process.

---

[146] To consider also the international policy dimension behind this development. The Demirel government considered the Soviet invasion of Afghanistan in December 1979 as a threat to Turkish interests. This led Turkey to develop a closer relationship with the U.S. government (Brown, L. C. (2006), p. 268).

[147] Hurriyet Daily News website, March 15th, 2011

[148] The military governed from September 1980 until the general elections held in November 1983. However, political parties of the pre-1980 period were excluded and their leaders regained their political rights much later, in 1987 (Gonen, L. (2006), p. 14).

[149] Reich, B. (1990), p. 396

[150] Kalaycioglu, E. (2002), p. 41

2.2.1. The deregulation process in Turkey

The Turkish deregulation story starts in early 1980 with the so-called "January 24th Measures", which broadly aimed at introducing the "Washington Consensus" principles in Turkey. I start the examination with our two major focus themes, i.e., the interest and exchange rate liberalization.

Turgut Ozal-led economic policy making team lifted, for the first time ever, interest rate ceilings on loans and deposits in July 1980, two months before the military intervention[151]. The aim was to achieve market-determined interest rates to avoid misallocation of resources, in line with "Washington Consensus" principles. This was a big step in the creation of financial markets. It had to be accompanied by letting the exchange rate find its market level by floating and by a restrictive monetary policy on the part of the central bank in order to fight inflation. Thus, the Central Bank of the Republic of Turkey (CBRT)[152] replaced multiple FX rates with a managed floating FX rate regime in April 1981[153]. A strict monetary policy to achieve price stability could then be termed successful in "Washington Consensus" terms. Reading actual figures, the rate of inflation was effectively reduced, in a couple of years, during the period of military government (Table 2.3). Nevertheless, none of this came easily. The consequent reduction in aggregate demand reduced corporate earnings[154]. Freed interest rates encouraged small and financially weaker brokers to offer higher interest rates on deposits, which they could only pay from the sale of new deposits. However, due to a lack of an adequate regulatory framework, the Turkish Central Bank was not able to monitor this behavior[155]. This was a typical Ponzi scheme[156] in Minskyan sense, as I will explain in section 3.1.3. A brokers' crisis developed in 1982, at which point the government intervened to close five small banks in default[157]. The bailout cost was 2.5 percent of GNP[158]. Government

---

[151] Atiyas, I. and Ersel, H. (1992), p. 3

[152] We will see in section 4.1.3 that the CBRT became "legally independent" only in April 2001.

[153] Onder, T. (2005), p. 303

[154] Atiyas, I. and Ersel, H. (1992), p. 3

[155] Ibid.

[156] Denizer, C. A., Gultekin, M. N. and Gultekin, N. B. (2000), p. 6

[157] Kibritçioglu, A. (2005), p. 141

[158] Denizer, C. A., Gultekin, M. N. and Gultekin, N. B. (2000), p. 7

authorities intervened to reregulate interest rates[159]! We observe that this passage from a state dominated to a deregulated economy ended in failure and in a return to state intervention. At fault was a regulatory failure in financial markets, which allowed unscrupulous brokers to develop unsound Ponzi schemes. Direct government regulation of interest rates continued until 1988 at which point the securities markets were relatively well-established and short-term interest rates started to be market determined again[160]. This episode shows that, while the 4th principle of the "Washington Consensus" was adopted, an inadequate institutional framework in banking sector impeded the proper functioning of financial markets.

Table 2.3: Turkey - Main Macroeconomic indicators, 1979-1995

	(1) GDP	(2) CPI	(3) CPI %	(4) DM/TL	(5) USD/TL	(6) Real FX rate	(7) CA/GDP	(8) Export/ Import
1979	-0.5	871	-	44.2	56.0	-	-1.7	-
1980	-2.8	1'886	116.6	120.3	102.4	-	-4.9	36.8
1981	4.9	2'564	35.9	28.9	46.8	-	-2.7	52.6
1982	3.6	3'259	27.1	33.8	39.9	95.8	-1.4	65.0
1983	5.0	539	30.9	29.8	45.2	89.6	-3.1	62.0
1984	6.7	800	48.5	38.6	62.7	82.8	-2.4	66.3
1985	4.2	1'160	50.4	64.9	42.6	83.2	-1.5	70.2
1986	7.0	1'561	37.0	66.3	28.9	78.6	-1.9	67.1
1987	9.0	2'168	39.6	64.5	27.9	77.2	-0.9	72.0
1988	2.3	3'801	71.7	60.1	66.5	77.7	1.8	81.4
1989	0.3	6'448	63.7	33.4	48.8	81.8	0.9	73.6
1990	9.2	455	62.2	42.7	22.9	94.5	-1.8	58.1
1991	1.1	754	68.7	71.5	60.2	91.4	0.2	64.6
1992	5.5	1'283	77.1	58.8	64.6	87.4	-0.6	64.3
1993	8.4	2'131	68.0	57.4	60.5	86.6	-3.4	52.1
1994	-5.0	4'396	104.4	195.7	169.9	66.7	1.9	77.8
1995	6.7	8'511	88.0	72.6	53.5	75.9	-1.4	60.6

Sources:

1. Constant GDP at 1987 prices, by "expenditures" approach, in percentage; Data from Turkish Statistical Institute[161]. For the years 1979 and 1980 the values are GNP at 1987 prices; Data from State Planning Organization, official website;

---

[159] Ibid.

[160] Denizer, C. A., Gultekin, M. N. and Gultekin, N. B. (2000), p. 7

[161] Turkish Statistical Institute (2009), p. 753

2. Consumer Price Index values: From 1978 to 1982 Ankara CPI (1968=100 base year); from 1983 to 1989 Turkey CPI (1978=100 base year); from 1990 to 1995 Turkey CPI (1987=100 base year). Annual averages of monthly changes; Data from CBRT, official website;
3. Consumer Price Index percentage change based on annual rate of change using 12-month averages. From 1979 to 1982 (base year 1968=100), from 1982 to 1987 (base year 1978=100), from 1988 to 1995 (base year 1987=100); Data from CBRT, official website;
4. DM/TL Exchange Rate change based on end-year bid-ask mid-value, in percentage, own calculations; Data from CBRT, official website;
5. USD/TL Exchange Rate change based on end-year bid-ask mid-value, in percentage, own calculations; Data from CBRT, official website;
6. Real FX rate, January 1982=100; the weights in the currency basket are 0.75 for USD and 0.25 for Euro. The relative price calculations use producer prices for the U.S.A and the Euro area and wholesale prices for Turkey; Data from State Planning Organization, official website;
7. Own calculations, Current Account data, in percentage, in USD, obtained from State Planning Organization, official website, transformed in TL with annual average TL/USD rate, CBRT daily data; GDP by expenditures, current TL prices; Data from Turkish Statistical Institute[162];
8. Export/Import ratio, in percentage; Data from State Institute of Statistics, official website.

In the aftermath of the 1982 brokers' crisis, policy makers recognized the need for institutional reform and as a result created the Capital Markets Board as the regulatory and supervisory authority in charge of securities markets[163]. In terms of Turkish Administrative Law, it was cast as a ministerial body[164] with a mandate to regulate primary markets for equities and bonds[165]. It began to work in 1983 with the principal objective of achieving a fair and orderly functioning of markets and protecting investors' rights. During the same year, the government created the Savings Deposit Insurance Fund (SDIF), which aimed at preventing the reemergence of liquidity and fraud problems

---

[162] Turkish Statistical Institute (2009), p. 741

[163] Atiyas, I. and Ersel, H. (1992), p. 7

[164] Zenginobuz, U. (2008), p. 477

[165] It was empowered by the Capital Market Law No. 2'499, published in the Official Gazette number 17'416, on July 30, 1981 (Capital Markets Board, official website).

previously experienced in the banking system[166]. Its mission was defined as follows[167]:

> "To insure saving deposits and participation funds in order to protect the rights of depositors and to contribute to the confidence and stability of the banking system and to insure that the banks and assets transferred to it are resolved in the most proper way."

The Turkish Central Bank had the mandate of administrating and representing the Savings Deposit Insurance Fund within the confines of regulation prepared by the Ministry[168].

While Turgut Ozal was in charge of economic affairs during the military rule, the political party he founded, ANAP, won the general elections held in November 1983. This democratically elected and militarily backed[169] single-party government introduced another set of regulations for secondary market operations[170]. Two decrees, issued between December 1983 and July 1984, lifted all quantitative restrictions on imports and liberalized capital controls[171]. As a consequence, restrictions concerning foreign exchange were lifted, allowing residents to open foreign currency accounts[172]. However, this was partial capital account liberalization, only permitting authorized banks,

---

[166] Atiyas, I. and Ersel, H. (1992), p. 4

[167] Saving Deposit Insurance Fund, official website

[168] Pazarbasioglu, C. (2005), p. 163

[169] Özal's political party ANAP won the general elections in 1983 at the expense of two parties openly backed by the military, and the military's overt opposition to his election. In fact, Kenan Evren, head of armed forces, had publicly declared his opposition to Ozal's party before the elections. Nevertheless, once elected, generals agreed on its economic policies, i.e., the Washington Consensus-led development scheme. Thus, the term "backing" is correct so far as the economic issues are concerned in the post-election period. There were, however, important contentious issues in the political sphere. For a detailed exposition of political context, see Evin, A. O. (2006), pp. 29, 30.

[170] Ersel, H. (1991), pp. 7, 8, Atiyas, I. and Ersel, H. (1992), p. 7

[171] Altinkemer, M. (1992), p. 1

[172] Ibid.

corporations holding investment incentive certificates and foreign trade companies to borrow freely in international markets[173].

The Ozal government introduced in 1985 a new Banking Law[174], addressing structural problems in the banking sector that had caused the brokers' crisis of 1982[175]. This was the first attempt to establish a capital adequacy ratio[176] (ratio of equity capital to risk-based assets) to maintain sufficient equity capital for losses that might arise due to a bank's risk exposure[177]. The law obliged banks to report non-performing loans separately but did not provide an independent regulatory framework to maintain reporting discipline. Instead, it named the Treasury as the principal institution responsible for bank supervision and regulation, as well as authorizing the Sworn Bank Auditors associated with the Treasury to examine banks' legal compliance and their financial standing[178]. Banks identified as having an unsatisfactory performance were to be reported to the Minister responsible for Economic Affairs. To note again a ministerial arm put in charge of the banking system, with subsequent moral hazard risks and the temptation of political inference in the monitoring of banks. An example demonstrating the broad and generalized authority of Ministry is found in the language of the Banking Law[179]:

> "It is able to take all measures to strengthen a bank's financial health."

Using this article as justification, more than fifteen banks, whose financial health was poor, were not declared bankrupt for a long time[180].

The government introduced several other market regulations in 1985[181] (auction system for government securities, the opening of the Istanbul Stock

---

173 Altinkemer, M. (1992), p. 1

174 Law No. 3'182, published on Official Gazette on May 2nd, 1985 (Yayla, H. E. (2006), p. 5)

175 Atiyas, I. and Ersel, H. (1992), p. 4

176 Ibid.

177 The banking sector's risk exposure is discussed in Section 3.3.2.2.

178 Atiyas, I. and Ersel, H. (1992), p. 4

179 Banking Act, No. 3'128, art. 62 (Soral, H. B., Iscan, T. B. and Hebb, G. (2005), p. 4)

180 In 1999, the IMF Stand-by agreement required the closing of five of them (Soral, H. B., Iscan, T. B. and Hebb, G. (2005), p. 5).

181 Ersel, H. (1991), pp.7, 8, Atiyas, I. and Ersel, H. (1992), p. 7

Exchange) and in 1986[182] (redefinition of the liquidity ratio for banks, starting of Open Market Operations by the Turkish Central Bank). More importantly, the Central Bank designed for the first time a monetary policy, aimed at controlling Central Bank's Short-term Cash Advance Facility to the Treasury. In 1986, the Central Bank was given the additional task of bank supervision, where analysis covered capital adequacy, asset quality, profitability and liquidity of the private commercial banking system[183]. Banks were also required to submit themselves to an external audit by independent auditing firms authorized by the Treasury and the Central Bank[184].

Briefly, while relations with the European Economic Community were suspended from 1980 to 1986 because of the military intervention, the government launched a series of important legal and institutional reforms in the securities market[185] and also signed three Stand-by agreements with the IMF, in 1980, 1983 and 1984[186]. These agreements aimed to apply the "Washington Consensus" principles to Turkey, through substantial reforms in exchange for supplying the needed credit. In Table 2.4, we observe the Stand-by agreements signed with the IMF from 1961 to 1984. To note that Turkey used a record high level of credit in 1980 with the initiation of the deregulation process.

Table 2.4: Turkey – IMF Stand-by agreements from 1961 to 1984

Number	Years	Duration	Credit effectively used (in million USD)
1	1961	12	24
2	1962	9	22
3	1963	11	32
4	1964	11	28
5	1965	12	0
6	1966	12	32
7	1967	11	40
8	1968	9	40
9	1969	12	15
10	1970	12	132

182 Ersel, H. (1991), pp.7, 8, Atiyas, I. and Ersel, H. (1992), p. 7

183 Atiyas, I. and Ersel, H. (1992), p. 4

184 Ibid., p. 5

185 Bayazitoglu, Y., Ersel, H. and Ozturk, E. (1991), p. 5

186 Under the Demirel government in 1980, and the Ozal government in 1983 and 1984.

11	1978 (1979)	24	132
12	1979 (1980)	12	338
13	1980	36	1'838
14	1983	12	83
15	1984 (1984)	12	248

Source: Ozçam, M. (2004), p. 2; In parenthesis is indicated the year in which such agreement was canceled.

Nevertheless, while deregulation process marked the initial phase of dismantling the state presence in the economy, political interference in monitoring, transparency and efficiency in auditing was far from international standards[187].

The Ozal government launched in 1987 a further step in foreign policy by making a formal application to join the European Community, reaffirming the country's commitment to long-term economic and political convergence with Europe[188]. However, there was no effort to introduce an EU-inspired de-politicized institutional framework. The use of the Turkish Central Bank's resources depended on political decisions, which continued to be a major factor fostering economic instability.

Thus, let me now examine, in the next section, the Turkish Central Bank's balance sheet to judge its degree of independence, as the latter is one of the essential EU requirements. In order to do this, I shall look at monetary and lending policies.

2.2.1.1. Turkish Central Bank's Analytical Balance Sheet and Monetary Policy

Central banks' balance sheets provide useful information regarding the health of the overall economy[189]. Movements in central bank assets and liabilities influence both financial markets and the real economy[190]. Central banks estimate the impact of changing money supply on the real economy (output, prices, trade, balance-of-payments, the FX rate and interest rates), which in turn influence each other. A review of monetary policy will show how money

---

187 I will examine in section 4.1.4, improvements in this regard in the aftermath of the February 2001 financial crisis.

188 Reich, B. (1990), p. 401

189 Onder, N. A. G. (2008), p. 18

190 Caruana, J. (2011), p. 2

supply was used during the transition period. We shall look at domestic borrowing and the interest rate to see how the fiscal deficit was financed.

Finally, we shall explore the reasons behind worsening macro indicators in the aftermath of the new reform program in the period from 1980 to 1986, i.e., unstable interest rates, leading to currency substitution, creating in turn circumstances for unstable foreign exchange rates and leading to unsustainable domestic debt dynamics. Blinder and Solow (1972)[191] and Sargent and Wallace (1981)[192] supported the view that bond financing of fiscal deficits allows a central bank to combat inflation in the short-term because public debts are not monetized. Nevertheless, as soon as the public debt ratio reaches unsustainable levels, the central bank will be obliged to monetize debt, which creates inflation. I will investigate whether this holds for the Turkish case.

To note in Table 2.5 that under "Domestic Assets" several items provided credit to the public sector and had become the source of the majority of Turkey's serious problems during this period: The "Short-term Cash Advance Facility to the Treasury"[193] was mainly used for the budgetary needs of the Treasury. "Credits to the banking sector" was made of SOEs' bills rediscounted through the banking sector (especially Ziraat Bank)[194]. Defaulting banks were transferred to the SDIF, leaving the Central Bank to bail them out. The "FX Revaluation Account" was composed of exchange rate differences to be invoiced to the Treasury at the end of the accounting period[195]. All these were needs of the public sector, and to cover them, the Central Bank had to create high-powered money. In fact, under "Reserve Money", the item "Currency Issued" accommodated the government's every need, which thus ranged from fiscal deficits to subsidies to farmers and bailing out defaulting banks.

Table 2.5: Structure of Turkish Central Bank's Balance Sheet

ASSETS	LIABILITIES
1) FOREIGN ASSETS	1) TOTAL FOREIGN LIABILITES

[191] Blinder, A. S. and Solow, R. M. (1972), pp. 3, 4

[192] Sargent, T. J. and Wallace, N. (1981), pp. 1-3

[193] The Treasury was allowed to borrow from the Central Bank up to 15 percent of government expenditure. This was called the "Short-term Cash Advance Facility", through which the Central Bank could extend domestic credit to the Treasury, which in turn sold interest free paper to the Central Bank (Ozatay (1997), p. 345).

[194] Osman, A. (2000), p. 7

[195] Ibid., p. 8

2) DOMESTIC ASSETS	Liabilities to non-residents
Cash Operations	Liabilities to Residents
2.1.1) Short-term Cash Advance Facility to the Treasury	2) CENTRAL BANK MONEY
2.1.2) Credits to Banking Sector	2.1) RESERVE MONEY
2.1.3) Credits to SDIF	2.1.1) Currency issued
2.1.4) Other items	2.1.2) Deposits of Banking Sector
FX Revaluation Account	2.1.3) Extra-budgetary Funds
IMF Emergency Assistance (Treasury)	2.1.4) Deposits of Non-Bank Sector
	2.2) OTHER CENTRAL BANK MONEY
	2.2.1) Open Market Operations
	2.2.2) TL Deposits of Public Sector

Source: Central Bank of Turkey

Figure 2.4 shows the impact of the deregulation process on the relative importance of domestic and foreign assets. "Foreign Assets" (including gold) increasingly replaced "Domestic Assets" from 1980 to mid-1990s. Liberalization of foreign trade in 1984 and complete liberalization of the capital account in 1989 were watershed events in regulatory law and contributed to these changes in "Asset" composition.

Figure 2.5 shows both the importance and the evolution of the Central Bank's "Short-term Cash Advance Facility" to the Treasury, relative to domestic debt stock and GNP. In other words, it shows the lack of independence of the Central Bank with regard to Treasury[196]. It is pertinent to ask whether monetary policy can be effective when the Central Bank cannot monitor the composition and the size of its balance sheet[197]. In this context, not only is the independence of the Central Bank undermined, but additional excessive money creation contributes to price instability. Nevertheless, it is possible to note in figure 2.5 the decreasing size of Central Bank's credit to Treasury from 1985 to 1990. The Central Bank's advances were gradually reduced through legislation after the 1994 crisis and abolished completely in 1997[198].

Let me now investigate the reasons behind the gradual change in the second half of the 1980s.

---

196 The CBRT Short-term Cash Advance Facilities were also used in the early 1980s as export subsidies. After 1984, the use of CBRT resources decreased to low levels and commercial banks provided export credits (Central Bank of the Republic of Turkey (2002b), p. 7).

197 Gros, D. (2004), p. 1

198 Guven, A. B. (2010), p. 13

Fig. 2.4: Relative composition of Domestic and Foreign Assets (1980-1995), in percentage

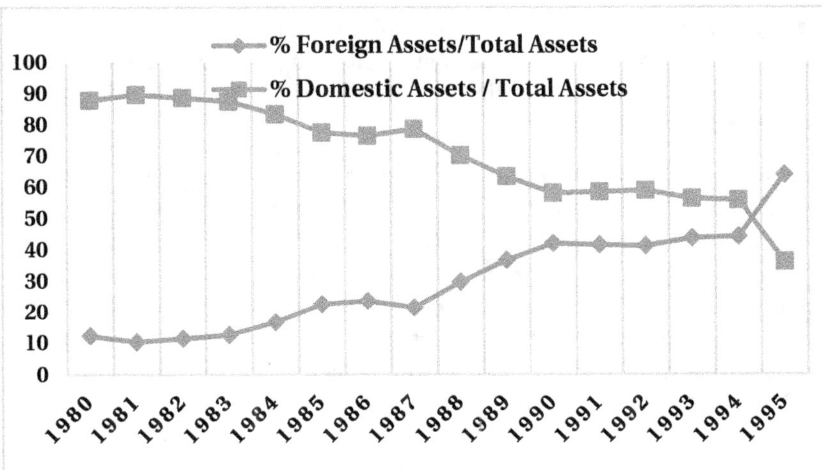

Source: Central Bank of Turkey, annual average of daily data

Fig. 2.5: Central Bank of Turkey – Money creation (1980-1997), in percentage

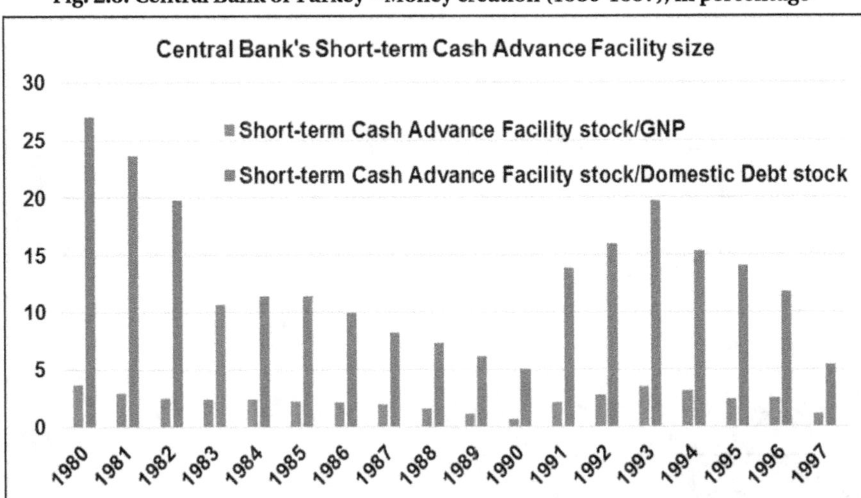

Source: Turkish Statistical Institute (2009), pp. 658, 659. The first column shows the ratio of the short-term cash advance over GNP; Whereas the second one shows the ratio over domestic debt stock.

Turkish Central Bank's monetary policy

The monetary policy from 1985 to 1988 was based on setting broad money (M2) in relation to targeted CPI and GDP rates for the following year[199]. The desired (M2) growth was to be achieved by controlling the expansion of both net domestic and net foreign assets. In fact, controlling the former meant that "Short-term Cash Advance Facility" was reduced by the sale of Turkish government bonds to the public[200].

To note, in Table 2.6, an increasing total domestic borrowing/GNP ratio and a declining M2/GNP ratio starting by the years 1984 and 1986 respectively, reflecting the policy change. Major buyers of government bonds were banks and other authorized institutions[201]. Almost simultaneously, the liquidity requirement ratio for banks was redefined at 17 percent and divided into two components: 5 percent highly liquid assets, (i.e., vault cash) and 12 percent in government securities[202]. This was a profitable solution for banks as they received interest on government securities.

---

[199] Cosar, N. and Bildirici, M. (2010), p. 104

[200] Kepenek, Y. and Yenturk, N. (2010), p. 233

[201] Candemir, H. B. (1994), p. 130

[202] Atiyas, I. and Ersel, H. (1992), p. 7

Table 2.6: Money supply and financial indicators as a percentage of GNP

	(1)[203] M1	(2) M2	(3) M2Y	(4) DEP. (5)+(6)	(5)[204] TL	(6) FX	(7) Dom. Borr.	(8) Bond Rec.	(9) Bonds Paym.	(10) T. Bill Rec.	(11) T. Bill Paym.
1979	15.4	18.3	-	-		-	1.4	1.1	0.4	0.6	0.5
1980	13.9	17.4	-	14.2	14.2	-	2.5	0.3	0.6	1.1	0.4
1981	12.1	20.4	-	-	-	-	0.2	0.3	0.3	2.1	1.6
1982	12.6	24.1	-	-	-		1.7	0.5	0.3	2.4	1.8
1983	13.9	23.6	-	-	-	-	1.9	1.4	0.2	0.6	1.3
1984	10.2	23.4	-	-	-	-	3.1	0.9	0.3	2.2	1.0
1985	9.7	24.2	26.3	26.1	22.7	3.3	3.2	1.9	0.5	3.4	2.8
1986	10.3	23.8	28.5	26.5	21.2	5.3	3.2	2.5	1.5	3.5	2.2
1987	11.5	23.5	30.7	28.0	20.6	7.4	3.8	2.7	1.5	5.3	4.1
1988	8.8	21.1	28.4	25.9	18.6	7.3	2.9	3.0	1.1	4.0	3.7
1989	8.5	20.5	26.6	24.4	18.3	6.1	3.7	3.9	1.3	3.3	2.9
1990	7.9	18.0	23.5	22.1	16.6	5.5	2.6	3.2	1.2	2.1	1.6
1991	7.4	18.5	26.5	24.9	16.7	8.2	4.1	1.8	1.5	5.4	3.4
1992	7.1	17.3	26.6	25.2	15.6	9.6	5.1	3.2	1.8	6.9	4.7
1993	6.5	14.1	23.7	22.5	12.6	9.9	5.3	3.2	1.7	8.6	7.5
1994	5.9	16.2	30.7	29.9	14.5	15.4	5.8	0.6	2.4	16.1	9.8
1995	4.9	16.0	30.7	30.2	14.2	16.0	4.8	2.8	1.7	14.6	12.1

Source: Columns (1) and (2) are obtained from Turkish Statistical institute[205]; Columns from (3) to (11) are obtained from the State Planning Organization; (4) Total Deposits in domestic and foreign currency; (5) Deposits in TL; (6) Deposits in FX); (7) Total Domestic Borrowing; (8) Government Bonds Receipt, (9) Government Bonds Payment; (10) Treasury Bills Receipt; (11) Treasury Bills Payment.

At the same time, the government became able to sell easily its securities to the commercial banking sector (Table 2.7). To note also that the liquidity ratio increased as time went by, thus the banking sector provided increasingly less credit to the private sector and started to become a major holder of government

---

203 Monetary Aggregates, definition: "In official money supply definitions prepared in line with Turkish Central Bank balance sheet and detailed accounts and banking system data, liabilities of monetary sector are identified in terms of degrees of liquidity. In this content, monetary liabilities of monetary sector define the monetary aggregates. And this is coherent with the European Central Bank definitions. Monetary Aggregates are:

M1= Currency in circulation (coins and banknotes issued – Banks' Vaults) + Demand deposits;

M2=M1+Time deposits (Turkish Lira, FX)

M3= M2+Funds received from Repo transactions + Money Market Funds" (Central Bank of the Republic of Turkey (2002a), p. 5)

204 Except official deposits and interbank deposits

205 Turkish Statistical Institute (2009), pp. 613, 614

debt[206]. We will observe later that this was the initial phase of a process during which the banking sector lost its intermediation function, instead of serving as a lender to the government, while the latter issued securities to cover budget deficits.

Table 2.7: Required Liquidity Ratio for banks, in percentage

	1986	1987	1988	1989	1990	1991	1992	1993	1994	1995
Total	17	17	27	30	30	35	35	35	35	35
Gov. securities	12	12	22	25	25	30	30	30	30	30
Cash	5	5	5	5	5	5	5	5	5	5

Source: Candemir, B. (1994), pp. 31, 33

Another important institutional change that affected the functioning of the banking system was the opening in 1986 of an interbank money market under the auspices of the Central Bank[207]. The purpose behind this move was to satisfy the short-term liquidity requirements of banks by mobilizing excess liquidity within the banking system itself[208].

The monetary program that the Central Bank designed in 1986 was again based on (M2) growth linked to the projected CPI and GDP expansion for the following year[209]. However, in the second half of 1987, M2 went beyond its growth limit[210]. One factor behind this monetary expansion was the general election held in November 1987. According to the Political Business Cycles (PBC) theory[211], "opportunistic" policy makers have incentives to stimulate the

---

[206] Onder, N. A. G. (2008), p. 5

[207] Bayazitoglu, Y., Ersel, H. and Ozturk, E. (1991), p. 4

[208] Ibid.

[209] Onder, N. A. G. (2008), p. 20

[210] Ibid.

[211] PBC theory appeared in the mid-1970s thanks to the seminal work of Nordhaus (1975) on "opportunistic" cycles created through monetary expansion in pre-election periods. Later, Hibbs (1977) introduced "partisan" models, which aimed to explain cycles induced by different preferences of inflation and unemployment trade-offs across parties, i.e., left-wing parties giving priority to lower unemployment and the right-wing to lower inflation (Alesina, A., and Roubini, N. (1992), p. 665). I will discuss the concept of central bank independence in section 4.1.2, which can potentially prevent or reduce the impact of political cycles on macroeconomic cycles.

economy to increase the probability of reelection[212]. To note in Figure 2.6 that, as expected, higher liquidity was associated with higher inflation.

Fig. 2.6: Co-movement between liquidity and inflation (Jan 1987-Apr 1988), in percentage

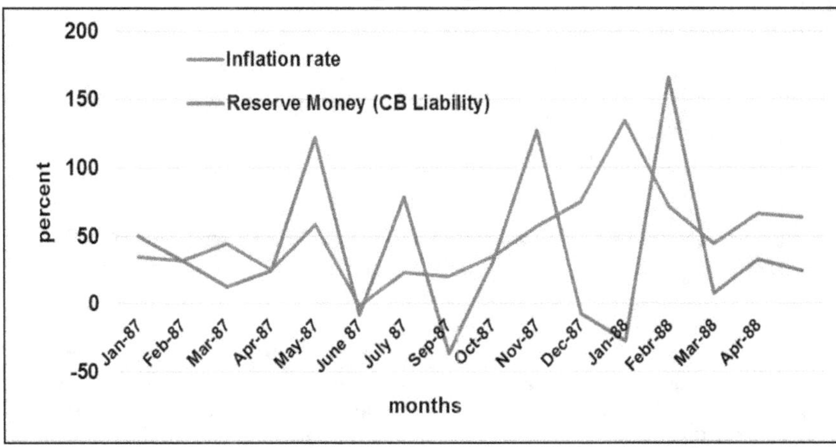

Source: Central Bank of the Republic of Turkey; Reserve Money shows the annualized rate of monthly changes, in percentage; Inflation rate is the annualized monthly percentage change of the Consumer Price Index. Reserve Money curve in the figure is the one more volatile than the other.

Turkish Central Bank aimed at maintaining a positive real interest rate for deposits as the "Washington Consensus" suggested. Nevertheless, "it was difficult", as John Williamson underlined[213], "to achieve and maintain positive and moderate market determined interest rates over time" due to chronic and unsustainable public sector deficits.

---

212 Alesina, A., and Roubini, N. (1992), p. 666

213 See Section 2.1, "Washington Consensus" point "4)".

Fig. 2.7: Comparing interest rates versus inflation rate changes (Jan 1987-Apr 1988), in percentage

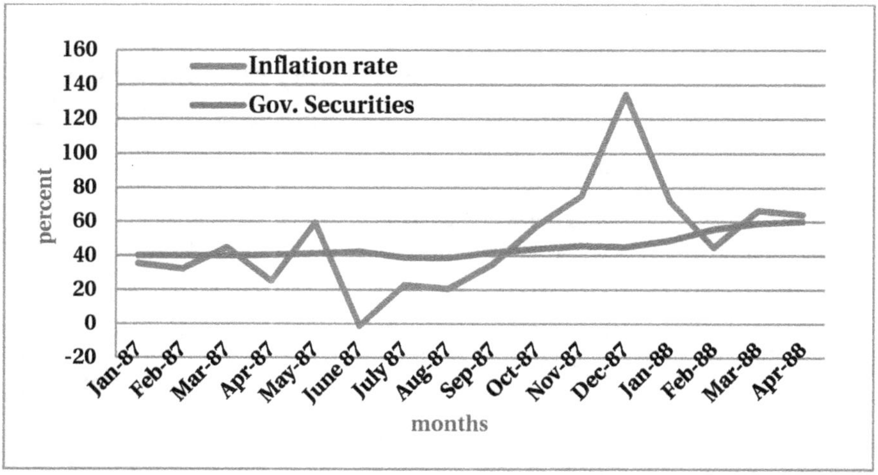

Source: Central Bank of the Republic of Turkey, Interest rate is the annualized value of the arithmetic monthly average of Treasury auctions; Inflation rate is the annualized monthly percentage change of the CPI. Government Securities curve in the figure is the one less volatile than the other.

For example, in the second half of the year 1987, real interest rates were frequently either negative or low when compared with the exchange rate (USD/TL) making foreign currency an attractive instrument for portfolio holders[214] (figures 2.7 and 2.8). We have to question whether the central bank policies can be effective when investors prefer to hold foreign currencies.

[214] Onder, N. A. G. (2008), p. 5

Fig. 2.8: Comparing real interest rates and DM/TL, USD/TL exchange rate (Jan 1987-Apr 1988), in percentage

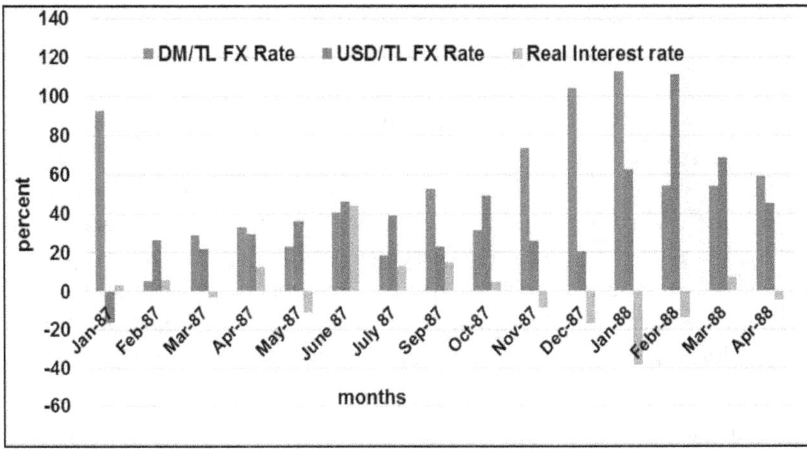

Source: Central Bank of Turkey. Real interest rate based on values in Fig. 2.7; DM/TL and USD/TL rates are the annualized monthly average of daily values. The first two columns in the figure are DM/TL and USD/TL FX rates, respectively. Whereas the third column represents the real interest rate.

To note that (M2) growth increased instability in both the inflation and exchange rates. General elections held in 1987 further exacerbated uncertainties. These rapidly degenerating circumstances led the government to issue new regulations on 4 February 1988, allowing higher interest rates for deposits and introducing a higher liquidity ratio for banks[215]. The latter was increased to 27 percent (of which 5 percent was vault cash, and 22 percent government securities)[216]. Although higher interest rates aimed at making the Turkish Lira more attractive and to decrease inflationary pressure by curbing excess demand[217], a higher liquidity ratio for banks meant that they had to hold more government securities. To note in Table 2.7 above, the increase in the required liquidity ratio for banks from 1987 to 1989. This also constituted an important way for the Central Bank to extend short-term cash advances to the Treasury[218]. Thus, while the Turkish Central Bank attempted to progressively reduce its practice of furnishing credit to the Treasury to meet fiscal deficit

215 Candemir, B. (1994), p. 131

216 Ibid., p. 132

217 Ibid.

218 Ibid.

demands, banks became major buyers of government securities in order to cover the fiscal deficit (Table 2.8). This was also convenient for banks, which were in difficulty in extending credits to the private sector[219]. In fact, high-interest rates meant also that it was more likely for them to encounter risky projects in the private sector. Thus, purchasing government securities was less risky than providing credits to the private sector[220]. Table 2.8 shows the percentage of government securities held by banks from 1987 to 1995. We observe that this ratio reached the lowest level in 1994, the year of the financial crisis. Thus, the decreasing trend of government securities held by banks from 1991 to 1994 is not to be necessarily associated with increased credit for the private sector, but rather with worsening macroeconomic conditions. I emphasize in this table the fact that, in the period considered, banks held a high proportion of government securities, i.e., more than 70 percent.

Table 2.8: Ratio of government securities held by banks over total securities issued by government, from 1987 to 1995, in percentage

Years	1987	1988	1989	1990	1991	1992	1993	1994	1995
Percent	77.7	90.5	90.2	85.9	92.8	79.1	77.8	71.5	81.6

Source: Turkish Undersecretariat of Treasury, official website, Debt Statistics

Concluding remarks

This chapter allowed me to investigate the first research question of the study:

> "Do deregulation of financial markets and elimination of exchange controls on capital movements create conditions for stable growth?".

Fig 5.20 in Chapter 5 and Fig. 6.1, in Conclusion, show that Turkey experienced unstable growth rates from complete liberalization of the capital account in 1989 to completion of regulatory reforms in 2002 and stable rates thereafter. This conducts me to argue that I can associate unstable growth rates

---

219 Candemir, B. (1994), p.132

220 Ibid.

with deregulated financial markets and elimination of exchange controls, in the absence of an adequate regulatory framework in Turkish financial markets. Nevertheless, to note that while these figures make evident the presence of such a correlation, this does not necessarily imply causation. In other words, while an adequate regulatory framework in financial markets can have an impact on stable growth rates from 2002 onwards, there might be other explanatory variables reinforcing growth stability, i.e., the EU full membership process itself. On the other hand, the first research question aims to introduce only an initial conceptual investigation rather than trying to explore a direct causality. I explained in Chapter 1 that the Turkish economy had been highly regulated for long decades. I show in this chapter that, nevertheless, deregulation (including lifting FX controls) did not create conditions for a stable growth. And I continue to investigate what Turkey needed to achieve stable growth rates.

More precisely, this second chapter of the book provides a perspective both on the "Washington Consensus" principles that were introduced as a benchmark for international requirements and on policy structure behind the Turkish financial deregulation process during the 1980s. It shows efforts of policy-makers to dismantle the state bureaucracy. However, a de-politicized institutional framework, or what I call in my study the 11th principle of "Washington Consensus", was absent. While the government showed significant efforts to reduce the use of Central Bank resources, it involved the banking system in financing public deficits. Nevertheless, we did not observe any substantial reform in the banking sector, which was forced to match public deficits instead of providing credits to the private sector. This scheme contradicted the dynamics behind a functioning market economy.

We will explore in Chapter 3 theoretical underpinnings behind the cyclical behavior of worldwide capital flows. These elements will be necessary to explain difficulties encountered by Turkey in adapting its financial market institutions and regulations to international standards.

While in Chapter 2 the "Washington Consensus" principles were introduced as a benchmark for international requirements, I will use the "Acquis Communautaire" in chapters 3, 4, and 5, as "EU requirements", a common element of both being the creation of a "functioning" market economy able to cope with competitive forces in international markets.

We will note that while Turkey applied for a full membership to the EU in 1987, the trend of the economy was not compatible with this ultimate goal. I can state that without EU-inspired institutional reforms in the banking sector, the situation could only worsen. This is what happened. We will observe that the 1994 and the 2001 financial crises were a serious shock to the economy. While the timing of the crises depended also on decisions of policy makers, it was unavoidable because the trend was unsustainable. I will question whether any sound institutional reform was put in place.

Chapter 3

Consequences of Deregulation in Turkish Financial Markets: Business Cycles and Financial Crises

Introduction

This chapter will lead me to investigate the 2nd research question of the study:

> "What is the role of institutions, culture, and tradition? What is the appropriate regulatory framework for an emerging market economy like Turkey?"

I start this chapter with a review of theoretical framework on both business cycles and currency crises because, in my opinion, in the absence of an adequate de-politicized institutional framework and high public deficits as was the case for Turkey, the deregulation process can feed cycles of boom and bust due to interest rate differentials and changing risk perceptions of investors, leading to instability.

In economics, as a simplification of reality, agents are supposed to make their decisions concerning supply and demand "rationally". Firms make their production/investment decisions and individuals purchase goods, services and securities. Such an ideal market is called "efficient" where prices provide accurate signals for resource allocation[221]. The rational expectations hypothesis, on the other hand, states that agents form expectations about the future based on their imperfect perception of the past and present. They will do their best to seize opportunities or avoid losses, but they know that the future is

---

221 Fama, E. (1969), p. 383

uncertain. On the whole, they tend to follow price signals which means that sometimes they get misled by collective madness. This implies that expectation is not an exact function of information variables[222]. Consequently, in real markets, agents strive to exploit market imperfections corresponding to such error terms in order to obtain extra profit.

To note that "Washington Consensus" principles were based broadly on such ideas as efficient markets defined above. However, markets can lead to boom-bust cycles, during which expansionary periods are terminated with a sudden deep recession, making emerging markets unstable or crisis-prone.

Let us first view Theories of Business Cycles in section 3.1 and then proceed, in section 3.2, to Currency Crises models that are conceptually based on the Mundell-Fleming model and also demonstrate features examined by the Austrian school. Thus, my aim in these two sections is to expand our theoretical understanding of boom-bust cycles in emerging economies attempting to adopt more open strategies for economic development. While international capital inflows can potentially feed the boom phase of a bubble they lead, sooner or later, to a rapid speculative outflow. On the other hand, the Mundell-Fleming model will serve as a framework making evident the interaction of exchange rate policy with other macroeconomic variables. We will then observe in section 3.3 that the creation of a boom phase in Turkey during the deregulation process from 1980 to 1989, led to a cycle of financial crises in 1994 and 2001. This section will examine the way regulatory reform changes were introduced in Turkey, i.e., the signature of the customs union with the EU, the creation of independent regulatory agencies both on competition and the banking sector.

We will observe how difficult it was to shake off seventy years of statist development policies and crony capitalism. It will be evident both the persistent presence of the traditional "state will come to our help" philosophy associated with the Turkish economic culture and the need for an adequate institutional framework.

---

[222] McCallum, B.T. (1980), pp. 718, 719

3.1. Review of Theories on Business Cycles

While I start with John Maynard Keynes, we will observe that the Austrian school and Hyman Minsky's approaches will provide us a wider perspective to narrate our story, also showing that the root causes of turbulences in markets have not changed much since the period of these authors.

3.1.1. Keynesian approach

John Maynard Keynes defined a credit cycle, in "A Treatise of Money" (1930), as the alternations of excess and deficit in investment over the volume of saving and the accompanying seesaw in the purchasing power of money due to these alternations[223]. He used as an example the credit cycles associated with the over-rapid investment in railways in the middle nineteenth century[224].

This shows also that bubbles due to investment higher than saving and its impact on investment and employment are not a new phenomenon. Then Keynes explained, in "The General Theory" (1936), the role of interest as follows[225]:

> "It seems then, that the rate of interest on money plays a peculiar part in setting a limit to the level of employment, since it sets a standard to which the marginal efficiency of a capital-asset must attain if it is to be newly produced."

Keynes further advanced the way an exogenous shock might raise interest rates and have a negative impact on growth and employment[226]:

> "A monetary economy, we shall find, is essentially one in which changing views about the future are capable of influencing the

---

223 Keynes, J.M. (1930a), p. 249

224 Keynes, J.M. (1930b), p. 146

225 Keynes, J.M. (1936), p. 222

226 Ibid., Preface, pp. XXII, XXIII

> quantity of employment and not merely its direction. But our method of analyzing the economic behavior of the present under the influence of changing ideas about the future is one which depends on the interaction of supply and demand. We are thus led to a more general theory, which includes the classical theory with which we are familiar, as a special case."

Regarding the irrational behavior of investors, Keynes added in a famous passage[227]:

> "Even apart from the instability due to speculation, there is the instability due to the characteristic of human nature that a large proportion of our positive activities depend on spontaneous optimism rather than a mathematical expectation, whether moral or hedonistic or economic. Most, probably, of our decisions to do something positive, the full consequences of which will be drawn out over many days to come, can only be taken as a result of "animal spirits"- of a spontaneous urge to action rather than inaction and not as the outcome of a weighted average of quantitative benefits multiplied by quantitative probabilities."

Clearly, there is plenty of room for "market madness" in this observation. Nevertheless, Keynes investigated in "The General Theory" (1936) the impact of financial instability on unemployment and income rather than the role that may be played by international capital flows in financial cycles or an analysis of boom-bust cycles[228]. Let me now focus on Austrian economists who saw in financial market manipulation the origin of boom-bust cycles in the real economy.

---

[227] Keynes, J. M. (1936), p. 161

[228] Ibid, pp. 313-332

3.1.2. From Knut Wicksell to Ludwig von Mises and Friedrich Hayek

Knut Wicksell's writings on monetary and trade cycle theory (1898 and 1935) take as a hypothesis the inter-temporal disequilibrium between present and future, which became the basic concept behind the Austrian business cycle theory[229]. More precisely, while savings and investment are coordinated in real terms in a barter economy, this is not always the case in an economy where money and bank credit are used[230]. Under certain circumstances, this may lead to disequilibrium when coordination between savings and investment are not assured. Knut Wicksell was the first to emphasize the distinction between money rate of interest and natural (or real) rate of interest.

Ludwig von Mises and Friedrich Hayek took inspiration from Wicksellian analysis in developing their trade cycle theory, which identified mistaken monetary policies as a factor generating volatile output[231]. The theory is based on an unsustainable boom created by the cheap credit policy of a central bank amplified by commercial bank credit rather than on a change in intertemporal preferences. In Wicksellian terms, the natural rate is "artificially" lowered. Consequently, resources are allocated to investments through greater savings which are not at all "voluntary". Friedrich Hayek in "Prices and Production" provided an analytical explanation of boom-bust cycles through the concept of "forced savings"[232]. According to Hayek, these "forced savings" signal a conflict between producers and consumers. After a certain time period, the disequilibrium created in inter-temporal markets converts such internal conflict into a bust.

Ludwig von Mises, in "Theory of Money and Credit" followed a similar approach to Knut Wicksell discussing the relationship between money rate of interest and natural rate of interest[233], focusing thus on dynamics between the two rates. However, their views diverged slightly: while Wicksell dealt with price level fluctuations, Mises explained business cycles through relative price shifts[234]. In fact, Mises argued that prices of consumption goods fall relative to

---

229 Leijonhufvud, A. (1997), p. 1

230 Festré, A. (2006), p. 333

231 Caporale (1993), p. 471

232 Hayek, F. A. (1931), pp. 135-157

233 Mises, L. V. (1934), pp. 180-185

234 Festré, A. (2006), p. 334

prices of production goods during the boom phase but eventually rise, leading to many bankruptcies and recession[235]. Mises's approach to interest rate changed over time. In fact, later in "Human Action" (1949), he introduced the term "originary" interest replacing the previously used "natural" rate of interest[236]:

> "It has been shown that time preference is a category inherent in every human action. Time preference manifests itself in the phenomenon of originary interest, i.e., the discount of future goods as against present goods.
>
> [...]
>
> Originary interest is the ratio of the value assigned to want-satisfaction in the immediate future and the value assigned to want-satisfaction in remote periods of the future. It manifests itself in the market economy in the discount of future goods as against present goods."

To note here is the emphasis on "time-preference" expressed as "forward-looking decisions" made by producers and consumers[237]. Mises introduced the "uncertainty" component through gross (or market) interest rates, the latter being different from "originary" rates[238]:

> "The market rates of interest on loans are not pure interest rates. Among the components contributing to their determination, there are also elements which are not interest. The money lender is always an entrepreneur. Every grant of credit is a speculative entrepreneurial venture, the success or failure of which is uncertain. The lender is always faced with the possibility that he may lose a part or the whole of the principal lent."

---

235 Garrison, R. W. (2004), p. 324

236 Mises, L. V. (1949), pp. 524-526

237 Festré, A. (2006), p. 342

238 Mises, L. V. (1949), p. 539

Mises explained the relationship between interest, credit expansion and the trade cycle by arguing that credit expansion by banks causes the gross (market) rate of interest to fall, which in turn influences the entrepreneur's calculation of a given project's profitability[239]. A lower rate is translated into an optimistic view about the probability of success of the investment project. In an attempt to realize profitable projects, credit expansion's boom-creating nature enters into action. Mises continued as follows[240]:

> "The boom can last only as long as the credit expansion progresses at an ever-accelerated pace. The boom comes to an end as soon as additional quantities of fiduciary media are no longer thrown upon the loan market. But it could not last forever even if inflation and credit expansion were to go on endlessly. It would then encounter the barriers which prevent the boundless expansion of circulation credit. It would lead to the crack-up boom and the breakdown of the whole monetary system."

According to Mises, "mal-investment" corresponds to a misallocation of resources due to an excess of resources during the early stages of production[241], which is coherent with Hayek's "forced savings" meaning. On the other hand, consumers who receive increased income will tend to consume more than during the pre-expansion period, provoking "over-consumption"[242]. In any case, such divergence between Mises's and Hayek's views does not seem a contradiction. Rather it emerges as a mutually reinforcing effort in exposing the dynamics behind an unsustainable credit-driven boom[243] due to distortions introduced through excessive money creation by monetary authorities. The result is that while prices contribute to inter-temporal economic coordination, the intervention of monetary authorities undermines this function. Austrian theory argues that the bust phase is inevitable because excessive expansion will eventually create inflationary pressures, inducing the central bank to raise

---

239 Mises, L. V. (1949), 552, 553

240 Ibid., p. 555

241 Mises, L. V. (1949), pp. 563, 569

242 Garrison, R. W. (2004), p. 328

243 Ibid.

interest rates. In a worst case scenario, hyperinflation destroys all savings, capital disappears leading real interest rates to unsustainable levels. Once profitable investment projects become unprofitable the consequent turbulence will be further accelerated when the "loss of confidence" and the credit crunch provoke "herd behavior"[244]. Thus, the Austrian theorists emphasize the microeconomic structure of production over time as a key factor. Once "mal-investment" occurs, attempts of monetary authorities to correct it through credit expansion undermine the "coordinating role" of interest rates, and the recession can only be postponed, not avoided.

We will later observe in sections 3.2.2 and 3.2.3 that concepts such as "loss of confidence" and "herd behavior" are basic elements behind the "Second and Third Generation Currency Crisis models" and are thus useful to explore the dynamics behind several currency crises during the 1990s. I will also use this framework to explain the 2001 Turkish currency crisis. In addition, the "coordinating role" of interest rates, as another important aspect of the central bank's role in the Turkish economy, composes one of the main pillars of my study.

Now let me have an overview of Hyman Minsky's approach, which is useful in exploring the dynamics behind the deregulated Turkish economy from the 1980s to the early 2000s.

3.1.3. Hyman Minsky: A post-Keynesian approach

Hyman Minsky's "financial instability hypothesis" is related to financially fueled boom-and-bust economic cycles[245] and it states that unregulated capitalism is unstable[246]. In boom periods investors take on ever higher risks and seek ever higher returns. When boom turns to bust, as it inevitably will, bankrupt investors have to sell their assets, causing a downward spiral and a liquidity crunch. Hyman Minsky, in an attempt to analyze dynamics behind financial instability, provided what he called, an "interpretation of the substance of Keynes's "General Theory"[247]. The basic Minsky cycle introduces income-debt relationships for economic units, such as "hedge", "speculative" and "Ponzi" finance, emphasizing the emergence of ever more fragile corporate

---

244 Oppers, S. A. (2002), p. 7

245 Barnes, P. (2010), p. 3

246 Oppers, S. A. (2002), p. 8

247 Minsky, H. P. (1992), p. 1

balance sheets at each phase through either reduced liquidity or increased debt-equity ratios. Minsky explains as follows[248]:

> "Hedge financing units are those which can fulfill all of their contractual payment obligations by their cash flows: The greater the weight of equity financing in the liability structure, the greater the likelihood that the unit is a hedge financing unit; Speculative finance units are units that can meet their payment commitments on "income account" on their liabilities, even as they cannot repay the principal out of income cash flows. Such units need to "roll-over" their liabilities (i.e., issue new debt to meet commitments on maturing debt); For Ponzi units, the cash flows from operations are not sufficient to fulfill either the repayment of principal or the interest due on outstanding debts by their cash flows from operations. Such units can sell assets or borrow. Borrowing to pay interest or selling assets to pay interest on common stock lowers the equity of a unit."

To note that if "hedge" financing dominates, the economy is safe and may maintain a system in equilibrium. On the other hand, when "speculative" financing dominates, risk exposure of an economy increases and when "Ponzi" financing dominates, the economy is in highly risky circumstances. These financial positions reflect also changing outcomes as a function of expectations, where initially expectations about future returns become increasingly optimistic and later, as expectations are disappointed, a rapid collapse becomes unavoidable. Within this "financial instability hypothesis" framework, Minsky argues that the degree of instability will depend on how effective regulations are[249]. In fact, a weak institutional framework will increase uncertainty, which in turn will influence negatively individual expectations, thus investors' decisions[250]. While Keynes argued that uncertainty and lack of

---

[248] Minsky, H. P. (1992), p. 7

[249] Sinapi, C. (2011), p. 7

[250] Filho, F. F. and Conceicao, C. A. (2003), p. 2

confidence of investors can dampen "animal spirits"[251], Minsky emphasized the role of regulations in providing credibility and continuity to the system[252] and he further advanced that though regulations are fundamental to "normal" functioning of the system, they are inherently subject to periodic systematic crises[253].

3.1.4. Mundell-Fleming model

The Mundell-Fleming model emphasizes on the role of exchange rates in affecting the whole economy through several channels, as it connects the national price system to global markets[254]. The exchange rate is thus a price influencing a wide range of price ratios, from tradable and non-tradable goods to capital goods and labor, and exports and imports (through, for example, the costs of intermediate inputs and capital goods)[255].

An earlier Keynesian approach to exchange rate movements was initially developed in 1936 by A. P. Lerner[256], who argued that the import/export price ratio can be manipulated by either an import or an export tax[257]. Studies during World War II and in the early 1950s include simple versions of the Keynesian income-expenditure model developed by Lloyd Metzler (1942), Fritz Machlup (1943) and James Meade (1951)[258]. In the early 1960s, Robert Mundell[259] and Marcus Fleming[260] went on to extend the Keynesian income-expenditure framework to economies open to international trade in goods and financial

---

[251] Keynes, J. M. (1936), p. 161

[252] Filho, F. F. and Conceicao, C. A. (2003), p. 10

[253] Ibid.

[254] Frenkel, R. and Taylor, L. (2006), p. 1

[255] Ibid.

[256] Lerner, A. P. (1936), pp. 306-313

[257] Frenkel, R. and Taylor, L. (2006), p. 2

[258] Frenkel, J. A. and Razin, A. (1987), p. 1

[259] Mundell R. A. (1960, 1961b, 1961c, 1963, 1964)

[260] Fleming, J. M. (1962)

assets[261], thus introducing the impact of capital mobility on macroeconomic policies under alternative exchange rate regimes[262].

According to the Mundell-Fleming framework, an economy cannot simultaneously maintain exchange rate stability, free capital movement, and an independent monetary policy[263]. It implies that only two of them can be attained at the same time, hence the term "Impossible Trinity" (Fig. 3.1). In current literature, the question of suitable exchange rate regimes for emerging economies is much discussed. It is worthwhile to discuss some aspects as far as the Turkish situation is concerned.

Fig. 3.1: The impossible Trinity concept

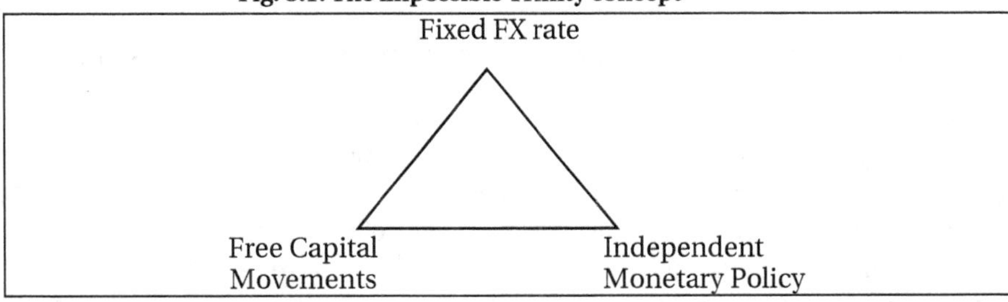

Source: Two seminal papers: Fleming (1962) and Mundell (1963)

Lawrence Summers (2000) emphasized that the choice of an appropriate exchange rate regime is an important element in minimizing the risk of currency crises and he argued in favor of a "bipolar" view, i.e., "a move away from the middle ground of pegged but adjustable fixed exchange rates toward the two corner regimes of either flexible exchange rates or a fixed exchange rate supported, if necessary, by a commitment to give up altogether an independent monetary policy"[264].

In line with this view, Stanley Fisher (2001) confirming the sentence above, considers "intermediate" regimes, which include "soft" pegs (i.e., crawling pegs and crawling bands) as crisis-prone and argues that they are not viable over long periods[265]. They both base their arguments on the Mundell-Fleming

---

261 Frenkel, J. A. and Razin, A. (1987), p. 1

262 Ibid.

263 Saxton, J. (2002), p. 11

264 Summers, L. H. (2000), p. 8

265 Fisher, S. (2002), pp. 8, 9

model. In fact, soft pegs are an attempt by a country open to international capital flows to have both a fixed rate and a monetary policy directed to domestic goals. It turns out that it is possible to achieve all three goals at once for some period of time[266]. Nevertheless, such combinations are unstable in the long term because they are internally contradictory[267]. In many cases, a soft peg is broken where the central bank pursues an expansionary monetary policy in favor of domestic goals[268] while avoiding inflation with sterilization policies. Mistakes in targeting the real supply of money can provide opportunities for arbitrage in foreign currency markets that create conditions for a currency crisis[269]. It may be possible to delay the crisis, even for long periods, however, the underlying conflict remains[270].

Why business cycle theories are useful for this study

These theories are useful for my analysis because they provide insight into the dynamics behind boom-bust cycles in an economy, making evident the root causes behind distortions. This will become an effective way of exploring factors behind financial crisis episodes experienced in 1994 and 2001 in Turkey. Though the "Washington Consensus" principles were essential for the transition to a free market economy, a politicized institutional framework led to volatile growth during the 1980s and the 1990s, due to inappropriate monetary policies. I thus introduce the theoretical framework that will be useful to investigate the impact of the 4th and 5th principles of "Washington Consensus", namely interest and exchange rates. Concepts such as "mal-investment", "forced savings" and "coordinating role of interest rates", will show the importance of a de-politicized central bank. This aspect is significant for my study as the EU requirements are based on the belief that an independent CB will pursue appropriate monetary policies, given the technical constraints imposed by the Mundell-Fleming framework.

The Minskyan approach provides perspective on how financial risk is underestimated in the beginning of a cycle, feeding a boom, until a highly leveraged situation and risk perception make the economy unstable, leading to

---

[266] Saxton, J. (2002), p. 12

[267] Ibid.

[268] Bubula, A. and Otker, I. (2003), p. 4

[269] Saxton, J. (2002), p. 15

[270] Ibid.

collapse. We consider that the quote from Minsky in the previous section corresponds to the Turkish situation in particular during the 1990s and the early 2000s, as Ponzi finance became unsustainable, increasing sovereign default risk.

The Minskyan framework is in many ways similar to the "mal-investment" concept of Mises. Nevertheless, Minsky places the origin of the financial crisis in the dynamics of capitalism itself, while Mises sees their origin in flawed monetary policies and banking laws. A combination of these two approaches is used in the next section devoted to Currency Crisis models, in an attempt to complete the theoretical perspective. This basic argument will then lead me to show in section 3.3 the causes behind volatile growth dynamics and make evident in Chapter 4 that, if there had been a de-politicized institutional framework, the "Washington Consensus" principles would have led to stable and not volatile growth. Briefly, in the absence of an adequate institutional framework, a bust phase can cause a speculative outflow of capital, a problem to which I now turn.

3.2. Currency Crisis Models

Financial crises in emerging markets have obliged economists and policy makers to draw lessons. Although there are common features behind many of them, several diverging aspects are present as well. Major examples include those experienced in Latin American countries in the 1970s and the 1980s, the 1992 European Exchange Rate Mechanism (ERM) crisis in Europe, the 1994 "Tequila" crisis in Mexico, the 1997 East Asian crisis, the 1998 Russian crisis. In 2001, crises in Argentina and Turkey had severe consequences. What these crises had in common was a sudden outflow of foreign capital and a "run on the currency" leading to sudden devaluations. This was because these countries followed a fixed exchange rate policy.

In the last decades, foreign exchange (FX) rate regimes for transition and developing economies have been at the center of policy debates. One of the major advantages of a fixed exchange rate regime is that it imposes discipline on monetary and fiscal authorities. However, if the authorities choose to ignore the disciplines implied by fixed exchange rates, countries can be obliged to abandon such a regime, usually in a sudden manner and in humiliating disarray.

Broadly speaking, in an economy with a fixed exchange rate regime, sudden capital outflows will cause a fall in international reserves leading to a currency crisis depending on the size of the sudden unexpected outflows. There are, generally, different factors behind such speculative attacks. The theoretical literature includes a variety of studies which consider different aspects. Many of them deal with devaluations. There are studies dealing with large and infrequent devaluations[271], others focus on small but frequent devaluations[272]. Some studies consider unsuccessful speculative attacks within the definition of a crisis which did not cause a devaluation but created a huge cost because they increased sharply domestic interest rates or decreased the level of international reserves[273]. Esquivel and Larrain (1998) take into consideration only successful speculative attacks. An unsuccessful attack means that the currency regime is not changed after the attack. Most currency crisis models focus on successful speculative attacks that obliged authorities to abandon the fixed exchange rate regime, albeit temporarily.

3.2.1. First Generation Models (FGMs)

Theoretical literature on currency crises follows Krugman's paper (1979), in which he shows that weak fundamentals cause currency crises[274]. The principal assumption behind the model is capital mobility and a fixed exchange rate regime. Domestic interest rates are considered equal to the international rates during the fixed rate period and to the international rates plus the rate of devaluation during the floating rate period, the latter showing up as a risk premium during the pre-crisis phase reflecting the risk of devaluation. For example, an excessive expansionary fiscal and monetary policy or a money financed budget deficit would imply a lower domestic interest rate compared with world rates. To prevent a capital outflow and avoid devaluation the central bank must intervene by selling international reserves, thus decreasing their level. If the expansionary monetary policy continues and the budget deficit becomes permanent, the central bank reserves gradually decline and the economy becomes vulnerable to speculative attacks, which lead to a currency crisis. Consequently, the authorities are obliged to devalue and to leave the fixed exchange rate regime.

---

[271] Edwards, S. and Montiel, P. (1989); Edwards, S. and Santaella, J. (1993); Frankel, J. A. and Rose, A. K. (1996); Milesi-Ferretti, G. M. and Razin, A. (1998)

[272] Flood, R. and Marion, N. (1994), Klein, M. W. and Marion, N. P. (1994)

[273] Eichengreen, B., Rose, A. K. and Wyplosz, C. (1995), Kaminsky and Reinhart (1999)

[274] Krugman, P. (1979), pp. 311-325

The Krugman (1979) framework, a restructured version of the Mundell-Fleming model, was further developed by Flood and Garber (1984) who introduced a small open economy, where prices of goods are set on world markets, thus purchasing power parity (PPP) holds[275]. Domestic residents can hold domestic or foreign money and domestic or foreign bonds. Monetary authority holds international reserves to keep the fixed exchange rate under control. That is to say[276]:

$$P = SP^* \tag{1}$$

where P is the domestic price level;

P^* is the foreign price level;

S is the nominal exchange rate.

For simplicity, it is assumed that P^* is fixed, i.e., $P^* = 1$. Thus, the price level is equal to the nominal foreign exchange rate. And, the domestic inflation rate is equal to the devaluation rate. Uncovered interest rate parity is represented by[277]:

$$i = i^* + S^* / S \tag{2}$$

where i is the domestic interest rate, i^* is the foreign one and S^* is the time derivative.

The monetary base (M) is composed of domestic credits (D) and FX reserves (R).

$$M = D + R \tag{3}$$

Moreover, it is assumed that government runs a constant budget deficit, which in turn is financed by a continuous rise of domestic credit. Reserve losses by the monetary authority match exactly domestic credit expansion. Thus, the following holds[278]:

$$R^\circ = -D^\circ = -\mu \tag{4}$$

---

275 Flood, R. and Garber, P.M. (1984), p. 2

276 Ibid

277 Flood, R. and Garber, P.M. (1984), p. 2

278 Ibid., p. 3

where D° is the derivative of D with respect to time and it represents change in domestic credit. That is to say, an increasing budget deficit leads to a continuous fall in reserves. When the level of reserves becomes close to zero, the government will have to abandon the fixed exchange rate.

To begin with, the exchange rate is fixed such that the "shadow" or "market" exchange rate[279] will diverge from the fixed one. However, monetary expansion led by continuous public sector deficits will push the "market" rate toward the fixed rate. Speculators will be aware that the exchange rate will be floated at time $t=T$, which is the optimal time for speculators to attack the currency. In other words, the fixed exchange rate will be kept as long as the divergence between the two rates is significant. As it approaches the fixed one, the speculative attack will become the dominant strategy[280]. In fact, each individual speculator is exposed to a loss by not selling out domestic currency if others do[281].

The main contribution of the "first generation" models is to show that speculative attacks are rational reactions of the market to inconsistent government policies. Such attacks restore the equilibrium of an economy with deteriorating fundamentals. This result is implied in the Mundell-Fleming model. In fact, with a fixed exchange rate regime and perfect capital mobility, expansionary monetary policy is ineffective.

Extensions to Krugman's approach

Krugman (1979) provides insight into the basic structure of a currency crisis. However, he assumes that monetary authorities do not try to prevent a crisis. Several authors developed extensions to the model assuming some government intervention, like sterilization, domestic borrowing, and interest rate policy. For example, Flood, Garber, and Kramer (1996)[282] argue that passive behavior of central bank is not realistic and they introduce "sterilization" as a commonly used reaction by monetary authorities. More precisely, they consider the case

---

[279] "Shadow" exchange rate can be defined as the rate that would be experienced if the exchange rate was not fixed or the one which ensures purchasing power parity "at home" and "abroad" (Flood, R. P., Garber, P. M. and Kramer, C. (1996), p. 227). I use the term "market" exchange rate interchangeably with the term "shadow" exchange rate.

[280] Jeanne, O. (2000), p. 14

[281] Ibid.

[282] Flood, R., Garber, P. and Kramer, C. (1996), p. 229

of the 1992 ERM crisis and that of the 1994 Mexican peso collapse, during which reserve losses before and at the time of attacks were sterilized. That is to say, the central bank expanded domestic credit (through open market purchases of domestic bonds) by the size of reserve losses and the attack did not influence the base money supply. Briefly, sterilization affects the bond market, rather than the money market. And, without any change in money demand, devaluation is avoided in the short-term[283].

Others[284] argue that monetary authorities could avoid reserve losses before the balance-of-payments (BOP) crisis by issuing domestic debt. Therefore, the equation (3) would become:

$$M = D + R - i\,B; \tag{5}$$

where i stands for domestic interest rates and B for bonds (instant maturity government debt).

In this way, bond issuance could completely finance the deficit and, therefore, $D = R = 0$. However, domestic debt B would increase, putting pressure on the inter-temporal budget constraint. Anyway, this situation cannot last forever because debt is paid back by new debt, at perhaps rising interest rates. A rational government would weigh costs and benefits and choose optimally whether to use this kind of intervention or to expose its economy to capital market shocks. In fact, crisis is unavoidable unless more fundamental measures are taken. For example, central banks can actively defend the domestic currency by raising short-term interest rates. This policy puts a break on the economy and postpones the crisis until the government adopts fundamental measures to regain credibility.

We observed in section 2.2.1.1 that bond financing of budget deficits gradually replaced domestic money creation in Turkey by the end-1980s, which led to unsustainable sovereign debt dynamics and crises.

3.2.2. Second Generation Models (SGMs)

The Krugman (1979) and Flood and Garber (1984) models describe how rational financial markets respond to unsustainable macroeconomic policies. They show that when monetary or fiscal policies are inconsistent with a fixed

---

283 However, to note that sterilization works better in cases where speculators expect a currency to appreciate. The central bank can easily sterilize incoming capital by selling bonds and accumulating reserves. It is much more difficult when capital is flowing out.

284 Calvo, G. A. (1996), p. 9; Calvo, G. And Vegh, C. (1999), p. 50

exchange rate, currency crises occur. These models, though providing important insights, do not explain underlying dynamics[285]. During the 1990s, the problem was not strictly speaking the weak fundamentals but their relationship with speculators' expectations. Krugman (1991) follows the Minskyan approach and attributes currency crises to market participants' expectations[286]. The year following the publication of Krugman (1991), the European ERM was exposed to a huge speculative attack. This event became subject to many other studies, i.e., the so-called Second Generation models, a major feature of which is that the occurrence of the speculative attack is triggered by the collective behavior of speculators and not by the policy actions of governments. For example, during the European Monetary System (EMS) crisis, the United Kingdom, and France did not follow excessively expansionary policies[287]. However, increasing unemployment and higher interest rates damaged the credibility of these countries as to whether they would respect their commitment to the EMS "tunnel". In fact, monetary authorities may always opt to float or not[288]. They will take this decision by weighing the benefits and costs of maintaining the fixed peg considering the overall economic conditions, based not only on fundamentals but also on beliefs of speculators. From this perspective, if speculators think that the policy maker is about to devalue, the attack starts. That is to say, the crisis is not determined only by fundamentals but it is also "self-fulfilling"[289]. In this context, the optimal policy of monetary authorities would be to float if speculators expect a devaluation or to keep the peg if not. The occurrence and timing of the crisis depend on the mood of the market. A rough analogy to speculators' "mood" could be what Keynes called "animal spirits" of entrepreneurs, which are not necessarily related to market fundamentals whatever they are!

However, fundamentalist and "self-fulfilling" views are not mutually exclusive. A currency becomes vulnerable to "self-fulfilling" speculation when fundamentals deteriorate[290]. On the other hand, an increase in devaluation expectations could force monetary authorities to raise interest rates, which in

---

[285] Jeanne, O. (2000), p. 2

[286] Krugman, P. (1991), p. 660

[287] Ibid.

[288] Ibid., p. 3

[289] Ibid., p. 4

[290] Krugman, P. (1991), p. 5

turn would make it costly to maintain the fixed exchange rate regime and fundamentals would worsen.

Thus, this perspective goes beyond an evaluation of movements of a few macro-fundamentals and it captures several other mutually reinforcing micro-factors, many of which are tacit, floating, subtle and specific to place and political environment, in turn depending on portfolio preferences of international investors offsetting their expected return against risk exposure in rapidly moving global markets.

To note that such interaction between macro-fundamentals and micro-factors introduces a further degree of uncertainty. Therefore, "multiple equilibria" become a major feature of the Second Generation models, which of course mean no equilibrium[291]. This was the price to pay for endogenizing the collective behavior of speculators, where each speculator has to determine how the economic conditions and expectations of other speculators will influence the policy makers' decisions about the exchange rate[292]. Thus, this approach, called also "escape clause", investigates under which circumstances it is convenient for the government to opt out or "escape" from a fixed exchange rate regime.

To explain this concept, I need to model expectations about a future monetary policy that considers the response of the monetary authorities to different variables. Let me consider the following model taken from Olivier Jeanne[293]:

$$D^e = F(X_1, X_2, \ldots) \tag{6}$$

where $X_1, X_2, \ldots$ are variables affecting the government's decision about monetary policy, like current account deficit, the unemployment rate or the state of the banking system.

Olivier Jeanne proposes to assume that the net benefit (NB) of maintaining a fixed exchange rate can be decomposed into two following terms[294]:

---

291 "Theory of Reflexivity" argued by George Soros is in the same spirit: it exposes the causal relationship between market expectations and the economic fundamentals running in both directions, so that the former may not be uniquely determined by the latter (Soros, G. (1994), pp. 46-80).

292 Jeanne, O. (2000), p. 19

293 Jeanne, O. (1997), p. 267

294 Jeanne, O. (1997), p. 267

$$\text{NB} = b^{t} - \eta(p_{t-1}) \tag{7}$$

where b_t = the gross benefit of the fixed peg;

(P_{t-1})= the probability held by speculators at *(t-1)* that the policy maker will devalue sometime in the future.

This equation shows that the benefit of a fixed exchange rate depends not only on economic conditions but also on the credibility of the monetary authority's commitment to the fixed exchange rate regime[295]. In fact:

b_t is determined by macroeconomic variables like current account balance, real exchange rates or the unemployment rate;

(p_{t-1}) implies that for given economic conditions, a higher p (a lower credibility) reduces the benefit of the peg. And lower credibility could force the monetary authorities to take costly decisions, like raising interest rates.

Consider the following model where the unemployment rate is given by the expectations augmented Philips curve[296]:

$$U_2 = \delta U_1 - \lambda\left(\pi - \pi^{e}\right) \tag{8}$$

where U_1 and U_2 are deviations of the unemployment rate from its natural level in periods one and two; π is the current level of inflation, whereas π^e is its expected level[297].

The monetary authority will decide to devalue or not to devalue by minimizing the following loss function *(L)*[298]:

$$L = (U_2)^2 + \varphi C \tag{9}$$

---

[295] Ibid.

[296] Jeanne, O. (2000), p. 23

[297] It is assumed that devaluation rate matches the inflation rate (Jeanne, O. (2000), p. 23)

[298] Ibid.

where φ_t is a dummy variable and is equal to 1 if monetary authority opts out, 0 otherwise; and C is the opting out cost and incorporates, i.e., loss of advantage of the fixed exchange rate regime or loss of reputation or credibility of central bank[299]. Speculators form their expectations with probability 1 or 0. Let us observe both of the cases:

Let us suppose that speculators do not expect any devaluation in the second period, i.e., $d^e=0$, where d is the devaluation rate. If the monetary authorities devalue, the loss function gives[300]:

$$L^D = (\delta U_1 - \lambda d)^2 + C; \tag{10}$$

If it does not devalue the loss function gives:

$$L^{ND} = (\delta U_1)^2 \tag{11}$$

A rational government will consider equations (10) and (11) to decide whether to devalue or not by estimating the case with the minimum loss.

1. $L^{ND} > L^D \Rightarrow \frac{C}{\lambda \lambda_d} - 2\delta U_1 < -\lambda d$ **=> government prefers devaluation**

2. $L^D > L^{ND} \Rightarrow \frac{C}{\lambda \lambda_d} - 2\delta U_1 > -\lambda d$ **=> government prefers to keep the fixed FX rate**

Now let me consider the case in which speculators do expect devaluation. If monetary authorities devalue, the loss function gives[301]:

$$L^D = (\delta U_1)^2 + C$$

And the loss in case it does not devalue:

$$L^{ND} = (\delta U_1 + \lambda d^e)^2$$

The decision of government will be based on the following equations[302]:

---

299 Jeanne, O. (1997), p. 268

300 Jeanne, O. (2000), p. 24

301 Ibid.

1. $L^{ND} > L^{D} \Rightarrow \frac{c}{\lambda \lambda_d} - 2\delta U_1 < \lambda d$ **=> government prefers devaluation**

2. $L^{D} > L^{ND} \Rightarrow \frac{c}{\lambda \lambda_d} - 2\delta U_1 > \lambda d$ **=> government prefers to keep the fixed FX rate**

To note that the variable $\frac{c}{\lambda \lambda_d} - 2\delta U_1$ is at the centre of the whole picture. I define it as "fundamental variable" Ω and summarize the above results as follows[303]:

1. $\Omega < -\lambda d$ => government prefers devaluation
2. $\Omega > -\lambda d$ => government prefers to keep the fixed FX rate
3. $\Omega < \lambda d$ => government prefers devaluation

(Cases 2 and 3: Multiple equilibria)

4. $\Omega > \lambda d$ => government prefers to keep the fixed FX rate
5. Observations[304]

- The variable Ω plays the same role as the "economic fundamentals" considered in the First Generation models;
- In cases 1) and 4) the government will not take into consideration the expectations of speculators. It will devalue in the case 1) and it will keep the fixed FX rate in the other;
- However, in cases 2) and 3) the outcome will depend on speculators expectations. In fact, in case of a speculative attack the government will devalue; if speculators do not expect a devaluation there will not be a speculative attack and the authorities will not devalue. Therefore, in this interval all depends on speculators' "spirits";
- The gross benefit of the fixed FX rate is a linear function of the opting out cost and of the unemployment rate. And the opting out cost may depend on

---

302 Ibid.

303 Jeanne, O. (2000), p. 25

304 Ibid.

other macroeconomic variables like current account balance or real exchange rate.

Discussion

The Second Generation models rely on the speculators' "mood", which can be influenced by "sunspot variables" such as:

- Certain hedge funds may be carefully observed by market participants. As a consequence, they may, in certain circumstances, affect market expectations[305];
- Large players play a similar role by taking a large position discreetly and then making public declarations that the fixed peg will not hold. This information may trigger a "self-fulfilling" and highly profitable attack[306];
- An exogenous event could become significant for market participants if they think that it is important. The 2001 Turkish currency crisis occurred because the Turkish Prime Minister abandoned a meeting in which the President was participating. Market participants interpreted this as a strong disagreement over economic reforms and attacked the currency[307].

Extensions to the Escape Clause Approach

The loss function in the model above could incorporate other factors, i.e.:

- Inflation increasing at rates higher than trading partners' could make the fixed exchange rate overvalued;
- Current account deficits could reach unsustainable levels;
- Political instability could rise at the approach of general elections or if a parliamentary majority is not sustainable due to disagreements between political parties.

And for many other similar reasons the parameters in the loss function could increase or change their value over time. In fact, different authors

---

305 I will examine this aspect in Section 3.2.3.1.

306 For a detailed examination of this issue, see Corsetti, G., Pesenti, P. and Roubini, N. (2001), pp. 1-21.

307 I will examine this event in Section 3.3.2.3.

attribute different weights to different explanatory factors: De Kock and Grilli (1993)[308] and Velasco (1996)[309] consider domestic debt. The central bank could prefer to devalue in order to decrease the real value of domestic debt. However, if the amount of domestic debt is in the "uncertainty zone", the government could face "self-fulfilling" attacks. Cole and Kehoe (2000)[310] focus on a similar model considering the amount of domestic debt and its maturity structure. Obstfeld (1994)[311] defines the devaluation rate as an endogenous variable determined by the relationship between inflation and unemployment rates. Drazen and Masson (1994)[312] consider a case in which speculators cannot estimate the level of opting-out cost. An increase in the unemployment rate reduces the credibility of the fixed exchange rate regime. However, if central bank insists keeping the fixed exchange rate, this could be interpreted by the market that the opting-out cost is too high and such a message could increase the credibility of the fixed exchange rate regime.

3.2.3. Third Generation Models (TGMs)

The 1997 East Asian currency crisis diverged from previous ones in some respects, hence the name "Third Generation", attributed by academic discussion to explaining it. In particular, "contagion" and interaction between "banking" and "currency" crises (or "twin" crises) became more pronounced[313]. However, I can still state that these models belong to the "escape-clause" category or Second Generation models due to strong reliance on the expectations of market participants or they may even be treated as an extension of Second Generation models with certain new interacting and rapidly evolving features.

The link between banking and currency crises was investigated by several authors well before the 1997 East Asia episode. While geographic contagion was experienced as early as the 1994 Mexican Tequila crisis, contagion phenomena started to produce a strong impact in the following years. For instance, the 1997 East Asian currency crisis and the 1998 Russian debt crisis tended to spread

---

308 De Kock, G. and Grilli, V. (1993), pp. 347-358

309 Velasco (1996), pp. 1023-1035

310 Cole, H. R. and Kehoe, T. J. (2000), pp. 309-330

311 Obstfeld, M. (1994), pp. 189-213

312 Drazen, A. and Masson, P. R. (1994), pp. 735-754

313 Jeanne, O. (2000), p. 6

very rapidly to neighboring countries[314]. Thus, to avoid any confusion that could derive from terminology I emphasize that these are Second Generation models with some additional features.

"Herd behavior", a major feature of these models, is not a new concept in economics. In fact, it presents similar dynamics to the Keynesian beauty contest[315], where the prize is awarded to the competitor whose choice most nearly corresponds to the average preferences of the competitors as a whole. The critical aspect here is to be able to anticipate what average opinion expects the average opinion to be.

"Herd behavior" can also be explained through "bandwagon effects", driven by the belief that other investors have privileged information[316]. They often ignore their own information and follow other investors' behavior thinking that others have had some news even though in fact they do not. Krugman (1998) defines "herding" and "contagion" of crises as follows[317]:

> "Herding: A wave of selling stocks, pushing the prices down, could be magnified through sheer imitation and turn into a stampede out of the currency. Aside from the biases and limitations of human cognition, herding occurs because of two other reasons. The first one is bandwagon effect driven by the awareness that investors have private information. The second answer is that much of the money invested in crisis-prone countries is managed by agents rather than directly by principals. All agents will want to act alike because they are compensated by their performances compared to others even if they have information that the market's judgment is in fact wrong.
> Contagion: Linkages between the countries explain contagion. A currency crisis in country A worsens the fundamentals in country

[314] Jeanne, O. (2000), p. 39

[315] Keynes (1936), p.156

[316] Krugman (1998), p. 1

[317] Ibid.

B. It prompts a competitive devaluation in order to remain competitive in trade."

In fact, a crisis can quickly spread to neighboring economies or to trading partners[318]. Major economic shifts in industrial countries can cause crises in emerging markets depending on the degree of their exposure to foreign borrowing, the size of their current account deficit and government debt, problems in the banking system and other factors that make the country vulnerable to international capital movements. Uncertainty about a central bank's commitment to keep a fixed exchange rate and its subsequent collapse suggest to the market that another country with similar macroeconomic circumstances might also abandon its fixed parity[319].

Another reason for contagion could be the interdependence of trading partners. The devaluation of several Exchange Rate Mechanism (ERM) currencies in 1992 increased the competitiveness of some countries with respect to others, influencing trade balances and employment prospects. For example, the devaluation of the Italian Lira in September 1992 decreased France's competitiveness compared with Italy, creating the expectation that the French franc would be devalued as well. Such expectation can trigger a capital flight.

A degradation of fundamentals increases the probability of a crisis. However, the timing of the crisis is unpredictable. It is difficult to measure, for example, the beliefs of market participants about the perceived health of the banking system or the political willingness to defend the fixed exchange rate. In this regard, this approach is similar to the Second Generation models. In fact, mere changes in investors' expectations can cause a speculative attack.

Some authors argue that currency crises lead to banking crises. For example, Mishkin[320] argues that if the banking system has a fragile structure and if a high proportion of debt is denominated in foreign currency, a devaluation of domestic currency will result in an increase in interest rates and rise in indebtedness. This would worsen balance sheets of firms and banks, causing a "twin" crisis. Others maintain that banking crises lead to currency

---

[318] Masson, P. (1998), p. 3

[319] Drazen, A. (1999), p. 6

[320] Mishkin, F. S. (1996), p. 42

crises. For example, Calvo (1996)[321], considering the 1994 Mexican crisis, argues that if central banks bailout defaulting banks by printing money, the fixed exchange rate cannot hold (a modified version of the Krugman (1979) model). Another group argues that banking and currency crises have some common causes. For example, Calvo and Vegh (1999)[322] show that exchange rate stabilization programs could become a cause of a currency crisis. In fact, while it is possible to stabilize exchange rate movements in short term, inflation rates converge slowly leading to real exchange variability. An appreciation leads to a widening current account deficit which, in turn, needs to be financed by foreign capital. If financial markets are convinced that the stabilization program cannot hold, a currency crisis can occur, leading to a banking crisis as well. Others argue that banking crises are highly correlated with currency crises and the causal link runs in both directions[323].

In both types of crises, financial liberalization and increased access to international capital markets accelerate the boom phase of the cycle. Deteriorating fundamentals shift market sentiment and "herd behavior" of investors could cause speculative attacks to spread to other economies ("spillover effect" or geographical contagion).

Studies investigating stabilization programs' impact on real currency appreciation and current account deficits are significant for our thesis, as the Turkish transition period involved such dynamics in line with Calvo and Vegh (1998) mentioned above. For example, I will examine in section 3.3.2.3 a stabilization program introduced in Turkey in 1999, which caused real currency appreciation leading to a current account deficit. The following quote from Kaminsky and Reinhart (1999)[324], that also introduces the impact of a fragile banking sector, provides insight into the 2001 Turkish currency crisis:

> "Theory and evidence exchange rate based stabilization plans have well-defined dynamics: Because inflation converges to international levels only gradually, there is a marked cumulative real exchange rate appreciation. Also, at the early stages of the

---

321 Calvo, G. (1996), p. 7

322 Calvo, G. and Vegh, C. (1999), pp. 3, 60

323 Goldfajn, I. and Valdes, R. (1997), p. 5; Kaminsky, G. L. and Reinhart, C. M. (1999), p. 474

324 Kaminsky, G. L. and Reinhart, C. M. (1999), p. 475

plan there is a boom in imports and economic activity, financed by borrowing abroad. As the current account deficit continues to widen, financial markets become convinced that the stabilization program is unsustainable, fueling an attack against the domestic currency. Since the boom is usually financed by a surge in bank credit, as banks borrow abroad, when the capital inflows become outflows and asset markets crash, the banking system caves in."

Conclusion

The way liquidity is provided is important. While central banks' key mandate is to provide liquidity, in some cases deregulated economies adopting international standards are exposed to free international capital flows, initially feeding the boom phase of a cycle, which terminates sooner or later with a recession or crisis. In some ways, the Austrian critique of fractional reserve banking, leading to excessive credit creation and a boom/bust cycle, foreshadows the consequences for a naively deregulated economy suddenly acquiring free access to international capital markets. The Business Cycle theories, the Mundell-Fleming and the Currency Crisis models provide us with additional theoretical tools whereby to understand the deregulated Turkish economy. Furthermore, introducing hedge funds in the next section will be useful for examining circumstances under which international capital movements can feed both deficits and bubbles, leading to volatile growth and creating an unsustainable cyclical trend. These highly leveraged institutions can potentially become a leading force in global markets, bearing risk in emerging markets in an attempt to make a higher profit. This section provides a preliminary overview, which will in turn be compared in Chapter 4 with the FDI flows, in order to discuss the impacts of these two types of capital flows and their contribution to financial (in)stability.

3.2.3.1. Hedge Funds

My aim in this section is to discuss key features of hedge funds in an attempt to gain insight into potential factors that can cause sudden movements in markets. Hedge funds are attentively observed by market participants in global markets because, in certain circumstances, they are able to affect market expectations. Thus, I conclude the section on Third Generation models with a discussion of these funds.

Hedge fund managers differ from other fund managers[325]. For instance, while the latter aim to eliminate "idiosyncratic risk" through portfolio diversification this is not always the aim of the former[326]. Thus, they can sometimes reinforce a "self-fulfilling" attack or "herd behavior".

The term "hedge fund" is used to describe any investment fund that uses "short selling"[327] and "leverage" for the purpose of hedging[328]. Unregulated hedge funds have acquired over time a highly leveraged nature[329]. They have not been subject to the same regulatory framework as other funds (i.e., mutual funds) which made them less transparent. Hedge funds have used, generally, dynamic trading strategies, which involved them in taking positions in different markets and adjusting investment portfolios frequently to benefit from changing expectations[330]. In fact, a significant proportion of their return has been due to "state-contingent" bets. Thus, developing "option strategies" has helped to capture such bets at least partially[331]. During the 1997 East Asian and the 1998 Russian crises, hedge funds were believed to have played a role in triggering these episodes[332]. Also, the 2001 Turkish financial crisis was precipitated by a "self-fulfilling" attack[333].

---

325 Nguyen, H. (2004), pp. 7, 8

326 See Annex 2 for an explanation of some distinguishing features of hedge funds regarding their investment strategies, i.e., their "alpha" driven behavior, which aims to exploit contrarian profit possibilities.

327 Short selling may be defined as the practice of selling a security the seller does not own at the time of the sale. Thus, the short seller bets on a stock price fall. His aim is to repurchase identical securities in the market to return them to the lender, in order to "close the position". However, this operation entails also risks. If the security price rises unexpectedly, the short seller will make a loss (Gruenewald, S., Wagner, A. F. and Weber, R. H. (2009), pp. 4, 5).

328 The first hedge fund in the history was founded in the U.S. in 1949 by Alfred Winslow Jones. This was an investment company specialized in purchasing undervalued stocks and selling short overvalued ones, with the objective of hedging, i.e., averaging out the portfolio's total risk exposure (Financial Stability Forum (2000), p. 80).

329 Ibid., p. 1

330 Financial Stability Forum (2000), p. 78

331 Agarwal, V. and Naik, N. Y. (2000), p. 6

332 Financial Stability Forum (2000), p. 1

333 Section 3.3.2.3, "Discussion" point "9)"

Impact of hedge funds on financial stability

The lack of information on hedge funds' activity makes it difficult to measure the impact of hedge funds on financial stability in emerging economies[334]. However, they perform several identifiable functions in the market that will be discussed below: First of all, they turn their portfolios over more frequently when compared with traditional funds, i.e., mutual funds. Thus, their short-term influence on markets can be larger than others[335]. Moreover, "macro" hedge funds try to exploit doubts regarding the sustainability of unsound macroeconomic policies, inducing them, for instance, to bet whether a fixed exchange rate regime in an emerging economy is sustainable[336]. However, while their expectations can potentially lead to "herd behavior" in markets, hedge funds, as active market participants, are more able than mutual funds to invest in less liquid markets and instruments. It is generally assumed that higher liquidity leads to more effective pricing. Their presence, therefore, allows new risk-return combinations, which may perhaps contribute to eliminating market inefficiencies and thereby lead to more "complete" financial markets[337]. However, they can assume highly risky positions due to leverage. While this aspect enables them to earn large profits, we note that their risk exposure can become extremely high and an unexpected event may cause equally large losses[338]. Thus, the counterparties, i.e., lenders, may also be in difficulty through "contagion" or "spill-over" effects.

The use of derivatives is another important aspect. Hedge funds originally operated by taking a "hedged" position against a particular event, expectation, or unexpected movement. However, over time many hedge funds became involved in operations far from this original purpose. In other words, hedge funds in many cases do not present a "hedged" nature[339]. In fact, derivatives are often used for speculative purposes, for example, an investor following a "positive feedback trading"[340]. In behavioral finance literature, this kind of

---

334 Garbaravicius, T. and Dierick, F. (2005), p. 43

335 Ibid.

336 Ibid.

337 Ibid., p. 5

338 Strömqvist, M. (2009), p. 89

339 Lhabitant, F. S. (2001), pp. 2, 3

340 also referred to as "momentum trading" or "trend-chasing" (Financial Stability Forum (2000), p. 145).

investor purchases assets in a rising market and sells them in a falling market[341], reinforcing the trend. Thus, the consequent shift may acquire a sudden non-linear direction from its fundamental value in the short-term. The magnitude of such a shift will also depend on the leverage used.

"Investment style" is another factor that can influence market dynamics. Hedge funds are typically involved (in particular "macro hedge funds") in taking strategic positions in response to shifting perceived economic performance and market inefficiencies[342]. Large strategic positions might, under certain circumstances become "self-fulfilling" (in line with the creation of "multiple equilibria" in the Second Generation models)[343].

It is also worth distinguishing the concept of "herd" from "style". "Herding" means that some funds imitate other funds' trade without having the same information. However, two funds following the same "style", having the same information and employing a similar trading strategy, are likely to have the same trades without any leader-follower relationship between them[344]. In the aftermath of the 1997 East Asian currency episode, the IMF investigated the role of hedge funds in triggering the crisis. This led to a study by Eichengreen et al. (1998), in which they questioned whether these funds can dominate or manipulate particular markets. They tested whether there was a significant tendency for other categories of investors to take the same positions as hedge funds in the current or immediately subsequent period. They found little evidence that hedge funds played a singular role in promoting "herd behavior"[345], arguing that their size was small compared with other institutional investors.

Nevertheless, the near-collapse of Long Term Capital Management (LTCM), a large hedge fund, during the Russian debt crisis in 1998, raised concerns regarding potential systemic risks generated by hedge funds. In the aftermath of this event, a U.S. government report recommended increased public disclosure by hedge funds arguing that more transparency would reduce "informational asymmetries" among market players[346].

---

341 Bohl, M. T. and Reitz, S. (2000), p. 1

342 Financial Stability Forum (2000), p. 123

343 Ibid., p. 124

344 Fung, W., Hsied, D. A. (2000), p. 6

345 Eichengreen et al. (1998), p. 11

346 Schwarcz, S. L. (2008), p. 218

Corsetti et al. (2001) investigated, in a wider perspective, the role of large players in currency crises[347]. They argued that marker power depends on the interaction of a variety of factors such as the size, the reputation for quality information, the ability to signal portfolio composition to the rest of the market and the ability to leverage. They took as a hypothesis the case in which large players' volume (or the estimated total size of hedge funds' net currency positions) is too small when compared with other institutional investors in the market and the amount of international reserves position of governments. They nevertheless argued that if markets think large players or hedge funds to have access to superior information, then even their modest short positions may lead others to "herd". They further advanced that, assuming "asymmetric information" among investors, even if large traders have less correct information when compared with small investors, their erratic forecasts can still influence other market participants' behavior given their size or position in the market[348]. In this regard, the Financial Stability Forum (2000) study argued that some macro hedge funds had a strong reputation in terms of information precision and the ability to forecast macro trends[349].

The Basel Committee on Banking Supervision preferred to use the term "highly leveraged institutions" when discussing risk components[350]. Leverage is the magnification of the rate of return (positive or negative) on a position or investment beyond the rate obtained by a direct investment of own funds in the cash market[351]. Its use can affect markets in two ways[352]: First of all, leverage creates and enhances the risk of default by borrowers, by definition. Moreover, it increases the potential for rapid deleveraging, which can cause turbulence in financial markets. For instance, if the rate of return on an investment to which borrowed funds have been committed turns out to be less than expected, the investor's equity may rapidly diminish and become insufficient to cover the loans. In the case of an unexpected price movement, a leveraged position will be closed faster by an investor than if it were not leveraged. The larger the leverage, the smaller is the price change that will be needed to trigger a reversal.

---

[347] Corsetti, G., Pesenti, P. and Roubini, N. (2001), p. 23

[348] Ibid., p. 17

[349] Corsetti, G., Pesenti, P. and Roubini, N. (2001), p. 23

[350] Basel Committee on Banking Supervision (2000), pp. 1-10

[351] Breuer, P. (2000), p. 5

[352] Ibid.

Thus, the larger the leveraged position is, the higher the impact may be of an exogenous destabilizing price movement[353].

To determine the potential for financial market turbulence, it is important to consider not only on-balance sheet leverage but also leverage implicit in off-balance sheet transactions, i.e., financial derivatives. Leverage is measured as the ratio of a firm's total assets relative to its equity[354]. In the case of on-balance sheet transactions, it is straightforward to calculate this ratio where increased bank loans will increase the size of assets over equity. However, in the case of off-balance sheet transactions, the level of risk of the leveraged position is more complicated to calculate.

Firms can be motivated to acquire leverage through derivatives for a variety of reasons. For instance, this operation is cheaper than an on-balance sheet transaction and it allows firms to assume a position with less capital[355]. Moreover, it can be argued that hedge funds prefer off-balance sheet transactions, which allow them to bear any risky position that their trade strategy allows while operating outside the supervision of regulators[356].

The Financial Stability Forum (2000) argued that most hedge funds used a moderate leverage ratio around 2: 1, with the highest leverage ratio among all investment styles being around 4: 1[357]. However, this is based on on-balance sheet transactions and it does not include risk exposure from off-balance sheet derivative transactions[358]. Regarding the LTCM, its leverage ratio of the trade[359] was between 40: 1 and 50: 1 before its collapse. The fund's overall leverage ratio fluctuated between 14: 1 and 31: 1 from June 1994 to December 1997[360], the latter ratio being evaluated as "extremely high" by the U.S. President's Working Group on Financial Markets[361].

---

[353] Breuer, P. (2000), p. 5

[354] Breuer, P. (2000), p. 5

[355] Ibid., p. 8

[356] Ibid., p. 3

[357] Financial Stability Forum (2000), p. 79

[358] Ibid., p. 153

[359] i.e., the total position to the amount of the LTCM's own capital devoted to the trade

[360] MacKenzie, D. (2003), p. 355

[361] US President's Working Group on Financial Markets (1999), p. 5

I end this section with a quote from by the Financial Stability Forum (2000) study[362]:

> "Under normal market conditions, highly leveraged institutions (HLIs) do not threaten the stability of medium-sized markets. Together with other market participants, HLIs can play an important role translating views about the fundamentals into prices and face the same incentives as other market participants to avoid outsized positions. Because of their ability and willingness to take leveraged positions, HLIs can be an important source of market liquidity and can, over time, contribute positively to market development.
>
> From time to time, large and concentrated positions may be established in medium-sized markets by HLIs. When this is the case, HLIs have the potential materially to influence market dynamics. The size and duration of the effects can be amplified through herding or through other market participants moving to the sidelines and depend critically on the strength of the fundamentals and the behavior of "ongoing" transactions in the domestic currency.
>
> The judgment as to whether in such cases HLIs positions are destabilizing has to be made on a case-by-case basis. Several members of the study group believe that large HLIs positions exacerbated the situations in several of the case study economies in 1998, contributing to potentially unstable market dynamics and significant spillovers.
>
> [....]
>
> The group is concerned about the possible impact on market dynamics of some of the aggressive practices cited in the case

---

362 Financial Stability Forum (2000), pp. 125, 126

> study economies during 1998; it is not, however, able to reach a conclusion on the scale of these practices, whether manipulation was involved and their impact on market integrity."

Despite all, some groups members believe that "manipulation can and does occur in foreign exchange markets and should be a serious source of concern for policy makers"[363].

3.2.3.2. Should "short selling" by hedge funds be restricted in a crisis?

Models can provide expected results as long as assumptions behind them are met. However, these assumptions are generally violated in real markets to different degrees. The theoretical framework I introduced will nonetheless be useful for a variety of reasons: First of all, it provides insight on the way money and credit are supplied and managed. Its interaction with an institutional framework in emerging economies has a significant impact on macroeconomic stability, one of my major focus themes. This aspect is crucially important for my study because the Turkish deregulation experience shows that short-term capital-led volatile growth was a major reason for instability and crises. The "Washington Consensus" prescription concerning liberalization of capital movements did not take into account the possibility that financial markets could change since Bretton Woods, becoming much larger and more volatile thanks to derivatives. While "Washington Consensus" was designed in 1989, both the number of hedge funds and capital under their management increased by the mid-1990s. I have to emphasize that speculators are liquidity providers and contribute to efficient pricing in markets, leading ideally to "completeness" of the latter. Moreover, they bear risk that others do not prefer to assume, allowing efficient risk sharing. Thus, thanks to financial derivatives, hedgers can find a counterparty wishing to take the opposite risk exposure at lower cost and in less time[364]. However, when deficit financing in an emerging market is supplied through global markets and the central bank is ineffective, rapid capital in and outflows can feed volatile growth cycles leading to instability, as the Turkish experience will show us.

On the other hand, an additional reason for instability can lie in the way derivatives themselves are used. While derivatives made the financial system safer for hedging purposes, also interventions of regulators in abnormal market

---

363 Financial Stability Forum (2000), pp. 125, 126

364 Miller, M. H. (1997), p. 8

circumstances are to be considered. For instance, the default of the investment bank Lehman Brothers in September 2008 put financial institutions' stocks under pressure and led securities regulators of a large number of countries to adopt emergency "short selling" restrictions[365]. To note that Turkey was not one of these countries[366]. A reason for this could be the fact that the 2008-2009 global recession did not have a severe impact on the Turkish economy. Nevertheless, it is worth to question whether the 2001 Turkish currency crisis, the most severe in Turkish history, needed an emergency "short selling" restriction. In fact, investors, including hedge funds, believed that a political dispute in February 2001 undermined the credibility of the reform program, triggering a "self-fulfilling" attack on the currency and a "short selling" of Turkish assets, which probably caused the crisis to deepen.

Whether "short selling" should be regulated is broadly a subset of a more general question[367]: when is it appropriate to regulate financial markets? First of all, I have to emphasize that any "short selling" restriction will impede all information to be fully reflected in prices, leading to allocative inefficiency[368]. As the primary goal of financial market regulation is to promote economic efficiency[369], the former is justified only when an unregulated market fails to produce an environment coherent with the public interest[370].

To note that it is a difficult task for policy makers to decide whether a temporary "short selling" ban needs to be introduced when a "self-fulfilling" attack is in play. When regulators introduce emergency "short selling" restrictions in an attempt to avoid the worsening of a crisis led by "herd behavior", they are at the same time aware of the fact that all this will be at the cost of inefficient pricing. In short, although hedge funds and derivatives have probably increased the speed and volume of capital flows, they are part of the modern financial system and have to be lived with. They cannot, by themselves,

---

[365] These were Australia, Austria, Belgium, Canada, Denmark, France, Germany, Greece, Hungary, Iceland, India, Indonesia, Ireland, Italy, Japan, Luxembourg, Netherlands, Norway, Pakistan, Portugal, Russia, Singapore, South Korea, Spain, Switzerland, Taiwan, the United Arab Emirates, the United Kingdom and the United States of America (Gruenewald, S., Wagner, A. F. and Weber, R. H. (2009), pp. 10-12).

[366] Ibid., p. 12

[367] Gruenewald, S., Wagner, A. F. and Weber, R. H. (2009), p. 15

[368] Ibid., p. 17

[369] Stigler, G. (1975), p. 88

[370] Gruenewald, S., Wagner, A. F. and Weber, R. H. (2009), p. 16

be blamed for crises and instability. The following quote from Merton Miller (1997) is relevant here[371]:

> "No derivatives-induced financial collapse really exists. Firms will continue to lose money on bad judgment and bad derivatives deals, just as they always have in deals on ordinary assets like stocks and real estate. And a major crack in one of the world's financial markets is always possible. But crashes in financial markets are policy disasters, tracing not to transactions between private sector parties, but to the deliberately deflationary actions of a central bank somewhere, usually overreacting to its previous policy errors in the other direction."

In line with the above quote, the 1994 Turkish financial crisis was triggered as a market reaction to a policy error. Similarly, the currency crisis of 2001 was another reaction of markets to a political crisis, which convinced global markets that structural reforms would not be achieved. Thus, turbulence or crises reflect the corrective mechanism of markets, reassessing an unsustainable trend in public policy.

Conclusion

This theoretical overview provides a perspective on the next section devoted to the two major financial crises, which shook Turkey in 1994 and 2001. It provides elements that are necessary to explain difficulties encountered by Turkey in adapting its financial market institutions and regulations to international standards.

My book decisively defends deregulated financial markets in Turkey, showing that the major reason for instability in Turkey for decades has been persistent and intense state intervention in economic decision-making. Nevertheless, I will also show that deregulation does not mean an absence of regulation, but a de-politicized regulatory framework within which the state introduces the rule of law and protects property rights. Moreover, an

---

371 Miller, M. H. (1997), p. 68

independent and thus de-politicized central bank will be able to face and minimize the negative effects of speculative capital movements.

To conclude, we will explore what sort of regulatory framework is suitable for Turkish financial markets and question why importing international standards did not always provide the expected outcome.

3.3. Cycles of Crises in Turkish Financial Markets

I now examine how Turkish financial markets collapsed in 1994 and 2001. I introduce both political and historical aspects when necessary, in an attempt to shed light on the country-specific circumstances behind the whole story.

3.3.1. Second phase from 1989 to 1994: Complete capital account liberalization and the 1994 financial crisis

Political stability was monitored by Generals during the 1980s. I should also not downplay the impact of political processes, with ANAP leader Turgut Ozal becoming an influential political figure during the whole decade and also in introducing the "Washington Consensus" principles. He was charged with economic affairs during the 43th Demirel and the 44th Ulusu governments (see Annex 3). Moreover, the Turgut Ozal-led militarily backed single-party civilian governments from 1983 to 1989 changed the shape of the whole economic structure.

To note in Table 3.1 one of the consequences of this "imposed" political stability. The wages/GNP ratio (col.1) decreased from 1979 to 1986. During this period, the military government severely restricted labor union activity and charged a state institution to settle the wage level[372]. The Turgut Ozal government maintained this real wage reduction policy. However, a relaxation of restrictions on strike activity allowed labor unions to become increasingly active after 1987[373]. In 1989, on the eve of his election in November to the post of President of the Republic, Prime Minister Turgut Ozal introduced two

---

[372] Celasun, M. (1994), p. 462

[373] Onis, Z. and Webb, S. B. (1992), p. 44

important changes that would significantly impact the economy[374]. First of all, wages in the public sector were allowed to increase in real terms[375]. This is the reason why we observe in Table 3.1 a decreasing wages/GNP ratio until 1986 and an increasing trend after 1989. This increase also signaled additional budget expenditures. Moreover, two important regulatory changes occurred in 1989:

1. Limiting high-powered money creation (March 1989): An accord signed between the Treasury and the CBRT, introduced a ceiling on the Short-term Cash Advance Facility, which was established at a much lower interest rate than the market rate. The CBRT was to charge the market rate once the advance exceeded this ceiling. This was an important institutional arrangement to limit excessive money creation[376];
2. Complete liberalization of capital account (August 1989)[377]: This reform represented a final step in eliminating economic controls of the pre-1980 period and helped accelerate the integration process with the EU and global markets by lifting all restrictions on capital movements and on borrowing by residents in international markets[378]. Briefly, Turkish stock and bond

---

374 Candemir, B. (1994), p. 16

375 Onis, Z. and Webb, S. B. (1992), p. 42

376 Bayazitoglu, Y., Ersel, H. and Ozturk, E. (1991), p. 11

377 Onder, T. (2005), p. 174

378 From August 1989, residents and non-residents were freely able to buy, sell and transfer foreign currencies. Residents were allowed to make payments for invisible transactions relating to all services to non-residents at home or abroad. Residents were allowed to accept foreign currency from non-residents for services rendered in Turkey and to transfer capital in order to establish or participate in commercial companies in the form of cash up to USD 5 million through banks and special finance institutions, or in kind, according to the provisions set forth in the customs legislation. Moreover, they were able to freely obtain credits in kind or in cash from abroad without term limits, provided that they utilized such credits through banks or special finance institutions. The Central Bank and the banks which held a "Gold Exchange Intermediation Certificate" were authorized to import unprocessed gold. Export and import of unprocessed gold was affected outside foreign trade regimes through declarations made to the Customs Administration. In June 1991, an amendment to the Decree No. 32 permitted residents to issue, introduce and sell securities in financial markets abroad, and following a second amendment introduced in March 1993, residents were entitled to purchase and sell all kinds of securities traded (not necessarily quoted) in foreign financial markets abroad through banks, special finance institutions and intermediary institutions authorized according to the Capital Market Legislation. The March 1993 amendments enlarged the coverage of securities by adding "other capital market instruments" among the capital and money market operations to be carried out by residents and non-residents in both domestic and foreign markets (Republic of Turkey, (1993), p. 8).

markets were completely accessible for non-resident investors without any restrictions on the repatriation of capital. Equivalently, domestic residents were allowed to purchase foreign securities without restrictions. In a final step, Turkey notified the IMF in April 1990 that it accepted the obligations of Article VIII, Sections 2, 3, and 4 of the IMF Articles of Agreement[379], and consequently the Turkish Lira was declared convertible[380].

Regarding the interest rate liberalization, we saw in section 2.1 that the "Washington Consensus" stated as follows[381]:

> "Two main principles should guide the level of interest rates. First, interest rates needed to be market-determined to avoid misallocation of resources. Second, positive real interest rates were necessary to discourage capital flight, to encourage savings and to make capital accumulation more likely."

To note, nevertheless, in Table 3.1 (col. 3) that there is a continuous increase in interest payments as a share of consolidated budget revenues, becoming thus an increasingly heavy burden on the economy. Thus, while capital account liberalization signified a milestone in the adaptation of Turkish financial market regulations to EU requirements, it created unexpected consequences as well. The absence of a sound institutional framework to oversee the economic transition brought together the necessary elements for a crisis. Table 3.1 shows the deterioration of the public sector budget deficit from 1990 to 1993, comprised mainly of, public sector wage bill (col. 1), interest payments (col. 3), SOE losses (col. 4) and military expenditures (col. 5). The latter increased significantly due to the government's effort to combat ethnic unrest threatening national security. Higher PSBR (col. 6) was financed through the sale of government securities, which in turn required higher interest rates (columns 7 and 8) further fostering fiscal costs (columns 2 and 3).

---

379 IMF (2002), p. 3

380 Altinkemer, M. (1992), p. 1

381 Williamson, J. (2000), p. 253

Table 3.1: Budget Balance and its components, PSBR and Interest Rates, in percentage

	(1) Wages	(2) Budg. bal.	(3) Int. p.	(4) SOE b. r.	(5) Milit.exp.	(6) PSBR	(7) Int. S.	(8) Int. C.	(9) Interb. rate	(10) CBRT rate	(11) Saving rate
1979	7.4	-3.1	3.5	-	-	7.2	-	-	-	10.75	20.00
1980	6.4	-3.1	3.6	-	-	8.8	-	-	-	26.00	33.00
1981	5.0	-1.5	5.4	-	-	4.0	-	-	-	31.50	35.00
1982	4.2	-1.5	6.1	-	-	3.5	-	-	-	31.50	50.00
1983	4.8	-2.2	9.2	-	-	4.9	-	-	-	48.50	45.00
1984	4.0	-4.4	15.7	-	-	5.4	-	-	-	52.00	45.00
1985	3.6	-2.3	14.9	-	-	3.6	-	-	-	52.00	55.00
1986	3.6	-2.8	19.7	-	-	3.7	49.8	51.7	39.9	48.00	48.00
1987	4.4	-3.5	22.5	2.9	-	6.1	43.0	45.6	42.4	45.00	58.00
1988	4.2	-3.1	29.3	2.1	2.9	4.8	57.2	59.5	46.8	54.00	83.90
1989	6.0	-3.3	27.2	1.8	3.2	5.3	53.9	59.8	26.9	54.00	58.80
1990	7.3	-3.0	25.3	3.5	3.5	7.3	49.7	54.0	62.7	50.75	59.40
1991	8.6	-5.3	24.9	4.3	3.8	9.9	69.8	80.5	59.9	54.50	72.70
1992	9.5	-4.3	23.2	4.0	3.9	10.5	74.6	87.7	67.8	54.50	74.20
1993	9.3	-6.7	33.2	3.7	3.9	10.2	79.3	87.6	69.9	54.50	74.80
1994	7.6	-3.9	40.0	1.9	4.1	6.2	109.9	164.4	92.1	64.00	95.56
1995	6.4	-4.0	41.3	-0.1	3.9	5.0	98.9	121.9	106.3	57.00	92.32

Sources:

1. Wages/GNP, data from State Planning Organization;
2. Consolidated Budget Balance/GDP, data from State Planning Organization;
3. Interest payment over consolidated budget revenues, data from State Planning Organization;
4. State Owned Enterprises borrowing requirements/ GDP ratio, data from Turkish Treasury;
5. Military Expenditures/GDP ratio, data from the World Bank[382];

---

382 Military expenditures data, from Stockholm International Peace Research Institute (SIPRI), are derived from the NATO definition, which includes all current and capital expenditures on the armed forces, including peacekeeping forces, defense ministries and other government agencies engaged in defense projects, paramilitary forces, if these are judged to be trained and equipped for military operations, and military space activities. Such expenditures include military and civil personnel, including retirement pensions of military personnel and social services for personnel, operation and maintenance, procurement, military research and development, and military aid (in the military expenditures of the donor country). Excluded are civil defense and current expenditures for previous military activities, such as for veterans' benefits, demobilization, conversion and destruction of weapons (World Bank official website, data from "indicators", "military expenditures").

6. Public Sector Borrowing Requirement over GNP ratio, data from State Planning Organization;
7. and (8) are simple average and compound average interest rates from domestic borrowing, data from Turkish Treasury;
8. Average interbank overnight interest rates, data from Turkish Central Bank;
9. Turkish Central Bank's discount rate;
10. One year maturity deposit saving rates, the rate of the last months of the years is used, data from Turkish Statistical institute[383].

Increased capital inflow was a direct result of capital account liberalization (Fig. 3.2), which in turn contributed to currency appreciation and a high current account deficit in 1993 (Table 2.3). Higher risk exposure of the economy due to worsening macro variables required higher interest rates to keep alive risk appetite of global investors that in effect became a heavy burden on both the PSBR and on the budget deficit side. All this was to be financed through both the CBRT resources (Fig. 2.5) and the bond market at higher interest rates (Table 3.1, columns 7 and 8). I emphasize thus the following point: real interest rates were positive to discourage capital flight, as predicted by the "Washington Consensus". However, they were continuously increasing and placing an unsustainable burden on public finances in the long term. However, no effort was made to introduce institutional reforms. Deregulation of markets allowed bond financing of budget deficits, without addressing the root causes of problems ranging from a politically managed central bank to a weak regulatory framework in the banking sector. Consequently, global markets requested increasingly higher interest in line with perceived higher sovereign default risk. Declining macro performance from 1989 to 1993 (Table 3.1) was exacerbated by additional factors, i.e., a volatile GDP (Fig. 3.3), which depended broadly on variable short-term capital inflows, in line with the instantaneously changing mood of global investors. In fact, FDI levels were traditionally low (Fig. 3.2). Figures 3.2 and 3.3 make also evident the co-movement between short-term capital inflows and growth. While the decline in 1991 had been because of the Gulf Crisis, I will now focus on the factors behind the 1994 capital outflow and crash.

---

[383] Turkish Statistical Institute (2009), p. 624

Fig. 3.2: Comparing Short-term Portfolio Investment versus FDI flows, in million USD

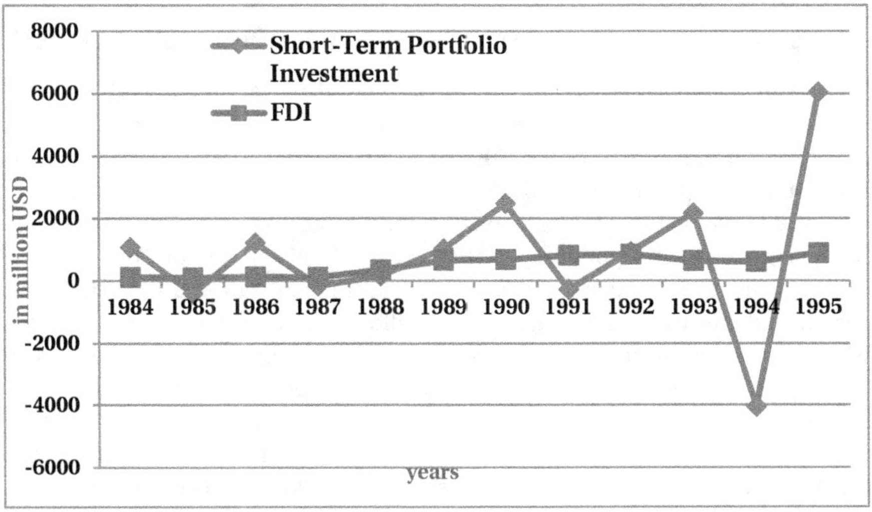

Source: Central Bank of Turkey, official website

Fig. 3.3: Growth rate dynamics from 1984 to 1995, in percentage

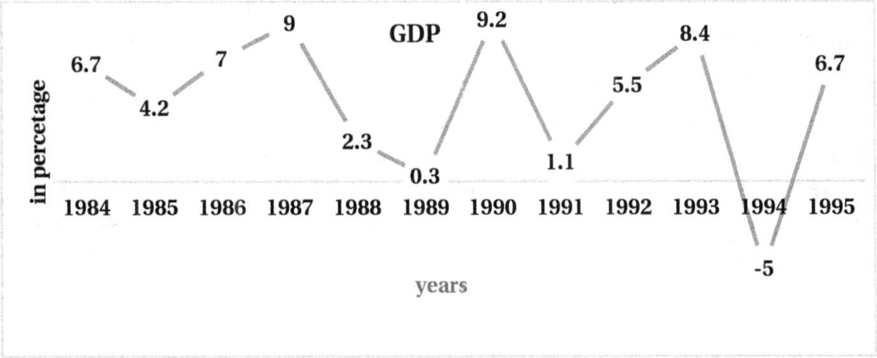

Source: Table 2.3, constant GDP, at 1987 prices, by "expenditures" approach

Discussion

1. How did the global markets price uncertainty from 1989 to 1993?

We saw in the previous section that the last Stand-by agreement with the IMF was signed in 1984 (Table 2.4)[384]. Although Turkey formally applied to join the European Community in 1987[385], there was no significant effort in adopting an EU-inspired de-politicized institutional framework. A referendum held during the same year lifted the pre-1980 political leaders' ban allowing their reappearance on the political scene[386]. Prime Minister Turgut Ozal became President in 1989 and complete capital account liberalization during the same year paved the way for short-term portfolio investment-led volatile growth, which depended on the mood of international investors. While global factors like the Gulf Crisis had a negative impact on the economy[387], domestic factors like the formation of a coalition government in the same year (see Annex 3) marked the initial phase of politically unstable circumstances. Uncertainty increased when President Turgut Ozal passed away in April 1993 and the Turkish political context was reshaped[388]. In May 1993, Prime Minister Suleyman Demirel was elected President and he appointed economics professor Tansu Ciller as Prime Minister. In September, the leader of opposition Ismet Inonu retired from politics and was replaced by Murat Karayalcin, a former mayor of Ankara and became vice-premier without being a member of Parliament[389]. Briefly, we observe the emergence of new political leaders, without much experience in politics: Tansu Ciller (DYP) as Prime Minister, Murat Karayalcin (SODEP) as vice-premier and Mesut Yilmaz (ANAP) as leader of the opposition.

Let me now look at how global markets priced these unstable circumstances from 1989 to 1993. To note in Table 3.1 that while PSBR/GNP ratio increased from 5.3 percent in 1989 to 10.2 percent in 1993, the compounded average interest rate on domestic borrowing increased from 59.8 percent in 1989 to 87.6 percent in 1993. The increasingly higher interest repayments (27.2 percent of

---

384 To note in Table 3.2 that the next Stand-by agreement was signed after the 1994 crisis.

385 Reich, B. (1990), p. 401

386 Gonen, L. (2006), p. 14

387 Celasun, O. (1997), p. 9

388 Hale, W. (2000), p. 200

389 Zurcker, E. J. (2004), p. 295

budget revenues in 1989 and 33.2 percent in 1993) had become a heavy burden on the economy. We also observe in figure 3.4 that real interest rates were higher than real GDP growth from 1991 to 1995. All these data show that market determined positive real interest rates, i.e., the 4th prescription of the "Washington Consensus", were about to kill off economic growth.

Fig. 3.4: Comparing real interest rates vs real GDP – from 1989 to 1998, in percentage

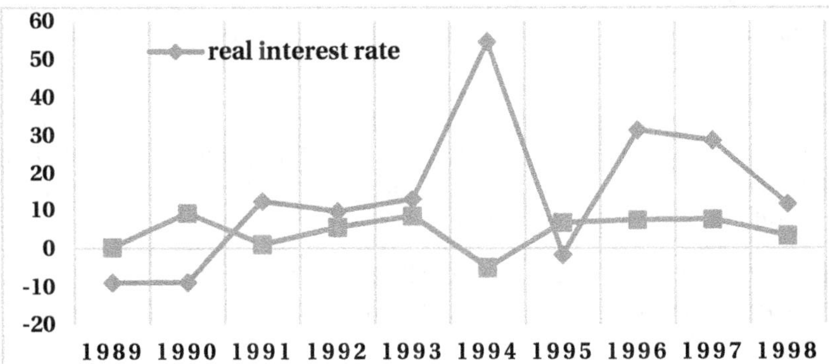

Source: Real Interest rate is based on the annualized value of the arithmetic monthly average of Treasury auctions and the annualized monthly percentage change of CPI, data from Turkish Central Bank; Real GDP is GDP by "expenditures" based on constant 1987 prices, data from State Planning Organization.

However, there was another important factor that had an impact on triggering the 1994 crisis: Government policy on interest rates[390]. Let us see, how deficit financing changed during the period before the crisis and caused a sudden capital flight.

2. Was the government or the Central Bank to determine the level of interest rates?

In June 1993, the new Prime Minister Tansu Ciller stated that the government intended to lower interest rates[391]. In fact, almost one third of consolidated budget revenues were spent on interest payments (Table 3.1, col.3). However, the way the Prime Minister tried to lower interest rates was far from international standards. This was accomplished through an attempt to fix a ceiling by law in defiance of market forces. This also meant that it was the

---

[390] Ozatay, F. (1997), p. 345

[391] Ibid.

politicians instead of the Central Bank who determined the level of interest rates. Steps to lower interest rates were adopted as follows[392]:

1. The government passed a law in Parliament wiping out the Treasury's accumulated "Short-term Cash Advance Facility" balance with the CBRT, an action that was illegal[393]. The Governor of Central Bank resigned (in early August 1993);

2. Before 1993, interest on government securities was exempt from taxes. The new government declared a 5 percent tax on revenue from all government securities[394];

3. In line with the new policy, the Treasury canceled most of the government bond auctions in November and December 1993 and changed the auction system at the beginning of 1994. Additionally, the Treasury fixed a maximum interest rate on government bonds[395];

4. The Central Bank's "Short-term Cash Advance Facility" provided the necessary means for financing ongoing immediate budgetary needs (fig. 2.5)[396].

All this meant that the government obliged the Central Bank to create more money, while the budget announced for 1994 did not include any policy to reduce the fiscal deficits[397]. Moreover, SOE goods' prices were not increased, but it was expected that the government would adjust prices after the local elections to be held in April 1994[398]. Meanwhile, increasing SOE losses amplified budget deficits. In these conditions, inflation expectations were high[399] and it was not rational for investors to hold domestic currency, which created a rush to buy foreign currency. We observe in Table 2.6, col.6 that the FX deposits/GNP ratio increased from 9.9 percent in 1993 to 15.4 percent in

---

392 Ozatay, F. (1997), p. 345

393 This allowed the Government to borrow almost twice the original amount (Ibid.).

394 Ozatay, F. (1997), p. 346

395 Ibid., p. 348

396 The Central Bank provided "Short-term Cash Advance Facility" to Treasury until 1997 (Guven, A. B. (2010), p. 13).

397 Celasun, O. (1997), p. 14

398 Ibid.

399 Ibid.

1994. More importantly, there was a significant demand for foreign currency by commercial banks, worried about their unhedged foreign exchange positions[400]. Fig. 3.5 shows that complete capital account liberalization in 1989 motivated commercial banks to make short-term profits by exploiting interest rate carry trades[401]. Their unhedged foreign exchange positions progressively increased, exceeding 100 percent of equity by the year 1993.

Fig. 3.5: Foreign Exchange positions of banks from 1988 to 2000, in percentage of equity

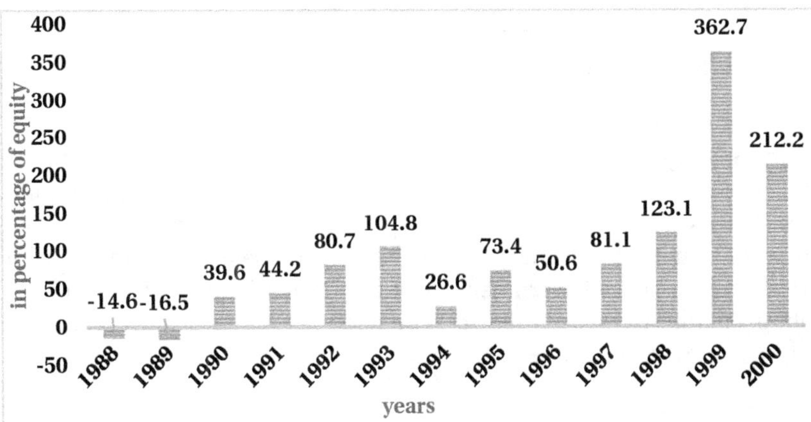

Source: Central Bank of Turkey

Looking at figures 3.5 and 3.6 together, it is straightforward to observe that from 1993 to 1994 the Central Bank was losing reserves while commercial banks were running large unhedged positions[402]. In fact, after December 1993 official CBRT reserves declined by more than 50 percent in a few months (observable in Fig. 3.6, decline from early December 1993 to late March 1994). Through its intervention in markets to defend the value of the domestic currency, the Turkish Central Bank was bailing out commercial banks[403].

---

400 Celasun, O. (1997), p. 17

401 Borrowing in foreign currency and investing in high-yielding Turkish government securities and making profit on interest rate differential while bearing the unhedged foreign currency risk exposure.

402 Celasun, O. (1997), p. 23

403 Ibid.

Fig. 3.6: CBRT's gross FX reserves, from December 1993 to March 1994, in million USD

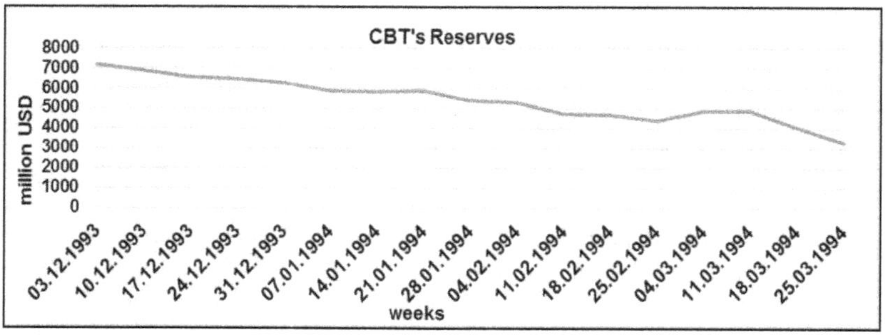

Source: Central Bank of Turkey

Briefly, in this atmosphere of deteriorating macroeconomic variables from 1989 to 1993, the government's dramatic attempt to control interest rates set off a crisis. These policy upheavals occurred during a period of high current account deficits (Table 2.3). Moreover, banks' high-risk exposure in foreign currency and maturity mismatch problems exacerbated the fragile debt situation[404]. Demand for government securities decreased dramatically and as a result, a funding crisis occurred in February 1994. Interest rates reached a peak of well over 400 percent (Fig. 3.7).

Fig. 3.7: Interbank Rates from December 1993 to May 1994, in percentage

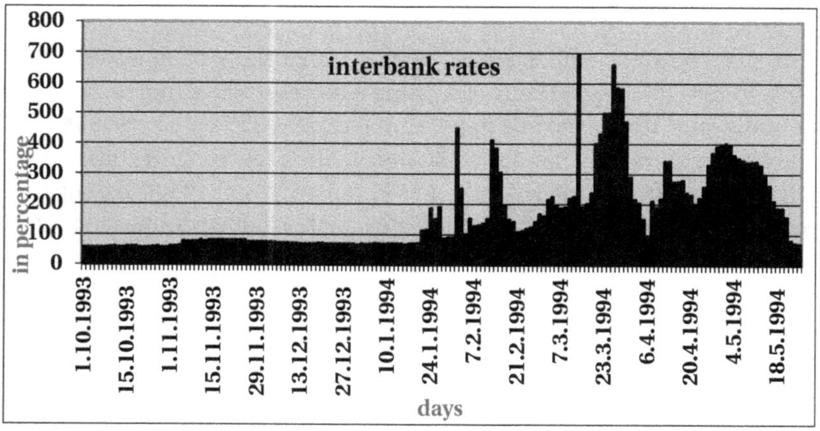

Source: Central Bank of Turkey

404 Celasun, O. (1997), p. 23

The turbulence had an overall impact on real activity. Non-performing loans increased significantly as well (Fig 3.8). Several banks' default risk increased. Three of them did indeed default[405]. Capital adequacy ratios of all banks decreased and the state banks lost 90 percent of their net worth[406].

Fig. 3.8: Proportion of Non-Performing Loans from 1988 to 2000, in percentage

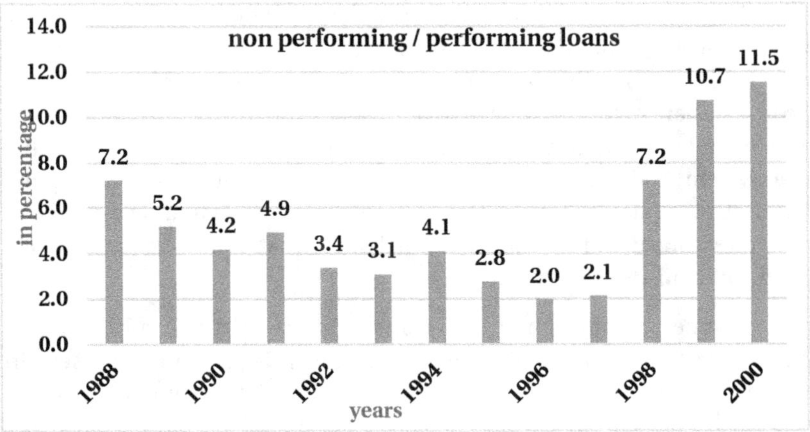

Source: Turkish Banking Association

To note that while markets were completely deregulated, it was difficult to change the economic culture associated with the traditional statist approach, as the February 1994 crisis shows us. The government intervention in defiance of both market forces and the CBRT regulations made evident the need for an adequate institutional and regulatory framework.

3. IMF to the rescue

The government's aim was to lower interest rates on government debt, which was a major factor behind the budget deficit. However, it did not take into consideration the fact that in an economy where capital accounts are liberalized, sudden policy changes (fixing maximum interest rates, canceling auctions, replacing debt financing by central bank resources) can increase demand for foreign currency and result in capital flight. In an economy open to

---

405 Ertugrul, A., Selcuk, F. (2001), p. 18

406 Ibid.

global markets the level of interest rates depends also on sovereign default risk perception of investors. In case the interest rates are not high enough to cover investors' expected return, a sudden capital flight can occur. In addition, attempting to dip into Central Bank resources to finance the budget deficit amounted to nothing more than the printing of new money.

As a result of all this, the government launched in the aftermath of the February 1994 crisis, a stabilization program on 5th April 1994, one week after the local elections. The program was based on reducing state expenditures, introducing fiscal discipline, increasing taxes and SOE goods' prices[407]. It also aimed to accelerate the privatization process, restricted the use of Central Bank resources to finance the chronic budget deficit and offered a 100 percent government guarantee on bank deposits to increase the credibility of the financial system[408]. Nevertheless, in the absence of reforms addressing the banking sector regulatory framework, the government guarantees on bank deposits were considered as contingent liabilities that would become public debt in case of bank defaults.

The government applied for an IMF loan on April 14th, which culminated in negotiations ending on July 8th (Table 3.2). The IMF program imposed, in addition to fiscal discipline, the regulation of the financial sector to address the moral hazard problem in private banks[409]. An initial 14-month Stand-by agreement in support of the government's economic and financial reform program for 1994-95 was eventually extended to 20 months at the request of Turkish authorities in April 1995[410].

---

[407] Celasun, O. (1997), p. 18

[408] Ibid., p. 17

[409] Karadag, R. (2010), p. 18

[410] See the request and approval of six months' extension on the IMF (1995) websites

Table 3.2: Turkey – IMF Stand-by agreements from 1994 to 2005

Number	Years	Duration (months)	Credit effectively used (million USD)
16	1994 (1996)	14	682
17	1999	36	17'254
18	2002	36	16'846
19	2005	36	4'748

Source: Ozçam, M. (2004), p. 2, Erdinc, Z. (2007), p. 8; In parenthesis is indicated the year in which the agreement was canceled.

Due to the currency depreciation during the crisis, the current account balance improved (Table 2.3). During this process, the Central Bank restricted domestic credits and increased its reserves[411] aiming at stability in exchange and interest rates in a high inflation environment. However, it attempted to control liquidity through short-term interest rates, which rose dramatically[412]. The government's program and the IMF agreement did not provide sustainable support to the real economy and in particular did not improve the fragile structure of the banking system. The Stand-by agreement was canceled in 1996[413] (Table 3.2). On the other hand, commercial banks greatly hindered progress by quickly returning to their old business practices, preferring to make short-term profits through interest rate carry trade opportunities, with the unhedged positions continuing to bear the foreign exchange risk (Fig. 3.5). We observe again that there was no structural reform on the agenda for the banking sector, which again began to look like an unlimited public debt liability.

This suggests that, while the cost of the crisis was high, the lesson had not been learned. Turkish economy needed structural institutional reforms. The 11th element to the "Washington Consensus" was crucial; in its absence, the economy could only shift from one crash to another. In fact, we will observe in section 3.3.2.2 that banking sector failure became a major factor behind the next currency crisis.

I now, for completeness, examine in the next section the 1994 crisis in the light of the theoretical framework of this study.

---

[411] Gumus, I. (2003), p. 7

[412] Ibid. p. 8

[413] Ozçam (2004), p. 2

4. Which model can best explain the 1994 financial crisis?

The reasons behind this crisis are quite similar to the Krugman (1979) model (or First Generation models) because the Turkish Central Bank was used to monetize the Government budget deficit[414]. However, in Turkey, a "managed floating" exchange rate regime was in place (Table 3.3). Whereas, all three generation models, discussed in section 3.2, assume a fixed exchange rate regime. Thus, despite similarities with the Krugman (1979) model, it is not possible to explain the 1994 Turkish crisis with any of these "generation" models"[415]. Nevertheless, I will examine dynamics behind this crisis using the Mundell-Fleming model that I described in section 3.1.4 on which was also based the Krugman (1979) model.

In Turkey, policy makers introduced full convertibility in 1989 in combination with "managed floating". Thus, under the Mundell-Fleming framework, the Turkish Central Bank could and did follow an independent monetary policy. However, this was not a politically independent monetary policy – quite the contrary in fact. As we observed in figure 2.5 above, the Turkish Central Bank had to create increasingly more money from 1991 to 1994 to meet the needs of the Treasury. This was also at a record level after the establishment of a bond market in the mid-1980s. The continuous increase of "Short-term Cash Advance Facility" during the years prior to the crisis illustrates that the Turkish Central Bank acted as a ministerial body related to the Treasury, without being able to undertake any autonomous initiative. Moreover, the government's intervention to artificially lower interest rates was another aspect of the Central Bank's complete subservience to its political masters.

The following FX rate regimes were practiced in Turkey from 1981 to 2011[416], which are to be taken into consideration in analyzing the Turkish crises under the Mundell-Fleming framework:

- Until April 1981: (multiple) fixed exchange rate regimes[417];
- from May 1981 to January 1998: managed floating (a floating rate regime)[418];

---

[414] Kansu, A. (2006), p. 170

[415] Ibid.

[416] Reinhart, C. M. and Rogoff, K. S. (2002), p. 100

[417] Ozatay, F. (1997), pp. 329, 330

- from February 1998 to February 2001: crawling band (an intermediate regime)[419];
- from February 2001 onwards: free floating (a floating rate regime).

Table 3.3 shows the Turkish regime changes within the main regime classes. I will discuss at the end of Chapter 3, in "concluding remarks" that the regimes can "de facto" diverge from this "de jure" classification, due to monetary authorities' decisions.

To note that while before 1981 in Turkey there were "multiple" fixed exchange rate regimes, a sort of "hard peg", after the introduction of the "Washington Consensus" principles both the "intermediate" and "floating rate" regimes were used.

To conclude, although the economy was completely accessible to global markets, decisions in the management of the economy were taken at the political level in defiance of market forces. Thus, a variety of factors ranging from inappropriate public policies and unhedged carry trade positions of the banking sector, to a weak regulatory framework, made the expected bond returns appear lower than the perceived sovereign risk. Investors preferred to sell-out Turkish assets, triggering the crisis. This shows that while the government's interest rate policy error was remarkable, we note, in a broader approach, that market reforms launched from 1980 onwards were incomplete, because they were based only on the deregulation of markets without introducing a de-politicized institutional framework, that is, Central Bank independence was not assured and the public sector continued in chronic deficit. In any case, although the 1994 crisis was a severe shock to the economy, it served to motivate the government to undertake radical decisions aimed at launching a new phase in the market reform process. In the aftermath of the crisis, the government introduced the Customs Union agreement with the EU, which had been under negotiation for many years. This was an important step in the process of full membership. It also showed that the intention of policy makers was to adopt EU-inspired market reforms.

---

418 Reinhart, C. M. and Rogoff, K. S. (2002), p. 100. During this period, policy makers introduced several regulations that had an impact on exchange rate practices. With the end of multiple rates in May 1981, the CBRT initiated to daily announce the FX rates, changing the rates 164 times in 1981, 245 times in 1982 and 246 times in 1983. Further liberalization in FX practices was introduced in July 1984. Additional regulations were introduced, for example, in 1988 and in the aftermath of the 1994 financial crisis. See for details, Arat, K. (2003), pp. 38-43

419 "Crawling band" regime around DM from February 1998 to January 1999 and around Euro until February 2001 (Reinhart, C. M. and Rogoff, K. S. (2002), p. 100)

I now examine in the next section the third phase of regulatory framework changes from 1995 to 2002. We will discover that another financial crash, this time more severe than the previous one, hit the economy in February 2001.

Table 3.3: "De Jure" Exchange Rate Regime Classification

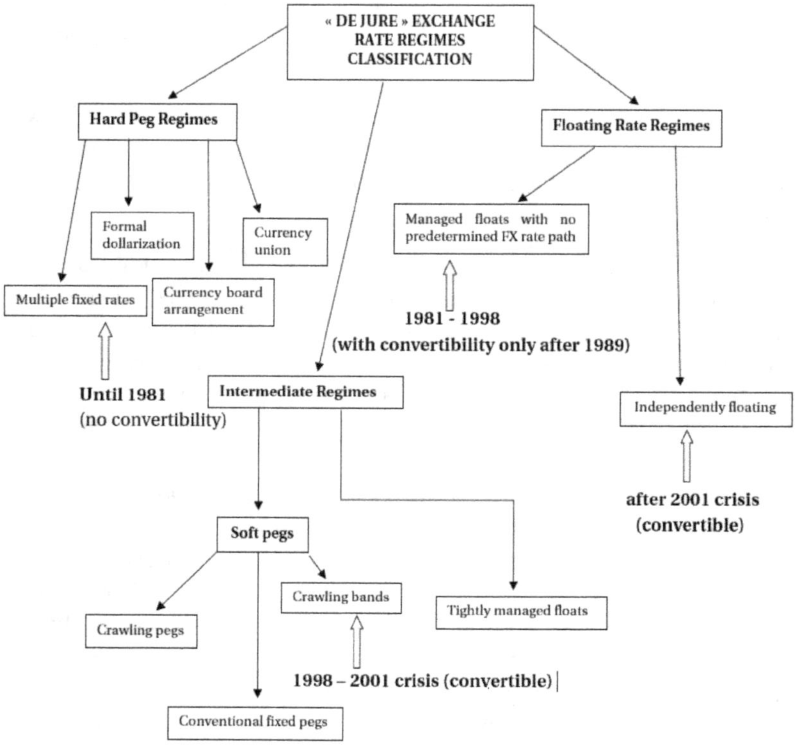

Source: Bubula, A. and Otker-Robe, I. (2002), pp. 14, 15

3.3.2. Third Phase from 1995 to 2002: Customs Union with the EU, banking sector's fragile structure and the 2001 currency crisis

This phase includes another series of market reforms, but this time reforms aimed to accomplish concrete steps towards full membership of the EU. Unfortunately, reforms did not initially target the banking sector but rather started with the Customs Union agreement with the EU. While the latter was a crucially important step in terminating traditional protectionist policies in Turkey, we will see that policy makers urged for a sound framework in banking sector only after a series of bank defaults in the late 1990s, too late to avoid another crisis. To note that the EU did not force Turkey to sign a Customs Union agreement in this stage of relations and that Turkey was the "demandeur". It was the first country to sign a Customs Union agreement with the EU without being a full member[420]. Apparently, it was less difficult for policy makers to launch a Customs Union than to achieve institutional and political reforms[421]. It seems that if the government had introduced an EU-inspired regulatory framework in the post-1994 crisis period when banks started again to take unhedged positions, perhaps it would have been possible to avoid the 2001 crash. Thus, while the Customs Union agreement was a significant step towards full membership of the EU, this was not the first priority to choose under these conditions. With hindsight, it seems clear that banking sector reforms should have preceded any further steps.

I first focus on implications of the customs union with the EU (section 3.3.2.1), then analyze the banking sector's structure (section 3.3.2.2) and finally the 2001 currency crisis (section 3.3.2.3).

3.3.2.1. Customs Union agreement

I start this section with a theoretical discussion on the customs union. Then, I will review the Agreement signed between Turkey and the EEC/EU, which will finally lead me to discuss the impact of this agreement on the Turkish economy.

Article XXIV of the GATT defines a customs union as a single customs territory that satisfies the following two conditions[422]: First, the members

420 Yilmaz, K. (2010), p. 1

421 Ibid.

422 World Trade Organization, official website

eliminate duties and other restrictive regulations on substantially all trade between them. Second, each member applies substantially the same duties and other trade regulations applied by each of the member states of the union to contracting parties not included in the union. Until the mid-20th century, the formation of a customs union was broadly associated with increasing economic welfare. Nevertheless, Jacob Viner introduced in 1950 a more accurate analysis showing that a customs union is a form of selective discrimination because it combines elements of free trade among members of the union and restrictions on trade with non-members, leading to either improving or worsening resource allocation and welfare[423]. This led James Meade, Richard Lipsey, and Kevin Lancaster to introduce their "theory of the second best", which showed that when there is more than one distortion of free market equilibria, the elimination of one of them does not necessarily improve welfare[424].

A customs union presents "static" and "dynamic" effects. While the former regards the situation before and after the elimination of tariffs, the latter is concerned with economic interdependencies over time.

"Static" effects of a customs union

Broadly, two types of static effects are classified as "production" and "consumption" effects. Regarding the former, Jacob Viner distinguished two types[425]:

- Trade creation: Elimination of tariffs between members of a union will shift supply from a high-cost domestic producer to a low-cost producer in another member of the union. Thus, a customs union involves the creation of some new trade and it improves international allocation of resources;
- Trade diversion: Elimination of tariffs between members of a union will shift supply from a low-cost non-member producer to a high-cost producer in a member of the union. Thus, a customs union worsens, in this case, the international allocation of resources.

To note that a customs union will have a positive welfare effect in case trade creation is higher than trade diversion.

---

423 Cherunilam, F. (2006), p. 292

424 Lipsey, R.G. and Lancaster, K. (1956), pp. 11-32

425 Ibid. p. 293

Similarly, the "consumption" effects have in turn positive and negative sides[426]. In fact, trade creation will have a positive consumption effect, as consumers will benefit from the positive production effects of the customs union, i.e., increased efficiency in resource allocation: The real income of consumers increase as a given amount of money income allows them to purchase more goods and services as prices decline. The opposite occurs in the case of trade diversion, leading to negative consumption effect[427].

"Dynamic" effects of a customs union

There may also be dynamic welfare consequences that influence in the long-term[428]. These include economies of scale, increased level of competition and stimulus of investment.

Customs Union as an EU Requirement

Chapter 29th of the Acquis Communautaire is in the Customs Union and it consists almost exclusively of legislation which is directly binding on the Member States[429]. It includes the EU Customs Code and its implementing provisions, the combined nomenclature, common customs tariff and provisions on tariff classification, customs duty relief, duty suspensions and certain tariff quotas, and other provisions such as those on customs control of counterfeit and pirated goods, drugs precursors, export of cultural goods as well as on mutual administrative assistance in customs matters and transit[430].

Let us overview what does the Treaty on the Functioning of the EU state regarding the customs union[431]:

"Art. 3: The Union shall have exclusive competence in the following areas:

- Customs union;
- The establishing of the competition rules necessary for the functioning of the internal market [....];

---

[426] Cherunilam, F. (2006), p. 294

[427] Ibid., p. 299

[428] Carbaugh, R .J. (2011), pp. 278, 279

[429] EU Commission official website, "Chapters of the Acquis"

[430] Ibid.

[431] Official Journal of the European Union (2012), pp. 51, 60, 61 and 62

Art. 30: Customs duties on imports and exports and charges having equivalent effect shall be prohibited between Member States. The prohibitions shall also apply to customs duties of a fiscal nature;

Art. 32: In carrying out the tasks entrusted to it under this Chapter the Commission shall be guided by:

- The need to promote trade between Member States and third countries;
- Developments in conditions of competition with the Union in so far as they lead to an improvement in the competitive capacity of undertakings [....];

Art. 34: Quantitative restrictions on imports and all measures having equivalent effect shall be prohibited between Member States;

Art. 35: Quantitative restrictions on exports and all measures having equivalent effect shall be prohibited between Member States;

Art. 37:

- Member States shall adjust any State monopolies of a commercial character so as to ensure that no discrimination regarding the conditions under which goods are procured and marketed exists between nationals of Member States [....];
- If a State monopoly of a commercial character has rules which are designed to make it easier to dispose of agricultural products or obtain for them the best returns, steps should be taken in applying the rules contained in this Article to ensure equivalent safeguards for the employment and standard of living of the producers concerned."

An overview on the Turkish case

The Customs Union signed with the EU in 1995 was the long sought after next step of an agreement first achieved in 1963 with the European Economic Community (EEC). In fact, while Greece signed an association agreement in 1961, Turkey signed the Ankara Agreement two years later[432]. The latter aimed at establishing a customs union between Turkey and the EEC, which would eventually lead to full membership[433]. Although the final goal was not intended as a promise, a customs union was considered a natural milestone of a closer

---

432 Muftuler, B. M. (2004), p. 31

433 Ibid.

relationship. Articles 2-5 of the Ankara Agreement[434] outlined the achievement of this end-result in three stages[435]:

1. A Preparatory Phase aimed to strengthen the Turkish economy through aid from the Community. The detailed rules for this stage were set in the Provisional and Financial Protocol to this Agreement;
2. A Transition Phase was designed to align the economic policies of Turkey with those of the Community in order to progressively establish a customs union between them;
3. The Final Phase was to begin with the finalization of the customs union and would have involved the Parties in a closer coordination of economic policies.

The EEC and Turkey enabled the Association Council[436] to make decisions regarding the way the "Acquis Communautaire"[437] would be transposed into national legislation. It includes, *inter alia*, international agreements concluded by the EU, such as the Ankara Agreement of 1963[438]. However, little enthusiasm existed at the time the Agreement was signed in regard to its implementation[439]. Turkey was reluctant to eliminate tariffs and other trade barriers on account of its Import Substitution Industrialization policy, whereas the EEC for their part did not lift restrictions on textile and agricultural products[440]. Moreover, relations were interrupted due to the military *coup* in 1980. Though the Generals allowed democratic elections in 1983, relations with the EEC resumed only in 1986 (see Annex 1). Turkey finally applied officially for full membership of the EU in 1987 during a new market deregulation process. Turkish policy makers wanted to send a clear signal that they were determined to abolish protectionist policies.

---

434 Republic of Turkey, Ministry of Foreign Affairs, official website, "Ankara Agreement"

435 Annex 1 presents chronological developments of Turkish–EU relations.

436 Association Council is composed of representatives of Member States, Turkey, members of the Council and the Commission (Cakir, E. A. (2002), p. 331).

437 The "Acquis" is a comprehensive set of rules defined as "the body of common rights and obligations, which bind all the member states together within the EU" (Commission of the European Communities (2000)).

438 Cakir, E. A. (2002), pp. 329, 330

439 Sozer, A. (2005), p. 4

440 Ibid.

The Ankara Agreement (art. 16) required that the parties should apply the provisions of the Rome Treaty for harmonization of their laws on competition[441]. Accordingly, in December 1994 the National Assembly approved the Competition Law[442], which also established a Competition Agency (art. 20). It stated that[443]:

> "in carrying out its duties, it shall have independent authority. No organ, authority, entity or person can give orders or directives that affect final decisions of the Agency."

Therefore, we observe that the Competition Agency was established as an Independent Regulatory Agency (IRA) far from political interference. Nevertheless, there were some caveats in the application. Two aspects warrant development:

- The Competition Law approved in December 1994 was an adaptation into national legislation of EU Competition Law[444]. It concerned prohibition of agreements, concerted practices, and decisions restricting competition (art.4)[445], prohibition of the abuse of dominant position (art.6)[446] and mergers and acquisitions significantly impeding competition in markets (art.7)[447]. However, while European legislation explicitly states that SOEs must respect competition rules as well, this was not the case for the version adopted into Turkish legislation[448].

---

441 Republic of Turkey, Ministry of Foreign Affairs, official website

442 Competition Authority (1994), p. 1

443 Ibid., p. 9

444 Mumcu, A. and Zenginobuz, U. (2001), p. 5

445 In line with the Article 85 of the Treaty of Rome or Article 81 of the Treaty of Amsterdam (Ibid., p. 6).

446 In line with the Article 86 of the Treaty of Rome or Article 82 of the Treaty of Amsterdam (Mumcu, A. and Zenginobuz, U. (2001), p. 8).

447 Ibid., p. 5

448 Article 90 of the Treaty of Rome, which was renumbered as Article 86 of the Treaty of Amsterdam, signed on 2nd October 1997 and entered into force on 1st May 1999. Treaty of Amsterdam amended certain provisions of the Treaty of Rome (Mumcu, A. and Zenginobuz, U. (2001), pp. 5, 6).

The following example provides insight into the consequences of this discrepancy between the "Acquis Communautaire"[449] and the Turkish version of Competition Law: During the first years of its existence, the Competition Board found that the Turkish Sugar Factories (TSF Inc.) was in a dominant position in the relevant market and violated articles 3 and 6 of the Competition Law by selling below cost[450]. This not only violated economic efficiency and profitability principals but caused financial distress for private sugar producers in the cities of Amasya, Konya and Kayseri[451]. Distorted pricing behavior from a SOE was pushing private producers out of business[452]. However, TSF Inc. refuted claims of violation of article 6 claiming that sale prices of sugar were determined by the relevant ministries on the basis of laws and concern for the public interest. This is an important aspect, as SOEs composed a significant market share in many sectors[453] and the transition process towards a functioning market economy cannot be successful nor can liberalization be effective without the elimination of the politically-backed market power of the SOEs;

- The Competition Authority enjoys financial and administrative autonomy and it is established as an independent institution by law[454]. It is composed of 11 members who are appointed by the Council of Ministers among candidates from different public institutions, for a renewable mandate of 6 years[455]. While this mandated requirement can reduce or potentially eliminate political influence, we must ask whether the Council of Ministers

---

449 Art. 102 of the Treaty on the Functioning of the EU states: "Any abuse by one or more undertakings of a dominant position within the internal market or in a substantial part of it shall be prohibited as incompatible with the internal market in so far as it may affect trade between Member States. Such abuse may consist in directly or indirectly imposing unfair purchase or selling prices or other unfair trading conditions. [...] " (Official Journal of the European Union (2012a), p. 89).

Whereas art. 106 is specifically on public undertakings: "In case of public undertakings and undertakings to which Member States grant special or exclusive rights, Member States shall neither enact nor maintain in force any measure contrary to the rules contained in the Treaties. [...]" (Official Journal of the European Union (2012a), p. 90)

450 Mumcu, A. and Zenginobuz, U. (2001), p. 21

451 Ibid.

452 Ibid.

453 Ibid., p. 20

454 Competition Authority (1994), p. 9

455 Mumcu, A. and Zenginobuz, U. (2001), p. 28

chooses the candidates on the basis of merit or is induced to select them with political affiliation in mind[456]. The Competition Authority, though officially independent, is a body potentially exposed to political interference by virtue of its close connection with the Council of Ministers.

Following the approval of the Competition Law, the National Assembly passed a number of legally binding laws in order to harmonize national legislation with the "Acquis Communautaire", including a Consumer Protection Act and certain articles of the Law of Intellectual and Artistic Works, in the first half of 1995[457]. Despite the fact that the Competition Board only began operating three years later in November 1997[458], the EU signed the Customs Union protocol in March 1995, the Turkish Parliament having already approved the Law and thus formally satisfying the Ankara Agreement requirements[459]. This episode shows that Turkey was dragging its feet as far as serious adaptation of its laws to the "Acquis" is concerned. It shows the wide cultural gap that still had to be closed. It also showed how lax the EU could sometimes be in applying its own standards.

The impact of the Customs Union Agreement on the Turkish economy

The EU countries have traditionally been an important trade partner for Turkey when compared with the rest of the world. Figure 3.9 shows that Turkish imports from the EU-27 ranged between 42.4 and 55.8 percent, while exports ranged between 55.2 and 58 percent from 1995 to 2006. The main trade partners have been Germany, Italy, France and the U.K. Figures 3.10 and 3.11 show evolution of trade with these partners in the same time period.

---

[456] Mumcu, A. and Zenginobuz, U. (2001), p. 28

[457] Cakir, E. A. (2002), p. 339

[458] In fact, members of the Board were not appointed until February 1997, (Zenginobuz, U. (2008), p. 479).

[459] Mumcu, A. and Zenginobuz, U. (2001), p. 1

Fig. 3.9: Proportion of Turkish import and export from the EU-27 over total values, in percentage

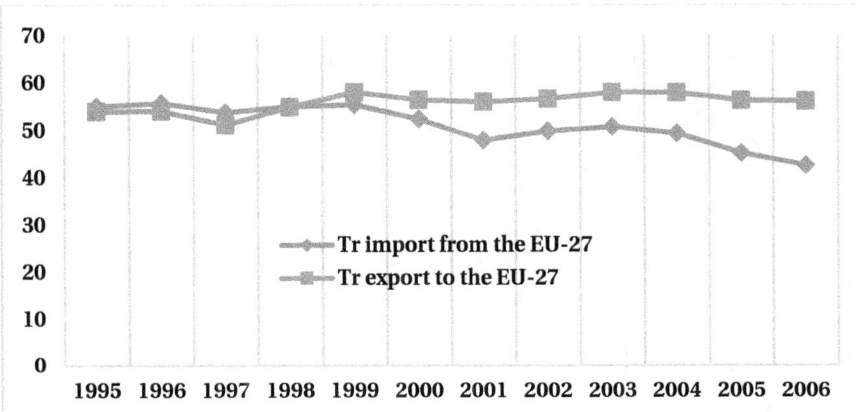

Source: State Planning Organization, Ministry of Economy

Fig. 3.10: Proportion of import from main EU trade partners over total import, in percentage

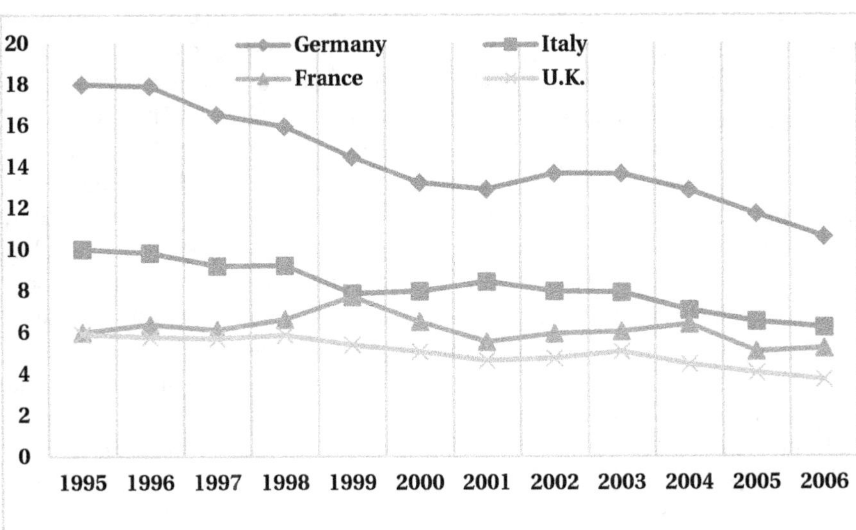

Source: State Planning Organization, Ministry of Economy

Fig. 3.11: Proportion of export to main EU trade partners over total export, in percentage

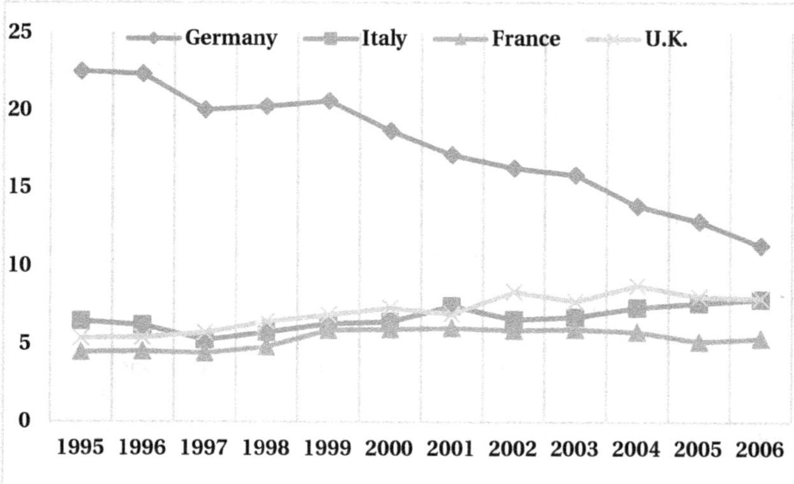

Source: State Planning Organization, Ministry of Economy

Empirical studies investigate mainly "static" effects of the customs union, as it is difficult to measure its long-term "dynamic" effects. For instance, Karaman and Ozkale (2007) evaluated foreign trade data and analyzed aggregate and disaggregated import demand by using panel data modeling[460]. They compared the Turkish import demand from EU countries with that from non-EU countries and found that the import demand is income elastic and price (exchange rate variable) inelastic[461]. More precisely, they argued that responsiveness to income changes decreased in the EU group and increased in the non-EU group, whereas they found evidence of price inelastic import demand in both groups. Regarding some import chapters selected for their study, they commented that customs union had been traded creative in machines and mechanical appliances, in the automotive sector and in electrical goods and machinery[462]. On the other hand, there was evidence of a marginal trade diversion effect on steel and iron imports. Moreover, in these sectors, imports from the EU have been less responsive to income changes but more responsive to price changes. There is no any empirical evidence on plastic and

460 Karaman, F.N., Ozkale, L. N. (2007), pp. 6-13

461 Ibid., p. 14

462 Ibid., pp. 14, 15

organic chemical imports. Briefly, the regression results differ among import chapters. For an accurate analysis, each chapter needs to be analyzed in its own dynamics. In any case, the analysis broadly suggests considerable trade creation but marginal trade diversion[463].

Some statistical data can also shed light on "static" effects on the economy. In fact, a direct impact of the Customs Union has been the decrease of tariff revenue when Turkey lowered its import tariffs from a simple average of 13.5 percent in 1995 to 3.6 percent in 1996, corresponding to a median tariff rate of 8.1 percent in 1995 and 1.2 percent in 1996[464]. This led to a decrease of the tariff revenues/total tax revenues ratio from 2.8 percent in 1995 to an average of 1 percent from 2004 to 2006[465]. Figure 3.12 illustrates the export/import ratio change over time of the 27 EU countries, some of which however were not a member of the EU in 1996. The figure also includes "total foreign trade" data with the rest of the world as Turkey had to lower tariff rates for third party countries, i.e., Free Trade Agreement (FTA) partners of the EU[466]. To note that, in the immediate period after the Customs Union, Turkish exports to the EU did not increase substantially to compensate for the increase in imported goods. One possible explanation for this is that the EU had already removed tariffs on imports from Turkey during the 1970s[467]. In fact, the Turkish market was not new for the European enterprises and the trade gap had widened by 2001. In any case, the expected welfare gain generated from a customs union is via trade creation, which applies on import flows and not on export flows.

463 Schmusch, S. (2008), p. 9

464 Taymaz, E. and Yilmaz, K. (2007), pp. 131, 132

465 Ibid., p. 132

466 Yilmaz, K. (2010), p. 3

467 Taymaz, E. and Yilmaz, K. (2007), p. 133

Figure 3.12: Export/Import Ratio change with the EU and the rest of the world, in percentage

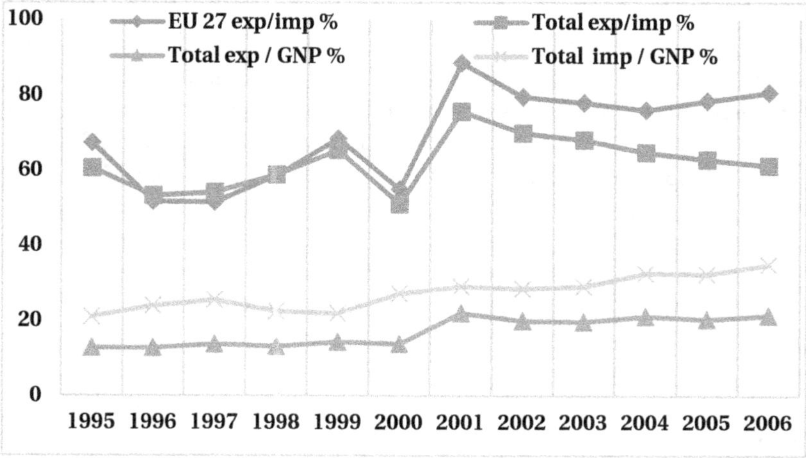

Source: State Planning Organization

Turkey had, during the 1990s, unstable political circumstances, volatile price indices and fluctuating interest rates, which in turn affected exchange rates and thus the overall trade volume. The Customs Union is only one of the explanatory variables in the figure above and this agreement must be evaluated in a wider perspective with a longer time horizon. It helped introduce and catalyze competitive behavior in markets and increased transparency, while through the implementation of a stable trade policy, it made the Turkish market more accessible by lowering or removing tariffs and non-tariff barriers[468].

The customs union with the EU was a huge step. Henceforth, it became imperative to adapt Turkey's market regulations and trade policy regime to European standards.

---

468 In addition to the EU countries, the Customs Union implied that the Most Favored Nation (MFN) tariff rates on tradable goods with non-preferential partners had to be reduced from an average of 22 percent in 1994 to 6.9 percent in 2001, GSP (Generalized System of Preferences) beneficiaries from 22 percent to 2.7 percent, and with the EU's Free Trade Agreements (FTA) partners from 22 percent to 1.34 percent (Kaminski, B. and Ng, F. (2007), p. 38).

Discussion 1: Problems emerging after the adoption of the EU Competition policy

The European Commission's Regular Reports in 1998 and 1999 argued that while price liberalization in the private sector was in place, the state was still playing a significant role in the pricing regime of SOEs and agricultural output[469]. It further advanced that roughly one third of the consumer price index was still subject to administrative pricing[470]. While agriculture sector's share of GNP fell from 33 percent in 1968 to 14 percent in 1996 (in favor of industry and services rising from 17.1 percent to 27.7 percent and 49.8 percent to 58.3 percent respectively), the sector still employed 42 percent of the population[471]. Turkish governments have traditionally pursued agricultural support policies both to maintain occupational levels in this cornerstone of the economy and to secure votes during elections[472]. This practice, in particular, was an important factor contributing to the acceleration of the public debt after mid-1980s, as discussed above[473].

Unsurprisingly, efforts to adopt pertinent EU legislation created problems in the agricultural sector. The majority of small farmers were not able to meet competitive prices, while modernization required structural changes[474]. In section 4.1.3 we will explore the creation of two Independent Regulatory Agencies for sugar and tobacco, two politically sensitive crops for which the IMF and the World Bank demanded privatization of the relevant SOEs. The degree of political independence of these agencies remains in question to this day. The presence of the Turkish state lingers on the economy and proves quite difficult to eliminate.

Discussion 2: The impact of customs union on Croatian economy

My study covers the EU-27, as I used data mainly until the year 2010. I would like to briefly overview here the impact of free trade to Croatia in a comparative perspective, which started the EU accession negotiations together with Turkey in October 2005 and became the 28th member state in July 2013.

---

[469] Commission of the European Communities (1999), p. 22

[470] Ibid., p. 23

[471] Ibid.

[472] Zenginobuz, U. (2008), p. 482

[473] Ibid.

[474] Commission of the European Communities (1999), p. 23

Croatia gained its independence in November 1991 by separating from the former Yugoslavia. The Stabilization Program that the government launched in October 1993 aimed at monitoring hyper-inflation and to establish macroeconomic stability. Whereas, the process of trade liberalization began officially in November 2000 with its accession to the WTO. Then, it signed the Stabilization and Association Agreement (SAA) and the European Free Trade Agreement (EFTA) with the EU in 2001, Free Trade Agreement (FTA) with Turkey in 2002, Central European Free Trade Agreement (CEFTA) in 2003 for closer cooperation[475] and it applied also for the EU membership in the same year. It became an official candidate in June 2004 and accession negotiations were opened together with Turkey on 3rd October 2005. Croatia adopted successfully *acquis communautaire* in the following years and joined the EU ten years after its membership application.

Thanks to the SAA that entered into force in 2005, Croatia's trade with the EU has gradually liberalized benefiting this small country from duty-free access to the EU for most of its agricultural exports (except for sugar, beef, and wine). Whereas, protection against EU agricultural products lasted until it joined the Union[476]. Full membership has also implied the adoption of the Common Agricultural Policy (CAP).

A 2013 European Commission study[477]estimated the impact of changes in trade and agricultural policies on major macroeconomic variables like international trade, production, and employment in Croatia, the EU and their main trading partners[478]. It shows that by adopting European trade regime and agricultural policy, this small economy would face changes in production and trade structure, i.e., at constant prices, its agricultural production would increase by 1.1 percent and food production decrease by 5.5 percent. Moreover, it would be exposed to strong price effects, declining the value of production at real prices in both agricultural and food-related sectors. In addition, Croatian primary agricultural goods exports to the EU would increase by 32 percent, while that of food products would fall by 20 percent. Wheat, vegetables and fruits, and beef would be the sectors that gain most due to trade diversion

---

[475] Holzner, M. (2013), p. 2

[476] Boulanger, P., Ferrari, E., Michakel, J. and Vinyes, C. (2013), p. 7

[477] The study used a CGE model MAGNET, which stands for Computable General Equilibrium model Modular Agricultural GeNeral Equilibrium Tool. Data for Croatia covers the period from 2007 to 2013 and estimates the impacts over the 5-year period after Croatia's accession in 2013.

[478] Boulanger, P., Ferrari, E., Michakel, J. and Vinyes, C. (2013), p. 10

effects from different countries to the EU. In contrary, imports of primary agricultural goods from the EU would fall by 3.2 percent, whereas those of food products would increase by 27 percent.

Through accession, protection for imports coming from the EU is replaced by an increase in protection of agricultural and food sectors for imports coming from third countries. This would lead to a decrease in total imports of agricultural products by 6.1 percent and an increase of food products by 11.2 percent. Simultaneously, total exports of Croatian agricultural products would increase by 7.4 percent and that for food products drop of 2 percent[479].

Among the disadvantages of EU full membership for Croatia, it is straightforward to note the reduction in customs revenue and the decrease in trade with CEFTA countries. The accession in 2013 has involved this country with the customs union and the adoption of the EU trading system that the member states apply to third countries[480]. Harmonization of Croatia's both tariff and non-tariff measures with those applied in the EU member states would affect also their trading partners[481]. In other words, abandoning the CEFTA and at the same time joining the EU would have a significant impact on foreign trade. For instance, Bosnia and Herzegovina is a traditionally important partner of Croatia composing around 13 percent of its total trade. An agricultural price increase thus would have a negative impact on its trade with this country.

On the other hand, Croatia has gained a better bargaining position thanks to the EU membership as its trade interest is represented by the European Commission. Also having the label of products manufactured in the EU has contributed to its image in international markets. In addition, competition in the domestic market would increase due to the duty-free access to competing products from the EU member states, which means an increase in intra-EU trade[482]. Membership has also allowed Croatia access to third countries having Free Trade Agreement with the EU. Moreover, it joined the European Economic Area and took over duty-free trade regime with Switzerland and customs union with Turkey, though the latter is not an important change as Croatia had already preferential trade agreements with these countries. It gained

479 Boulanger, P., Ferrari, E., Michakel, J. and Vinyes, C. (2013), p. 37

480 Stulec, I, Bakovic and Vuckovi, V. (2014), p. 383

481 Boulanger, P., Ferrari, E., Michakel, J. and Vinyes, C. (2013), p. 7

482 Details on products with the largest increase and decrease in average tariff rates see Stulec, I, Bakovic and Vuckovi, V. (2014), p. 386

preferential trade arrangements with several Mediterranean, Latin American, Asian, African, Caribbean and Pacific countries as well as customs union with Andorra, Monaco, and San Marino[483]. The Croatian trade agreements with CEFTA, EFTA and with Turkey do not apply anymore. However, as the EU signed the SAA with some CEFTA countries (i.e., Albania, Bosnia and Herzegovina, Montenegro, Macedonia, and Serbia) Croatia has to apply the same agreement with these countries[484].

According to empirical research, the EU membership would have the following effects on the Croatian economy[485]: An increase in the foreign trade deficit with the EU member states in the short-term (though this would be rebalanced in the long-term), a decline of exports to CEFTA countries, a decline in the CPI and GDP in Croatia. In addition, trade diversion effects may occur both for Croatia and the EU in case imports from more efficient non-EU producers would be substituted by imports from less efficient producers within the EU countries. The net effects are to be tested over some longer period as it will depend also on economic, social and political factors.

Concluding remarks: Let us now turn to the Turkish case and examine other difficulties that the economy had to experience during the 1990s.

Briefly, the Customs Union with the EU showed that Turkish agriculture was not able to face competition in the EU without urgently needed structural reforms. The need for structural reforms was also urgent in the financial sector. As we saw in section 2.2.1.1, since the late 1980s, banks held a high proportion of government debt (Table 2.8), effectively financing the fiscal deficit and themselves encountering serious difficulties during the whole decade. The 1999 European Commission's Regular Report stated that[486]:

> "Turkey has most of the hallmarks of a market economy, possessing a well-developed institutional and legislative framework, a dynamic private sector and liberal trade rules. The economy has considerable potential for growth and has shown

---

483 Stulec, I, Bakovic and Vuckovi, V. (2014), p. 386

484 Ibid., p. 387

485 Ibid., p. 389

486 Commission of the European Communities (1999), p. 29

> great adaptability, particularly in the context of the customs union, which has contributed significantly to its modernization. These factors should, in theory enable Turkey in the medium-term to acquire a viable market economy able to withstand the pressure of competition. However, if it is to be able to run its economy efficiently and make the most of its advantages, it must establish a credible, durable framework of macroeconomic stability and a climate in which the financial sector can genuinely act as an intermediary."

In reality, while Turkey had adopted a large number of EU directives into the national legislation, the banking sector had lost its "intermediation" function between the financial and the real sector. It served mainly to finance the budget deficit through the purchase of government securities thus replacing the Turkish Central Bank that had traditionally created high-powered money for the same purpose.

I examine, in the next section, vulnerabilities of the banking sector during the 1990s, which also became one of the major factors behind the 2001 financial crisis.

3.3.2.2. Banking sector's fragile structure after the deregulation process from 1980 to 1989

In this section, we will explore the composition of the banking sector, factors behind its profitability, the relationship between state banks and agricultural subsidies, the impact of the latter on budget deficits and the interaction between government securities, interest rates and foreign exchange rates, which will pave the path towards investigating dynamics behind the next 2001 currency crisis.

Table 3.4 shows that the number of state-owned banks decreased during the 1990s. Regarding private banks, their number increased after the full liberalization of the capital account in 1989. This can also be attributed to weaknesses in granting licenses, which made an entrance into the sector relatively easy, whereas license revocation was difficult[487]. Industrial groups, in

---

[487] BRSA (2010), p. 9

particular, took advantage of this opportunity, helping to explain the increase in the number of private banks from 24 in 1989 to 38 in 1998. Nonetheless, at the same time, a growing number of banks[488] were being transferred to the Savings Deposit Insurance Fund (SDIF) during the period from 1998 to 2000, signaling serious problems and growing moral hazard.

Table 3.4: Number of banks from 1989 to 2000

	1989	**1990**	**1991**	**1992**	**1993**	**1994**	**1995**	**1996**	**1997**	**1998**	**1999**	**2000**
Banks(1)	53	56	55	57	58	55	55	56	59	60	62	61
SOBs (2)	8	8	8	6	6	6	5	5	5	4	4	4
PBs (3)	24	25	26	31	32	29	32	33	36	38	31	28
SDIF (4)	-	-	-	-	-	-	-	-	1	2	8	11
Foreign	21	23	21	20	20	20	18	18	18	18	19	18
D. Bs.(5)	9	10	10	12	12	12	13	13	13	15	19	18
Total (6)	62	66	65	69	70	67	68	69	72	75	81	79

Source: Banks Association of Turkey

(1) Commercial banks; (2) State owned commercial banks; (3) Privately owned commercial banks; (4) Commercial banks under SDIF; (5) Development and investment banks; finally (6) is the sum of (1) and (5).

The impact of the liberalization process on the ownership structure of banks is straightforward. Table 3.5 shows that the proportion of state-owned banks decreased in favor of banks owned privately by residents and non-residents. To note that while the number of state-owned banks decreased during the 1990s, they still accounted for more than 1/3rd of total assets by the year 2000.

---

488 BRSA (2003), p. 10

Table 3.5: Structure of banking sector, in percentage of total assets

	1989	1990	1991	1992	1993	1994	1995	1996	1997	1998	1999	2000
Banks(1)	90.8	91.2	91.5	92.7	92.9	91.8	92.6	94.0	94.6	95.3	95.2	95.6
SOBs (2)	45.6	44.8	42.4	43.1	36.9	39.6	37.7	38.3	34.6	34.9	34.9	34.2
PBs (3)	42.5	43.5	45.9	46.0	52.3	49.2	52.0	52.7	55.4	53.3	46.0	47.4
SDIF (4)	0.0	0.0	0.0	0.0	0.0	0.0	0.0	0.0	0.0	2.6	9.1	8.5
Foreign	2.7	2.9	3.1	3.7	3.8	3.0	2.9	3.0	4.7	4.4	5.2	5.4
D. Bs.(5)	9.2	8.8	8.5	7.3	7.1	8.2	7.4	6.0	5.4	4.7	4.8	4.4
SOBs (6)	6.7	6.5	6.3	5.3	5.1	6.0	5.7	4.5	4.1	3.6	3.4	3.3
PBs (7)	2.3	2.1	2.1	1.8	1.8	1.9	1.5	1.3	1.1	0.9	0.9	0.9
Foreign	0.2	0.2	0.2	0.2	0.3	0.2	0.2	0.2	0.2	0.2	0.4	0.3
Total (8)	100.0	100.0	100.0	100.0	100.0	100.0	100.0	100.0	100.0	100.0	100.0	100.0

Source: Banks Association of Turkey

(1) Commercial banks; (2) State owned commercial banks; (3) Privately owned commercial banks; (4) Commercial banks under SDIF; (5) Development and investment banks; (6) State owned development and investment banks; (7) privately owned development and investment banks; finally (8) is the sum of (1) and (5).

However, it is important to ask whether profitability and efficiency criteria were met. To note in Table 3.6 that despite a recovery in the aftermath of the 1994 crisis, external and domestic factors from 1997 to 1999 negatively affected the whole economy. My first point of observation focuses around a decrease in the average number of Loans (Ls) and an increase of Non-Performing Loans (NPLs), which compared with a decreased share of income from credit means that the banks' essential function of intermediation between financial markets and the real sector became less pronounced[489], while simultaneously maintaining their role in financing the government budget deficit. Figure 3.13 shows the increasing portion of government securities and the decreasing portion of loans when compared with banks' assets from the early 1980s to early 2000s. This means that through deregulation of markets, banks lost their intermediation function between financial and real private sector and made more and more profit from lending to the government.

489 BRSA (2010), p. 11

Table 3.6: Asset Quality and profitability, in percentage

	1989	1990	1991	1992	1993	1994	1995	1996	1997	1998	1999	2000
L/A (1)	42.2	47.0	43.9	41.8	41.4	39.1	42.5	43.1	45.5	38.3	30.1	30.6
NPL/L (2)	5.2	4.2	4.9	3.4	3.1	4.1	2.8	2.0	2.1	7.2	10.7	11.5
Int. /tot. (3)	-	51.7	48.2	48.7	46.7	36.2	42.0	41.1	42.1	32.2	21.6	19.6
Int. /tot. int. (4)	-	69.2	67.4	64.0	63.7	61.7	62.8	60.6	61.3	46.6	37.2	38.0
Int. G.S./ int. income (5)	-	20.4	21.1	23.1	25.6	23.0	23.9	24.5	21.9	22.2	24.7	19.4
Income/ assets (6)	2.3	2.8	2.1	2.7	3.4	1.9	3.9	3.9	3.7	3.9	1.2	-2.0
Net income/ assets (7)	1.9	2.5	1.9	2.2	2.8	1.4	2.9	3.1	2.7	2.3	-0.5	-2.8

Source: Banks Association of Turkey, BRSA (2010), p.12

1. Ratio of total loans to total assets;
2. Ratio of non-performing loans to total loans;
3. Ratio of credit interest income to total income;
4. Ratio of Interest received from credits to total interest incomes;
5. Ratio of Interest received from government securities to total interest income;
6. Ratio of Income before tax to average of total assets;
7. Ratio of net income to average of total assets.

Figure 3.13: Crowding-out of private sector by government securities, in percentage

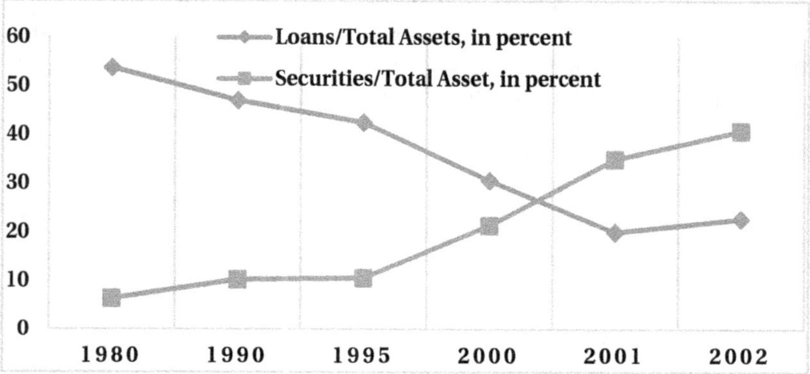

Source: Banking Supervision and Regulation Agency, Pazarbasioglu, C. (2003), p. 4

Regarding asset quality indicators, while the NPL/L ratio in Table 3.6 corresponds to the overall banking sector, Table 3.7 makes a comparison of NPL/L between state-owned and private banks.

Table 3.7: Banks' Non Performing Loans (NPLs) to Total Loans (Ls) Ratio, in percentage

NPL/L	1989	1990	1991	1992	1993	1994	1995	1996	1997	1998	1999	2000
SOBs	6.6	5.7	7.2	4.1	4.5	4.0	3.0	2.4	2.5	5.6	10.0	12.5
PBs	3.7	2.6	2.7	2.3	1.8	2.6	1.8	1.6	2.0	2.4	3.6	6.1

Source: Banks Association of Turkey; SOBs and PBs stand for "state-owned banks" and "private banks", respectively.

The state banks' losses were mainly due to subsidized credits to the agricultural sector. Moreover, this explains why in the case of two major state banks' (Ziraat Bank and Halk Bank) total write-offs of receivables amounted to 3 percent of GDP in 1996 and exceeded 13 percent of GDP in 1999[490].

These bank losses did not receive compensation from budget resources. I conclude that official data on the budget deficit that we observe in Table 3.8 is only a portion of the whole. It is an incomplete representation of reality: State-owned banks had to cover their losses by borrowing from the market at short-term and at high-interest rates, further aggravating the long-term cost to the government[491] (Table 3.8).

Table 3.8: Key Macro Indicators from 1989 to 2001

	1989	1990	1991	1992	1993	1994	1995	1996	1997	1998	1999	2000	2001
BUDGET(1)	-3.3	-3.0	-5.3	-4.3	-6.7	-3.9	-4.0	-8.3	-7.6	-7.3	-11.9	-10.9	-16.9
DOMESTIC BORROW.													
simple (2)	53.9	49.7	69.8	74.6	79.3	110.0	98.9	107.8	110.7	102.0	94.0	36.6	75.9
comp. (3)	59.8	54.0	80.5	87.7	87.6	164.4	121.9	135.2	127.2	122.5	109.5	38.0	96.2
mat. (4)	233	236	211	211	257	119	206	195	349	233	479	410	148
INFLATION RATE (5)	65.7	62.1	62.5	70.4	65.3	84.8	103.5	81.3	80.7	90.7	70.5	63.0	48.4
FX RATE													
DM/TL (6)	39.5	43.4	55.0	76.0	50.1	178.8	72.5	68.6	61.9	70.5	52.8	29.5	90.2
USD/TL (7)	48.8	22.9	60.2	64.6	60.5	169.9	53.5	77.9	86.9	71.6	61.0	48.4	96.5
Real (8)	106.4	123.1	128.2	126.1	133.8	101.3	110.0	114.0	121.6	132.9	140.3	152.0	123.1

---

490 BRSA (2010), p. 10

491 Ibid.

Source: State Planning Organization

1. Budget Balance/GDP ratio, in percentage;
2. Interest rate based on domestic borrowing, average simple rate, in percentage;
3. Interest rate based on domestic borrowing, average compound rate, in percentage;
4. Average maturity of public debt (in days);
5. Inflation rate based on consumer price index (CPI), yearly average percentage change based on monthly changes; for the period 1987-1994 is used index value 1987=100; for the period from 1995 to 2001 is used index value 1994= 100;
6. Annual change based on year average DM/TL exchange rate, in percentage;
7. Annual change based on year average USD/TL exchange rate, in percentage;
8. Real Exchange Rate Index based on 1 USD +1.5 Euro basket in the relative price calculations. Turkey uses the consumer price index, whereas the USA and Euro area use the producer price index to derive the real exchange rate from the nominal.

Unstable macro indicators that we note in Table 3.8, from budget deficits to inflation and interest rates, led again the Turkish government to ask for the IMF assistance, this time on a Staff Monitoring Program[492]. Thus, policy makers were engaged for a strict monetary policy with a target inflation rate[493] accompanied by a reduced budget deficit and structural reforms[494]. Thanks to the disinflation program, the inflation rate based on CPI followed a decreasing trend starting in 1998 (Table 3.8). However, budget deficit and interest rates remained at high levels and the latter continued to be sensitive to domestic and external factors (Fig. 3.14), and in turn fostered volatile economic circumstances. External factors included a decreased level of global liquidity. The Russian government declared a default in August 1998 and LTCM, major hedge fund we mentioned in section 3.2.3.1, collapsed in the following months, due to its highly-leveraged position on Russian government securities. Global investors were worried about possible "contagion" effects in Turkey from the 1998 Russian debt crisis. Moreover, domestic economic and political[495] uncertainties in addition to structural weaknesses in the banking sector were perceived as significant risk factors: The Turkish government was rolling over its debt amidst exacerbated and worsening global liquidity circumstances. These uncertainties increased the perception of sovereign default risk and

---

[492] IMF Staff Monitoring Program (1998), IMF website

[493] Ertugrul, A. and Selcuk, F. (2001), p. 20

[494] Onis, Z. (2002), p. 15

[495] To note in Annex 3 that short-term coalition and minority governments was a major feature of the 1990s.

decreased expected returns for global investors, while the liquidity needed to cover deficits depended on investor confidence and market expectations.

Despite these circumstances, Moody's announced on 30th November 1999 that it had changed the outlook for foreign currency bonds and bank deposits from stable to positive[496]. There were two major factors behind this reappraisal[497]: The expectation of an IMF stabilization program and improving Turkish-EU relations. Turkey signed a "Letter of Intent" with the IMF on December 9th, 1999 and became an official candidate for full EU membership the very next day at the Helsinki Summit on December 10th-11th[498].

The Commission adopted in July 2000 a single framework for coordinating all sources of European Community pre-accession financial assistance for Turkey. This regulation also provided the legal basis for Accession Partnership for Turkey[499]. All funds were pre-accession oriented[500] and reforms were to be supported through structural adjustment facilities. The objective was to help Turkey undertake major structural reforms in line with the "Acquis Communataire"[501].

---

496 Moody's official website

497 Alper, E. (2001), p. 4

498 Ibid.

499 Commission of the European Communities (2000), p. 8

500 Half of the funds were to be allocated for structural and sectoral reforms aiming in particular to harmonize Turkish legislation and practices with the "Acquis Communautaire"; Whereas the other half of the appropriations were intended to finance other measures promoting Turkey's integration into the EU, that is to say, to help the Turkish administration and institutions to develop the capacity to implement the "Acquis" (through institution building) and to assist Turkey in mobilizing investments needed to align its industry and infrastructure with Community standards (through investment support and regional/rural development) (Commission of the European Communities (2000), p. 8).

501 Commission of the European Communities (2000), p. 9

Fig. 3.14: Interest Rates on Government Securities, in percentage

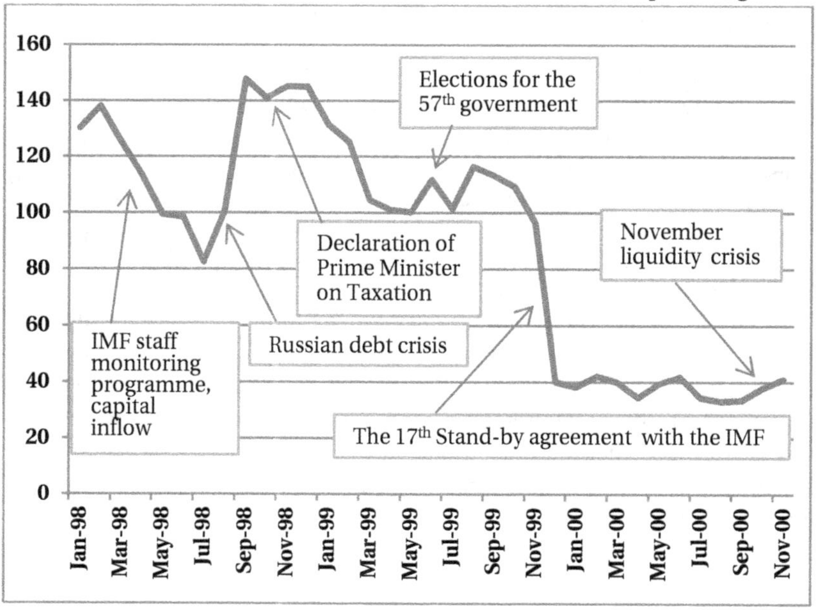

Source: Turkish Central Bank, State Planning Organization, Banks Association of Turkey

But, while improving relations with the IMF and the EU increased investor confidence, unhedged foreign exchange positions of Turkish banks reached a peak in 1999 (Table 3.9). In fact, unstable foreign exchange rates during the 1990s (Table 3.8) were caused by a lack of confidence in the local currency by both households and banks.

Table 3.9: Capital Adequacy Ratios (CARs) and Households' Deposits from 1989 to 2001

	1989	1990	1991	1992	1993	1994	1995	1996	1997	1998	1999	2000	2001
CARs													
eq./ass. (1)	9.4	10.1	9.6	8.6	9.3	8.4	8.9	8.9	9.4	13.0	8.2	9.3	20.8
FX/eq. (2)	-16.5	39.6	44.2	80.7	104.8	26.6	73.4	50.6	81.1	123.1	362.7	212.2	-
DEPOSITS													
FX dep. (3)	6.1	5.5	8.2	9.6	9.9	15.4	16.0	17.5	18.7	17.8	23.5	20.2	31.8
TL dep. (4)	18.3	16.6	16.7	15.6	12.6	14.5	14.2	18.7	18.4	20.4	27.7	24.4	25.0

Source: Banks Association of Turkey (BRSA (2010))

1. (Shareholders' equity + total income)/total assets, in percentage;
2. FX position/shareholders' equity, in percentage;
3. Household deposits at banks in FX/GNP, in percentage;
4. Household deposits at banks in TL/GNP (excluding government and interbank deposits), in percentage.

While households suffered from the effects of unstable inflation rates that made real interest rates unpredictable and as a consequence giving the impression that foreign currency was an attractive portfolio investment, the banks attempted to make profit from interest rate carry trades as we observed in Figure 3.13. The 1999 European Commission's Regular Report argued somewhat optimistically that[502]:

> "The Turkish Banking sector follows the universal banking model. Significant efforts have been made to align the banking legislative framework on Community standards. Provisions on solvency ratios, annual and consolidated accounts, capital adequacy, consolidated supervision and money laundering are in line with the equivalent Community measures. Some others need further alignment. It can be assumed that in the near future the main legislative framework will be in place."

In fact, Turkish policy makers had accomplished a substantial amount of "paper" progress in transposing the EU standards into the national legislation, but there were many weak points. Firstly, there remained a multitude of

[502] Commission of the European Communities (1999), p. 36

agencies concerned with supervision and regulation of the banking system[503]: Although two institutions were formally charged with supervision, namely, the Undersecretariat of Treasury and the Central Bank, in practice the Capital Markets Board, the Ministry of Finance and the Prime Minister's Office were also involved in the process[504]. Differences in the application of accounting and independent auditing standards further weakened an effective implementation of regulations[505].

Turkish policy makers introduced a new Banking Law to restructure the banking sector regulatory framework in June 1999, which also mandated the creation of an independent regulatory agency, the Banking Regulation and Supervision Agency (BRSA)[506]. Passing of the law in parliament and the establishment of the BRSA were carried out with the assistance of the IMF, although at that time no official stand-by agreement had been signed[507]. The limit on commercial banks' net open FX position was lowered to 20 percent of capital in September[508]. The Letter of Intent for the Stand-by Agreement from the Turkish government to the IMF in December 1999 stated[509]:

> "The Banks Act will be amended to increase transparency and independence in the operation of the Agency, to strengthen key prudential regulations, and to provide all of the tools needed for the improved resolution of problem banks. The BRSA will be made fully autonomous by removing the involvement of the Council of Ministers from all decisions in the area of supervision, other than the appointment of the members of the Board.
>
> [....]

---

503 BRSA (2010), p. 16

504 Ibid.

505 Ibid.

506 IMF (1999), "Letter of Intent" dated 9th December 1999, Section 52, IMF official website

507 Zenginobuz, U. (2008), p. 480

508 IMF (1999), "Letter of Intent" dated 9th December 1999, Section 52, IMF official website

509 Ibid., Section 53

The Board of the BRSA will be named by end-March 2000 (a structural performance criterion) and the BRSA is expected to be in full operation by end-August 2000."

In addition, the Capital Market Board, which was founded in 1981 and "related" to the Ministry of Finance, gained full administrative and financial independence in 1999[510] and was effectively transformed into an Independent Regulatory Agency. The following year the Banking Supervision and Regulation Agency started its operations and the Saving Deposit Insurance Fund[511] was transferred to its responsibility. Table 3.10 makes evident that the BRSA replaced all ministerial agencies as an independent institution in banking supervision and interacting also with two other independent institutions, i.e., the CMB and the CBRT by the years 2000 and 2001, respectively.

Table 3.10: Agencies concerned with supervision of the banking system, in the pre- and post-reform period and their degree of independence

	Treasury	CBRT (2)	CMB (3)	Min. Fin. (4)	Pr. M. Off. (5)	SDIF (6)	BRSA (7)
1981-1999	**ministerial**	**related to Treasury**	**related to Min. of Finance**	**ministerial**	**ministerial**	**related to CBRT**	-
1999	**ministerial**	**related to Treasury**	*IRA*	**ministerial**	**ministerial**	**related to CBRT**	IRA
2000	**ministerial**	**related to Treasury**	*IRA*	**ministerial**	**ministerial**	*related to BRSA*	*IRA*
From 2001 onwards	ministerial	*Independent status*	*IRA*	ministerial	ministerial	*related to BRSA*	*IRA*

Source: BDDK (2010), p. 16; where (1) stands for the Undersecretariat of Treasury, (2) Central Bank of the Republic of Turkey, (3) Capital Market Board, (4) Ministry of Finance, (5) Prime Minister's Office, (6) Saving Deposit and Insurance Fund and (7) Banking Regulation and Supervision Agency. In bold are shown ministerial agencies involved with economic decision-making, and in italics are shown independent institutions operational in economic management; Whereas, those smaller in size make evident agencies that have not any impact on economic decision-making or that were not operational yet, i.e., the Parliament established the BRSA in 1999 but it became operational in 2000.

---

510 Law No. 4'487 of 1999 (Zenginobuz, U. (2008), p. 478)

511 which was founded in 1983 and functioned under the authority of the Central Bank.

Briefly, by the year 1999 independent regulatory agencies had started to appear. We will observe in section 4.1.4 that others were created during this period as well. This was an important progress in introducing a sound institutional framework. In my opinion, this is the 11th principle that the original "Washington Consensus" prescriptions should have included. Thus, 1999 is an important year not only because the Capital Markets Board gained a de-politicized structure, but also the creation of an IRA in the banking sector meant that a crucial sector for the functioning of markets would soon have a de-politicized framework.

I recall that, while markets were deregulated during the 1980s and the 1990s, the Turkish banking sector replaced the Central Bank in financing budget deficits, losing its intermediation function in the economy. The creation of an IRA in this sector marked the initial phase of a new era. We will see in the next section that the Banking Supervision and Regulation Agency became operational only in late-August 2000, in a period when the Turkish economy was already shifting towards a collapse due to the failure of a major government securities holding bank in a highly unhedged position. The November 2000 liquidity crisis and February 2001 currency crisis were thus unavoidable. However, we will observe in Chapter 4 that in the aftermath of the 2001 currency crisis, this agency played a crucial role in achieving financial market reforms and contributed to the functioning of markets in line with international standards.

Let me now examine in the next section how the economy shifted into a banking sector-led currency crisis.

3.3.2.3. Dynamics behind the February 2001 Currency Crisis

The most severe financial crisis Turkey experienced in its history occurred during the implementation of a Stabilization Program agreed with the IMF in December 1999, obliging the authorities to abandon it. This section begins with an overview of this program as a starting point to investigate dynamics behind the crisis.

The December 1999 IMF Stabilization Program

A. "A major target is to decrease the inflation rate to a single digit by the end of 2002;

B. A pre-announced foreign exchange (FX) rate path with respect to the existing basket will be introduced. It will be announced for the period 1st January 2000 – 31st December 2000, during which the depreciation rate will be 20 percent, equal to the target WPI inflation. The daily FX rate adjustments, within each month, will be constant;

C. There will be no band around the FX rate path for the first 18 months following the introduction of this regime. A gradual shift towards a more flexible regime will begin on 1st July 2001 when a progressively widening band around the central FX rate path will be introduced. This band will widen at a rate of 15 percent per year. Thus, the total width of the band will reach 7.5 percent by end-December 2001, 15 percent by end-June 2002 and 22.5 percent by end-December 2002;

D. The CBRTs' stock of net domestic assets (NDA) at the end of each quarter will not exceed the December 1999 level. During each quarter NDA will remain broadly constant (short-term fluctuations around 5 percent of total base money at the end of preceding quarter is allowed);

E. Within this context, all base money created through the balance-of-payments and domestic interest rates will be fully market determined. Capital in and outflows will not be sterilized. The interbank interest rates posted by the Turkish Central Bank will be adjusted daily in line with the movements of overnight money market rates;

F. During the second half of 2001, as a gradually widening band is introduced around the pre-announced FX rate path more flexibility will be given to NDA policy so as to allow a gradual shift from a monetary framework centered entirely on the FX rate to one that allows greater flexibility in pursuing the inflation target."

The same agreement also introduced a comprehensive "structural reform" into the agenda covering a wide range of areas from banking and agricultural sectors to pension reform and tax policy[512]:

> "Our structural reform program aims at making sustainable over the medium-term the fiscal adjustment lowering the burden of interest payments on public sector debt, improving transparency and economic efficiency and reducing the contingent liabilities of the public sector. All these are essential to create an environment where high growth rates could be sustained in a low inflation environment."

---

[512] IMF (1999), "Letter of Intent" dated December, 9th, 1999, Section 38

Discussion

1. What were the initial objectives of the Stabilization Program?

The Stabilization Program was in line with "Washington Consensus" principles as well as EU requirements, i.e., it aimed at macro stability and a functioning market economy.

2. Were the Program's targets achievable?

Regarding point (A), the aim was to achieve an inflation rate lower than 10 percent by year end-2002. Figure 3.15 shows that this was an achievable target. In fact, the annual rate of inflation decreased from 68.9 percent in January to 39 percent in December 2000. Thus, it is straightforward to observe the positive impact of the program on macro variables such as a rapidly decreasing inflation rate, a relatively stable exchange rate and lower interest rates (Table 3.8). This, in turn, reduced uncertainty relative to inflation and exchange rate risk and lowered the future burden of interest payments on the public debt. Moreover, low-interest rates had a positive impact on consumption and investment, helping improve GDP growth rates from a low of -3.4 percent in 1999 to +6.8 percent in 2000[513]. The program was thus successful in the short-term, as far as the targeted macroeconomic variables were concerned. In addition, it did not allow the Central Bank to expand its domestic assets and increase money supply, which was a chronic problem for Turkey during the previous decades.

3. What problems were encountered? Why did the current account deficit worsen?

Point (B) introduced restrictions on exchange rate movements, defining the ceiling for domestic currency depreciation as 20 percent, equal to the target Wholesale Price Index (WPI) inflation rate for the year 2000. Although this target was not achieved, the exchange rate depreciated by 24.4 percent from 1st January to 31st December 2000, close to the 20 percent target range. Figure 3.15 shows the annual average exchange rate change. However, the differential between price levels and exchange rate caused a real appreciation (Table 3.8),

---

[513] Constant GDP, by expenditures approach based on 1998 prices (Turkish Statistical Institute (2009), p. 762). These data are a new series produced by the Turkish Statistical Institute in line with the European System of Accounts (ESA-95). While I will discuss the reform in the field of statistics in section 5.1, to note here that the GDP data I use, for the period from 1998 onwards, is in line with the EU definition. Thus, it diverges, though slightly, from the data series that I used in Table 2.3.

thereby increasing the current account deficit in 2000 (Table 3.11). In this set of circumstances, the view of Calvo and Vegh (1998) introduced in the section on Third Generation models needs to be discussed[514]. The reason why many exchange rate stabilization programs may end with balance-of-payments crisis is that the exchange rate is pegged to a major currency at the beginning of the program, while the inflation rate slowly converges to targeted levels. Thus, when the local currency begins to appreciate in real terms, imports boom and widening current account deficits develop[515].

Fig. 3.15: Inflation and exchange rate trends during the IMF disinflation program, in percentage

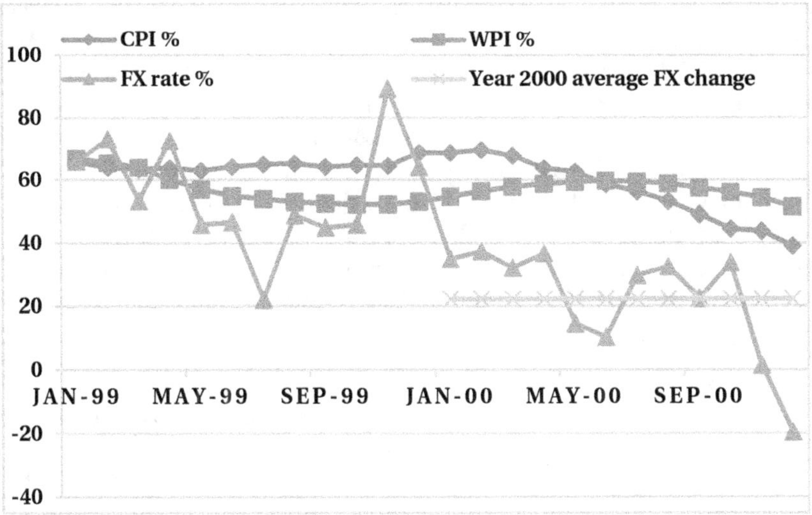

Source: CPI % is the CPI percentage change over the same month of the previous year; WPI % is the WPI percentage change over the same month of the previous year, data from State Planning Organization; FX rate % is the bid USD/TL monthly percentage change, data from Turkish Central Bank

In Turkey, the FDI level was traditionally low, but the economy attracted short-term portfolio investment, which covered the current account deficits. From the point of view of a non-resident investor, as long as the peg was maintained through the IMF Program, the rate of depreciation was predictable and nominal interest rates were attractive. The IMF Stabilization Program had a

---

514 Section 3.2.3

515 Calvo, G. A. and Vegh, C. A. (1999), pp. 3, 11, 45

strong impact on interest rates which decreased from a level of around 100 percent in 1999 (Table 3.8) to less than 40 percent in 2000. The determinants behind capital inflow were, broadly, the risk-free rate (i.e., U.S. government securities with the same maturity) plus a risk premium for investing in Turkey.

I can decompose the risk premium as follows[516]:

Risk premium = exchange rate risk + sovereign default risk

The IMF Stability Program significantly reduced exchange rate risk during the year 2000 while the closer relationship with the EU had a positive impact on perceived sovereign default risk, thus reducing the risk premium. In other words, the IMF Stabilization Program was successful in terms of targeted macro fundamentals. However, overall country risk exposure increased when financial indicators revealed that the economy was based on a fragile structure. As we saw in section 2.1, several authors emphasized that an economy becomes crisis-prone as current account deficits rise. In addition, I introduce here Rodrik and Velasco (1999) who argue that crisis probability increases with a rising current account deficit/GDP ratio[517] and domestic debt/GDP ratio[518]. Moreover, they advance that the short-term debt/reserves ratio is a "robust predictor of financial crisis"[519]. To note in Table 3.11 that both the current account deficit/GNP ratio and the short-term debt/reserves ratio increased sharply in 2000. Regarding the domestic debt/GNP ratio, Table 3.12 illustrates its increasing level from 1999 to 2001.

Table 3.11: Selected indicators showing major risk factors from 1995 to 2001, in percentage

	1995	1996	1997	1998	1999	2000	2001
CA/GNP (1)	-1.4	-1.3	-1.4	1.0	-0.7	-4.8	1.4
Sh. term f. debt/res. (2)	128.7	104.2	95.1	105.4	98.9	127.6	85.9
M2Y/res. (3)	354.0	314.1	287.8	321.8	329.4	381.4	380.6
Currency Subs. (4)	1.1	0.9	1.0	0.9	0.8	0.8	1.3

Source: State Planning Organization and Undersecretariat of Treasury

516 Alper, E. (2001), p. 5

517 The CA deficit/GDP ratio is an important explanatory variable according to Borensztein et al. (1999) and Bussière and Mulder (1999) as well.

518 Rodrik, D. and Velasco, A. (1999), p. 17

519 Ibid., p. 2

1. Ratio of current account balance to GNP;
2. Ratio of short-term foreign debt to Central Bank's international reserves;
3. Ratio of M2Y to Central Bank's international reserves;
4. Currency substitution, proxied as ratio of foreign exchange deposits to domestic currency deposits.

There was another item, thus, in addition to budget deficits that needed to be financed through global markets: The current account deficit. According to Point (E) of the Stabilization Program, domestic interest rates were to be determined by global markets. The latter became the unique providers of liquidity to the economy. Expectations of global investors depended not only on macro variables but were also influenced by institutional and regulatory weaknesses, particularly in the banking sector and by what happens elsewhere. They were global investors after all. In other words, the Central Bank was curtailed in supervising the financial system limiting its ability to provide (or absorb) excess liquidity in the market, while global investors noticed that banks benefiting from implicit government guarantees increased the risk of sovereign default.

To note in Table 3.12 the increasing share of domestic debt from the early 1990s to the early 2000s. Preliminary observations reveal that both the proportion of government securities/GNP and domestic debt/GNP ratios increased during the whole decade. While government securities composed an increasingly significant proportion of domestic debt, another method of domestic borrowing used by the Treasury was to create arrears with SOEs, social security organizations, farmers, and contractors[520]. These arrears were later settled with government securities issued without auction process[521].

[520] Osman, A. (2000), p. 7

[521] Ibid.

Table 3.12: Domestic debt, in percentage

	1989	1990	1991	1992	1993	1994	1995	1996	1997	1998	1999	2000	2001
Gvt. Bonds (1)	4.7	4.7	3.8	3.7	3.6	0.9	2.8	4.0	7.7	7.1	21.7	21.8	22.8
Tr. Bills (2)	1.5	1.4	2.9	3.8	3.2	7.8	6.5	8.8	8.1	10.6	4.1	1.6	10.0
(1)+(2)	6.2	6.1	6.7	7.5	6.8	8.7	9.3	12.8	15.8	17.7	25.8	23.4	32.8
Debt (3)	18.2	14.4	15.4	17.6	17.9	20.6	17.3	21.0	21.4	21.7	29.3	29.0	69.2
(1)+(2)/(3)	34.4	42.5	43.3	42.9	38.5	42.4	53.8	61.1	73.9	81.9	88.1	80.8	47.4
CBRT adv. (4)	1.1	0.7	2.1	2.8	3.5	3.1	2.4	2.5	1.1	-	-	-	-
CBRT adv./ Debt (5)	6.1	5.0	13.9	16.0	19.7	15.3	14.1	11.8	5.4	-	-	-	-

Source: Turkish Central Bank, State Planning Organization

Notes to Table 3.12:

1. Ratio of Government Bonds to GNP[522];
2. Ratio of Treasury Bills to GNP[523];
3. Ratio of domestic debt stock to GNP;
4. Ratio of Turkish Central Bank's Short-term Cash Advance Facility stock to GNP;
5. Ratio of Turkish Central Bank's Short-term Cash Advance Facility stock to Treasury to Domestic Debt Stock.

To conclude, though the IMF Stabilization Program targets were perhaps achievable, foreign investors became increasingly reluctant to hold Turkish securities in the second half of 2000 leading to a liquidity crisis in November 2000. It was evident that the expected risk premium was higher than that offered by government securities, due to increasing current account deficits and rising domestic debt.

4. What other sovereign risk factors were perceived by global investors?

The items we observed on the ASSETS side of the Central Bank's Balance Sheet, in section 2.2.1.1, show additional risk factors. Regarding the Treasury's borrowing from the Central Bank, the latter was not allowed to provide "Short-term Cash Advance Facility" to the former to finance the budget deficit after

---

522 "Government bonds" are Government Debt Securities issued by the Undersecretariat of Treasury with one year or more due date (Isbank website).

523 "Treasury Bills" are Government Debt Securities issued by the Undersecretariat of Treasury with less than a year of due date (Isbank website).

1997[524]. However, this was not the only way the Treasury borrowed from the Central Bank. A portion of the government budget deficit figured as losses in the balance sheets of state-owned banks like Ziraat and Halk Banks due to subsidies to farmers, while these banks were not allowed to default. This is the item that we observed in Table 2.5 "Credits to Banking Sector" on the ASSETS side of the Central Bank's Balance Sheet, financed through "Currency Issued" on its LIABILITIES side.

On the other hand, while the government introduced a full guarantee for bank deposits in the aftermath of the 1994 crisis, to protect investors against an unexpected bank default, this also caused moral hazard as liabilities in the banking sector reached high levels in the second half of the 1990s. We observed in Table 3.4 that 22 banks were transferred to the Savings Deposit Insurance Fund (SDIF) from 1997 to 2000. The item "Credits to SDIF" on the ASSETS side of the CBRT's balance sheet in Table 2.5 was to match all losses from defaulting banks, again by creating money on the LIABILITIES side. This aspect is crucially important in judging the risk perception of investors. The weak regulatory framework in the banking sector was well-known and was a major cause of uncertainty, which further fed into the negative subjective evaluation of investors. In the case of an unexpected increase in the number of defaulting banks, it was up to the Central Bank to serve the Treasury in bailing them out. Thus, while the Central Bank's Short-term Cash Advance Facility was not allowed after 1997, there were other financial needs of the Treasury forcing the Central Bank to create high-powered money.

5. Why did the IMF Stabilization Program motivate banks to take unhedged positions?

Since banks were used to making an easy profit through interest rate carry trades[525], rapidly decreasing international interest rates created irresistible profitability gaps for many of them. Because exchange rates were predictable, banks consciously chose to increase the volume of their unhedged positions. Despite a regulation on commercial banks introduced in September 1999 limited the open foreign currency position to 20 percent of bank capital, this proportion reached 205 percent by September 2000, for which inadequate auditing was to blame[526]. Although many banks argued that they hedged their

524 Guven, A. B. (2010), p. 13

525 The most widely used currencies were the Japanese yen, the U.S. dollar, the Australian dollar and the Swiss franc (Kozlovskis, K. (2011), p. 1142).

526 Uygur, E. (2001), p. 15

positions through forward contracts, these were either realized with firms in the same holding group or constituted a small and relatively unimportant proportion of their total positions[527]. Thus, while regulations aimed to prevent unhedged positions and banks looked as though they had hedged their positions, in reality, they were exposed to risk. The effectiveness of monitoring depended on the regulatory framework, but the quality of auditing and risk management tools was not up to international standards.

6. Why did the Central Bank violate the terms of the Stabilization Program?

As a result, global investors became reluctant to hold Turkish assets and the "soft" peg regime came under attack. The Turkish Central Bank intervened in FX markets to prevent a "self-fulfilling" attack[528]. I now describe the circumstances that led to the November 2000 liquidity crisis as follows: One of the private commercial banks, Demirbank, was in an excessively high unhedged position[529]. Its paid up capital was equivalent to around USD 300 million[530]. However, the value of the Turkish government securities it possessed was an estimated USD 7.5 billion, equivalent to almost 10 percent of the total government debt[531]. It had financed this "investment" through short-term borrowing on international markets[532].

As the exchange rate began to slip and the unhedged risk of Demirbank was publicly known, its foreign creditors stopped lending, thereby putting pressure on other banks with open positions and causing panic sales of Treasury bonds, thus raising interest rates dramatically[533]. This event helps explain higher interbank interest rates and the growing standard deviation between min and max rates from August/September 2000 (Table 3.13). The initial phase of the November 2000 liquidity crisis developed due to Demirbank's failure to borrow in the overnight market on November 20th[534]. The Central Bank respected the

527 Uygur, E. (2001), p. 16

528 Ertugrul, A. and Selcuk, F. (2001), p. 22; Ozatay, F. and Sak, G. (2002), p. 23

529 Ertugrul, A. and Selcuk, F. (2001), p. 22

530 Gencay, R. and Selcuk, F. (2003), p. 2

531 Uygur, E. (2001), p. 16

532 Ertugrul, A. and Selcuk, F. (2001), p. 22

533 Gencay, R. and Selcuk, F. (2003), p. 2

534 Ozatay, F. and Sak, G. (2002), p. 22

IMF program's net domestic assets (NDA) rule, at point (D), and did not lend to Demirbank[535]. Consequently, Demirbank had to sell a proportion of its government securities causing a rise in secondary market interest rates[536]. The overall trend led to the expectation that the currency peg might not hold, which in turn triggered an outflow in short-term portfolio investment and created the conditions for a liquidity crisis on November 22nd. The Central Bank started to provide liquidity to cash-strapped private banks to remedy the situation, violating article (D) of the Stabilization Program[537]. However, this additional liquidity was quickly converted into foreign currency precipitating the collapse of the exchange rate. The Central Bank stopped providing liquidity when interbank rates on Turkish lira (TL) reached an untenable 873 percent in December[538] (Table 3.13).

On December 5th, the IMF agreed to an additional loan of USD 7.5 billion, which was also the same day that Demirbank was transferred to the SDIF[539].

---

535 Ozatay, F. and Sak, G. (2002), p. 22

536 Ibid., p. 24

537 Gencay, R. and Selcuk, F. (2003), p. 2

538 Ibid.

539 Ertugrul, A. and Selcuk, F. (2001), p. 22

Table 3.13: Interest, inflation, and exchange rates, from September 1999 to March 2001, in percentage

	Interbank rates (1)				Gvt. Sec. (2)		Inflation (3)		FX (4)	FX (5)
	Min	Max	Aver.	St. D.	Simp.	Comp.	CPI	WPI	DM	USD
1999										
Sept	57.5	71.0	67.2	4.6	85.7	113.2	64.3	52.4	57.3	41.8
Oct	65.5	69.6	69.5	1.1	83.0	109.3	64.7	52.1	45.3	49.5
Nov	68.7	70.0	69.8	0.3	73.4	96.4	64.6	52.1	34.6	91.4
Dec	69.9	70.0	70.0	0.1	-	-	68.8	53.1	55.2	61.7
2000										
Jan	18.9	64.6	35.9	10.3	37.2	38.3	68.9	54.6	11.6	39.5
Feb	26.3	83.2	49.2	14.1	39.8	42.1	69.7	56.3	12.9	30.5
Mar	26.4	68.1	39.1	9.0	38.1	39.9	67.9	57.8	16.2	33.6
Avr	18.9	45.9	36.2	6.6	33.7	34.5	63.8	58.7	-4.7	43.4
May	32.1	56.3	41.3	6.6	36.8	39.4	62.7	59.3	32.0	10.7
June	26.4	75.8	42.0	11.7	41.5	41.9	58.6	59.7	34.2	6.6
July	13.6	38.8	26.0	5.1	32.7	34.5	56.2	59.4	-5.3	33.8
Aug	22.1	92.6	35.6	16.9	32.8	33.2	53.2	58.8	-6.7	33.9
Sept	23.7	79.7	46.2	14.1	36.0	33.6	49.0	57.5	5.8	22.8
Oct	25.8	71.2	38.4	9.7	37.5	38.0	44.4	56.0	-18.2	30.3
Nov	27.9	315.9	79.5	67.6	39.0	41.0	43.8	54.3	28.1	-1.0
Dec	61.8	873.1	199.0	239.0	-	-	39.0	51.4	55.5	-18.0
2001										
Jan	31.1	76.8	42.2	12.5	57.7	64.9	35.9	48.0	11.2	8.3
Feb	36.6	4'018.6	436.0	983.8	76.2	110.3	33.4	44.5	396.4	433.0
Mar	80.0	96.6	81.9	4.1	125.0	193.7	37.5	42.1	147.2	130.0

Sources:

1. Interbank rates, data from Turkish Central Bank;
2. Simple and compound average interest rates from government securities. Own calculations from Treasury auctions, data from Turkish Central Bank;
3. Consumer Price Index and Wholesale Production Index percentage change (1994=100 base year) over the same month of the previous year, data from State Planning Organization;
4. DM rate change is based on the annualized end-month bid-ask mid-value change of DM/TL FX rate, data from Turkish Central Bank. A (-) sign means appreciation of TL against DM. We note that from 1st January to 31st December 2000 the TL depreciated against DM by 14.1 percent, instead of 20 percent allowed by the 1999 Stabilization Program;
5. USD rate change is based on the annualized end-month bid-ask mid-value change of USD/TL FX rate, data from Turkish Central Bank. A (-) sign means appreciation of TL against USD. We note that from 1st January to 31st December 2000 the TL depreciated against DM by 24.4 percent, instead of 20 percent allowed by the 1999 Stabilization

Program, and then the "intermediate" exchange rate regime collapsed in February 2001.

7. How was the February 2001 currency crisis triggered?

But the crisis was not yet over: It was followed in February 2001 by another one. We observed that during the November 2000 liquidity crisis, the Turkish Central Bank intervened, expanding Net Domestic Assets and violating the Stabilization Program. However, the authorities maintained the pegged exchange rate regime thanks to assistance from the IMF[540]. Moreover, this helped a capital inflow in particular in January 2001 and the Central Bank reserves returned to pre-liquidity crisis levels[541]. Nevertheless, the overall economic circumstances continued to be fragile and markets were not convinced about the capability of the Treasury to roll-over domestic debt[542]. The banking system was fragile and structural reforms were needed to deal with the chronic public deficit, to convince markets of the sustainability of domestic debt and by extension of the crawling peg exchange rate regime.

On the other hand, we observe a major critique to the theoretical basis of the 1999 IMF Stabilization Program from Stanley Fisher, the then Deputy Director of the IMF (2001) who based his criticism on the experiences of the November 2000 liquidity shock in Turkey and of the 2001 crisis in Argentina[543]. In line with Lawrence Summers's "bipolar" view mentioned in section 3.1.4, he considered "intermediate" regimes (such as Turkey's under the 1999 IMF Stabilization Program) as crisis-prone and argued that they are not viable over long periods[544]. Thus, while suggesting either full flexibility or full dollarization, he expressed doubts regarding the sustainability of the crawling peg in Turkey[545]. His paper "Exchange Rate Regimes: Is the Bipolar View Correct" was published one month before the Turkish February 2001 currency crisis, where he stated[546]:

---

540 Gençay, R. and Selçuk, F. (2003), p. 3

541 Ibid.

542 Ibid.

543 Voyvoda, E. and Yeldan, E. (2005), p. 2

544 Fisher, S. (2001), pp. 8, 9

545 Voyvoda, E. and Yeldan, E. (2005), p. 3

546 Fisher (2001), p. 3

> "For countries open to international capital flows soft pegs are not sustainable, but a wide variety of flexible exchange rate arrangements remains possible and it is to be expected that policy in most countries will not be indifferent to exchange rate movements."

He further advanced as follows[547]:

> "The need to move away from a soft peg is one of the reasons an exit mechanism was built into the Turkish stabilization and reform program that began in December 1999. The intention is that a band around the crawling peg will begin broadening in the middle of 2001 and continue broadening through the end of 2002, until the exchange rate regime approaches more a managed float than a peg. The difficulties that Turkey experienced in 2000 relate to more banking sector problems and the failure to undertake corrective fiscal actions when the current account widened, than to the design of the exchange rate arrangement and corrective measures in both these regards have been agreed and are being implemented."

In fact, the sixth point (F) of the 1999 IMF Stabilization Program introduced a gradual widening of the exchange rate band in the second half of 2001 and thus aimed at a higher flexibility in exchange rate movements. Unfortunately, this phase of the program was never achieved because the whole system collapsed well before. Why? What were the problems the Turkish financial markets had to face in spite of the Stabilization Program's positive impact on macro variables? In fact, we observe in Table 3.13 above that, interbank rates were reduced in January 2001 after the turbulence of December 2000, inflation followed a decreasing trend, while exchange rates were under control. In spite of difficulties, the Stabilization Program seemed to be providing the expected results. What was the problem that triggered the currency crash in February 2001?

---

547 Fisher (2001), p. 20

Significantly, there was an inconsistency between the interest and exchange rate changes[548]. We observe in Table 3.13 that during the year 2000, interest rates on government securities mirrored more or less the rate of depreciation of the TL until November 2000. However, the default of a major market maker of government securities, Demirbank, called into question the debt roll-over capability of the Treasury[549]. In the first auction of February 2001, interest rates reached 70 percent while the upper limit of the annual rate of TL depreciation against a basket of USD and Euro was announced to be 12 percent in 2001[550]. Thus, the level of interest rates was inconsistent with the pre-announced rate of TL depreciation[551]. As market confidence was lost because of defaulting banks, the sustainability of the peg was questioned as well. I discussed in section 2.1, the relationship between the public sector deficit and foreign liabilities of the banking sector in presence of bailout guarantees in the case of Thailand. I emphasized that implicit government guarantees encouraging excessive risk-taking created moral hazard, which became a major cause triggering the 1997 East Asian currency crises because forward-looking investors carefully estimated future government expenditures. It was straightforward to observe that in the absence of structural reforms, more banks would default and increase the fiscal deficit. Turkish case presented a similar fragility, thus, the rest of the story is simple: Any negative event or news under these circumstances could have triggered a "self-fulfilling" attack.

A domestic debt auction of the Treasury was to be held on 20th February 2001 aiming to borrow more or less USD 5 billion (approximately 10 percent of the total domestic debt) in order to roll-over the USD 7 billion domestic debt maturing the day after[552]. However, a political dispute arose on February 19th, during a routine but key meeting of top political and military leaders[553], between Prime Minister Bulent Ecevit and President Ahmet Necdet Sezer over how to fight public sector corruption[554]. The Prime Minister declared to the media that this was a "serious political crisis"[555]. Though the dispute was not in

548 Ozatay, F. and Sak, G. (2002), p. 25

549 Ibid.

550 Ibid.

551 Ibid.

552 Gençay, R. and Selçuk, F., p. 3

553 The so-called "National Security Council" meeting

554 Feridun, M. (2004), p. 41

555 Gençay, R. and Selçuk, F., p. 3

any way related to economic policy, global investors believed that structural reforms would not be achieved and, in such a fragile economic situation, the intermediate exchange rate regime would not hold. This was sufficient to trigger a "self-fulfilling" speculative attack on the exchange rate.

Though the Central Bank defended the currency, interbank interest rates reached a peak of 4'018 percent within three days (Table 3.13). Thus, it had to float in an attempt to avoid losing reserves[556]. Credibility was lost and it was estimated that the cost of maintaining the peg was higher than its potential benefit. A few days later, another local bank, Ulusalbank, controlled by the same group that owned the Demirbank, was declared bankrupt[557].

7. Examining the 1999 Turkey-IMF Stabilization Program in the light of the Mundell-Fleming (M-F) model

Let me start this section with a quote from John Williamson, who, in explaining the "competitive exchange rate" argument of the "Washington Consensus" principles, stated as follows[558]:

> "I suspect that by 1989 a majority of economists, in Washington and elsewhere, were already in favor of either firmly fixed or freely floating exchange rates and hostile to the sort of intermediate regime that in my judgment gives the best promise of maintaining a competitive exchange rate in the medium-term. My own preference remains an intermediate regime of limited flexibility."

In line with the view above, the 1999 Turkey-IMF Stabilization Program introduced at point (B) a crawling peg (intermediate) regime, while the economy was completely open to international capital movements. I question whether the Central Bank's policy can be effective within this framework. The view of Lawrence Summers (2000), who argued in favor of a "bipolar" view, that

556 Bredenkamp, H., Joseffson, M. and Lindgren, C. J. (2007), p. 1

557 Gençay, R. and Selçuk, F., p. 4

558 Section 2.1, the 5th "Washington Consensus" principle

I introduced in section 3.1.4, can provide a good starting point for this discussion[559]:

> "The choice of appropriate exchange rate regime, which, for economies with access to international capital markets, increasingly means a move away from the middle ground of pegged but adjustable fixed exchange rates toward the two corner regimes of either flexible exchange rates or a fixed exchange rate."

I examined the 1994 financial crisis and argued that due to the managed floating regime in combination with free capital movements, the Turkish Central Bank was "independent" in terms of the Mundell-Fleming framework[560]. However, the 1999 IMF Stabilization Program changed this. The CBRT was committed to defending a particular range of FX values for the TL under the crawling peg system. Stanley Fisher (2002) argued that prior to the crises of Mexico (1994), Brazil (1999), Argentina (2000) and Turkey (2001), each of these economies introduced a peg, which was initially part of a policy package to reduce inflation. He commented as follows[561]:

> "These crises reinforced the conclusion that the impossible trinity makes a softly pegged exchange rate non-viable when the capital account is open.
>
> [....]
>
> A country may succeed for some time in living with the impossible trinity particularly if the exchange rate is undervalued. But when the capital account is open, a pegged exchange rate is crisis-prone, vulnerable to a speculative attack,

---

559 Summers, L. H. (2000), p. 8

560 though this was not a politically independent monetary policy as the Turkish Central Bank had to create high- powered money to meet the needs of the Treasury (see Fig. 2.5).

561 Fisher, S. (2002), p. 3

> possibly producing a second generation crisis, in which the measures necessary to defend the peg are not politically viable."

But which factors in this scheme increase the likelihood of a crisis? To answer this question let us suppose that the central bank attempts to achieve a monetary policy in favor of domestic goals through sterilized intervention (i.e., to adjust the real supply of money to real changes in demand)[562]. Eventual mistakes in targeting the real supply of money can provide opportunities for arbitrage in foreign currency markets, which creates conditions for a currency crisis[563]. For this reason, the fifth point (E) of the 1999 Stabilization Program forbade sterilization in order to remove the likelihood of such a "mistake". This aspect, though aiming to prevent an eventual Mundell-Fleming inconsistency, also means that the Central Bank must "wait and see" without being able to take any initiative.

The 1999 Stabilization Program envisaged an "ineffective" Central Bank for a certain period of time while gradually removing the exchange rate band. In fact, the sixth point (F) meant that the peg introduced in the first 18 months was to be gradually widened in the second 18 months: the exchange rate band that we observe in Fig. 3.15 was to continue from January 2000 to June 2001, whereas from July 2001 to December 2002 the band was to widen every 6 months by 7.5 percent. Thus, the Stabilization Program envisaged an "exit" strategy from the soft peg during the second 18 months of the Program, allowing more space for an independent monetary policy on the part of the Central Bank. Unfortunately, the program did not survive the first 18 months due to the crisis that was triggered during the 14th month.

According to Stanley Fisher's (2002) comments after the February 2001 currency crisis[564], stabilization programs through an exchange rate anchor had been successful in lowering the high inflation rate. He continued[565]:

> "But doing so, without an exit mechanism is very risky. And it is risky even if an exit strategy is specified as the case of Turkey in

---

562 Saxton, J. (2002), p. 10

563 Ibid.

564 To note that the quote of Stanley Fisher in the previous section was prior to the February 2001 crisis.

565 Fisher, S. (2002), p. 7

> 2000-2001 shows. So, I conclude that while an exchange rate peg could be used in future to help disinflate, the commitment would have to be quite short-lived if it were not to result in a pegged exchange rate type crisis."

To conclude, while the 1999 IMF Stabilization Program contained a gradual "exit" strategy from the soft peg towards a more managed float, in points "C" and "F", to be realized from mid-2001 to end-2002, markets did not wait and forced the Central Bank to float well before.

The way the capital outflow occurred is important for this study. In fact, a more serious political crisis occurred in April 2007 at the end of President Ahmet Necdet Sezer's mandate[566]. The candidacy of pro-Islamist Abdullah Gul aroused severe reactions both from secularists and the military high command. This led to a political shock on 27th April 2007 that was considerably more severe than the 19th February 2001 political crisis[567]. What was the reaction of markets? Although the stock market and the domestic currency lost value the day after, they stabilized rapidly[568]. It did not lead to an economic shock at all! Why? The major reason is that market confidence was not lost[569].

But how did the policy makers achieve this? We will explore in Chapter 4 the response to this question. For the moment, I examine in the next section, which currency crisis model can explain the 2001 currency crisis.

7. Explanation of 2001 currency crisis through the optic of Generation Models – The First Generation currency crisis framework

I begin with the First Generation models (FGMs) and ask whether the dynamics behind the 2001 crisis fit this framework. Krugman (1979) and Flood and Garber (1984) showed that weak fundamentals cause currency crises, i.e., a chronic budget deficit financed by continuous money creation and central bank intervention through the sale of reserves to avoid devaluation. These models

---

566 Bredenkamp, H., Joseffson, M. and Lindgren, C. J. (2007), p. 1

567 Ibid.

568 Ibid.

569 Ibid.

put emphasis on the continuous deterioration of macro fundamentals forcing the central bank to gradually decrease the level of international reserves[570].

Let us see whether this was the case for Turkey during the pre-crisis period. Table 3.8 shows that budget deficits reached excessively high levels from 1998 to 2001 and interest payments absorbed respectively 61 percent and 80 percent of consolidated budget revenues in 2000 and 2001. This was an excessively high number and the situation was unsustainable. However, we observed in Fig. 2.5 and Table 3.12 that Turkish Central Bank did not provide Short-term Cash Advance Facility to the Treasury after 1997[571], thus, the budget deficit, though excessively high, was not money-financed, but rather financed by borrowing from the market. Base money was created through capital inflows. Nevertheless, we observe in Figure 3.16 that the depletion of international reserves in the period prior to the crisis was not gradual, but sudden. Therefore, the hypothesis behind the First Generation models (money-financed budget deficits and gradually declining reserves) was not realized[572].

Fig. 3.16: Turkish Central Bank gross FX reserves, from January 1998 to July 2001, in million USD

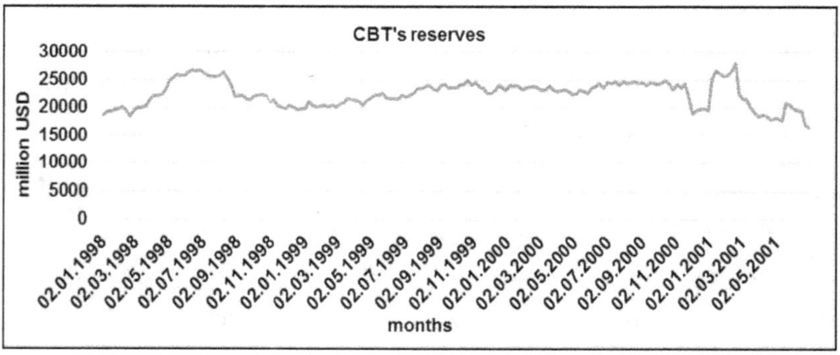

Source: Central Bank of the Republic of Turkey, official website, weekly data

On the other hand, the inflation rate was reduced from 1998 to 2001 and the average depreciation rate was lower than the average CPI change for the year 2000 (Table 3.8), thanks to the IMF Stabilization Program. Moreover, the maturity structure of government securities increased during the two years

570 Ozatay, F. and Sak, G. (2002), p. 5

571 Guven, A. B. (2010), p. 13

572 Ozatay, F. and Sak, G. (2002), p. 6

preceding the crisis (Fig. 3.17). Thus, it is not possible to state that all macroeconomic fundamentals were deteriorating. Average inflation and interest rates were lower in early 2001, before the February 2001 crisis, compared to their level in late 1999 (Table 3.13).

Fig. 3.17: Maturity structure of Government Securities, in days

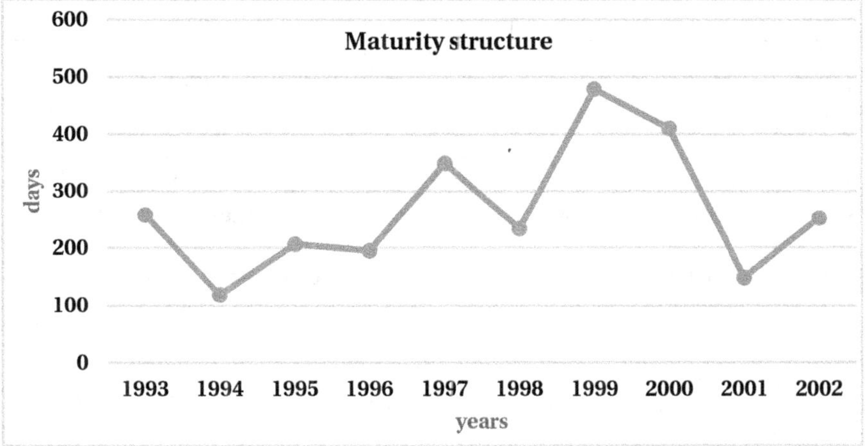

Source: State Planning Organization

To summarize, while some macro fundamentals improved thanks to the 1999 IMF Stabilization Program, the crisis occurred in early 2001 and not in late 1999. Why? To note that the First Generation models are not sufficient to explain the February 2001 Turkish currency crisis[573].

I investigate now whether there were other factors such as market expectations feeding a "self-fulfilling" crisis. For example, the appreciating currency in Table 3.14 and worsening current account balance deserve further investigation. What about of a relationship between the banking sector's high-risk exposure and its possible impact on the developing currency crisis? Can this last aspect have triggered a "self-fulfilling" attack?

---

[573] Ozatay, F. and Sak, G. (2002), p. 9

Table 3.14: Budget and current account balance, real exchange rates, from 1993 to 2002

	Budget (1)	Pr. Budget (2)	Int. rep. (3)	Real FX (4)	Exp./Imp. (5)	CA bal. (6)
1993	-6.7	-0.9	33.1	133.8	52.1	-3.60
1994	-3.9	3.8	40.0	101.3	77.8	1.99
1995	-4.0	3.3	41.3	110.0	60.6	-1.38
1996	-8.3	1.7	55.4	114.0	53.2	-1.33
1997	-7.6	0.1	39.6	121.6	54.1	-1.37
1998	-7.3	4.3	52.8	132.9	58.7	0.96
1999	-12.0	2.0	57.0	140.3	65.4	-0.73
2000	-11.0	5.0	61.0	152.0	51.0	-4.91
2001	-16.9	6.4	80.0	123.1	75.7	2.33
2002	-15.2	3.7	68.7	137.7	69.9	-0.99

Source: State Planning Organization, Turkish Statistical Institute

1. Consolidated budget balance/GNP ratio, in percentage, data from State Planning Organization;
2. Primary budget balance/GNP ratio, in percentage, data from State Planning Organization;
3. Interest repayments/consolidated budget revenues, in percentage, data from State Planning Organization;
4. Real FX rate, January 1987=100; the weights in the currency basket are 0.75 for USD and 0.25 for Euro. In the relative price calculations is used producer prices for the U.S.A and the Euro area and wholesale prices for Turkey, data from State Planning Organization;
5. Export/Import ratio, in percentage, data from Turkish Statistical Institute (2009), p. 478;
6. Current account balance/GNP ratio, in percentage, data from Turkish Statistical Institute (2009), p. 514.

The Second Generation currency crisis framework

I examine now whether the SGM framework is more helpful to understand the dynamics behind the Turkish experience in certain respects. To observe that these models do not associate a crisis event only with weak fundamentals as is the case for Krugman (1979)'s First Generation models, but instead introduce the concept of "expectations" of global investors. As we saw in section 3.2.3, Guillermo Calvo and Carlos Vegh (1998)[574] examined a sample of emerging markets (Argentina, Brazil, Chile, Mexico and Uruguay), where exchange rate

[574] Calvo, G. and Vegh, C. (1999), p. 11

based stabilization programs were introduced. The following quote can shed light on my analysis[575]:

> "Most exchange rate based stabilization programs end in balance-of-payment crises. These programs typically unleash dynamics –consumption booms, sustained real appreciation, current account deficits– which call into question their sustainability. This, in turn, fuels speculation of a possible abandonment of the exchange rate anchor. Once the survival of the program has been called into question, financial factors – such as a large stock of short-term debt– often aggravate the situation and may induce self-fulfilling crises."

In line with this quote, I now investigate factors that could have an impact on market participants' "expectations", namely the "sustainability" of the current account deficit and the public debt:

1. Current account deficit: Guillermo Calvo and Carlos Vegh (1998) identified a common pattern in their sample of emerging markets mentioned above. These countries were all implementing exchange rate based stabilization programs. In each case, a slow convergence of the rate of inflation to the devaluation rate led to the appreciation of the domestic currency and a deteriorating trade and current account balance. We observed the same tendency in Turkey during the 1999 IMF Stabilization Program. Fig. 3.15 and Table 3.13 show that the inflation rate fell more slowly than the currency. The result was an appreciating currency in real terms, a decreasing export/import ratio and a worsening current account deficit (Table 3.14);

2. Public debt: Table 3.15 shows increasing debt after complete capital account liberalization in 1989. To note that consolidated budget deficits constituted an important part of the public sector debt since the early 1980s[576]. While more than half of the domestic debt was financed through sale of government securities in the second half of the 1990s (Table 3.15), instead of domestic credit expansion, we observe in Table 3.14 that a

---

575 Calvo, G. and Vegh, C. (1999), p. 11

576 Consolidated public sector debt includes also the accumulated debts of SOEs, special funds and municipalities (Ozatay, F. and Sak, G. (2002), p. 36).

significant amount of budget revenues in the three years previous to the 2001 currency crisis was devoted to serving the debt. One result was growing investor suspicion that authorities would not honor their commitments. This translated into increasing interest rates on government securities due to higher sovereign default risk perception by investors. Sustainability of the public debt was increasingly questioned[577].

Table 3.15: Debt profile of Turkey, from 1989 to 2002, in percentage

	1989	1990	1991	1992	1993	1994	1995	1996	1997	1998	1999	2000	2001	2002
D.debt (1)	13.7	10.8	11.5	13.2	13.4	15.4	13.0	15.9	16.2	16.5	21.9	21.9	50.9	42.8
E.debt (2)	30.8	26.1	26.7	27.8	29.6	38.8	33.6	32.6	33.2	35.6	41.7	44.7	57.7	56.2
(1)+(2)	44,5	36.9	38.2	41.0	43.0	54.2	46.6	48.5	49.4	52.1	63.6	66.6	108.6	99.0
Gov. sec/D. debt(3)	34.4	42.5	43.3	42.9	38.5	42.4	53.8	61.1	73.9	81.9	88.1	80.8	47.4	-
Gov. sec. banks (4)	90.2	85.9	92.8	79.1	77.8	71.5	81.6	84.4	89.5	86.8	85.3	75.9	74.5	-

Source: Turkish Treasury - Debt Statistics and State Planning Organization

1. Ratio of domestic debt stock to GDP, data from Turkish Treasury;
2. Ratio of gross external debt stock to GDP, includes debt of public and private sector and that of the Central Bank, data from Turkish Treasury;
3. Ratio of government securities (government bonds + treasury bills) to domestic debt stock, data from State Planning Organization;
4. Proportion of government securities held by banks, data from State Planning Organization.

While the sustainability of current account deficits and public debt is an issue necessitating further research, the important aspect to emphasize for this study is that markets were judging the sustainability of public deficits, eventually triggering a "self-fulfilling" attack on the currency, a major feature of Second Generation models.

To conclude, the Second Generation models present elements useful in exploring factors behind the 2001 currency crisis, in particular emphasizing the

---

577 (Ozatay, F. and Sak, G. (2002), p. 19

impact of expectations of investors, making thus evident the "self-fulfilling" feature of the crash. To note that while the CBRT preferred to keep the currency peg during the November 2000 liquidity crisis, it preferred to float during the February 2001 crisis, because the cost of keeping the peg was considered higher than floating[578]. Thus, in addition to the credibility problem of the public debt, the credibility of Central Bank's commitment to the currency peg was also in play.

Nevertheless, further investigation will be necessary as a weak institutional framework in banking sector also had a significant impact in triggering the "self-fulfilling" attack[579]. Thus, it will be useful to examine whether the Third Generation models can contribute to our understanding[580].

The Third Generation currency crisis framework

Let us now see whether Third Generation models can explain the 2001 currency crisis. These are an extension of the Second Generation models because they are also based on expectations of markets and on the same "self-fulfilling" mood of investors. Some of their additional features provide insight on the Turkish case, namely the relationship between the banking sector and currency crises and "herd behavior" of investors. Regarding the former aspect, we have already seen that banks were involved in purchasing a high proportion of government debt. Moreover, during the 1990s they lost their essential function of intermediation between the financial and the real sector and continued to prefer easy profits from interest rate carry trades. This is also one of the reasons why the 2000 IMF Stabilization Program had such a pronounced negative impact on banks' profitability. In fact, rapidly decreasing domestic interest rates increased pressure on many banks, triggering the liquidity crisis of November 2000. The Demirbank case discussed above was an important example in this regard. However, a broader question persisted in the minds of global investors: How many banks would default? This question inevitably involved speculation on the future government deficits due to the 100 percent bailout guarantee for failing banks introduced in 1994 in the aftermath of the previous crisis. Thus, one crisis leads to another when the root causes of problems are not addressed, i.e., the achievement of needed institutional reforms. In addition to increased moral hazard, it became vital to estimate the

---

[578] Kansu, A. (2006), p. 203

[579] Ozatay, F. and Sak, G. (2002), p. 10

[580] Kansu, A. (2006), p. 203

size of the losses, which would negatively impact the budget deficit and increase the public sector borrowing requirement. The default of Demirbank in November 2000 confirmed that possessing USD 7.5 billion in unhedged positions and subsequent default resulted in an IMF loan of the same amount.

The relationship between the banking sector's foreign liabilities and future extra public sector deficits due to government bailout guarantees, convinced global investors that they could expect the following[581]: Future defaults would be financed by the government increasing thus public debt. This, in turn, would lead to a sovereign debt crisis, triggering a move out of Turkish assets and forcing the authorities to abandon the flexible pegged exchange regime, as in the case of the 1997 East Asian currency crisis. It is possible to argue that, despite the difficulty to conclusively prove the hypothesis, "prospective deficits" reinforce the idea that pegged FX rate regimes will not hold[582]. While undergoing turbulent macro conditions and amid a fragile banking system, the political dispute previously mentioned acted as a "sunspot" variable (disconnected from fundamentals[583]) and focussed anticipations, culminating in a sudden loss of confidence[584]. A massive wave of Turkish assets was dumped on the market, just as the Third Generation models predicted. The Turkish 2001 crisis was simultaneously a currency, banking, and an anticipated government debt crisis.

Conclusion: Although the First Generation models cannot help in explaining the 2001 financial crisis, the Second and Third Generation models provide insights on the dynamics behind it[585].

7. Market-determined interest rates-sovereign default risk-functioning market economy

The point (E) of the 1999 IMF Stabilization program maintained that interest rates should be market determined in order to achieve appropriate conditions for a "functioning" market economy. However, market-determined interest rates, though necessary, cannot provide the expected results in the presence of a weak institutional framework, in particular in the banking sector combined

---

581 Ozatay, F. and Sak, G. (2002), p. 19

582 Burnside, C., Eichenbaum, M. and Rebelo, S. (2001), p. 1158

583 Arias, G. (2003), p. 6

584 Wälti, S. (2003), p. 11

585 Kansu, A. (2006), p. 206

with fundamental macroeconomic disequilibrium in the shape of chronic public sector deficits, which increase the perception of the risk of sovereign default. Under these circumstances, the risk premium on interest rates had to be sufficient to cover this added risk. However, this just increased the budget deficit and increased the likelihood of sovereign default, precipitating capital flight, and a liquidity crisis.

8. Failure in achieving structural reforms?

In Section 3.3.2.3 we saw that "structural reforms" were introduced through the 1999 IMF Stabilization Program, in addition to changes in "monetary and exchange rate policy". Were the reforms in the banking sector achieved? What about Central Bank independence? The following quote from the "letter of intent" in the aftermath of the November 2000 liquidity crisis covers these aspects[586]:

> "The increased flexibility in managing monetary policy that will gradually become available as of the second half of 2001 will be used by the Turkish Central Bank with the primary goal of sustaining disinflation. We will thus start a gradual shift from a monetary policy centered on the exchange rate to one centered on formal inflation targeting, which has been successfully adopted by several other countries. As a necessary step to support this shift, a new central bank law will be enacted by end-April 2001 (a condition for the completion of the eighth review) with the goal of designating price stability as the primary monetary policy objective of the Turkish Central Bank, enhancing its operational independence in the pursuit of that objective, increasing its degree of accountability for monetary policy decisions and enhancing the transparency of monetary policy formulation. All this will also be necessary to make the central bank legislation consistent with the Maastricht Treaty, with a view to Turkey's prospective participation in the EU."

---

586 IMF (2000) website, "Letter of Intent" dated 18th December 2000, Section 30

The same letter of intent (of 18th December 2000) emphasized the fact that the Banking Regulation and Supervision Agency (BRSA) had become fully operational by late August 2000, that banking supervision departments at the Treasury and the Central Bank had been closed and that the Saving Deposit Insurance Fund had become an independent legal entity administrated by the BRSA[587].

While this was a significant effort, a comprehensive reform of the banking sector had not yet been achieved, as the currency crisis triggered two months later would show. Nevertheless, we can state that, despite the huge cost of the collapse, the February 2001 currency crisis accelerated the structural reform process, as we will observe in Chapter 4.

9. Post-February 2001 currency crisis period: expansionary policies or "Washington Consensus" again?

Regarding the results of Second Generation models, Krugman (2001) argued as follows[588]:

> "If a speculative attack drives a currency off its peg, this does not imply a negative shock to employment and output. Indeed, in this case, the contrary should be true: because the policy constraint of a peg is removed, the result is actually positive for short-run economics."

However, on the contrary, output decreased in Turkey by 5.7 percent in 2001[589]. Similarly, Flood and Marion (2000) noted that Second Generation models predict expansionary policies in the post-speculative attack period, in line with investors' expectations[590]. However, in Turkey after the 2001 currency crisis, monetary policy was not expansionary[591]. In the "Letter of Intent"

---

587 IMF (2000) website, "Letter of Intent" dated 18th December 2000, sections from 47 to 60

588 Krugman (2001), pp. 6, 7

589 Constant GDP by Expenditure approach, in line with the ESA-95 definition, at 1998 prices (Turkish Statistical Institute (2009), p.762).

590 Flood, R. and Marion, N. (2000), p. 246

591 Ozatay, F. Sak, G. (2002), p. 11

addressed to the IMF in May 2001, the government[592] emphasized that priority was to be given to fiscal discipline[593], thus it continued to follow the "Washington Consensus" principles. However, this time government put emphasis on structural regulatory and institutional reforms, in line also with EU requirements.

Now, I focus on the post-crisis period in an attempt to explain the logic behind the new policy.

Conclusion

This chapter aimed, among others, to investigate the 2nd research question of the study:

> "What is the role of institutions, culture, and tradition? What is the appropriate regulatory framework for an emerging market economy like Turkey?"

I discussed the theoretical underpinnings behind the cyclical behavior of worldwide capital flows in sections 3.1 and 3.2 and examined the factors behind the 1994 and 2001 crises in Turkey, in sections 3.3.1, 3.3.2.2 and 3.3.2.3. I argued that, in line with the Minskian perspective, a weak institutional framework was a major factor generating uncertainty, and overestimated expected returns in the boom phase were replaced by "herd behaviour" or "bandwagon effect" in the bust phase, leading to market madness or, in term of Keynes, to "animal spirits". The need for effective regulations was evident[594].

I analyzed the exchange rate regimes prior to the crises (i.e., a floating regime in the period preceding the 1994 crisis and an "intermediate" one in the period preceding the 2001 crisis). I discussed whether the Turkish monetary policy was compatible with other policy options using the Mundell-Fleming framework. Although "intermediate" regimes seem more crisis-prone, it is worth to note the following aspects:

---

592 The 57th Bulent Ecevit coalition government lasted from 28th May 1999 to 18th November 2002 (Annex 3).

593 IMF (2001) website, "Letter of Intent" dated 3rd May 2001.

594 Sinapi, C. (2011), p. 7

1. While the choice of exchange rate regime should allow the Central Bank to conduct an effective monetary policy, the Central Bank's monetary policies should, in turn, be coherent with whichever exchange rate regime is chosen;

2. I discussed, at the end of section 3.3.1, the "de jure" IMF exchange rate classification, which distinguished broadly between three main categories: Hard peg regimes, "intermediate" regimes and floating rate regimes. Though this classification offers the possibility to analyze the different degrees of monetary autonomy afforded by each regime, it fails to capture the differences between the foreign exchange rate regimes officially adopted and what the authorities were actually doing in practice[595]. For example, while countries can announce pegged exchange rate regimes and make frequent devaluations, they can also claim to have a floating regime but manage their exchange rates along a predetermined path, in an attempt to avoid the political costs of visible devaluations if the peg were officially established[596]. The consequent divergence between "de jure" and "de facto" regimes adds to the confusion.

To note that the frequency of intervention was much higher than that reported by G7 countries in the 1990s and early 2000[597]. For instance, the Turkish Central Bank intervened in foreign exchange markets in 68 percent of business days, from 1st November 1993 to 31st December 2003, whereas in Japan, monetary authorities intervened in only 7 percent of business days from April 1991 to December 2002[598].

Nevertheless, my discussion here goes beyond the choice of exchange rate regime. In other words, while I discussed the Turkish Central Bank's autonomy under the exchange rate regime chosen, my aim is not to investigate what the "de facto" regime due to Central Bank interventions was, but to show the following: Regardless of the exchange rate regime that was chosen, without an EU-inspired institutional framework, a capital flight-led crisis was unavoidable in the post-1989 full capital account liberalization period. I called this the 11th element of the "Washington Consensus" framework, without which the original 10 prescriptions, though essential, were not sufficient to produce the expected

---

[595] Bubula, A. and Otker-Robe, I. (2002), p. 5

[596] Ibid., p. 6

[597] Herrera, A. M. and Ozbay, P. (2005), p. 2

[598] The data set used contains daily Turkish Lira/USD spot exchange rate, the interbank overnight interest rate for Turkey, the daily values of CBRT foreign exchange purchases and sales and the US Federal funds rate (Herrera, A. M. and Ozbay, P. (2005), pp. 2-4).

results, leading to volatile growth cycles and crises. Thus, if a sound regulatory framework had been introduced from the beginning of the deregulation process, a stable growth and a functioning market could have perhaps been achieved. In other words, this chapter allowed us to make more evident an answer to the 2nd research question: The implementation of the "Washington Consensus" principles could not produce the expected economic performance as long as an "appropriate" institutional and regulatory framework is not put in place.

Nonetheless, it is never too late. I will examine, in Chapter 4, the completion of reforms in particular on central bank independence and creation of independent supervisory institutions. This context shows also that I associate the term "appropriate" with a de-politicized institutional framework which can potentially change traditional expectations of economic agents. In fact, the statist approach in economic management made part of the Turkish culture until 1980, which led economic agents to expect a state intervention in case of difficulties. The 1994 and 2001 financial crashes I examined in this chapter showed that despite political efforts in introducing reforms in central banking during the 1980s, this crucially important institution produced a poor performance in economic policy making. While in August 1993 the government intervened in defiance of market forces and of CBRT regulations, increasing the fragility of the economy and thus preparing conditions for the February 1994 crisis, the CBRT was again ineffective in the eve of the 2001 crisis. On the other hand, the inter-country risk aversion of economic agents is another important aspect as it seems that Turkish agents traditionally had been more risk inclined when compared with advanced economies in the EU. In fact, not only the central bank behavior depended on political decisions but also there was not a derivatives market during the 1980s and the 1990s allowing economic agents to hedge their risk exposure. We will observe in Chapter 4 how the Turkish Central Bank gained its independent status in 2001 and a derivatives market became operational in 2006. This will make clear the meaning of "appropriate" institutional and regulatory framework that I first discussed in Chapter 1 (Section 1.6).

Then, Chapter 5 will examine the impact of these reforms on economic performance.

Chapter 4

Institutional Transformation

Introduction

I will investigate, in this chapter, the 3rd research question of the study:

> "What is the role of monetary stability and the attitude of the central bank? How do central bank policies affect the vulnerability of an economy? Is its independence important?"

In chapters 2 and 3, I examined attempts by Turkish policy makers to adopt the "Washington Consensus" rules with the assistance of the IMF. We observed that after the 1994 financial crisis, recovery began in 1995 and the Customs Union agreement became an important next step in adopting an EU-inspired regulatory framework. Nevertheless, a variety of exogenous and endogenous factors negatively affected the economy, namely decreasing global liquidity due to the East Asian and Russian crises in 1997-1998, the earthquakes that struck Turkey in 1999 and several bank failures in the late 1990s that only worsened the already unstable macro trend and led the Turkish economy to the most severe currency crisis of its history in February 2001.

I begin this chapter with a quote from Hernando de Soto which is important for my analysis[599]:

> "Deregulation involves de-politicizing the economy in order to protect the state from the manipulation of redistributive combines and the economy from politicians, just as the church was separated from the state."

In the light of this quote, I will examine in Chapter 4 the EU-inspired regulatory framework from 1999 to 2002. A major feature of this period is that

---

599 De Soto, H. (1989), p. 249

the structural reforms initiated by coalition governments of the 1990s were successfully completed. I will thus examine both the Turkish Central Bank independence and the creation of EU-inspired independent supervisory institutions in different sectors from banking to agriculture and state aid and observe their impact on overall macro stability. I will also focus on privatizations and FDI flows which grew after 2004 and I will overview the situation of property rights as political efforts in encouraging mortgages by 2007 is an important reform that can influence also the financial markets in the near future. Thus, while the section 4.1 will focus on a de-politicized institutional framework, section 4.2 will examine political efforts to adopt the EU-inspired standards on privatizations, FDI and property rights over time.

4.1. Adapting EU requirements to Turkish conditions: a de-politicized regulatory framework in economic management

I will focus, in this section, on adoption of the EU-inspired regulations in reforming the Turkish Central Bank and the creation of independent supervisory institutions. Section 4.1.1 starts with a review of EU requirements on monetary policy. Then, section 4.1.2 introduces a theoretical discussion aiming to define central bank independence. Section 4.1.3 examines how the Turkish Central Bank gained its independence and section 4.1.4 focuses on the creation of independent regulatory agencies.

4.1.1. Central Bank Independence and Inflation Targeting Monetary Policy as an EU Requirement

Chapter 17th of the *Acquis Communautaire* is on Economic and Monetary Policy and it contains specific rules requiring the independence of central banks in Member States, prohibiting direct financing of the public sector by the central banks and prohibiting privileged access of the public sector to financial institutions[600]. It further states that new Member States are also committed to

---

[600] EU Commission, Chapters of the Acquis, official website

complying with the criteria laid down in the Treaty in order to be able to adopt the Euro in due course after accession[601].

Regarding the price stability objective, achievable through an "independent" central bank, the Treaty on the Functioning of the EU states, among others, as follows[602]:

> "Art. 119: 1) For the purposes set out in Article 3 of the Treaty on European Union[603], the activities of the Member States and the Union shall include, as provided in the Treaties[604], the adoption of an economic policy which is based on the close coordination of Member States' economic policies, on the internal market and on the definition of common objectives, and conducted in accordance with the principle of an open market economy with free competition; 2) Concurrently with the foregoing, and as provided in the Treaties and in accordance with the procedures set out therein, these activities shall include a single currency, the Euro, and the definition and conduct of a single monetary policy and exchange rate policy, the primary objective of both of which shall be to maintain price stability and, without prejudice to this objective, to support the general economic policies in the Union, in accordance with the principle of an open market economy with free competition; 3) These activities of the Member States

[601] EU Commission, Chapters of the Acquis, official website

[602] Official Journal of the European Union (2012a), pp. 96, 97

[603] Art. 3 of the Treaty of the EU states on economic issues: "The Union shall establish an internal market. It shall work for the sustainable development of Europe based on balanced economic growth and price stability, a highly competitive social market economy, aiming at full employment and social progress, and a high level of protection and improvement of the quality of the environment. It shall promote scientific and technological advance. [....]" (Official Journal of the European Union (2012a), p. 17)

[604] Art. 1 of the Treaty of the EU defines the term "Treaties" as follows: "The Union shall be founded on the present Treaty and on the Treaty on the Functioning of the European Union (hereinafter referred to as 'the Treaties'). Those two Treaties shall have the same legal value. The Union shall replace and succeed the European Community." (Official Journal of the European Union (2012a), p. 16)

> and the Union shall entail compliance with the following guiding principles: stable prices, sound public finances and monetary conditions and a sustainable balance-of-payments."

Moreover, the Protocol No. 13 on the "convergence criteria" states as follows[605]:

> "Art. 1: The criterion on price stability referred to in the first indent of Article 140 (1) of the Treaty on the Functioning of the European Union[606] shall mean that a Member State has a price performance that is sustainable and an average rate of inflation, observed over a period of one year before the examination, that

---

[605] Official Journal of the European Union (2012a), p. 281

[606] Art. 140 (1) states: "Once every two years, or at the request of a Member State with a derogation, the Commission and the European Central Bank shall report to the Council on the progress made by the Member States with a derogation in fulfilling their obligations regarding the achievement of economic and monetary union. These reports shall include an examination of the compatibility between the national legislation of each of these Member States, including the statutes of its national central bank, and Articles 130 and 131 and the Statute of the European System of Central Banks and of the ECB. The reports shall also examine the achievement of a high degree of sustainable convergence by reference to the fulfillment by each Member State of the following criteria:

a) the achievement of a high degree of price stability; this will be apparent from a rate of inflation, which is close to that of, at most, the three best performing Member States in terms of price stability;

b) the sustainability of the government financial position; this will be apparent from having achieved a government budgetary position without a deficit that is excessive as determined in accordance with Article 126 (6);

c) the observance of the normal fluctuation margins provided for by the exchange rate mechanism of the European Monetary System, for at least two years, without devaluing against the Euro;

d) the durability of convergence achieved by the Member State with a derogation and of its participation in the exchange rate mechanism being reflected in the long-term interest rate levels.

The four criteria mentioned in this paragraph and the relevant periods over which they are to be respected are developed further in a Protocol annexed to the Treaties. The reports of the Commission and the European Central Bank shall also take account of the results of the integration of markets, the situation and development of the balances-of-payments on current account and an examination of the development of unit labor costs and other price indices." Official Journal of the European Union (2012a), pp. 108, 109

does not exceed by more than 1 ½ percentage points that of, at most, the three best-performing Member States in terms of price stability. Inflation shall be measured by means of the consumer price index on a comparable basis taking into account differences in national definitions."

4.1.2. Central Bank Independence

In this section, I will investigate what "independence" means. Despite a long debate among economists in attempting to define this concept, no single definition is right for all countries[607]. In fact, an institution owned by state cannot be entirely independent of government.

I will first discuss why central bank independence is so important and how it can be measured. I will emphasize that the concept of "independence" cannot be defined as a single index measure but rather as a multidimensional set of characteristics that, in some combination, can reinforce central bank's ability in achieving price stability[608]. On the other hand, more independent central banks tend to be more transparent, the latter, in turn, is associated with institutional quality[609] that I attempted to define in section 1.6. Thus, I will also introduce the concept of transparency. Finally, I will expose some quantitative measures aiming to show the degree of Turkish Central Bank's independence and transparency.

Why is central bank independence important?

This concept is important because it is a major institutional reform aiming to achieve price stability. I emphasized in chapters 2 and 3 that monetary expansion driven by political factors had been the main cause of high and persistent inflation in Turkey from 1970s to early 2000s.

---

607 Siklos, P. L. (2008), p. 802

608 Ibid., p. 811

609 Crowe, C. and Meade, E. E., (2008), p. 1

Let us first explore what are government incentives for monetary expansion. Cukierman (1992) classifies them into four categories: Employment, revenue, balance-of-payments and financial stability[610].

1. Employment: The government and the public are drawn into a trade-off between inflation and unemployment[611] leading to the so-called time-inconsistency problem. While politicians (in particular left-wing)[612] prefer more employment before the private agents' contracts are set, they have an incentive to inflate afterwards[613];

2. Revenue: Inefficient public sector-led development policies leading to loss-making SOEs can produce substantial pressure on budget balance. If financial markets are not developed and access to foreign financing is limited, the government can have an incentive to create high-powered money for deficit financing;

3. Balance-of-payments: Emerging countries rapidly opening their economies to international markets can become vulnerable to balance-of-payments crises in particular in presence of high deficits, low international reserves and a fragile domestic financial system. Although in many cases structural and fiscal adjustments are needed, policy makers may urge for a competitive devaluation;

4. Financial instability: A variety of aspects ranging from non-performing loans in banking sector and subsidized credits provided from state-owned banks to further loans to insolvent SOEs can force a politically managed central bank to create high-powered money, i.e., in bailing out insolvent banks.

All these motives can create inflationary pressure over time, and delegating monetary policy to an independent central bank may reduce inflationary bias. In fact, politicians can be severely constrained in their monetary policy manipulation by the autonomy of the central bank and this would prevent (or reduce) the impact of electoral cycles on macroeconomic variables. The literature on political business cycles (PBCs) mainly focused on the following two aspects:

---

610 Maliszewski, W. S. (2000), p. 750-752

611 Eijffinger, S. C. W. and De Haan, J. (1996), p. 5

612 Alesina, A., Cohen, G. D. and Roubini, N. (1991), p. 26

613 Maliszewski, W. S. (2000), p. 751

1. Opportunistic behavior: Nordhaus (1975) introduced the idea of opportunistic PBC, where politicians have an incentive to introduce expansionary monetary policies in the pre-election period leading to higher inflation and restrictive policies afterwards[614]. This approach assumes that voters are naïve and backward looking, i.e., they evaluate politicians by examining performance retrospectively and they do not attempt to predict future performance[615]. They evaluate positively higher growth and lower unemployment and they do not understand the economic model, which relates inflation and unemployment[616]. We observed an example of opportunistic PBC in Turkish case in Fig. 2.6, where the pre-November 1987 elections monetary expansion accelerated price instability;
2. Partisan (or ideological) behavior: Hibbs (1977) emphasized systematic differences among political parties in their ideology and their economic goals[617]. Parties tend to introduce policies consistent with the economic interests and preferences of their constituencies[618] as voters choose those best representing their preferences[619]. Diverging political views can have an impact on monetary policy as left-wing governments are generally thought to give priority to lower unemployment, while right-wing governments are supposed to be more concerned with price stability[620].

Finally, central bank independence can contribute to fiscal discipline without any additional costs in terms of volatile or reduced GDP[621].

How to measure central bank independence?

Measuring central bank independence is not an easy task, as researchers need to question which proxy to choose to quantify the elements that define the relationship between a government and a central bank[622]. Thus, creating a

614 Alesina, A., and Roubini, N. (1992), p. 666

615 Nordhaus, W. D. (1990), p. 3

616 Alesina, A., Cohen, G. D. and Roubini, N. (1991), p. 3

617 Ibid.

618 Nordhaus, W. D. (1990), p. 40

619 Ibid., p. 4

620 Eijffinger, S. C. W. and De Haan, J. (1996), p. 12

621 Dumiter, F. C. (2011), p. 107

622 Siklos, P. L. (2008), p. 807

central bank index is a subjective process and studies using an index to measure independence can produce diverging results depending on proxies chosen and subjective weights given to these proxies[623].

Several studies[624] during the 1980s and the early 1990s that aimed to rank central bank independence developed indices considering mainly the "legal" independence[625], which is an important element as the enforcement of the law is a main source of credibility. It is possible to create indicators, for example, by decoding information from central bank statutes. Legal characteristics of a central bank are mainly[626]:

- The appointment, the dismissal, and term of office of the chief executive officer of the bank;
- The policy formulation concerning the resolution of conflicts between the executive branch and the central bank over the monetary policy;
- The objectives of the central bank;
- Restrictions on the ability of the central bank to lend to the public sector, such as direct advance and securitized lending.

Grilli, Masciandro, and Tabellini (1991) compared the monetary regimes of eighteen industrial economies from 1950 to 1989 basing their analysis on "political" and "economic" independence. They constructed their index of "political" independence in function of the following three elements[627]:

- Procedures for appointing the members of the central bank governing bodies;
- Relationship between the central bank and the government;
- Policy goals of the central bank with respect to monetary policy.

---

623 Sheppard, P. (2008), p. 4

624 For instance, studies of Bade, R. and Parkin, M. (1980), Alesina, A. (1988), Masciandro, D. and Tabellini, G. (1988) and Grilli, V., Masciandro, D. and Tabellini, G. (1991)

625 Cukierman, A., Webb, S. B. and Neyapti, B. (1992), p. 355

626 Ibid., pp. 356, 357

627 Eijffinger, S. and Schaling, E. (1992), p. 28

They evaluated the degree of "political" independence using the following criteria[628]:

- Are the appointment procedures of governor and board members independent from political influence? Are they appointed for more than five years?
- Do government representatives participate in the board?
- Does the board need government approval for monetary policy?
- Does the statute of the bank require price stability among its goals and does it strengthen the banks' position against government in case of a conflict?

Grilli, Masciandro, and Tabellini (1991) weighted equally these attributes and ranked the eighteen central banks from 1 (least independent) to 6 (most independent)[629].

Regarding the "economic" independence Grilli, Masciandro and Tabellini (1991) investigated its capacity in choosing the instruments of monetary policy. They associated the central bank autonomy with two features:

1. Monetary financing: The influence of politicians in determining the amount to borrow from the central bank is an important aspect as it has an impact on the monetary base. Thus, greater is the government influence on monetary financing of deficits, lower is the central bank independence. To measure the independence under this aspect they investigated whether the direct credit facility is automatic, at market interest rates, temporary and of limited amount;
2. Monetary instruments: This aspect focuses on the influence of politicians, for instance, on the level of interest rates. It investigates more precisely if the discount rate is set by the central bank, if the central bank participates in the primary market for government securities and whether the banking supervision is entrusted to the central bank alone or not.

On the basis of scores given to these criteria, Grilli, Masciandro and Tabellini (1991) constructed the "economic" independence index ranked from 1 (least independent) to 7 (most independent).

Nevertheless, the legal statute is only one of the determinants of actual independence. Hence, the distinction between *de jure* independence and *de*

---

[628] Eijffinger, S. and Schaling, E. (1992), p. 29

[629] Ibid.

facto independence as the provision of the law can diverge from actual practices[630]. Cukierman (1992) and Cukierman, Webb and Neyapti (1992) extended the analysis to developing countries and introduced two behavioral indices of central bank independence[631]. These are the turnover of central bank governors and questionnaire-based index:

1. Turnover of central bank governors[632]: The turnover rate represents the average of the changes in governors over time or TOR=1/average tenure[633]. This indicator presumes that high turnover rates of central bank governor indicate a lower level of independence as frequently changing governors would increase the likelihood of having a governor who would follow politicians' will. Moreover, this would discourage the governor in introducing monetary policies longer than the election cycle. On the other hand, a low rate of turnover does not necessarily imply a high level of independence as a subservient governor may also stay in office for a long time;

2. Questionnaire-based index[634]: Questions sent to specialists in central banks aim to investigate the practice rather than the law on issues ranging, for instance, from the degree of actual tenure overlap between the governor and the political authorities, limitations on lending in practice to the actual priority given to price stability. While the nature of responses is entirely subjective, these are useful in identifying divergence between legal and actual independence. While each response is coded with a different number, different weights given to questions influence also the sum of results.

Transparency

The concept of central bank independence implies, inevitably, "accountability" and "transparency" issues, which are key elements in succeeding in inflation targeting policy. In fact, an independent central bank should be both "accountable" keeping the public regularly informed and "transparent" by disclosing information related to economic policy making process. Eijffinger

---

[630] Siklos, P. L. (2008), p. 803

[631] Maliszewski, W. S. (2000), p. 752

[632] Cukierman, A., Webb, S. B. and Neyapti, B. (1992), p. 363

[633] Dumiter, F. C. (2010), p. 4

[634] Cukierman, A., Webb, S. B. and Neyapti, B. (1992), p. 366, 367

and Geraats (2002)[635] distinguish five aspects of transparency: political, economic, procedural, policy and operational.

1. Political transparency is related to the openness about the policy objectives including formal objectives of monetary policy, i.e., quantitative targets;
2. Economic transparency refers to economic information used for monetary policy, including economic forecasts and evaluating the impact of its decisions;
3. Procedural transparency is about the internal decision-making process, for instance, whether it provides information how it reaches policy decisions, including the release of minutes or voting decisions;
4. Policy transparency is about the release of information on the policy decision, i.e., whether the public is informed immediately with a detailed explanation of the logic behind this decision;
5. Operational transparency is related to the transmission of the policy decision in practice, whether it involves a discussion of the accuracy of its past forecasts and accounting for errors in policy.

Crowe and Meade (2007)[636] constructed a transparency index including two questions for each of the five categories above (Table 4.1).

[635] Eijffinger, S. C. W. and Geraats, P. M. (2002), pp. 2, 3

[636] Crowe, C. and Meade, E. E. (2007), p. 81

Table 4.1: Transparency Measure

Categories	Questions
Political	Is there a statutory objective?
	Is there an explicit numerical target for prices or inflation?
Economic	Does the CB publish surveys to be used to estimate inflation expectations?
	Does the CB publish any forward-looking analyses, i.e., forecasts?
Procedural	Does the CB publish minutes of policy meetings?
	Does the CB publish voting patterns of the monetary policy committee?
Policy	Does the CB publish explanations on the same day that policy changes?
	Does the CB publish an explanation on its meetings days even when there is no change in policy?
Operational	Does the CB publish a discussion of risks to the outlook or forecast?
	Does the CB publish a discussion of shocks or forecast errors after the fact?

Source: Crowe, C., and Meade, E. E. (2007). The overall transparency index is defined as an unweighted average of five categories. Coding is based on giving a numerical value to the answers: 0, 1 or in some cases 5.

Finally, Table 4.2 shows the scores based on two studies, Cukierman, Webb and Neyapti (1992) and Crowe and Meade (2007), aiming to provide insight on the degree of independence and transparency of the Turkish Central Bank, comparing the 1980s with other time frames in the 1990s and the 2000s. It is possible to note a lower Turnover Rate from 1995 to 2004 when compared with the1980s, which indicates a higher level of independence gained over time, according to one of the CWN (1992) behavioral indices of central bank independence (CBI). Regarding the "legal" independence (CWN, (1992)), it is straightforward to observe the following changes under different aspects from 1980s to 2003:

- appointments: higher degree of CBI;
- policy formulation: higher degree of CBI;
- policy objective: no change;
- limits on CB lending to government: higher degree of CBI.

The CWN and un-weighted CWNU indices compare the 1980s with 2003 and show a higher degree of independence over time.

Regarding the transparency of the Turkish Central Bank, a comparison between 1998 and 2006 shows that only under political transparency there is no any change. However, under all other aspects (economic, procedural, policy and operational and transparency index) there is an improvement.

Table 4.2: Index Scores (Turkey) on Central Bank Independence and Transparency

CBI	turn0	turn1	q10	q20	q30	q40	cwn0	q11	q21	q31	q41	cwn1	cwnu0	cwnu1
	0.40	0.20	0.52	0.48	0.60	0.38	0.46	0.65	1.00	0.60	1.00	0.85	0.44	0.87
Trans.	**q10**	**q20**	**q30**	**q40**	**q50**	**trans0**	**q11**	**q21**	**q31**	**q41**	**q51**	**trans1**		
	1	0.5	0	0	0	0.3	1	1	0.5	1	0.5	0.8		

Source: Crowe, C. and Meade, E. E. (2008)

Definitions of data

turn0	Turnover of central bank governor, 1980-1989 sample (CWN)
turn1	Turnover of central bank governor, 1995-2004 sample (Crowe-Meade)
q10	CBI aspect 1 (appointments), 1980-1989 sample (CWN)
q20	CBI aspect 2 (policy formulation), 1980-1989 sample (CWN)
q30	CBI aspect 3 (policy objective), 1980-1989 sample (CWN)
q40	CBI aspect 4 (limits on CB lending to government), 1980-1989 sample (CWN)
cwn0	CBI, 1980-1989 sample (CWN)
q11	CBI aspect 1 (appointments), 2003 sample (Crowe-Meade)
q21	CBI aspect 2 (policy formulation), 2003 sample (Crowe-Meade)
q31	CBI aspect 3 (policy objective), 2003 sample (Crowe-Meade)
q41	CBI aspect 4 (limits on CB lending to government), 2003 sample (Crowe-Meade)
cwn1	CBI, 2003 sample (Crowe-Meade)
cwnu0	CBI, 1980-1989 sample, un-weighted (see Cukierman, 1992)
cwnu1	CBI, 2003 sample, un-weighted (see Cukierman, 1992)
q10	Transparency category 1 (political), 1998 sample
q20	Transparency category 2 (economic), 1998 sample
q30	Transparency category 3 (procedural), 1998 sample
q40	Transparency category 4 (policy), 1998 sample
q50	Transparency category 5 (operational), 1998 sample
trans0	Transparency index, 1998 sample
q11	Transparency category 1 (political), 2006 sample
q21	Transparency category 2 (economic), 2006 sample
q31	Transparency category 3 (procedural), 2006 sample
q41	Transparency category 4 (policy), 2006 sample
q51	Transparency category 5 (operational), 2006 sample
trans1	Transparency index, 2006 sample

To conclude, the Turkish Central Bank became more independent and transparent in the post-2002 period, according to Table 4.2.

I examine now, in the next section, which reforms led the Turkish Central Bank to achieve this result.

4.1.3. EU-inspired regulatory reforms and the CBRT's "legal" independence

Turning back to our story, we noted at the end of Chapter 3 that in the aftermath of the February 2001 currency crisis, the government gave priority to fiscal discipline, instead of introducing an expansionary policy. That is to say, it followed a "Washington Consensus" principle again! But this time was different. Why? Let us see the rest of the story.

Immediately after the crisis, Kemal Dervis left his position as Vice-Chairman of the World Bank, to take up the post of Minister of Economic Affairs[637]. On 2nd March 2001, the government adopted a package of financial and economic reforms[638]. On March 8th, the Council of the European Union formally approved the Accession Partnership[639]. Finally, the Turkish government adopted its "National Program for the Adoption of the Acquis" on March 19th, which implied a wide range of political and economic reforms[640]. In April 2001, Law No. 4'651 established the full autonomy of the Central Bank as the unique authority over monetary policy and the exchange rate regime[641]. Its primary objective was redefined as to achieve and maintain price stability[642]. The new law also established a "Monetary Policy Committee", where the Treasury had no voting rights[643]. The government displayed a strong political will in the

---

637 Yeldan, E. (2003), p. 3

638 Commission of the European Communities (2001), p. 14

639 Republic of Turkey, Ministry of Foreign Affairs, official website, Section 7

640 Commission of the European Communities (2001), p. 8

641 Guven, A. B. (2010), p. 14

642 Central Bank of Turkey, official website, Law No. 4'651

643 Republic of Turkey (2002), p. 25

"Letter of Intent" of May 2001[644] in the pursuit of reform of which the major goals included[645]:

- an independent central bank aiming to achieve price stability;
- a floating FX rate regime;
- fiscal discipline targeting a pre-specified primary budget surplus;
- a restructured financial sector, aiming to diversify risks, introducing reforms on public banks, taking control of connected lending practices and including repo (repurchase agreement) in the banks' balance sheet definitions, making these transactions evident in the bank reports[646].

To note that in this period the Turkish Central Bank gained the necessary tools to effectively exercise its independence when analyzed from both a political and economic viewpoint.

Let me begin from the political perspective. As I mentioned before, a protocol introduced in 1997 abolishing the Turkish Central Bank's Short-term Cash Advance Facility to the Treasury was an important step. In addition, the Law No. 4'651 of April 2001 declared its de-politicized status, as the sole institution charged with monetary policy. Henceforth, the Treasury would have to raise cash on the market.

In economic terms, the floating exchange rate regime made possible an independent monetary policy within the Mundell-Fleming framework. The previous crawling peg (an intermediate regime) limited monetary policy under full convertibility. The intervention of Turkish Central Bank on 22nd November 2000, to refinance the collapsing banking system not only violated the NDA ceiling introduced by the IMF Stabilization Program[647], but also the Mundell-Fleming framework. In fact, under full convertibility and a pegged exchange rate regime, the Turkish Central Bank's intervention was an attempt to achieve all three goals simultaneously and, according to the Mundell-Fleming model, was bound to end in a foreign exchange crisis. Thus, in line with the Stanley Fischer "bipolar" view, which suggested either a fixed or a floating regime, but not an intermediate one (section 3.1.4), the choice of a floating FX rate regime

---

644 IMF (2001) website, "Letter of Intent" dated 3rd May 2001

645 Atiyas, I. and Emil, F. (2005), p. 41

646 Atiyas, I. et al. (2005), p. 41

647 See point (D) of the December 1999 IMF Stabilization program, in the beginning of section 3.3.2.3.

after the February 2001 currency crisis also accorded full flexibility to the CBRT in its monetary policy.

I conclude that a fixed exchange rate regime is perhaps one of the most harmful of all government interventions in markets. It shields the whole economy from market realities, causing huge mal-investment. Table 3.11 shows also that the exchange rate peg in the beginning of 2000 created huge current account deficits, whereas the free-float regime after the February 2001 currency crisis led the economy to a current account surplus.

Adaptation to EU requirements concerning Central Bank Independence

Let us have a look at the European Commission's Regular Report (2001) concerning the Turkish Central Bank's independence[648]:

> "Confronted with two financial crises, Turkey has been unable to make further progress towards achieving a functioning market economy. Considerable parts of its economy are, however, already competing in the EU market, under the framework of the customs union with the EC. The two financial crises put an end to the preceding economic stabilization program. [....]
>
> Turkey has made some progress in the adoption of the EMU "acquis". The independence of the Central Bank has been increased in April 2001. As regards direct public sector financing by the central bank, the provisions preventing the Bank from granting, advancing or extending credit to the Treasury, public establishments and institutions have been reinforced. The Bank may not purchase debt instruments issued by the Treasury and public establishments and institutions on the primary market. Turkey has taken important steps to increase the independence of the Central Bank, but further measures are needed to align with the "acquis" in this area. The Central Bank Law is

648 Commission of the European Communities (2001), pp. 45, 65, 66

> incompatible with the "acquis" as far as the determination of the inflation target is concerned since this is decided upon in agreement with the Government. Other amendments may be needed to ensure full compliance with the "acquis" in the area of personal and institutional independence."

The European Commission's Progress Report (2009)[649] reiterated these concerns: The Turkish Central Bank could still refinance banks bailed out and taken over by the Saving Deposit Insurance Fund. To note that there is still no change in the legal framework concerning this aspect by late 2016.

Let me now investigate what was the degree of independence of the CBRT under "economic" criteria considered by **Grilli, Masciandro and Tabellini (1991), i.e., monetary financing and monetary instruments** (section 4.1.2).

Capacity of the CBRT in choosing instruments of monetary policy

1. Monetary Financing: The size of CBRT's balance sheet

I examined in section 2.2.1.1 the relationship between the size of a central bank's balance sheet and its independence. I emphasized that taking control of the size of its balance sheet became a major objective of the Turkish Central Bank only in the second half of the 1980s and I also showed that the Turkish Central Bank was not able to achieve this goal during the 1990s. In fact, until 1997, it was still creating money for the Treasury and in the late 1990s several bank defaults were again covered through Central Bank high-powered money creation. However, it is straightforward to observe in Table 4.3 a decline in the asset size of the Turkish Central Bank in the post-2001 currency crisis period and infer that the radical post-2001 crisis reforms were, in fact, being implemented.

How the Turkish Central Bank finally succeeded in achieving this major goal, considering it had failed since the beginning of the deregulation process? The answer lies in the missing 11th element of the Washington Consensus: The adoption of the EU-inspired regulatory framework.

We will observe in the next section that significant improvements were achieved also in the Turkish banking sector.

---

[649] Commission of the European Communities (2009), p. 59

Table 4.3: Ratio of Assets/GDP in financial sector during the 2000s, in percentage

	2000	2001	2002	2003	2004	2005	2006	2007	2008	2009
CBRT	18.5	34.5	21.1	16.8	13.4	13.9	13.8	12.6	11.9	11.5
Banks	63.8	72.2	60.7	54.9	54.8	62.7	65.9	69.0	77.1	87.4
Leasing (1)	1.3	1.2	1.1	1.1	1.2	0.9	1.3	1.6	1.8	1.5
Factoring (2)	0.8	0.6	0.6	0.6	0.7	0.8	0.8	0.9	0.8	1.1
Cons. Fin. (3)	0.0	0.0	0.1	0.2	0.3	0.4	0.4	0.5	0.5	0.5
Insurance (4)	1.5	1.7	1.5	1.6	1.8	2.2	2.3	2.6	2.8	3.5
Pension C. (5)	0.0	0.0	0.0	0.7	0.8	0.9	0.9	1.1	1.3	1.6
Sec. Ins. (6)	0.3	0.3	0.3	0.3	0.2	0.4	0.4	0.5	0.4	0.5
Sec. Tr. (7)	0.0	0.0	0.0	0.0	0.1	0.1	0.1	0.1	0.1	0.1
Sec. Funds (8)	1.2	2.0	2.7	4.4	4.4	4.5	2.9	3.1	2.5	3.1
BIST Cap. (9)	28.0	28.6	16.1	21.1	23.7	33.6	30.3	39.9	19.1	36.8
Real Est. (10)	0.5	0.5	0.3	0.3	0.3	0.3	0.3	0.5	0.5	0.5
Total	116.0	141.4	104.6	102.1	101.5	120.8	119.5	132.4	118.9	148.2

Source: Banking Regulation and Supervision Agency, (2009), p. 2

(1) Financial Leasing Companies; (2) Factoring Companies; (3) Consumer Financial Companies; (4) Insurance companies; (5) Individual Pension Companies; (6) Securities Intermediation Insurance; (7) Securities Investment Trust; (8) Securities Investment Funds; (9) Borsa Istanbul Market Capitalization; (10) Real Estate Investment Trust.

2. Monetary Instruments: Short-term interest rates

To note that, in the aftermath of the February 2001 currency crisis, the Central Bank Act of April 2001 officially defined the mandate of Turkish Central Bank as an independent institution and introduced a transitional period to an inflation targeting regime (called "implicit inflation targeting" regime) that lasted from the beginning of 2002 to late 2005[650]. The major aim of the Turkish Central Bank during this period was to enhance the credibility of its monetary policy, which depended on a variety of factors, ranging from the level of public debt to improvements in the banking sector and whether the latter would react properly to its policy signals[651]. During this period, structural reforms achieved in different areas (such as the redesigned agricultural support system or the restructured banking system) had a significant impact in reducing the size of the public debt to sustainable levels in line with EU standards. While I will discuss this aspect in section 5.1, I wish to emphasize here the fact that structural reforms in the public sector were also essential for the Central Bank in its attempt to gain credibility. In high public debt circumstances a central

650 Ersel, H. and Ozatay, F. (2008), p. 4

651 Ibid., pp. 8-10

bank raising its short-term interest rates to fight inflation can be misinterpreted by markets as a sign that public debt is not sustainable and result in capital flight[652]. To note that the Central Bank and the Government jointly announced official inflation and monetary targets from 2002 to 2005 and the former used short-term interest rates to achieve a monetary base consistent with these targets, which were in line with the 18th IMF Stand-by agreement (Table 3.2)[653]. Moreover, the rationale behind any decision taken on interest rates was explained to the public through public *communiqués*[654]. However, it diverged from an "explicit inflation targeting" regime in several ways: For instance, inflation targets were set jointly with the government[655], the meeting days of the monetary policy committee were not announced to the public, final decisions were not made by voting in the monetary policy committee but rather by the governor, vice governor and directors of government departments. The monetary policy committee's role was consultative only[656].

In addition to reduced public debt, a variety of other factors had an impact in raising the credibility of the Turkish Central Bank, including the government's request for a Stand-by agreement with the IMF that was to cover the period from 2005 to 2007[657], with particular focus on fiscal and monetary discipline and reforms in financial services and social security. To note also that from 2004 to 2005, the EU candidacy enhanced the confidence of markets that structural reforms would effectively be implemented, which in turn raised the credibility of the Turkish Central Bank in its monetary and inflation targeting policy[658].

Six zeros were deleted from the Turkish Lira at the beginning of 2005[659]. This monetary reform, although having a limited psychological impact, also contributed to signal the initial phase of a new era, where markets could have confidence in the overall economic management of the country. The IMF also

---

[652] Ersel, H. and Ozatay, F. (2008), p. 8

[653] Kara, A. H. (2006), p. 10

[654] Ersel, H. and Ozatay, F. (2008), p. 11

[655] Central Bank of the Republic of Turkey (2005), p. 1

[656] Ersel, H. and Ozatay, F. (2008), p. 11

[657] Ibid., p. 15

[658] Ibid.

[659] Central Bank of the Republic of Turkey (2005), p. 2

monitored the monetary base, the level of international reserves and net domestic assets as part of its performance criteria[660].

By 2005, a variety of factors from increased predictability of relatively stable macro variables[661] to increased credibility of the Turkish Central Bank, in line with progress achieved in its independence, meant that the preconditions of the inflation targeting regime had, to a large extent, been met and it was appropriate to start an "explicit inflation targeting" regime at the beginning of 2006[662].

I argued in the beginning of this section, nevertheless, that the Banking Law still allowed the Central Bank to finance the Savings Deposit Insurance Fund. It asserted that this aspect undermined its full independence. I also emphasized that, by late 2016, there is still no change in legislation concerning Central Bank bank bailouts. Though the Turkish banking sector stood on a secure basis by the mid-2010s when compared with the early 2000s, in the case of an eventual bank default the Central Bank can potentially, under current legislation, create money. Though the likelihood of this situation (occurrence of bank defaults and Central Bank intervention through money creation) is low at least as of the date of manuscript 2016, this aspect contradicts, from a legal point of view, its independent status.

I indeed emphasized in section 3.3.2.2 that the banking sector, prior to the 2001 financial crisis, lost its intermediation function between the financial and the real sector and became the main purchaser of government securities, borrowing on international markets at low-interest rates and lending to the Government at high ones, ignoring the exchange rate risk. Who bore this risk? Banks were convinced that the government would bail them out. This overall shift in the banking sector's function within the economy was, therefore, the result of moral hazard in an open capital market and was also a major factor increasing the overall risk exposure for the country. However, the founding of IRAs from 2001 onwards helped to correct some of these weaknesses. Specifically for the banking sector, we will observe from letter "a" to "d" in the next section that the Banking Regulatory and Supervisory Agency (BRSA) introduced regulations to adopt EU requirements, such as restructuring state-owned banks and introducing an effective supervisory framework.

---

660 BRSA (2010), p. 36

661 I will observe in figures 5.1, 5.2 and tables 5.1, 5.2 that Turkey met Maastricht criteria by 2004-2005 and showed better performance when compared with the average of EU-27 member states in the second half of the 2000s.

662 Central Bank of the Republic of Turkey (2005), pp. 1, 2

Table 4.3 shows that while the assets of commercial banks declined from 2000 to 2004 due to the November 2000 and February 2001 crises, the sector answered strongly to the adoption of EU-inspired regulatory changes after this date[663]. Table 4.4 compares this performance with selected EU countries' growth. It is possible to observe in the last two columns that the percentage in asset size from 2002 and 2004 to 2008 in Turkey was much higher than the EU-27 average. It was lower only than Hungary from 2002 to 2008 and than Greece from 2004 to 2008.

Table 4.4: Total Assets, comparison with selected EU countries

	2002	2003	2004	2005	2006	2007	2008	%change 2002-08	%change 2004-08
Turkey	127	146	172	255	269	340	343	170	99
EU-27	25'312	26'519	29'038	32'898	36'820	41'072	42'209	67	45
Czech R.	79	78	87	101	115	140	155	96	78
Hungary	44	55	68	78	94	109	125	184	84
Poland	125	112	142	163	190	236	263	110	85
Greece	202	213	230	281	315	383	462	129	101
Portugal	310	349	345	360	397	440	482	55	40

Source: BRSA (2009), p. 19; Values are in billion Euros, except the last two columns showing the percentage changes from 2002 to 2008 and from 2004 to 2008.

Similarly, Table 4.5 compares Turkey with selected EU countries with respect to loans in order to see to what extent the banking sector regained its intermediation function within the economy. To note in the last two columns that the percentage change in loan size from 2002 and 2004 to 2008 in Turkey was the highest in our sample of countries and well above the EU-27.

---

663 Banking Regulation and Supervision Agency (2009), p. 3

Table 4.5: Total Loans, comparison with selected EU countries

	2002	2003	2004	2005	2006	2007	2008	%change 2002-08	%change 2004-08
Turkey	30	40	57	100	118	167	172	573.3	202
EU-27	11'076	12'673	13'679	15'447	17'144	19'299	19'275	174.0	41
Czech R.	29	31	33	41	52	67	77	265.5	133
Hungary	26	32	40	47	56	66	76	292.3	90
Poland	61	57	67	78	96	134	158	259.0	136
Greece	95	110	128	148	167	199	221	232.6	73
Portugal	183	186	195	209	231	258	281	153.6	44

Source: BRSA (2009), p. 25; values in billion Euros except the last two columns showing the percentage change from 2002 to 2008 and from 2004 to 2008

Concluding remarks

I examined the CBRT's independence under "legal" and "economic" aspects. I argued that regarding the former, political will followed the EU requirements after the 2001 crisis. Whereas, regarding the latter, I discussed the Turkish situation in line with Grilli, Masciandaro and Tabellini (1991)'s "economic" independence criteria who investigated its capacity in choosing the instruments of monetary policy, associating the central bank autonomy with two features: Monetary financing (the size of its balance sheet) and monetary instruments (short-term interest rates). I argued that while monetary financing of budget deficits ended by 1997 (section 2.2.1.1, Fig. 2.5), eventual bank defaults can still be financed by the CBRT, although the occurrence of such defaults seems unlikely by 2016. Regarding the monetary instruments, I emphasized two aspects: First, the CBRT had a policy objective, i.e., the inflation targeting monetary policy. Second, the CBRT was allowed to use short-term interest rates to achieve this monetary goal. Nevertheless, the degree of CBRT independence was to be improved over time, in line also with macroeconomic variables, i.e., the level of public debt, which in turn would have an impact on the credibility of this institution. The "implicit" and "explicit" inflation targeting periods show this gradual improvement in the degree of its independence. For instance, while during the initial phase known as "implicit" inflation targeting, the CBRT set jointly with the government the inflation targets, it became autonomous under this aspect by the beginning of 2006, in line also with macroeconomic improvements and enhanced credibility before markets. This sheds light also on the relationship between the CBRT and the government, which is one of the elements in evaluating the "political" independence of a central bank in Grilli, Masciandaro, and Tabellini (1991) (section 4.1.2). These remarks provide me useful elements in drawing a response to the 3rd research question:

> "What is the role of monetary stability and the attitude of the central bank? How do central bank policies affect the vulnerability of an economy? Is its independence important?".

To note that the aim of a floating exchange rate regime is a stable but free market exchange rate, due to stable, balanced policies at all levels. On the other hand, I discussed in section 3.1 theories on business cycles where Ludwig von Mises emphasized the "coordinating role" of interest rates. This was lost in Turkey during the 1980s and the 1990s, as interest rates followed a volatile trend to satisfy risk appetite of global investors, instead of playing a role of coordination between savings and investments. However, improvements in CBRT independence from 2001 to 2006 allowed this institution to use short-term interest rates to achieve monetary stability, in words of Ludwig von Mises the "coordinating role" of interest rates.

We will observe in Chapter 5 that this had a significant impact in addressing the overall vulnerability of Turkish economy by diminishing false market signals to investors.

4.1.4. Independent Regulatory Agencies (IRAs)

We observed in the previous section that the CBRT gained "legal" independence in 2001. Then, its gradually increasing level of independence reached the highest degree by the year 2006. The government was in the hands of a single-party from 2002 onwards, achieving political stability and also having a significant impact in implementing reforms and enhancing credibility before global markets. We will nevertheless observe that the banking sector gained a sound framework only in the second half of the 2000s.

I will examine in this section the IRAs created, of which in particular the one in the banking sector is strictly related to the reforms in central banking analyzed in the previous section. The IRA aiming to monitor the state aid in agriculture and another in telecommunications are important as they shed light on the way state intervenes in the economy and antitrust rules are regulated. While I introduce all of the IRAs created from 1999 to 2002 to provide complete information regarding the EU-inspired institutions introduced in this period, I will mainly focus on the IRA in the banking sector in line with the scope of the book. Moreover, IRAs on state aid and telecommunications are important as far as the creation of competitive forces in markets and privatizations issues are concerned.

The creation of regulatory agencies in Turkey was not unprecedented: For example, the Capital Market Board (CMB) was established in 1981 as a regulatory agency but it was a ministerial body. Nonetheless, at the insistence of the IMF, it became independent from the Ministry in 1999, permitting me to state that the CMB functioned as an IRA after this date. There were two IRAs created in the aftermath of the 1994 financial crisis, the Competition Agency (an essential part of the customs union with the EU, see section 3.3.2.1) and in the same spirit the Higher Board for Radio and Television, which was enabled to regulate the broadcasting market[664]. The government established six more from 1999 to 2002:

(1) Banking Regulation and Supervision Agency (1999);

(2) and (3) Agencies in Sugar, Tobacco, and Alcoholic Beverages sectors (2001-2002), in the context of State Aid to agriculture;

(4) Telecommunication Agency (2000);

(5) Energy Markets Regulatory Agency (2001);

(6) Public Procurement Agency (2002).

To note again the IMF assistance in the creation of IRAs, in spite of the fact that these were not an implication of the "Washington Consensus", but instead addressed weaknesses in the banking regulatory framework and introduced the "Acquis Communautaire". This aspect is the main distinguishing feature of this period. Although the IMF assistance is notable in both parts, I highlight in Chapter 4 structural institutional reforms, which were not emphasized in the original "Washington Consensus" but constitute basic elements of the EU regulatory framework. This is the reason why I argue that these were "EU-inspired", although in particular, the IRAs created in the banking and telecommunication sectors were also part of IMF conditionality. I will also argue that those in sugar, tobacco, and alcoholic beverages were not imposed by the IMF, though the latter insisted in dismantling the state presence in these sectors. Instead, we will see that the Turkish government created them to maintain, perhaps, the state presence in these sectors, an issue, which deserves further investigation. Thus, the common denominator between these IRAs, aside from their *de-jure* independence, is their mandate to fulfill EU requirements in Turkish legislation through the introduction of appropriate regulations and institutions. It is to this that I now turn.

---

664 Zenginobuz, U. (2008), p. 478

(1) Banking Regulation and Supervision Agency (1999)

Financial sector reforms comprise an important part of EU requirements for full membership. Turkish policy makers established the BRSA as a financially and administratively independent institution to oversee these reforms, as an IRA consistent with the EU framework[665]. It began operations only at the end of August 2000[666], just in time to preside over Turkey's most spectacular banking crisis in its history due to interest rate carry trades and unhedged FX positions described in Chapter 3. As we observed in section 3.3.2.3 (points 5 and 6 of "Discussion") Demirbank's highly risky position caused a rise in interest rates, which led to the November 2000 liquidity crisis (Table 3.13). In the aftermath of the February 2001 financial crisis, the BRSA announced the Banking Sector Restructuring Program whose major aim was to adopt regulations that would promote a surely "efficient, competitive and sound banking sector"[667]. In this section, I will begin with an overview of this program. A comparison of the results with a sample of EU countries will then highlight apparent divergences. The Program was based on four points[668]:

a. Restructuring state-owned banks

The cost of credit subsidies to the agricultural sector had become enormous for state banks by the late 1990s due to large differences between market costs and subsidized prices and rates[669]. I argued in section 3.3.2.2 that these losses exceeded 13 percent of the GDP by 1999. The 57th Bulent Ecevit coalition government suspended agricultural price support subsidies in the aftermath of the currency crisis on 3rd July 2001[670]. Efficiency in the banking sector was also somewhat improved thanks to the merger of Emlak and Ziraat Banks (Table 4.6)[671]. Reform of state banks contributed to raising their efficiency in terms of organization, human resources, technology, financial control and risk management, all in line with the requirements of modern banking and

---

665 Pazarbasioglu, C. (2005), p. 162

666 BRSA (2002), p. 2

667 Pazarbasioglu, C. (2005), p. 162

668 Ibid.

669 OECD (2001), p. 89

670 BRSA (2003), p. 5

671 Ibid., p. 6

international competition[672]. Table 4.6 shows that nearly one-third of branches were suppressed and more than half of the personnel had to leave their posts.

Table 4.6: State-owned banks' restructuring from 2000 to 2002

	Dec. 2000	Dec. 2002	percentage change
Nb. branches	2'494	1'685	-32.4
-Ziraat	1'287	1'139	-11.5
-Halk	804	546	-54.8
-Emlak	403	-	-
Nb. personnel	61'601	30'399	-50.7
-Ziraat	36'576	22'099	-39.6
-Halk	10'000	8'300	-66.8
-Emlak	15'025	-	-

Source: BRSA (2003), p. 7

b. Ensuring resolution on the intervened banks without money creation

The Turkish Central Bank had monitored the Saving Deposits and Insurance Fund (SDIF) since its creation in 1983 when it received its initial mandate to insure saving deposits. After the 1994 financial crisis the SDIF, thus the CBRT, was also charged with injecting funds into banks requiring support and it received 22 failing banks from 1997 to 2000 (Table 3.4). The BRSA took over the control of the SDIF in end of August 2000[673]. Table 4.7 shows that the bailing out cost of defaulting banks was huge. It corresponded to 18.7 percent of GDP by the year 2001.

How was this financed? Premiums collected from the banking sector and proceeds from the sale of defaulting banks covered only a small proportion (equivalent to 1.7 percent of GDP)[674]. For the rest, the Treasury issued government securities (17 percent of GDP)[675]. This additional public debt was due to the full government guarantee introduced in the aftermath of the 1994 crisis (section 3.3.1, discussion point "3"), in the absence of an adequate regulatory framework in the banking sector.

---

672 Pazarbasioglu, C. (2005), p. 163

673 Ibid.

674 Ibid., p. 164

675 Ibid., p. 163

Table 4.7: Ratio of State Banks' Losses to GDP, in percentage

	Ratio to GDP
State Banks' Losses due to subsidized lending	12.8
Capital Support to State Banks	2.0
Resolution of SDIF Banks	18.7
-Public Resources (government securities)	17.0
-Private Resources	1.7
TOTAL	33.5

Source: Pazarbasioglu, C. (2005), p. 163, Banking Regulation and Supervision Agency

c. Strengthening private banks

The BRSA introduced a variety of regulations on aspects ranging from limiting foreign currency open positions to encouraging mergers and acquisitions and obliging banks to introduce triple auditing practices[676]. For instance, the regulations published in February and March 2002 obliged banks to be subject to three separate audits[677]: An independent audit company was to undertake the first audit. Then, another independent audit company, which was to be selected by the BRSA would conduct a second evaluation. The BRSA itself would be involved in the third and final audit[678]. The aim was to improve the quality of the supervision process through independent "stress tests". Table 4.8 illustrates pre-audit and post-audit results for 25 private banks in 2001 on three selected key indicators. Triple audit results showed that the capital adequacy ratio was lower by 6.5 percentage points and the proportion of non-performing loans was 18 percentage points higher than the pre-audit position.

Table 4.8: Pre- and post-audit results for private banks - 2001

	Pre-audit	Post-audit
Capital Adequacy Ratio (CAR) (in percentage)	21.3	14.8
Non-Performing Loans/Loans (in percentage)	7.0	25.0
Loans (in billion TL)	29.2	24.0

Source: Banking Regulation and Supervision Agency

---

676 Pazarbasioglu, C. (2005), p. 164

677 Ibid.

678 BRSA (2010), p. 56

d. Realization of an effective regulatory and supervisory framework

The liberalization process, macro volatility, and successive financial crises meant that companies needed to manage their risks better, hence the need and increased interest in risk modeling and use of financial derivatives. These were essential structures of modern banking. The BRSA aimed to prevent, starting by January 2001, the frequently used practice of forward contracts in institutions belonging to the same group, leading to a "fictitious hedge", which in reality concentrated risk instead of spreading it. In February 2001, the BRSA published a "Regulation on Measurement and Evaluation of Capital Adequacy of Banks", determining the procedures and principles for calculating capital adequacy for banks bearing significant market risks, including interest rate risk and exchange rate risk[679]. In June 2001, amendments to the 1999 Bank Law introduced a "Consolidated Equity" definition in line with the equity definition in EU directives[680]. Thus, credit limits were to be calculated in line with EU standards. In January 2002, options, futures and other financial derivatives were included in the definition of credit[681]. The BRSA introduced an additional regulation in January 2002, which included risk measurement and calculation of capital requirements related to the risk structure of option-type derivative products in line with international best practices. Another regulation, the "Act on Restructuring of Debts to the Financial Sector" promoted the establishment of "bad banks" to manage and ultimately try to sell off non-performing loans of banks and encourage debt restructuring[682].

Concluding remarks

To note that the February 2001 currency crisis, in conjunction with IMF and EU-inspired supervision and regulatory changes, had a major impact on the banking sector[683]. These improvements and significant progress in the Central Bank's independence (sections 4.1.2 and 4.1.3) show us another important aspect: A banking sector that has regained its intermediation function between the financial sector and the real sector, can further increase its efficiency through an effective interaction with an independent central bank. We

---

679 BRSA (2010), p. 62

680 Ibid., p. 62

681 Ibid., p. 64

682 Ibid., p. 63

683 Ibid., p. 17

observed that in Turkey the latter started a "full-fledged inflation targeting" policy in January 2006. Under these circumstances, an effective Central Bank communication policy, where the banking system can interpret its policy signals, paves the way for a functioning market economy. This new regulatory and institutional framework corresponded to what we have called the needed "11th element of the Washington Consensus".

We will observe in Chapter 5 the significant impact of these reforms on both macro variables and the risk structure of the economy. Some caveats, nevertheless, must be considered, as I will show that the inflation targeting policy also led to an appreciating currency, once more creating current account imbalances.

Let us now look at how the Turkish government tackled its structural deficit – the root cause of all the previous economic instability. I start with the agricultural sector.

(2) and (3) Agencies in Sugar, Tobacco, and Alcoholic Beverages sectors (2001-2002): Reform of State Aid to agriculture to meet EU requirements and emerging problems

State aid to agriculture was a Turkish "way of life", and a heavy burden on the state budget. Subsidized credits to the agricultural sector were directed through state-owned banks. Thus, not only did the state-owned banks fully expect to have their failing agricultural loans covered by the Treasury, but agricultural units never expected to have to repay their loans. Such pervasive state aid was clearly contrary to a fully functioning market economy. Consequently, the overall question of state aid was a particularly important aspect in the EU negotiating process (although the EU itself is not unknown for subsidizing agriculture[684]). The 1998 and 1999 EU Commission's regular reports on Turkey

---

684 The following article of the Treaty on the Functioning of the EU provides insight on EU`s approach regarding the compatibility of state aids with the internal markets: "Art. 107: 1) Save as otherwise provided in the Treaties, any aid granted by a Member State or through State resources in any form whatsoever, which distorts or threatens to distort competition by favoring certain undertakings or the production of certain goods shall, in so far as it affects trade between Member States, be incompatible with the internal market;

argued that there was no effective control on state aid based on EU principles[685] and that Turkey needed to align its legislation with the "Acquis Communautaire" in this area[686]. In an attempt to achieve this goal, the Turkish government began to implement an agricultural policy reform in 2000, which consisted of replacing many agricultural price support systems with direct

---

2) The following shall be compatible with the internal market: a) aid having a social character, granted to individual consumers, provided that such aid is granted without discrimination related to the origin of the products concerned; b) aid to make good the damage caused by natural disasters or exceptional occurrences; c) aid granted to the economy of certain areas of the Federal Republic of Germany affected by the division of Germany, in so far as such aid is required in order to compensate for the economic disadvantages caused by that division. Five years after the entry into force of the Treaty of Lisbon, the Council, acting on a proposal from the Commission, may adopt a decision repealing this point;

3) The following may be considered to be compatible with the internal market: a) aid to promote the economic development of areas where the standard of living is abnormally low or where there is serious underemployment, and of the regions referred to in Article 349, in view of their structural, economic and social situation; b) aid to promote the execution of an important project of common European interest or to remedy a serious disturbance in the economy of a Member State; c) aid to facilitate the development of certain economic activities or of certain economic areas, where such aid does not adversely affect trading conditions to an extent contrary to the common interest; d) aid to promote culture and heritage conservation, where such aid does not affect trading conditions and competition in the Union to an extent that is contrary to the common interest; e) such other categories of aid as may be specified by decision of the Council on a proposal from the Commission. " (Official Journal of the European Union (2012a), p. 96)

685 Commission of the European Communities (1998), p. 39, Commission of European Communities (1999), p. 26

686 The EU Commission has a mandate to review all systems of state aid in its Members. Art. 108 of the Treaty on the Functioning of the EU states:

"1) The Commission shall, in cooperation with Member States, keep under constant review all systems of aid existing in those States. It shall propose to the latter any appropriate measures required by the progressive development or by the functioning of the internal market; 2) If, after giving notice to the parties concerned to submit their comments, the Commission finds that aid granted by a State or through State resources is not compatible with the internal market having regard to Article 107, or that such aid is being misused, it shall decide that the State concerned shall abolish or alter such aid within a period of time to be determined by the Commission. If the State concerned does not comply with this decision within the prescribed time, the Commission or any other interested State may, in derogation from the provisions of Articles 258 and 259, refer the matter to the Court of Justice of the European Union direct. On application by a Member State, the Council may, acting unanimously, decide that aid which that State is granting or intends to grant shall be considered to be compatible with the internal market, in derogation from the provisions of Article 107 or from the regulations provided for in Article 109, if such a decision is justified by exceptional circumstances. [....]" (Official Journal of the European Union (2012a), pp. 91, 92)

income supplements[687]. Priority was given to reducing state involvement in agriculture. To note, however, that Turkish legislation diverged in part from that of the EU[688]. For instance, the Competition Agency in Turkey, unlike the EU Commission, was not authorized to supervise state aid. Although the Competition Agency was operational from 1997, various public institutions (Undersecretariat of Treasury, Undersecretariat of Foreign Trade, Eximbank and other authorized institutions) continued to issue subsidies to the agricultural sector.

Briefly, the creation of a Competition Agency was a precondition to implement the Customs Union with the EU. However, traditional state intervention in agriculture continued to contradict Turkey's commitments under the Customs Union because it subsidized lending distorted prices, impeding the formation of competitive forces in markets. It is worth taking as examples, two important agricultural products, sugar, and tobacco, that provided mass employment and required state aid, which manifested itself under several forms ranging from subsidized inputs and politically established prices to investment credits[689]. However, it was the presence of public monopolies in these sectors, which was incompatible with the EU criterion of a functioning market economy. For example, the 2001 European Commission Regular Report on Turkey noted that the state monopoly on trade in alcoholic beverages and tobacco products violated Turkey's prior commitment under the Customs Union[690]. It further advanced that Parliament had adopted new regulations in order to restructure this sector, introducing an IRA in the tobacco sector and paving the path for privatizations. However, the President of Republic did not approve these regulations because of social consequences for tobacco growers[691]. Thus, the proposed Tobacco and Alcoholic Beverages Market Agency was delayed until 2002.

While the creation of an IRA in the tobacco sector took time, the government succeeded in establishing an IRA in the sugar sector by June 2001 and initiated the privatization process for the major state monopoly of Turkish Sugar Factories Inc. (TSF A.S.). In an interview made for this study[692], Sahin

---

687 Commission of the European Communities (2002), p. 78

688 Republic of Turkey (2001), pp. 174-178

689 Commission of the European Communities (1999), p. 26

690 Commission of the European Communities (2001), p. 57

691 Ibid., p. 59

692 E-mail and telephone interviews held from 5th to 7th March 2011

Yavuz, an expert at the Competition Agency, stated that while privatization and competition were both obligations under the EU process, neither of these two IRAs, respectively in the sugar and tobacco sectors were required under the context of "Acquis Communautaire". He further mentioned that after the end of monopoly and the creation of these agencies, several former employees of the monopolies found their way onto the Sugar IRA's executive body. While the Competition Agency contested this conflict of interest, its decisions were not binding for the Sugar IRA. It seems as if the government created these two agencies only to introduce a new form of state presence in these sectors, where politicians were traditionally involved for reasons ranging from employment generation to securing votes before elections[693]. This episode shows how difficult is to change "deep culture", while changing laws and creating IRAs is relatively easy.

On the other hand, while creation of an IRA on state aid was an EU requirement, it was neglected. In June 2001, the government decided to establish an independent body responsible for monitoring state aid to be effective as of January 2003[694]. Nevertheless, Turkey neither adopted the EU state aid legislation nor created an independent state aid monitoring authority during the following years[695]. The chapter on competition of the EU negotiation process was suspended in 2006[696]. The reopening depended on the alignment of Turkey's national legislation regarding state aid with EU competition law.

New law on State Aid in 2010: A solution?

Turkish government introduced a legal framework for state aid, which also created the State Aids Supervisory and Regulatory Agency in 2010, with the objective to reopen the chapter on competition[697]. However, the framework was still far from complying with EU standards under two aspects: The new agency was established under the auspices of the Undersecretariat of Treasury. The Government argued that domestic conditions in every member country varied in this regard. In the Czech Republic, the state aid authority was created

---

693 Commission of the European Communities (2000), p. 8

694 Commission of the European Communities (2001), p. 56

695 Commission of the European Communities (2003, 2004, 2005, 2006, 2008)

696 The European Council decided to partially suspend negotiation talks on eight chapters (Annex 1), one of them being on the customs union (Archick, K. and Kim, J. (2008), p. 5).

697 EU Harmonization Committee, the Turkish Parliament official website

within the Competition Agency, and in Bulgaria within the Ministry of Economic Affairs[698]. The new law was also not applicable to state aids to agriculture and fisheries. Thus, although the motivation of the government to continue negotiations on an important chapter like competition was evident, it continued to reserve the question of state aid to agriculture for political reasons.

Let me now examine improvements in the regulatory framework in the telecommunications and energy sectors, which were on the agenda of the 1999 IMF Stabilization Program.

(4) Telecommunication Agency (2000) and Privatization of Turk Telekom

Reform of Turkey's financial system was not occurring as an isolated phenomenon but was part of a massive program covering many segments of the economy. Sometimes reforms in one area impacted other areas. This was the case with the privatization of Turk Telekom, which became an important issue not only because the EU-inspired regulatory framework created a new competitive market, but it was also considered an important source of revenue for budgetary needs during the year 2000. Thus, the credibility of the December 1999 IMF Stabilization Program partly depended on this. A strong relationship between privatization receipts and public debt management was evident. The sale of Turk Telekom was expected to generate USD 2-2.5 billion, composing around 1 percent of GNP[699]. The revenue was to be transferred directly to the Treasury to meet budgetary needs[700].

To achieve a de-politicized management in the telecommunications sector was a major challenge. In fact, policy makers had to overcome several obstacles in trying to meet the EU regulatory framework while complying with Turkish laws and the Constitution. During this process, the government founded the Telecommunications Agency as an IRA, in 2000, which was also part of an agreement signed with the World Bank[701].

---

698 EU Harmonization Committee, the Turkish Parliament official website

699 IMF (1999), "Letter of Intent" dated 9th December 1999, Section 23

700 Ibid.

701 Zenginobuz, U. (2008), p. 477

I start this section with an overview of the privatization process of the Turk Telekom, initiated in 1994 and achieved only in 2005. This example will show the levels of difficulty encountered introducing structural changes in Turkey.

In the aftermath of the February 1994 financial crisis, the government introduced a Stabilization Program with the IMF[702] on April 5th, which gave priority to the privatization of SOEs, taking also into consideration the need for a legal framework for the privatization of Turk Telekom[703]. The government's motivation was based both on financial stress and on pressure from the international financial institutions. In fact, the IMF imposed the Stabilization Program, while the World Bank collaborated by contributing USD 100 million in loans[704]. These combined efforts thus introduced international standards. On 5th May 1994, Parliament approved Law No. 3'987, allowing the government to proceed with decree-laws on the privatization process within the following three months. The government issued Decree Laws No. 530, 531 and 532 on 30th May 1994. Turk Telekom was established as an SOE through Law No. 4'000 on 6th June 1994[705] and it was included in the privatization portfolio[706]. However, Law No. 3'987 was annulled by the Constitutional Court on 7th July 1994 and consequently, the decree-laws mentioned above were invalidated[707]. In fact, during this initial phase of Turk Telekom's privatization, an adequate framework limiting its monopoly power and encouraging competition was still absent. The Constitutional Court's decision was published in the Official Gazette on 5th August 1994. The main concerns raised by the Court in its decision included the following[708]:

1. Law No. 3987 gave the Government the authority to issue decree-laws with almost no limitations. This was equivalent to delegating the legislative authority to the executive, and was thus not constitutional;

---

[702] Section 3.3.1, "Discussion" point 3)

[703] Ayyildiz, E. (2005), p. 35

[704] Muftuler, B. M. (1997), p. 104

[705] Atiyas, I. and Dogan, P. (2010), p. 263

[706] Up to this date telecommunication services were carried out by a state monopoly called "Posts, Telegraph and Telephone (PTT)", a nation-wide monopoly providing postal and telecommunication services. It was subject to Law No. 406 of 1924 (Telegram and Telephone Law).

[707] Atiyas, I. (2009), p. 3

[708] Ibid., pp. 7, 8

2. Transferring to foreigners control over public services that had strategic value, such as telecommunications and electricity, was unconstitutional;
3. The privatization of natural monopolies would have created private monopolies, which was unconstitutional. Thus, it was necessary to show what sort of measures would be undertaken to ensure oversight and control.

Several government attempts, made in the following years, did not yield any institutional reform to comply with the Constitutional Court's decisions. Finally, international pressure played an important role. During the first month of the IMF's Stabilization Program, in January 2000, Parliament approved the Telecommunication Law (No. 4'502) and decided on the termination of monopoly rights of Turk Telekom by the end of 2003. It also introduced an institutional change by establishing an independent regulatory body, the Telecommunication Agency[709]. The Telecommunication Agency was to have an independent source of finance. The members of the governing body were to be appointed for fixed terms and could not be removed. Its decisions could not be modified by the Ministry, but only by the high administrative court. However, in September 2000 the auction for Turk Telekom failed, causing serious problems because its sale was expected to generate significant revenues to meet the fiscal deficit. The credibility of the 2000 IMF Stabilization Program was in play. Some commentators argued that the auction failure affected investor confidence causing the short-term capital outflows from September to November 2000, which precipitated the ensuing financial crisis[710]. The sudden increase in interest rates in September 2000 (Table 3.13) shows that this could indeed be another factor in the worsening trend. Another tender launched in December 2000 failed as well, showing that investors were increasingly nervous[711]. According to Atiyas and Dogan (2009), they were also discouraged by the regulatory uncertainty and perhaps also the loss of monopoly status by 2003.

Impact of EU regulatory framework

The EU rules contributed to Turkish telecommunications reform in two ways: Increased competition and reduced regulatory uncertainty[712]. The privatization

---

[709] Atiyas, I. (2009), p. 17

[710] Atiyas, I. and Dogan, P. (2009), p. 5

[711] Ibid., p. 6

[712] Ibid., p. 15

process during the 1990s was pursued in the absence of competition considerations. In the 2000s, however, efforts were made to introduce an EU-inspired regulatory framework in order to promote competition. In the absence of such regulation, "natural" monopolies have no incentive to provide access to potential entrants[713]. The EU framework insured reasonable access to networks on a non-discriminatory basis, which prevented turning a state monopoly into a private one. In the end, the Turk Telekom privatization process followed this model. All of this took a long time. Under a risk/return perspective, in the case of regulatory uncertainty, investors show lower willingness to pay for the same expected return, needing to be compensated for extra uncertainty[714]. This explains, in part, the failure of tenders in 2000. In fact, investors were not informed about what type of regulatory obligations they would have to face in the post-privatization phase. Although the policy makers introduced an EU-inspired regulatory framework (Law No. 4'502) and created the Telecommunications Agency as an IRA in 2000, the Agency became independent from the Ministry only in 2001.

Regarding the political dynamics behind this, I emphasize the fact that the governments during the 1980s and the 1990s pursued policies aiming at dismantling public ownership in line with the "Washington Consensus", but they did not create a legal framework promoting competition[715]. The rush privatization during the 1990s turned into a long struggle between Parliament, governments and the Constitutional Court leading to political disputes among coalition partners. Moreover, in such conditions, the whole process was treated as an opportunity for revenue generation, while the main goals (increase in long-term productivity and efficiency) were neglected.

Nevertheless, the July 2002 elections produced a pro-market single-party government (AKP) committed to accelerating privatization and FDI flows. Henceforth, a new phase in the privatization process began. The main features of this period were stable political circumstances favorable to competition, capable of introducing the EU-inspired regulations. The single-party government floated 51 percent of Turk Telekom in 2003, while Law No. 5'189 removed the upper limit on foreign ownership only in 2004, in line with the new FDI policy[716]. Thus, a variety of factors such as decreasing regulatory

---

713 Atiyas, I. and Dogan, P. (2009), p. 16

714 Atiyas, I. and Dogan, p. (2009), p. 15

715 Ibid., p. 6

716 I will discuss in section 4.2.2, the improvements introduced in regulatory framework in 2004 aiming to attract FDI.

uncertainty, together with political and economic stability, gradually contributed to reducing risk perception of investors, leading to a successful privatization tender in 2005[717].

Comparing the Turkish Telecom's regulatory framework with a sample of EU countries

A scorecard comparing institutional capacities in various EU countries and Turkey was published by the European Competitive Telecommunications Association (ECTA)[718] for the years 2008 and 2009. To note in Table 4.9 that Turkey's overall performance[719] is second to last, with bad results for "regulatory environment"[720], and close to average results for "institutional framework"[721]. Regarding the "efficiency" of National Regulatory Authorities (NRAs), the length of time they have been in operation may be relevant[722]. Turkey, as well as Poland and the Czech Republic, had only recently established regulatory agencies and all present a poor performance for "Efficiency of NRA" and "Total results", whereas the United Kingdom, which pioneered this type of institution in the 1980s, showed the best performance of all.

---

[717] The Oger Telecoms Venture Groups (a consortium led by Saudi Oger and Telecom Italia) won the tender for Turk Telekom held in July 2005 and the sale was concluded in December. The 55 percent block sale provided revenue of USD 6.55 billion, a record gain for Turkey in privatization transactions (Bardadioglu and Cetinkaya (2007), p. 7).

[718] "The Scorecard is based on responses submitted by National Regulatory Authorities ("NRAs") and ECTA members to a detailed questionnaire by various stakeholders, consisting of 118 questions grouped in five sections: (1) Overall institutional environment; (2) Key enablers for market entry and network roll out; (3) The NRA's regulatory processes; (4) Application of regulation by the NRA; And (5) regulatory and market outcomes. [....]

On the basis of consolidated responses received for each country from the various stakeholders, a comparative quantitative analysis was carried out, resulting in an overall score for the effectiveness of the regulatory environment in each country." (ECTA, (2009), p. 2)

[719] Ibid., p. 3

[720] ECTA, (2009), p. 7

[721] Ibid., p. 6

[722] Ibid., p. 38

Table 4.9: Comparing the degree of institutional quality in 2008-2009

	Inst. fr. (1)	Reg. env. (2)	Effic. (3)	Appl. reg. (4)	Cond. (5)	Tot. (6)
Turkey	(57) 68	(9) 41	(21) 31	(12) 25	(40) 49	(140) 213
Czech R.	(71) 61	(31) 31	(40) 25	(17) 19	(49) 56	(190) 192
Hungary	(71) 75	(52) 51	(54) 35	(33) 34	(71) 71	(282) 264
Poland	(47) 45	(26) 55	(35) 25	(13) 34	(58) 84	(180) 243
Greece	(78) 69	(35) 45	(40) 33	(28) 49	(65) 55	(247) 251
U.K.	(73) 69	(76) 72	(62) 51	(62) 64	(101) 112	(373) 368

Source: European Competitive Telecommunication Association (2009), pp. 1-39; (1) Institutional Framework; (2) Regulatory Environment; (3) Efficiency of National Regulatory Authorities (NRAs); (4) Application of Regulation by the NRAs; (5) Economic Market Conditions; (6) Total results. The values in parenthesis represent the score in 2008. A higher score corresponds to a higher effectiveness.

(5) Energy Markets Regulatory Agency (2001)

Pro-market reform of electricity and natural gas markets was also a precondition for the IMF's support for Turkey[723]. Together with the sale of Turk Telekom, the expected total proceeds from privatization was USD 7.6 billion, composing 3.5 percent of GNP[724]. The Electricity Market Law, enacted in February 2001, was part of the process aimed to change the national legislation to comply with EU standards. This law introduced free market rules and aimed at restructuring the sector[725]. It also created an independent Energy Market Regulatory Authority in order to ensure a de-politicized decision-making process and to increase the degree of competition and transparency. This was an important step forward in achieving a functioning market economy, increasing capital inflows and promoting a shift towards a longer-term foreign capital. It represented a major break with the inward looking state-sponsored policy framework of the past.

However, the 2008 European Commission Progress Report on Turkey argued that competition remained limited in both the electricity and energy markets and that the Regulatory Agency should implement the regulations more rigorously[726].

---

723 Commission of the European Communities (2001), p. 70

724 IMF (1999), "Letter of Intent" dated 9th December 1999, Section 23

725 State Planning Organization (2001), p. 49

726 Commission of the European Communities (2008), p. 57

(6) Public Procurement Agency (2002)

The government adopted the new Public Procurement Law in 2003 creating an IRA whose main mandate was to serve as a complaints office in all matters related to public procurement and to develop and enact all secondary regulations. However, this law was not in conformity with the "Acquis" in several respects. To begin with, a large number of public entities were exempted from the overall scope of the law and, in 2003, the bidding periods were reduced. The 2004 amendments caused restrictions on competition and full transparency, i.e., it introduced higher thresholds for contract awards notices and there was no information on criteria used.

The 2004 EU Commission Regular Report on Turkey stated that these restrictions were not coherent with the "Acquis"[727]. The 2006 EU Commission Regular Report stated that while the Public Procurement Agency updated thresholds and financial limits for procurement, these remained above EU levels and reduced the opportunity for foreign bidders to apply. Furthermore, bureaucratic procedures prevented wider access to public tenders[728]. The 2008 EU Commission Regular Report argued that a 15 percent price advantage for domestic bidders contradicted the EU principles[729].

In late 2009, the Public Procurement Agency drafted a bill, to be approved by the Parliament, in line with the "Acquis Communautaire", lifting all barriers to foreign interests to bid in public procurement tenders[730]. However, the bill included an article that introduced a transition period for the abolition of the threshold for foreigners. It stated that a threshold value for foreigners could be established as long as Turkey was not a full member of the EU.

In conclusion, although the EU introduced some changes in this area, divergences were still evident in late 2009. While lifting this threshold could have increased FDI flows to Turkey, it seems that Turkish policy makers preferred to retain this conditionality during the negotiations for full membership. This episode shows that national sentiment is still much alive in economic policy supported by both public opinion and domestic lobbies.

---

[727] Commission of the European Communities (2004), p. 81

[728] Commission of the European Communities (2006), p. 36

[729] Commission of the European Communities (2008), p. 43

[730] Today's Zaman (26th November 2009) website

Concluding remarks

The rigor of EU requirements, along with pressure added by the IMF and WB, favored an isomorphic process in Turkey, as discussed in section 2.2. As the case of Turkey shows, while the transition process was initiated by the International Financial Institutions and the EU and best international practices were transferred to Turkey, local divergences stemming from politics, culture, tradition and history proved to be obstacles in achieving expected outcomes. In an attempt to draw some conclusions, let me now discuss the following aspects:

1. Was Turkey too slow in adopting financial reforms? Was the reform process incomplete?

I have considered in this study two major benchmarks, which served as a blueprint for Turkey's transition process to a free market economy. In Chapter 2, I examined the "Washington Consensus" principles, which proposed mainly a deregulated free market economy. The basic logic behind this was that markets are a more efficient instrument for allocating resources than even the wisest regulators or legislators[731]. However, for markets to function efficiently, they must also be competitive. In fact, in Chapter 4, I introduced the EU-inspired regulatory framework, one of the major aims of which is to achieve a functioning market. This implicitly implies creating circumstances for effective competition. Nevertheless, I emphasized the fact that the Competition Agency, created as an obligation of the Customs Union agreement with the EU in 1995, became operational only in 1997 and even then had difficulty in reining in state monopolies and monitoring state aids. Thus, I can state the following:

Conclusion 1: From 1980 to 1997, Turkish financial markets, although completely deregulated, were not effectively competitive.

When competition is ineffective, the government's aim should be to eliminate impediments to competition and to make the ongoing government intervention unnecessary[732]. This was the case in Turkey from 1980 to 2000, which finally saw the establishment of a number of independent regulatory agencies. Particularly important IRAs for my study, in addition to the Competition Agency, include the Capital Markets Board, which became independent from the Ministry of Finance in 1999 and the Banking Regulatory and Supervisory Agency which became operational in late August 2000. This

---

[731] Stelzer, I.M. (2001), p. 13

[732] Ibid., p. 14

reform process was in line with the spirit of another quote from Hernando de Soto:

> "The political sphere, for its part, must be independent of the economic power structure."
>
> [....]
>
> "Deregulation would mean freeing public resources so that the state could use them to ensure that strict, efficient rules of the game were imposed."

Conclusion 2: From 1980 to 2000, the banking sector not only lacked a sound regulatory framework but was also encouraged by the government to finance the public sector deficit. A banking sector that has lost its intermediation function between the financial and the private sector can only impede the achievement of a functioning market economy. Furthermore, the more the government borrowed from the banks the more the banks took unhedged loans on international capital markets, in the end leading to a collapse of confidence.

After the 1994 financial crisis, the government adopted the Customs Union with the EU, but insufficient attention was given to correcting the public sector deficit and to reforming the banking sector.

Conclusion 3: The reform process from 1980 to 2001 was not only slow but was also incomplete, thus contributing to the occurrence of the 1994 and 2001 crises. For example, efforts of policy makers to prevent the monetization of the state budget deficit directly, simply shifted the state financing problem from the use of CBRT resources onto the banking sector with the disastrous consequences that I have discussed.

Among reasons behind this unsatisfactory state of affairs, it is not possible to neglect the political cycles impeding the implementation of proper reforms. After the military government that ruled from 1980 to 1983, the following three major political cycles had a significant impact on the economic decision-making process:

- the single-party ANAP (center-right) governments from 1983 to 1991;

- nine coalition governments from 1991 to 2002[733];
- and the single-party pro-Islamist AKP governments from 2002 onwards.

The unstable period from 1991 to 2002 produced two major financial crises, both of them caused by disorderly public finances. Finally, I can state that the Turkish economy entered into a new phase after the February 2001 currency crisis, during which the IMF and EU-inspired regulatory rules were actually implemented, gaining the confidence of markets. This aspect is crucially important as the interaction between reforms and market confidence can further contribute to the functioning of markets. Turkish policy makers each time introduced radical reforms after crises, i.e., Customs Union in 1995, central bank independence and banking sector restructuring in 2001.

Conclusion 4: Crises themselves give rise to further reforms. Turkey, along with the rest of the world, staggered on from one crisis to another, in a constant process of trial and error. Sometimes errors and crises are the only way to learn to design better institutions as the Turkish case shows us.

2. Was the EU financial regulatory "acquis" itself inadequate?

Let me now ask whether the EU financial regulatory framework presents some gaps. The development of a single or integrated market in financial services in the EU has always been one of its major goals[734]. To address this issue, a Committee of Wise Men was established at the request of the European Council. It identified obstacles to the construction of an integrated financial services market in the EU, in the so-called "Lamfalussy Report" of 2001[735]. While this report argued that the EU legislative system was slow and that the transposition and implementation of EU Directives by member states took excessive time[736], it also highlighted efforts to harmonize regulations within the EU area[737]. One outcome was the Markets in Financial Instruments Directive (MiFID), which aims to supervise the market conduct in the EU and started to be implemented in 2007[738]. MiFID became known as the "Lamfalussy

733 Grand National Assembly of Turkey and Inter-Parliamentary Union (IPU) websites

734 Hertig, G. and Lee, R. (2003), p. 3

735 Ibid.

736 Ibid., p. 4

737 Arthur, T. and Booth, P. (2010), p. 84

738 Ibid., p. 90

Directive"[739]. To note, among the objectives of this directive, promoting cross-border competition, regulating investment banks and over-the-counter markets[740]. New standards for derivatives were also included under the MiFID[741]. However, the 2008-2009 global recession and 2010-2011 European financial crises have shown problems similar to those experienced in Turkey in some member states, notably unsustainable public debt financed largely through the private banking system. The origins of this development are to be found, at least in part, in Basel II regulations, which were supposed to make banks sounder! Concerns were thus raised in the EU regarding the need to introduce further regulations on hedge funds and other private investment funds[742]. While this study is not directly concerned with the global recession of the late 2000s, I nevertheless argue that even in the EU, there are diverging views on what the regulatory framework should be. It seems that first of all, an intellectual effort is needed to identify which institutions should be regulated and how[743]. While under certain circumstances, regulations may be judged as necessary, we have to question whether market failures alone can justify state intervention in the presence of such obvious regulatory failures[744].

This study is in the process of adopting EU regulations in Turkey. Regulation is an ongoing process, especially in the EU, where Directives must be translated into national law. With this purpose, the Turkish Grand National Assembly created an "EU Harmonization Committee" in 2003. Nevertheless, we should be aware of the fact that even in the EU, the adaptation of national legislation to EU directives is a lengthy and complicated process. Moreover, these regulations cannot always avoid failures. During this study, I hope to have shown that a promising approach is to empower independent regulatory agencies with a bottom-up approach to adopting and adapting new regulations, within a general framework of respect for the rule of law and economic realities.

---

[739] Markets in Financial Instruments Directive (2007), EU Business official website

[740] Arthur, T. and Booth, P. (2010), p. 90

[741] Ibid., p. 91

[742] Ibid., p. 28

[743] Ibid., p. 45

[744] Ibid., pp. 125, 126

3. Political support for reform

Identifying the sort of regulation an emerging market like Turkey needs to adopt is not the end of the story, but rather only the initial phase of a long path because Turkey has been adapting an imperfect model from the EU to its own specific circumstances, the latter creating an additional bias. Improvements can be achieved only thanks to the ability to adapt and change in the light of experience, as the Turkish case shows us. When Turkey turned its back on an inward looking state-sponsored economic development model in 1980, it started a long process of trial and error towards a functioning market economy. Three IMF bailouts, a customs union with the EU and later accession negotiations, have all played a part in Turkey's transition process. However, these reforms can never be perfectly "completed" as they always need to be adapted, not only to specific local conditions but also to changes in conditions over time. In the end, Turkey had to find the political will to pursue this path.

On the other hand, I emphasize that dynamics behind political will to pursue reforms requires further research, as the post-2002 reform process has been led by pro-Islamist AKP party. To note that the leaders of the latter were, during the 1980s and 1990s, in favor of Islamic customs and rules in political and daily life contradicting thus certain basic principles of the EU. While full EU membership is a long and complicated process, it seems that the pro-Islamist interest groups in the country can benefit at least from the initial phase of this process. For instance, the military presence in political life always protected the secular basis of the Republic and outlawed anti-secular activities. It seems that the EU membership process can now outlaw the military influence in political life. Thus, the short-term and long-term objectives of the pro-Islamist AKP party can diverge, making the whole EU full membership process more complex. Nevertheless, this political will, whatever objective it pursued in the long term, has been sufficient to reinforce EU-inspired reforms in the short-run, from 2002 onwards. Time alone will tell whether the AKP can genuinely combine a de-politicized modern economy with a pro-Islamist approach, as Islamic customs and rules contradict both the EU and the traditional Turkish secular lifestyle. Nevertheless, the pro-Islamist Fethullah Gulen terrorist organization-led unsuccessful military intervention on 15th July 2016 show that anti-secular pro-Islamist interest groups were largely allowed to be infiltrated into the state apparatus, from armed and police forces to justice and education during the AKP single party governments, from 2002 onwards. This also signals an attempt to achieve a wide-scale internal transformation of Turkey towards political Islam, during the ongoing EU negotiations process!

I now turn to another important step in achieving a functioning market economy: The privatization of state-owned enterprises. I mentioned in the previous section that privatization of the telecommunications and energy sectors were essential elements of the 1999 IMF Stabilization Program. I will show, in the next section, how the privatization process accelerated after 2004.

4.2. Regulatory Reforms on Privatizations, FDI and Property Rights

I emphasized in section 1.6 that the Copenhagen (economic) criteria for full membership require, first of all, "the existence of a functioning market economy", i.e., "the existence of a broad consensus about the essentials of economic policy" and "macroeconomic stability". This study mainly focused on the CBRT independence to fulfill these two conditions for being a functioning market economy.

The Copenhagen (economic) criteria for full membership require also "the capacity to cope with competitive pressures and market forces within the Union". In this section, I will examine the adoption of the EU-inspired rules to create a competitive regulatory framework and to eliminate administrative obstacles, aiming both to encourage privatizations and to attract FDI. I will also overview the property rights situation since the beginning of the foundation of the Republic. This will shed light also on some historical features and political aspects that are important in evaluating the institutional transformation from a traditionally statist approach to a free market one. On the other hand, the creation of a mortgage market from 2007 onwards can have a positive impact on financial markets in the near future, as Turkey never had a developed credit market. I will examine in sub-sections 4.2.1, 4.2.2 and 4.2.3, respectively major topics of this section.

4.2.1. Privatizations

Introduction

In this section, let me first review the legal basis behind the privatization process from 1980 to 1998 during which gross privatization revenues totaled USD 4.5 billion[745]. I shall compare this period with 1999-2010, during which

---

[745] Ficici, A. (2001), p. 1

receipts from privatization reached USD 42 billion. An examination of the dynamics behind these two periods will provide insight on problems related to the Turkish case. Thus, I will examine, in sub-section 4.2.1.1, improvements in the composition of the privatization portfolio after the adoption of the EU-inspired institutional framework from 1999 to 2002 as well as the growing share of FDI in recently privatized SOEs. To note that overall progress in the privatization process clearly brought improved efficiency and promoted the creation of a functioning market economy.

Legal basis of the privatization process: an adequate framework to promote competition in markets?

The Turkish story on privatization starts with the center-right AP government's decision to introduce "Washington Consensus" principles on 24th January 1980, of which one of the leading policy recommendations was privatization of inefficient SOEs. This implied a shift away from public ownership inward looking development plans to a free market open economy based supply-side approach, where state action was to be kept to a minimum. However, the political, economic and social disorders led to a military *coup* on 12th September 1980. The generals dissolved the parliament, political parties, trade unions and civil society organizations. However, TUSIAD –an NGO founded by major corporate holdings– remained untouched[746]. In 1983, the armed forces stepped aside and supported a single-party government led by Turgut Ozal, a former TUSIAD member, leader of the newly founded political party ANAP and winner of 1983 elections[747]. Several ministers in his cabinet (including the minister of finance, customs and justice, and two state ministers) had close ties with TUSIAD[748]. Thus, the privileged status of leading family holdings was maintained as a major interest group.

Thanks to TUSIAD support, in addition to that of generals, Turgut Ozal managed unpopular reforms through decree-laws in a context where political opposition was highly limited due to armed forces' monitoring. The government put special emphasis on privatization together with capital account and foreign trade liberalization in 1984. Traditionally, all imports were regulated by import programs implying a variety of trade restricting measures

---

746 Karadag, R. (2010), p. 13

747 We observed in sections 2.2.1 and 3.3.1 that Turgut Ozal was a key figure in introducing the "Washington Consensus" principles in 24th January 1980 and implementing them during the whole decade.

748 Karadag, R. (2010), p. 16

from import quotas, import bans to tariffs and tariff-like taxes and surcharges. Partial reforms in 1981 and a major one in 1984 lifted almost all import quotas and bans[749]. On the other hand, the government policy to promote exports ranged from a depreciating real exchange rate to providing subsidized export credits. While in the early 1980s the government used the CBRT resources to promote exports, after 1984 the CBRT Short-term Cash Advance Facility decreased to low levels and commercial banks became major lenders in the export credit market[750]. The deregulation process involved increased reliance on private actors and market forces taking over functions and responsibilities that were previously regarded as properly being within the governmental sphere[751]. Hence, the pricing policy of the SOEs became crucially important[752]. Their prices were adjusted frequently from 1980 to 1984 to meet financial targets set by the IMF and corresponding to the liberalization process. However, they were still subject to political constraints imposed by the government. The first laws on the privatization of SOEs were introduced in 1984, a few months after the formation of the democratically elected single-party ANAP government[753]. The government nominated, two years later, the New York-based Morgan Guaranty Bank to carry out the privatization process[754]. It prepared a privatization master plan and proposed the following:

- transferring the decision-making process from the public to private sector;
- promoting competition, improving efficiency and increasing the productivity of SOEs;
- enabling a wider distribution of share ownership;
- reducing the financial burden of the SOEs in the general budget;
- and raising revenue for the Treasury.

---

749 Olgun, H. and Togan, S. (1989), pp. 949, 950

750 Central Bank of the Republic of Turkey (2002b), p. 7

751 Feigenbaum, H., Henig, J. and Hamnett, C. (2003), p. 1

752 Celasun, M. and Arslan, I. (2001), p. 230

753 Law No. 2'983 (Law on the encouragement of savings and acceleration of public investments) and the Decree-Law No. 233 adopted on, respectively, 29th February and 8th June 1984 (Privatization Administration, Turkish Prime Ministry, Republic of Turkey official website).

754 Yeldan, E. (2005), p. 12

Furthermore, the Master Plan included a study of the Turkish legal system to determine the factors that might present legal issues in the privatization process[755]. It concluded that the Turkish Constitution and relevant laws did not outlaw privatization. However, it also noted that specific laws did not exist to guide a privatization process. Despite this vagueness of legal circumstances, the government attempted to carry out the process without making the necessary constitutional and legal changes. Turgut Ozal preferred ruling by decree[756], effectively replacing parliamentary procedures and constraints in order to accelerate the liberalization process and to overcome interest group pressures. Opposing groups led mainly by left-wing political parties, contested this procedure, arguing that the law-making power belonged to parliament and not to the government leaders. However, ANAP as a single-party government, supported by the military, maintained its policy and enacted a more comprehensive legal basis in 1986[757], explaining objectives and methods of the privatization program. The overall legal framework became only more complex because it attempted to quickly address the needs of circumstances through decree-laws and amendments. It created new bodies or transferred their mandates, making the whole framework appear disorganized[758]. To note that there were no Independent Regulatory Agencies at that time. The sole regulatory agency created in 1982, the Capital Market Board, was "related" to Ministry and became independent only in 1999.

During the 1990s, former political leaders were back on the scene, involved in several coalition governments, reflecting a highly fragmented political picture[759]. Coalition partners provoked disputes to redistribute and claim state resources that Turgut Ozal alone had controlled during the previous decade. The result was scandals due to some politicians' relationship with bankers and even criminal organizations in an attempt to influence privatization auctions[760]. Oyak, contrary to its initial mandate to function as a pension fund[761], became a conglomerate with large holdings in several sectors ranging

---

755 Ertuna, O. (1998), p. 15

756 Onis, Z. (2004), p. 2

757 Decree Law concerning the Denationalization of Public Economic Enterprises, enacted on 28th May 1986 (Privatization Administration, Turkish Prime Ministry, Republic of Turkey, official website).

758 Atiyas, I. (2009), p. 6

759 See Annex 3

760 Atiyas, I. and Emil, F. (2005), pp. 17, 18

761 See under the "Historical background on the Turkish economy" of section 2.2

from iron and steel, petroleum, cement, and automotive industries to insurance, investment, banking, and tourism.

Frequently changing coalition governments impeded successful privatization. The reason behind this was not only statist-minded opponents but also strongly pro-market politicians who supported the privatization process while in power but strove to impede it when they were in the opposition[762]. Patronage politics was one of the features of Turkish political life with parties behaving as networks serving their clients by channeling public resources to their supporters. Opponents utilized the weaknesses in the legal framework and contested the procedure before the Constitutional Court[763], resulting in ineffectiveness. For example, in the first half of 1989, 90 percent of Citosan, a large cement SOE, was sold to Société Ciment Français and 70 percent of Usas, an airline catering service, was sold to Scandinavian Airlines. The two opposition parties, the pro-market (center-right) DYP and statist (center-left) SHP appealed to the Constitutional Court and succeeded in blocking the deals. The DYP-SHP government of 1991 to 1995 would promote the privatization process, which in turn was contested by opposition forces[764].

After the 1994 financial crisis, the IMF Stabilization Program, adopted on April 5th of the same year, attempted to de-politicize the pricing mechanism by permitting SOE management to raise prices in line with costs in order to get them to behave like normal market-driven firms. We saw in section 4.1.4 the difficulties encountered while privatizing Turk Telekom[765]. The Turkish Constitution did not rule out privatization as long as it was accompanied by an appropriate legal framework to impede the formation of private monopolies[766]. The Constitutional Court's decisions invalidating the government's privatization process, although an obstacle to the implementation of the privatization program, encouraged policy makers to establish institutions for a functioning competitive system. In fact, as we have already seen in the previous

---

762 Ercan, M. R. and Onis, Z. (2000), p. 17

763 Ibid., p. 32, Atiyas, I. (2009), p. 7

764 Atiyas, I. (2009), p. 7

765 Ayyildiz, E. (2005), p. 35

766 Article 167 of the Turkish Constitution titled "Supervision of Markets and Regulation of Foreign Trade" states: "The State is entrusted with the duty and responsibility to take the measures that ensure and improve the proper and organized functioning of markets for money, credit, capital, goods and services, and to prevent monopolization and cartelization likely to emerge in markets *de facto* or as a result of agreement" (International Constitutional Law official website).

section on the privatization of Turk Telekom, the privatization of a state monopoly does not always automatically lead to a competitive market structure. In the case of natural monopolies, firms' expected efficiency gains depend on an environment that is both regulated and competitive[767]. In the absence of an adequate regulatory framework coherent with the country's institutional endowment, a state monopoly could be transformed into a private monopoly without achieving any real change in efficiency[768].

The enactment of a new law on privatization and the establishment of an authority enforcing competition were deemed necessary to satisfy not only article 167 of the Constitution, but also the Customs Union being negotiated at the same time with the EU[769]. Hence, we see that internal and external forces were behind the two laws enacted in 1994[770]:

1. The Privatization Law (No. 4'046) entered into force on 27th November 1994. This law provided an adequate framework, funds, and appropriate mechanisms to accelerate the privatization process. It established the "Privatization High Council" and the "Privatization Administration" to facilitate the decision-making process[771];
2. The Law on the Protection of Competition[772] entered into force on 13th December 1994, using articles 81 and 82[773] of the Treaty of Rome as a

---

767 I provide in Annex 4 the needed regulatory options on pricing methodologies in case of natural monopolies. Whereas, in this section our central concern is with the majority of privatization cases, i.e., on normal products for which there was no justification for public ownership from an economic theory point of view. In other words, there was not much need for post-privatization regulation.

768 Aybar, C. B., Guney, E. S. and Suel, H. (1998), p. 30

769 In section 3.3.2, we saw that the Customs Union agreement with the EU was signed on 6th March 1995 and entered into force on 1st January 1996.

770 The EEC-Turkey Association Agreement (Ankara Agreement) of 12th September 1963 provides (art.16) that principles cited under the clauses of the Treaty of Rome relating to competition, tax and harmonization of legislation apply to the partnership (Turkish Competition Authority official website).

771 The "Privatization High Council" was the ultimate decision-making body. It was headed by the Prime Minister. The "Privatization Administration" was the executive body for the privatization process. It was a legal public entity with its own budget, reporting directly to the Prime Minister. Its principal duty was to execute the decisions of Privatization High Council (Privatization Administration, Turkish Prime Ministry, Republic of Turkey official website, "Privatization Endeavor in Turkey").

772 Law on the Protection of Competition (1994), p. 1

773 Official Journal of the European Union (2006), pp. 73-75, available on Official Journal of the European Union website.

source[774]. Its main effect was the introduction of EU antitrust rules. The Competition Agency was established as the body responsible for implementing the new law[775].

4.2.1.1. Privatization portfolio composition and FDI proportion

I will examine in this section the sectors, which became subject to privatization from 1980 to 2010. Figure 4.1 shows the gross privatization revenues to GDP ratio in the pre- and post-institutional and regulatory reform period. Overall receipts were negligible during the 1990s despite the 1994 privatization law and the 1995 Customs Union agreement. We observe peaks in 1998 and 2000, but these were related to single specific privatization revenues, namely, minority asset sales of Is Bank in 1998 and GSM sales of Turk Telekom in 2000. However, after the completion of regulatory and institutional reforms, identified with the introduction of a "regulatory state" through the creation of IRAs, gross accumulated revenue reached USD 42 billion by 2010[776]. Table 4.10 provides a breakdown of privatization revenues corresponding to methods used from 1985 to 2010, where the sum of Block and Asset sales compose 80 percent of the total privatization revenues, while Table 4.11 illustrates the composition of sectors within the sum of Block and Asset Sales. I consider only privatization implementations through Block Sales and Asset Sales because the "BIST sale" and "public offering" involve small shares among many investors. However, my aim is also to highlight the FDI proportion of privatized SOEs, the definition of which excludes investors with shares smaller than 10 percent in the privatized firm. This is why I do not take privatization revenues through "BIST sale" and "public offering" into consideration.

---

774 Turkish Competition Authority, official website

775 It began its operations in November 1997 (Zenginobuz, U. (2008), p. 480).

776 Privatization Administration, Turkish Prime Ministry, Republic of Turkey official website

Fig. 4.1: Privatization revenues from 1980s to 2010, in percentage of GDP

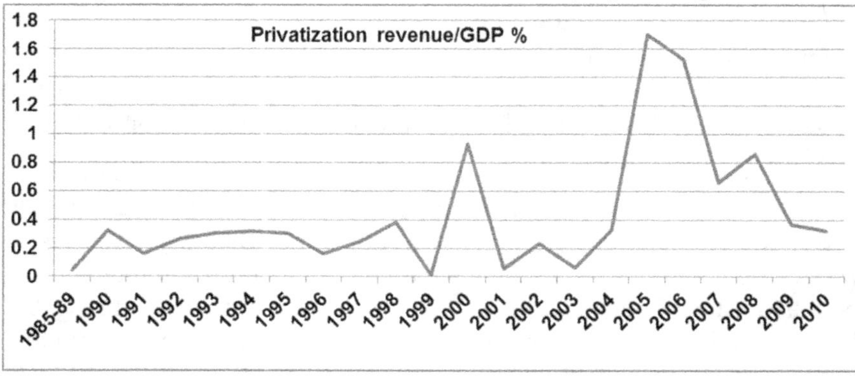

Source: Privatization Administration, World Bank

Table 4.10: Privatization revenues according to method used, 1985-2010

	USD	Percentage
Block Sale	20'257'066'639	48.2
Asset Sale	13'389'424'251	31.8
ISE Sale	1'261'053'768	3.0
Public Offering	7'091'202'610	16.9
Total	41'998'747'268	99.9

Source: Privatization Administration, Turkish Prime Ministry, Republic of Turkey official website; BIST stands for Borsa Istanbul

In Table 4.11, the remaining sectors included in "others" composed each less than 1 percent of the total (block and asset sales) and covered a variety of sectors ranging from tire manufacturing, automobile distributor, pulp and paper production, sugar processing, textile and electricity production, to maritime, airport handling services, tourism and supermarket chains[777].

777 Privatization Administration, Turkish Prime Ministry, Republic of Turkey official website

Table 4.11: Sub-division of sectors composing Block and Asset sales, 1985-2010

Block + Asset Sales	Percentage
Petro-chemicals	22.4
Turk Telekom	19.5
Banking and Insurance	14.4
Iron and Steel	9.1
Cigarettes and Alcoholic beverages	8.2
Cements	2.7
Mining	2.1
Others	21.6
Total	100.0

Source: Privatization Administration, Turkish Prime Ministry, Republic of Turkey official website

The completion of 1999-2002 regulatory reforms and the consequent EU-inspired competitive market conditions were a major factor behind the accelerated privatization process, starting in the year 2004. All these reforms[778] contributed to reducing regulatory uncertainty. We observe a historical peak in 2005 due to the sale of Turk Telekom[779] (see Fig. 4.3) to non-resident investors (constituting 87.5 percent of total "block and asset sale" revenue and 65.3 percent of FDI flows for 2005). This was the highest revenue received from the privatization of an SOE.

What was the proportion of FDI flows within privatization revenues?

Regulatory reforms increased the attractiveness of Turkey's business environment, influencing both resident and non-resident investors' decisions. We observed in Table 4.10 that the block and asset sales generated USD 33.6 billion in privatization revenue, of which 33.9 percent (USD 11.4 billion) corresponded to FDI flows from 1985 to 2010 (Fig. 4.2). Table 4.12 provides information on the composition of the latter within the same period. To note that a significant amount of FDI related to privatization was received in the

---

[778] including reforms in the banking sector (as we saw in section 4.1.4) and government policy to attract FDI flows (as we will see in section 4.2.2.3)

[779] The IRA created in 2000 in the telecommunications sector adopted a regulation introducing the Price Cap mechanism for tariffs in September 2001, the most widely used method in Europe. Turk Telekom became subject to Price Cap method in January 2002 (Commission of the European Communities (2002), pp. 75, 105). The overview on pricing methods in Annex 4 provides insight on incentive mechanisms aiming to enhance competition. The logic behind this offers a wider perspective on policy makers' efforts to satisfy the Constitutional Court's preoccupation with the measures to be taken to avoid an eventual private monopoly.

second half of the 2000s. Thus, Figure 4.3 shows FDI and privatization revenue relative to GDP and the proportion of the former in the latter. Through these data, I prove the following: The statist development policies inherited from the 1930s led policy makers in the 1980s to deregulate markets in line with "Washington Consensus" principles. However, EU-inspired "regulatory state" was not present in Turkey in the 1980s and 1990s, during which privatization episodes without competitive market conditions led the Constitutional Court to annul several cases. Weak privatization receipts and FDI flows also show that regulatory uncertainty together with macroeconomic instability was a major obstacle in effectively terminating public monopolies in favor of the private initiative. However, the regulatory reforms completed from 1999 to 2002 created circumstances in which the Turkish regulatory state could supervise the interaction between private economic agents, both resident and non-resident. The substantial shift in privatization revenues and FDI flows shows a reduction in economic nationalism inherited from the 1930s.

Fig. 4.2: Block + Asset Sales: FDI composition, in percentage

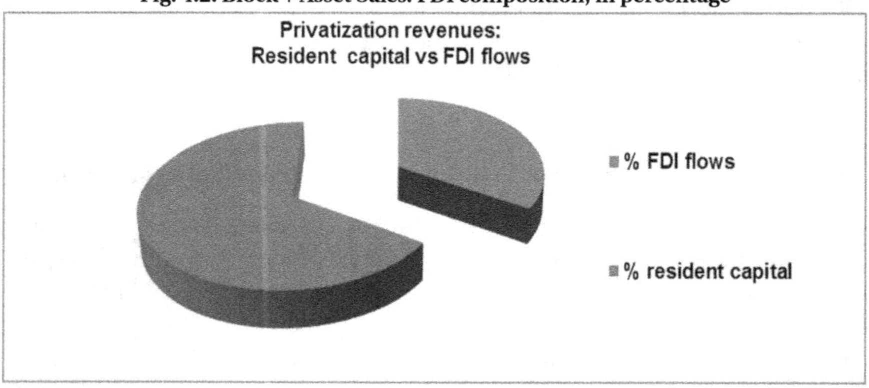

Source: Privatization Administration, Turkish Prime Ministry, Republic of Turkey and Central Bank of Turkey official websites

Table 4.12: List of Privatized Corporate holdings

Date	TR Company	FDI Company	Sector	Million USD
Block Sales			9'075.6	
09.08.1989	Afyon Cimento	Société Ciment Français	Ciment	13.0
08.09.1989	Ankara Cimento	Société Ciment Français	Ciment	33.0
08.09.1989	Balikesir Cimento	Société Ciment Français	Ciment	23.0
08.09.1989	Pinarhisar Cimento	Société Ciment Français	Ciment	25.0
08.09.1989	Soke Cimento	Société Ciment Français	Ciment	11.0
22.02.1991	USAS	SAS	Airport Serv.	14.5
22.02.1991	TOFAS	FIAT Auto Spa	Otomotive	13.2
17.05.1991	Turk Kablo	NOKIA Int. Finnish Fund	Telec.	11.0
01.07.1991	Gunes Sigorta	Gan International	Insurance	18.9
01.03.1993	Netas	Northern Telekom	Telec.	26.0
19.08.1993	Teletas	Alcatel B.V.	Telec.	21.0
10.12.1993	AEG Eti AS	AEG Aktiengesellschhaft	Electronics	2.2
21.06.1994	AEG Eti AS	AEG Aktiengesellschhaft	Electronics	5.9
14.11.2005	Turk Telekom AS	Oger Telecoms	Telec.	6'550.0
16.05.2006	Basak Sigorta AS	Groupama International	Insurance	204.4
16.05.2006	Basak Emeklilik AS	Groupama International	Pension Fund	63.6
20.05.2008	PETKIM	Socar&Turcas-Incaz OGG	Petro-chem.	2'040.0
Asset Sales				2'320.0
24.06.2008	TEKEL Cigarettes Industry A.S.	BRITISH AMERICAN TOBACCO A.Ş.	Cigarettes	1'720.0
11.02.2009	Sakarya Electricity Distribution A.S.	Akcez O.G.G.	Electricity	600.0
Total (Block Sale + Asset Sale)				11'395.6

Source: Privatization Administration, Turkish Prime Ministry, Republic of Turkey official website

Fig. 4.3: Privatization revenues versus FDI flow size, in percentage, 1985-2010

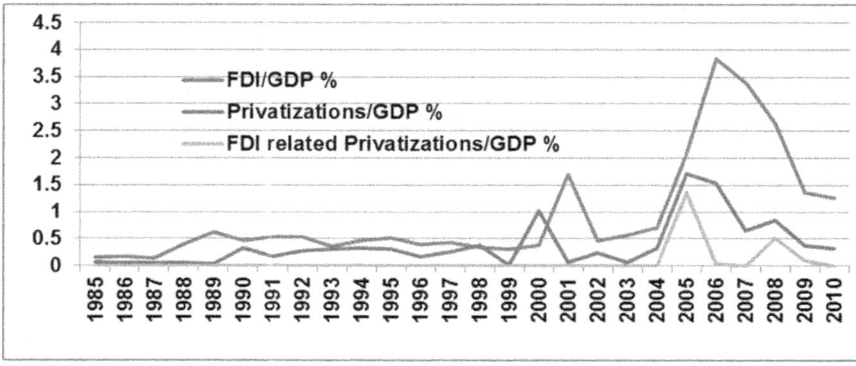

Source: Turkish Prime Ministry, Privatization Administration, and Turkish Central Bank official websites

Concluding remarks

In a final segment, let me examine how the changing state bureaucracy viewed the EU-inspired reforms regarding FDI flows.

Major reasons behind the delays in the structural reform process of the 1990s

We observed in chapters 2 and 3 that, despite the pursuit of privatization during the 1980s and 1990s, there lacked an adequate institutional framework allowing competition in line with the EU principles. Moreover, reforms became operational only after long delays. For instance, policy makers created the Competition Agency in 1994 in accordance with the Customs Union agreement with the EU. However, coalition governments and industrial groups prevented the Agency from becoming operational until 1997. Why?

During the government formation process, the primary concern of politicians was which ministries would be able to monitor which agencies[780]. However, successful structural reform requires cooperation among all state agencies. Let us suppose a coalition government composed of three political parties, where A controlled the Treasury, B controlled the Privatization Administration and C controlled public banks, each striving to channel state resources in favor of its own constituency. Let us suppose that A and B belong

[780] Atiyas, I. and Dogan, P. (2009), p. 5

to reformist parties but C prefers to provide cheap credit to farmers. In such a case A and B would also prefer not to become reformist. In fact, if one party thinks that another (or the other two) will not respect reforms, it is also convenient for this party not to respect them, because through unilateral efforts, not only will reforms be unsuccessful, but the reformist party also loses votes[781]. Thus, if there is no cooperation among coalition partners, the following non-cooperative Nash equilibrium emerges: It is convenient for each party to avoid the introduction of reforms or to impede their functioning. This was, in fact, one of the major reasons behind the delays in the reform process in Turkey during the 1990s.

Changing politico-bureaucratic circumstances in the 2000s

To note that, despite its harmful impact on the economy and society, the February 2001 crisis broke this negative equilibrium[782], where each coalition partner continued to give priority to the interests of its constituency at the expense of state resources. After the most severe currency crisis of Turkish history, electors no longer voted for old politicians, considering them corrupt and responsible for the crisis, and the pro-Islamist AKP won the 2002 general elections, thereby creating a new equilibrium. Due to its nature as a single-party government, cooperation among state agencies was now easily achieved.

Let me now examine, in the next section, the impact of institutional reforms in an area closely related to privatizations: FDI flows. In fact, an increase in privatization revenues during 2004-2005 coincided with record-breaking FDI flows in the same period. We observed in the previous section that a portion of privatization revenues was due to inward FDI flows.

During the 2000s, not only was the state bureaucracy reshaped, but also emerged a new interest group favored by the pro-Islamist AKP government: A new Islamist business *élite* began to replace the military and TUSIAD member family holdings. Undoubtedly, increased FDI flows also constitute a new interest group, which shows that the Turkish economy gained the confidence of global investors, thanks to regulatory and institutional reforms.

Thus, I examine, in the next section, the reasons why Turkey had traditionally been unable to attract FDI in the previous decades, what

---

781 Atiyas, I. and Emil, F. (2005), p. 11

782 Ibid.

circumstances ultimately made reforms possible and what progress was achieved in attracting FDI inflows during the 2000s. I will consider inward FDI flows as a barometer of the effectiveness of EU-inspired regulatory and institutional reforms.

4.2.2. FDI

Introduction

Governments constantly seek to improve the investment climate as their countries compete with others in an attempt to attract FDI. While Turkey had historically experienced very low FDI levels[783], a more general liberalization program initiated in 1980[784] aimed among other things to attract FDI. To note in Figure 4.4 that full capital account liberalization in 1989 had a positive impact.

Fig. 4.4: FDI inflows during the 1980s, in million USD

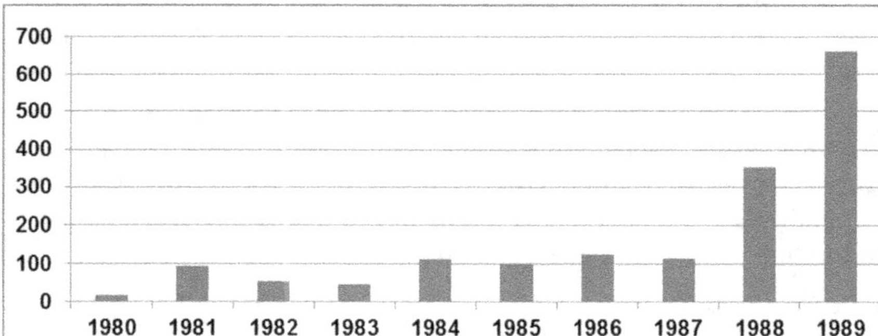

Source: World Bank

Nevertheless, despite increased FDI flows after 1989, the level was still low when compared with my sample of EU countries for the same period. Table 4.13 shows that FDI flows to three EU countries (Greece, Portugal, and Spain) were higher than those to Turkey, until the second half of the 2000s, with a

---

[783] By the end-1960s the cumulative FDI stock was only USD 17.3 million, reaching USD 228.1 million by the end-1970s (Erdilek, A. (2006), p. 12).

[784] Foreign Capital Framework Decree No. 8/126 of 25th January 1980 and Foreign Capital Framework Decree No. 86/10'353, of 13th March 1986, were major pieces of legislation introduced during the 1980s, amending Law No. 6'224 of 1954, thus aiming to attract FDI (Atac, O. A. and Aydin, N. (1990), p. 569).

significant difference with respect to Spain and Portugal. A comparison with Poland, Hungary, and the Czech Republic which did not join the EU until 1st May 2004, is even more surprising, given that the liberalization process in Turkey started one decade before these countries had left the socialist regime. They succeeded in attracting more FDI than Turkey only a few years after opening their economies to the rest of the world[785]. Thus, comparing the FDI flows to Turkey to those of Poland, Hungary and the Czech Republic by 1995 leads me to the following question: Why could Turkey not attract FDI during the 1990s?

Table 4.13: FDI flows, in million USD, Turkey versus a sample of EU members, 1989-2009

	Turkey	Greece	Portugal	Spain	Poland	Hungary	Czech R.
1989	663	752	1'736	8'428	11	-	-
1990	684	1'050	2'610	13'983	89	553	-
1991	810	1'135	2'448	12'492	291	1'462	-
1992	844	1'144	1'873	13'275	678	1'479	-
1993	636	977	1'533	9'681	1'715	2'349	654
1994	608	981	1'269	9'215	1'875	1'144	878
1995	885	1'053	684	8'085	3'659.	4'804	2'567
1996	722	1'058	1'346	9'623	4'498	3'288	1'435
1997	805	984	2'356	8'937	4'908	4'154	1'286
1998	940	-	3'004	14'282	6'365	3'343	3'700
1999	783	567	1'167	18'523	7'270	3'307	6'312
2000	982	1'083	6'681	38'835	9'343	2'770	4'987
2001	335	1'585	6'173	28'163	5'714	3'943	5'640
2002	108	53	1'754	39'993	4'131	3'012	8'496
2003	170	1'331	7'254	25'606	4'589	2'177	2'021
2004	2'785	2'105	1'660	24'791	12'716	4'281	4'977
2005	10'031	657	4'058	24'572	10'309	7'626	11'602
2006	20'185	5'400	10'968	31'171	19'876	19'522	5'521
2007	22'047	1'958	2'969	66'682	23'651	70'843	10'606
2008	18'269	5'303	4'681	74'226	14'978	66'893	6'572
2009	7'849	2'419	2'807	6'451	13'796	2'783	2'665

Source: World Bank

785 The Polish market had FDI inflows during the 1980s as well, although amounts were low, whereas starting by 1990 with a more liberalized economy, flows increased considerably. Hungary became accessible in 1991, the Czech Republic in 1993.

Several events occurred during the 1990s, which caused the Turkish economy to appear either more or less attractive to foreign investors during the 1990s:

- The currency crises of 1980 and 1994 were severe shocks to economy, increasing the overall country risk exposure and harming Turkey's reputation for proper macroeconomic management;
- Further legal framework changes aimed at making the Turkish market more accessible to foreigners were undertaken in the mid-1990s[786];
- The Customs Union agreement with the EU, enacted in 1996, was a further step towards integration with global markets[787];
- The 1997 East Asian and the 1998 Russian crises caused capital flight from emerging markets, including Turkey;
- An amendment to the Constitution in August 1999, allowing international arbitration for non-resident investors made Turkey a more attractive location;
- The European Council's Helsinki Summit accepted Turkey as a candidate country for a full EU membership on 11th December 1999.

All these events occurred during a politically unstable period with nine fragile coalition governments being formed during the span of a decade. Pro-Islamist trends and ethnic terrorism were additional factors polarizing and fragmenting the political landscape. Under these unstable macro and political circumstances, the regulatory and institutional framework, though showing some improvements, was far from achieving international standards. In fact, while markets were already completely deregulated there were no independent regulatory agencies (IRAs) to ensure the effective functioning of institutions and markets (see chapters 2 and 3). From a non-resident's perspective, investing in Turkey was still highly risky with an unpredictable return due to volatile macro conditions and rapidly changing governments. Institutional uncertainty was an additional factor increasing risk. Moreover, when the size of the Turkish

---

[786] Decree 95/6'990 of 7th June 1995 replaced Decree 92/2'789 issued on 4th March 1992. The latter empowered the General Directorate of Foreign Investment of Treasury to approve foreign investment related operations and transactions. These included reviewing and registering licensing, franchising, know-how, technical assistance and management agreements (for details, see Paksoy, S. (1996), pp. 243-247, available on Paksoy website).

[787] Examined in Chapter 3, section 3.3.2.1

economy and its population are taken into consideration, divergence from other countries in the sample was even bigger. In fact, Turkey is the most populated country in the sample and has the highest GDP after Spain. Tables 4.14 and 4.15 provide a comparison of the relative values of FDI flows. To note that Turkish relative FDI (per capita and with respect to GDP) figures became comparable with other countries in the sample in the post-regulatory reform period, only by the year 2005.

Table 4.14: FDI per capita, in USD, Turkey versus a sample of EU members, 1989-2009

	TR	GR	PORT	SP	POL	HUN	CZ. R.
1989	1'202	7'452	17'479	21'740	29	-	-
1990	1'219	10'333	26'374	36'006	233	5'338	-
1991	1'419	11'062	24'644	32'082	760	14'095	-
1992	1'452	11'031	18'803	33'981	1'767	14'264	-
1993	1'075	9'335	15'378	24'704	4'459	22'686	6'333
1994	1'010	9'295	12'699	23'452	4'864	11'061	8'496
1995	1'445	9'902	6'827	20'528	9'482	46'511	24'853
1996	1'159	9'879	13'395	24'376	11'647	31'896	13'914
1997	1'271	9'130	23'358	22'578	12'698	40'375	12'485
1998	1'459	-	29'660	35'956	16'461	32'562	35'941
1999	1'196	5'212	11'476	46'394	18'805	32'309	61'388
2000	1'478	9'924	65'291	96'309	24'297	27'128	48'637
2001	4'970	14'475	59'981	69'163	14'939	382'712	55'171
2002	1'581	482	16'924	96'803	10'805	29'658	83'260
2003	2'454	12'080	69'484	60'962	12'011	21'494	19'802
2004	3'964	19'029	15'812	58'071	33'303	42'364	48'725
2005	14'094	5'922	38'473	56'621	27'011	75'603	113'346
2006	28'000	48'443	103'630	70'658	52'111	193'839	53'770
2007	30'199	17'499	27'996	148'581	62'042	704'502	102'631
2008	24'716	47'197	44'069	162'935	39'285	666'385	63'049
2009	10'491	21'441	26'406	14'037	36'162	27'771	25'410

Source: World Bank, abbreviated country names stand for respectively, Turkey, Greece, Portugal, Spain, Poland, Hungary and the Czech Republic

Table 4.15: FDI/GDP ratio, in percentage, Turkey versus a sample of EU members, 1989-2009

	TR	GR	PORT	SP	POL	HUN	CZ. R.
1989	0.6	1.0	2.9	2.1	0.01	-	-
1990	0.5	1.1	3.5	2.7	0.2	1.7	-
1991	0.5	1.1	2.9	2.2	0.4	4.4	-
1992	0.5	1.0	1.8	2.2	0.8	4.0	-
1993	0,4	0.9	1.7	1.9	2.0	6.1	1.9
1994	0.5	0.9	1.3	1.8	1.9	2.8	2.1
1995	0.5	0.8	0.6	1.4	2.6	10.8	4.6
1996	0.4	0.8	1.1	1.5	2.9	7.3	2.3
1997	0.4	0.7	2.1	1.6	3.1	9.1	2.3
1998	0.3	-	2.5	2.4	3.7	7.1	36.0
1999	0.3	0.4	1.0	3.0	4.3	6.9	10.5
2000	0.4	0.9	5.7	6.7	5.5	5.8	8.8
2001	1.7	1.2	5.1	4.6	3.0	7.4	9.1
2002	0.5	0.03	1.3	5.8	2.1	4.5	11.3
2003	0.6	0.7	4.5	2.9	2.1	2.6	2.2
2004	0.7	0.9	0.9	2.4	5.0	4.2	4.5
2005	2.1	0.3	2.1	2.2	3.4	6.9	9.3
2006	3.8	2.0	5.5	2.5	5.8	17.3	3.9
2007	3.4	0.6	1.3	4.6	5.6	51.1	6.1
2008	2.5	1.5	1.9	4.7	2.8	43.2	3.0
2009	1.3	0.7	1.2	0.4	3.2	2.2	1.4

Source: World Bank, abbreviated country names stand for respectively, Turkey, Greece, Portugal, Spain, Poland, Hungary and the Czech Republic

In addition, Turkey's ranking in the World Bank's Doing Business Index improved during this period (Table 4.16).

Table 4.16: Doing Business Ranking

	Nb. of countries	Turkey's ranking
2006	155	84
2007	175	65
2008	178	60
2009	181	59
2010	183	60

Source: Doing Business 2010, World Bank, Undersecretariat of Treasury

Let me investigate now what factors allowed Turkey to attract FDI at levels comparable with my sample of countries by 2004. How did the Turkish investment climate improve? What were the major dynamics behind its enhanced FDI attractiveness? To answer these questions, I first investigate unnecessary costs related to administrative and bureaucratic procedures on the eve of the February 2001 currency crisis. Then, I will turn to the principal reforms introduced after the crisis.

4.2.2.1. Estimating the cost of administrative barriers to FDI

State involvement together with economic nationalism since the 1930s made, over the course of many decades, administrative procedures a serious obstacle for investors[788]. Many of these procedures lacked a clear sense and had become meaningless formalities, creating thus only uncertainty and encouraging corruption. This means increased costs for investors and also discourages them because it makes both the riskiness and expected return of investment difficult to estimate. Despite the difficulty of quantifying the costs of these factors, a Price Waterhouse Coopers (PWC) study attempted to measure opacity[789] and its costs for a sample of countries, including Turkey, and found that unfavorable administrative conditions had a strongly negative impact in attracting FDI. A high degree of opacity raises the cost of doing business and curtails the availability of investment capital[790]. The study was published in January 2001 and provides information on the relationship between regulatory weaknesses, sovereign risk and obstacles to attracting FDI on the eve of the February 2001 Turkish currency crisis. The survey-based opacity scores were transformed into a metric allowing a meaningful economic interpretation[791]. The study attempted to illuminate two aspects:

1. **Impact of risk premia on bond spreads**: A regression analysis examined the incremental impact of opacity on sovereign bond spreads. The extra risk premium to induce investors to invest in a country provided a concrete measure (in basis points) of the marginal price of opacity. Table 4.17 shows that investors required 9.82 percent more on Turkish sovereign bonds, due to opacity factors, than the benchmark risk-free US sovereign bonds. To

---

[788] FIAS (2001), p. 1

[789] The study defined opacity as “the lack of clear, accurate, formal, easily discernable and widely accepted practices”. It took into consideration five factors, arguing that “there may be corruption in government bureaucracy that allows bribery or favoritism, the laws governing contracts or property rights may be unclear, conflicting or incomplete, economic policies (fiscal, monetary and tax-related) may be vague or change unpredictably, accounting standards may be weak or inconsistent, making it difficult to obtain accurate financial data, business regulations may be unclear, inconsistent or irregularly applied” (Barth, J. R., Hall, T. W., Kurtzman, J., Wei, S. J. and Yago, G. (2001), p. 6).

[790] Ibid., p. 6

[791] Ibid., p. 21

note that this premium was higher than those of all other countries in the sample, except for Russia;

2. **Corporate tax measure**: The study ran another regression, this time aiming to convert the "cost of opacity" into an equivalent marginal corporate tax increase. Let us look at the data provided in Table 4.17, where Singapore was taken as the benchmark country. For Turkey, the failure to reduce its opacity to the level of Singapore was equivalent to raising the corporate income tax rate by 36 percent. This investigation suggested that a high degree of opacity can easily offset the benefit of a tax cut to attract FDI. This also means that domestic reforms aiming to reduce opacity may be effective in attracting FDI without reducing tax revenue to the government[792].

Table 4.17: The cost of opacity[793]

	TR	GR	PO	HU	CZ	RUS	BR	MEX	UK	USA	SING
Risk premium	982	557	724	370	899	1'225	645	308	63	0	0
Corp. Tax Equivalent	36	22	28	17	33	43	25	15	7	5	0

Source: PriceWaterHouseCoopers (2001), p. 10, abbreviated country names stand for, respectively, Turkey, Greece, Poland, Hungary, Czech Republic, Russian Federation, Brazil, Mexico, the United Kingdom, the USA and Singapore; Risk premium is in basis points, whereas Corporate Tax Equivalent is in percentage.

4.2.2.2. Examining administrative barriers to FDI in Turkey by 2001

Let me now examine the administrative barriers leading foreign investors to require, according to the PWC (2001) study, a 9.82 percent premium on Turkish sovereign bonds. In another important study, the Foreign Investment Advisory Service (FIAS)[794] analyzed administrative obstacles to FDI in Turkey affecting investors' risk perception. The study was based on interviews with domestic and foreign investors, public officials and administrators and was conducted in March 2001. It also included a review of laws and documents relating to FDI[795]. The following problems were identified:

---

792 Barth, J.R., Hall, T.W., Kurtzman, J., Wei, S.J. and Yago, G. (2001), p. 26

793 Ibid., p. 10

794 FIAS is a joint service of the International Finance Corporation and the World Bank. It advises developing country governments on how to attract and retain FDI flows and maximize their impact on development (FIAS (2001), p. ii).

795 Ibid., p. 1

Government control rather than service orientation[796]

Regulatory policies lead to excessive control instead of contributing to a functioning market mechanism. These policies are based on mistrust rather than aiming to provide an incentive for private business.

Complex and frequently changing regulations lack coordination between bureaucracies[797]

A large majority of investors ranked complexity and non-transparency of government regulatory policies as a major factor that affected their ability to establish and operate a business in Turkey[798]. On average, 20 percent of management's time was spent in dealing with bureaucracy and administrative procedures, compared to 8 percent in Central and Eastern Europe and only 4 percent in Latin America[799]. Overlapping institutional structures and legal mandates created confusion among investors regarding each institution's specific mandate[800]. Major features of this mechanism, far from international best practices, ranged from excessive documentation requirements and customs formalities to duplication of approvals and inspections.

Corruption

Investors reported a high level of corruption[801]. In fact, the aspects mentioned above created circumstances for informal payments to accelerate procedures (to both institutions and individuals). Many firms also reported employing several full-time staff dedicated to dealing with government procedures. Over 65 percent of investors surveyed, reported using specialized consultants or 'paper followers' with knowledge of procedures and contacts in Ankara to deal with bureaucracy more effectively[802]. Such payments were formalized through salaries paid to consultants or to other "middle men". These conditions

---

[796] FIAS (2001), p. X

[797] Ibid., p. 38

[798] Ibid., p. 131

[799] Ibid., p. 4

[800] Ibid., p. X

[801] Ibid., p. XI

[802] Ibid., p. 6

affected the overall competitiveness of Turkey since all these procedures caused unjustified additional financial costs of starting and running a business.

Discouraging procedures

An example of discouraging procedures will show the sort of obstacles without any clear purpose that were common in Turkey. To start the registration procedure, a foreign investor needed an investment approval from the General Directorate for Foreign Investment (GDFI). One of the documentation requirements was the proof that USD 50'000 or an equivalent sum had been deposited in Turkey[803]. It is important to note that neither investment approval nor the USD 50'000 was required in any EU members, including those that joined the EU during the 2000s, namely the Czech Republic, Hungary, and Poland[804]. Requiring a minimum deposit was not best practice, as FDI should be welcomed, and a lower amount might have been a starting point for an additional investment in the future. Moreover, this was only a formality because the procedure obliged the investor to show that the sum had been transferred to Turkey, but they could withdraw it after obtaining the GDFI approval! Regarding time spent on registration procedures, it would have typically taken a minimum of ten weeks in Turkey[805]. By contrast, in Latvia, company registration took three to fifteen days, in Estonia two to three weeks and four weeks in Hungary[806].

Suggestions of the FIAS report

The overall report emphasized the fact that, to attract FDI flows, Turkey needed to offer a competitive cost structure. It recommended the following actions be taken: Removing administrative barriers, strengthening private and public sector consultation and establishing an inter-ministerial committee to oversee and to implement the priority policy actions at the highest level and a coordination body to follow-up the implementation process on a regular basis.

---

[803] FIAS (2001), p. 35

[804] Ibid., p. 37

[805] Ibid., p. 35

[806] Ibid., p. 35

4.2.2.3. Turkish government's efforts to adopt EU-inspired standards

While one of the major features of the post-2001 currency crisis period was to continue to implement the "Washington Consensus" principles, policy makers gave priority to improving the regulatory framework. The reason behind this strategy was not only to make Turkey EU-compatible –a process accelerated by the Customs Union agreement in 1995– but also to benefit from advantages of FDI. The PCW (2001) study above showed that, in the past decades, excessive interest payments on public debt were also due to regulatory and institutional problems. It was time, therefore, to change the investment climate and to seize the opportunity to attract more FDI as the other EU countries had done. Lowering the size of the public debt and increasing of FDI would do this.

What was the Turkish authorities' response to the FIAS (2001) report?

The government introduced a program[807] in line with the report, which aimed at private sector-led growth, a smaller but more transparent and effective public sector, an accelerated privatization process and an improved investment climate. Moreover, in an attempt to address international investors' reluctance due to uncertainties under regulatory aspects, the government issued a decree[808] as part of a national strategy to stimulate competitiveness and to increase the overall level of income and productivity[809]. This decree established the YOIKK, a coordinating body[810] composed of representatives of senior public and private sector decision-makers. Its major task was to remove regulatory and administrative barriers to private investment.

The EU-sponsored "Twinning" Project, FIAS (2001) report and "Acquis Communautaire"

"Twinning" is an institution-building instrument of the European Commission in the context of enlargement of the EU[811]. It aims to assist candidate countries in strengthening their administrative and judicial capacity to implement the

---

807 The "Reform Program to Improve the Investment Environment in Turkey", in November 2001 (Dutz, M., Us, M. and Yilmaz, K. (2005), p. 284)

808 "The Decree on Improving the Investment Climate in Turkey", 11th December 2001 (Ibid.)

809 Ibid.

810 YOIKK is the initials of "Coordination Council for the Improvement of the Investment Climate", in Turkish.

811 Commission of the European Communities (2009), p. 10

"Acquis Communautaire" as future EU member states. The Turkish Undersecretariat of Treasury ran a twinning project with the German Federal Ministry of Economics and Technology, a benchmark member state of the EU, which aimed at commenting on the YOIKK reform process accomplishments and recommending ways for further improvement[812].

The FIAS recommendations were also consistent with the "Acquis Communautaire", which required Turkey to remove administrative barriers, to promote free capital movements and to enhance its FDI attractiveness in its path towards EU membership. Regarding FDI access to Turkey, the 2002 EU Commission's Regular Report highlighted several aspects of Turkish laws which were not EU-compliant. It argued that in the field of capital movements, though there was a certain degree of alignment with the "Acquis", significant restrictions still limited participation of foreigners in Turkish enterprises and the acquisition of real estate[813]. It advanced that:

> "Regulations concerning the acquisition of real estate by non-nationals (foreign natural persons) and foreign legal persons exist. The acquisition of real estate by foreign natural persons is bound to the principle of reciprocity between Turkey and other countries. In addition, foreign real persons are prohibited from acquiring real estate in villages (Village Law) and near military and security areas (Prohibited Military and Security Areas Law). Acquisitions over 30 hectares are subject to the permission from the Council of Ministers. Concerning legal entities, foreign firms are permitted to acquire real estate in Turkey pursuant to foreign investment legislation and provided that the real estate to be acquired is related to the investor's permitted activities. Foreign-controlled enterprises are prohibited from engaging in real estate trading. The Tourism Law and Petroleum Law include

---

[812] This twinning project was titled "Towards Improving the Investment Climate in Turkey: Comments on the YOIKK Reform Process". It was sponsored by the EU and the report was published in 2006 (YOIKK official website, and European Union (2006), pp. 1, 2).

[813] Commission of the European Communities (2002), pp. 72, 73

> exemptions to the restrictions stipulated in the Village Law. Turkey should bring this legislation into line with the Acquis.
> An authorization system for investment is still in place and capital of USD 50'000 must be provided to establish a company or open a branch in Turkey. A new foreign investment law is expected to replace the present system by a registration system and remove the minimum amount required for investing in Turkey."

In the same spirit, the Council of European Union's Decision on the Principles, Priorities, Intermediate Objectives and Conditions contained in the Accession Partnership with Turkey (19th May 2003) explicitly stated for the first time two recommendations regarding FDI, declaring that Turkey should[814]:

> "Facilitate and promote the inflow of foreign direct investments.
> [....]
> And remove all restrictions affecting FDI (originating from the EU) in all sectors in Turkey. "

What was the Turkish authorities' response to the Council's recommendations?

The Turkish government's prompt response in the following weeks demonstrated a solid political will to achieve radical reforms. A new FDI law, in line with the EU requirements, entered into force on 17th June 2003 and replaced the previous law of 1954[815]. Major changes included:

- It guaranteed national treatment for foreign investors and repealed the minimum capital requirements of USD 50'000 for foreigners to establish a company in Turkey;
- It replaced the previous FDI approval system with a simple registration;

---

814 Council of the European Union (2003), pp. 44, 45

815 Law No. 6'224 (Law for Encouragement of Foreign Capital) enacted on 18th January 1954 (Undersecretariat of Treasury (2003), official website).

- It granted foreign investors full convertibility in transferring their capital and earnings;
- It banned nationalization without fair compensation;
- It recognized foreign investors' right to international arbitration;
- It adopted international standards[816] in producing FDI statistical data[817] regarding the definition of a foreign investor and FDI[818] in line with international standards. From now on, a foreign investor was associated with his country of residence, i.e., being non-resident in the economy. As for FDI, it was defined as an acquisition of 10 percent of a company, consistent with the IMF/OECD definition;
- Turkey also participated in a 2003 Survey of Implementation of Methodological Standards for Direct Investment (SIMSDI), led by the IMF and OECD in the second half of 2003[819].

The new legal framework was in line with international standards and prospects, contributing to the announcement in December 2004 by the European Council that the negotiations for full membership were to begin in October 2005. Legal framework improvements and further steps towards the EU membership added to investor confidence. In addition, improvements in reducing bureaucratic procedures increased the competitiveness of Turkish investment climate. Table 4.18 shows that with the reforms introduced, the

---

816 The OECD Benchmark Definition provides operational guidance on how FDI data should be compiled, to meet internationally accepted standards, setting the world standard for direct investment statistics (OECD (2008), p. 14). This description is consistent with the underlying concepts and definitions of the International Monetary Fund's (IMF) Balance of Payments and International Investment Position Manual 6th Edition (BPM6) (IMF (2009), pp. 100, 101).

817 The compilation of the balance-of-payments statistics and international investment position is regulated by the Article 43 of 1970 Central Bank Law No. 1'211, as amended by Law No. 4'651 of 25th April 2001. Thus, this article provides the legal basis for data collection of FDI (Sisik, Y. (2006), p. 3).

818 FDI Inward and Outward Transaction Data (Balance of Payments) and Inward and Outward Position data (International Investment Position)

819 The IMF and the OECD have since 1997, conducted a SIMSDI in order to measure the extent to which statistical systems have implemented the recommendations on direct investment statistics. This evaluation tool also provides standardized information on data sources and collection methods supporting the exchange of FDI data amongst reporting economies for multilateral comparisons. Turkey participated in the 2nd and the 3rd surveys realized in 2001 and 2003 during which the IMF and the OECD introduced a revision to update the SIMSDI information, marking a significant improvement in the availability and compilation of FDI statistics (IMF and OECD (2003), pp. 1-3).

number of procedures to start a business were significantly reduced by 2005. Similarly, Table 4.19 illustrates that the time needed to start a business became the shortest in the sample from 2005 to 2008, comparable to the Czech Republic and Portugal.

Table 4.18: Starting a business (number of procedures)

	2004	2005	2006	2007	2008	2009	2010
Turkey	13	6	6	6	6	6	6
Greece	15	15	15	15	15	15	15
Portugal	11	11	11	8	7	6	6
Spain	10	10	10	10	10	10	10
Poland	4	4	4	4	4	4	4
Hungary	10	10	10	10	10	10	6
Czech	6	6	6	6	6	4	4
Slovak	10	10	10	10	9	9	9
Ireland	10	9	9	9	9	6	6
Brazil	17	17	17	17	18	18	16

Source: Doing Business, World Bank

Table 4.19: Starting a business: Time (number of days)

	2004	2005	2006	2007	2008	2009	2010
Turkey	38	6	6	6	6	6	6
Greece	38	38	38	38	38	19	19
Portugal	78	78	54	8	7	6	6
Spain	114	114	47	47	47	47	47
Poland	18	18	18	13	13	13	13
Hungary	31	31	31	31	31	31	32
Czech	52	52	38	38	16	5	4
Slovak	40	40	40	24	17	20	20
Ireland	103	52	25	25	25	16	16
Brazil	152	152	152	152	152	152	120

Source: Doing Business, World Bank

Industrial and Intellectual Property Rights (IIPRs)

Full harmonization and implementation of the IIPRs is a topic of crucial importance within the framework of EU integration process[820] and it has a significant impact on FDI flows. Understanding this necessity, Turkey introduced measures to increase its institutional capacity in this area[821]. Reforms initiated in 2004 brought the Turkish legal basis closer to the EU standards[822]. By March 2005, some nine specialized courts of the first instance specialized in the area of industrial and intellectual property rights were established, with judges trained on these topics[823]. Moreover, a number of twinning projects (see below) were launched to bring Turkish institutions (from courts to customs and police) up to standard. From 2003 to 2009, the total number of patent applications and patents granted increased by 528 percent and 375 percent respectively, 94 percent of which were delivered to foreign investors.

---

[820] Article 118 of the Treaty on the Functioning of the EU states: "In the context of the establishment and functioning of the internal market, the European Parliament and the Council, acting in accordance with the ordinary legislative procedure, shall establish measures for the creation of European intellectual property rights to provide uniform protection of intellectual property rights throughout the Union and for the setting up of centralized Union-wide authorization, coordination and supervision arrangements. The Council, acting in accordance with a special legislative procedure, shall by means of regulations establish language arrangements for the European intellectual property rights. The Council shall act unanimously after consulting the European Parliament." (Official Journal of the European Union (2012a), p. 96)

[821] Under the Customs Union of 1995, Turkey undertook an initiative to harmonize its national existing law in regards with "intellectual, industrial and commercial property rights" with current EU legislation and international (WIPO/WTO) standards. Comprehensive reforms towards this objective were enacted (EC-Turkey Association Council (1995), pp. 55-58).

[822] Law No. 5'101 of March 2004 amended the Law on Intellectual and Artistic Works, Law No. 5'846 of 1951.

[823] Voss, J. and Murphy, D. (2006), p. 197

Fig. 4.5: Patents granted to domestic and foreign investors

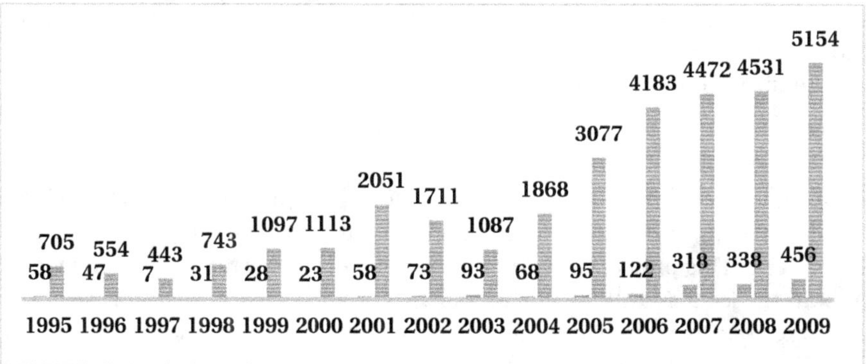

Source: Turkish Patent Institute; The first and the second columns represent patents granted to domestic and foreign investors, respectively.

What problems arose from EU-inspired IIPR reforms?

The European Commission's Progress Report (2005) noted that while Turkish legislation on industrial property protection had largely been brought into line with EU and WTO requirements and efforts towards complete convergence were proceeding, doubts remained as to Turkey's administrative capacity to actually implement the new legislation[824]. This required an efficient operation and coordination of various enforcement agencies, notably the Turkish Patent Institute, Customs, Civil, Criminal and Administrative Courts, public prosecutors and police forces[825]. Despite these shortcomings, Turkey was ranked sixth in 2007 among 29 European Patent Office (EPO) member countries with 6'189 patent applications[826].

Twinning Projects on IIPRs

Twining projects launched between Turkey and the EU, constitute a significant effort to adapt the "acquis" to Turkish conditions. For example, the "Turkey-EU pre-accession financial assistance program" allowed the Turkish Government to run a project in collaboration with the EU[827] from May 2006 to November

---

824 Commission of the European Communities (2005), p. 66

825 Voss, J. and Murphy, D. (2006), pp. 197, 198

826 Undersecretariat of Treasury (2009a), p. 52

827 Named "Support to Turkey's Efforts in the Full Alignment and Enforcement in the Field of IPR with a Focus on Fight Against Piracy".

2007, in order to raise the effectiveness of its civil service judicial and executive administrations. This elaborate program included workshops and seminars for judges and prosecutors to improve the efficiency of the judicial system in terms of the protection of IPRs, as well as training for customs officers. The Government established a Coordination Council for IIPRs in May 2008 to implement the program[828].

Another "Twinning Project" was launched in March 2010 between the Turkish Patent Institute and the German International Legal Cooperation Institute[829]. This project used Germany as one of the best models in the world in both the legal and IIPR fields to transfer administrative and legal know-how to Turkey[830]. Once the decision-making procedures were aligned with EU best practices, a particularly important outcome was an environment of higher-level protection of IPRs as well as a decrease in the workload of the Turkish courts. In order to support Turkey's efforts in this area, more than 50 high-ranking experts from the EU, among them judges from the German Federal Supreme Court and the German Federal Patent Court, as well as members of the Office of Harmonization for the Internal Market participated in the project during the thirteen month implementation period[831]. In addition, customs, police, and other institutions were integrated into the project. The EU allocated 1.2 million Euros to this project, with the Turkish Patent Institute and the Ministry of Justice allocating considerable amounts as well[832].

Concluding remarks

We observed in this chapter that in addition to privatization revenues, the FDI flows increased in 2004-2005. The reforms of 2000-2005 finally convinced global investors that Turkey was a good place to invest in the long-term, while the deregulation process during the 1980s and the 1990s attracted only short-term capital flows thereby creating instability. Thus, the EU-inspired regulatory reforms, the 11th element of the "Washington Consensus", were essential in allowing the economy to benefit from the IMF's original ten policy

---

828 Undersecretariat of Treasury (2009), p. 53

829 Called "Supporting Turkey for Enhancing Implementation and Enforcement of IPRs in Turkey" (Turkish Patent Institute, official website)

830 Ibid.

831 Ibid.

832 Ibid.

prescriptions. Priority was at last given to rule of law and protection of property rights. The latter aspect also covered protection of industrial and intellectual property rights, which is significant because investors prefer not only stable macroeconomic circumstances but also secure conditions where intellectual property rights are protected. We observed in the Fig. 4.5 the increased demand for patents from non-resident investors after 2004, which shows the desire for a safe investment environment. While industrial and intellectual property rights composed one of the elements introduced through the Customs Union in 1995, there were serious shortcomings in implementing these norms. In this respect, the twinning projects in collaboration with benchmark EU countries in the late 2000s were crucially important in providing effective assistance to the authorities responsible for the implementation of these EU-inspired legally binding rules.

Turkey is traditionally familiar with transferring institutions from the West to Turkish conditions. While changing laws is relatively easy because it depends also on politicians' decisions, to achieve the hoped for results require an accurate adaptation of legally binding rules to local conditions. I mentioned Twinning projects run with Germany, a benchmark country for international best practices, aiming to improve both investment climate and respect of IIPRs, to point out efforts that can be highly beneficial for a candidate country like Turkey to reduce and eliminate the institutional gap with the EU member states.

As I discussed political efforts in adopting the EU standards on the IIPRs, let me now overview, in the next section, the situation of property rights broadly since the beginning of the foundation of the Republic. I introduce both historical and political aspects in examining this issue. While the former aims to shed light on traditional approach to property rights in an economy where state presence had always been dominant in shaping the whole economy, the latter will enlarge our view on some factors allowing a pro-Islamist party to dominate the political scene by the mid-1990s, i.e., delivering services at micro level addressing the material needs of the urban poor. Nevertheless, my major aim is to examine the adoption of EU-inspired rules and to emphasize political efforts in creating a mortgage market in Turkey by the late 2000s.

4.2.3. An overview on Property Rights in Turkey: The neglected 10th "Washington Consensus" prescription

Introduction: Why property rights and land registry are important issues?

While I focused in this Chapter on the 11th "Washington Consensus" prescription, I now overview what was the situation of property rights and under which aspects it was neglected in Turkey. This will enlarge our view also regarding the policies followed over decades to adapt another set of Western rules to Turkish conditions.

Property rights are an important element in achieving and reinforcing a functioning market economy. Hernando de Soto argued in "Mystery of Capital (2000)"[833] that one of the reasons why macroeconomic and structural adjustment reforms in developing countries are not working is because to create capital requires a complex system of legal property. Nevertheless, when records and maps are outdated it is not clear who owns what and where, who is responsible for losses and fraud. This leads to uncertainty and has a negative impact on exchange economy, also because there are no recognizable rules. This topic is important for my study because the 10th prescription of the "Washington Consensus" referred to property rights, which were neglected in Turkey during the implementation of these prescriptions in the 1980s and the 1990s.

I will investigate in this section how appropriate was the respect of property rights in Turkey. Inequality, in particular in the Eastern regions of the country, was a result of a semi-feudal agricultural structure from the beginning of the Turkish Republic. We observed in Chapter 4 that the agricultural sector was still unable to face competitive forces of the EU by the 2000s. I showed that this dependence on state intervention became a major reason for economic instability in Turkey for several decades and still contradicted the "Acquis Communautaire" in the early 2010s. Thus, an overview of the property rights, land registry, and cadastre situation is crucially important for discovering additional factors that had impeded development in agriculture, making this sector dependent on state intervention through subsidized lending. While the section 4.2.3.1 will examine land registry and cadastre from the 1920s to 1980s, the section 4.2.3.2 will overview the situation from the 1980s to the 2010s.

---

833 De Soto, H. (2000), pp. 25, 26, 58

Moreover, the absence of a developed mortgage market in Turkey is another significant aspect, which allows me to argue that capital had never been efficiently used since the foundation of the Republic. In Hernando de Soto's terms[834], "institutions that give life to capital and that allow the individuals to secure the interests of third parties with their work and assets" had not existed in Turkey. Thus, the Mortgage Law introduced in 2007 is another crucially important aspect that can contribute to the creation of additional wealth in the country[835]. This will be the focus of section 4.2.3.3.

4.2.3.1. Evolution of Property Rights and Land Registry and Cadastre until the 1980s

Under the Ottoman Empire, lands were traditionally maintained under state ownership and individuals possessed only usage rights[836]. The Empire's land ownership system prevented the formation of feudal forms of government in the Ottoman period. This system continued until 1858 when the Land Law introduced the transition to private ownership[837]. Nevertheless, statistical data relating to years 1912-1913 in Anatolia, covering a total of one million families living in rural areas, show great inequality[838]:

- The top 5 percent of the population held 65 percent of total lands (of which the richest 1 percent held 39 percent of land);
- 95 percent of families had 35 percent of total lands (of which 8 percent did not possess any land at all).

When Kemal Ataturk founded the Republic of Turkey in 1923, 80 percent of the population lived in rural areas, earning their livelihood directly or indirectly from land, while the land ownership system inherited from the Ottoman period was clearly biased[839]. Moreover, 70 percent of the working population was directly occupied in the agricultural sector, which in turn composed almost 50 percent of GNP. Kemal Ataturk emphasized the need for each farmer to own enough land to sustain his family and distributed land to farmers in need, either

---

834 De Soto, H. (2000), p. 13

835 Ibid.

836 Demir, O. and Coruhlu, Y. E. (2008), p. 5'561

837 Ibid., p. 5'562

838 Demirel, Z. and Gulsever, F. Z. (2007), pp. 2, 3

839 Inci, I. (2010), pp. 345, 346

without payment or by payment extending over ten years, which contributed to reducing inequality to a certain extent. It is worth emphasizing that the land distributed to farmers belonged to the state, whereas land belonging to big landowners remained untouched and in Eastern regions a semi-feudal system persisted.

Kemal Ataturk gave priority to a series of reforms, including creating a land registry. The first Turkish Constitution of 1924 reinforced private property rights, making nationalization of property more difficult[840]. Initial efforts led to organizing a cadastre under the General Directorate of Land Registry and aimed to determine property and boundaries of real estate[841]. Kemal Ataturk completely abolished the Ottoman land system[842] by adopting the Swiss Civil Code in 1926[843] and the so constituted Turkish Civil Code introduced a land registry system integrated with cadastre maps. Its aim was to define rights and responsibilities pertaining to real estate in the country[844]. The government introduced the Cadastre and Land Registry Law in 1934[845] and two years later designed the institutional framework of the Turkish Cadastral system: The General Directorate of Land Registry and Cadastre was affiliated with the Ministry of Public Works and Settlement. This institution was charged with organizing the implementation of land registry and cadastre works[846].

Nevertheless, due to persistent inequality in land ownership, Ataturk announced in 1936 that making farmers landowners was necessary for nation-wide development[847]. In line with this, Prime Minister Ismet Inonu declared in 1937 that obliging farmers to work on others' land under bad conditions had led to inefficiencies[848]. He further said that while the objective of government can never be to violate the property rights of large landowners, priority was to be given to a more equitable ownership. This signaled that the government

---

840 Inci, I. (2010), p. 350

841 Law No. 474 in 1924 and Law No. 658 in 1925 (Demir, O. and Coruhlu, Y. E. (2008), p. 5562)

842 Demirel, Z. and Gulsever, F. Z. (2007), p. 3

843 Kokturk, E. (2002), p. 1

844 Cete, M., Palancioglu, H. M., Geymen, A. and Alkan, M. (2010), p. 626

845 Demir, O. and Cete, M. (2004), p. 389

846 Cete, M., Palancioglu, H. M., Geymen, A. and Alkan, M. (2010), pp. 626, 627

847 Inci, I. (2010), p. 354

848 Ibid.

could eventually nationalize private property of large landowners for the purpose of reducing social inequality[849].

The Turkish Constitution recognized the possibility to provide land to farmers. Article 44 of Turkish Constitution states[850]:

> "The state shall take the necessary measures to maintain and develop efficient land cultivation, to prevent its loss through erosion and to provide land to farmers with insufficient land of their own or no land."

Amendments introduced to the Constitution during the same year (1937) made possible nationalization of lands with the purpose of making landless farmers landowners, also with the possibility of payment over time. This was also the year when the statist principle[851] was included in the Constitution[852]. However, Kemal Ataturk passed away in 1938 and the Second World War made large-scale land reform impossible. In the period from the foundation of the Republic in 1923 to 1944, a considerable amount of land was nevertheless distributed to landless farmers, 91 percent of which was realized before the death of Kemal Ataturk[853]. Nevertheless, this had only a minor effect in reducing the persistent inequality. Finally, in the aftermath of the Second World War, the "Making Farmers Landowners Law" came into effect in 1945[854]. This law aimed to provide land to landless farmers from:

- Land in the State's possession or in private ownership;

[849] Inci, I. (2010), p. 355

[850] International Constitutional Law website, consulted on 20th October 2011.

[851] Kemal Ataturk defined statism as a system peculiar to Turkey based on private initiative but placing on the state responsibility to launch economic development. It was a system different from both liberalism and Marxism. Given the then ongoing world economic crisis and Turkey's domestic conditions, this was seen as the best approach to increase national welfare (Altiparmak, A. (2002), p. 39).

[852] To note that Turks lost World War I together with Germans. While John Maynard Keynes explains in "The Economic Consequences of the Peace" the difficulty of German reparations, Turkey suffered between the two World Wars from a huge debt inherited from the Ottomans after 1923 (see Annex 1). In addition, inequality in distribution of land and lack of capital formation led to protectionist policies during the 1930s (For German reparations see Keynes, J. M. (1919), pp. 71-142).

[853] Inci, I. (2010), p. 357

[854] Demirel, Z. and Gulsever, F. Z. (2007), p. 3

- Surplus land, common to villages, towns, and cities;
- Land obtained from dried lakes or filled rivers.

In addition, it became possible to expropriate the land of private persons, municipalities, foundations and corporate bodies in order to distribute it to farmers[855]. While the law aimed to reduce economic inequality, it was also intended to destabilize the large landowners and reinforce the popularity of the single political party, the CHP[856].

To summarize, efforts for a substantial land reform that began in the second half of the 1930s led to a law in 1945, which had an important impact on Turkish political life. Failing to change the semi-feudal nature of Turkish agriculture, it created confrontation on an ideological level rather than a substantial economic reform. Political views diverged on the way property rights were to be designed. The opposing team, among them Celal Bayar and Adnan Menderes, left the CHP and founded the Democratic Party (DP) in January 1946[857]. To note that Celal Bayar was the former prime minister and loyal commander of Ataturk and Adnan Menderes was a landlord in the Western part of Turkey and a lawyer[858]. The DP supported a more liberal policy[859]. It introduced a law addressing cadastral works in rural areas[860]. Nevertheless, this also had become a second law addressing cadastral works creating duplication problems[861]. This situation lasted until Law No. 3'402 introduced in 1985, which incorporated cadastral laws and regulations into one law[862]. That is to say, from 1950 to 1985 the legal framework was not clear, creating a further degree of uncertainty.

---

855 Demirel, Z. and Gulsever, F. Z. (2007), p. 3

856 This is the comment of Sevket Pamuk, professor of Turkish Economic History at the Bogazici Universtiy, during an interview I held in June 2010.

857 Baytal, Y. (2007), p. 549

858 Yilmaz, S. (2009), p. 149

859 Adnan Menderes-led DP governed from 1950 to 1960, until the first military intervention (Grand National Assembly of Turkey and Inter-Parliamentary Union (IPU) official websites).

860 The Land Titling Law introduced in 1950 (Law No. 5'602) (Demir, O. and Coruhlu, Y. E. (2008), p. 5562).

861 Law No. 766 of 1950 was changed in 1964 and 1966 (Cagla, H., Akkus, S., Civcik, E. and Ozugur, I. (2011), p. 2).

862 Aydin, C. C. (2008), p. 6972

Conclusive remarks: What do we learn from all this?

Let me now first draw conclusions from Turkish experience prior to the 1980s, which will increase our understanding. Then in the next section, I will discuss reforms on cadastral works from the 1980s to 2010s.

1. What was the approach to property rights? What major policies were followed?

Before the foundation of the Republic of Turkey on 29th October 1923, two important events designed economic policies that would be undertaken in the early years of the Republic:

- The Izmir Economic Congress (17th February – 4th March 1923) promoted private initiative while emphasizing the need to avoid monopolistic tendencies[863]. Moreover, foreign capital was allowed as long as it contributed to economic development and respected Turkish law;
- The Lausanne Peace Treaty (24th July 1923), the founding charter of the Republic of Turkey. It also provided a repayment scheme for the inherited Ottoman debt, saddling the young republic with a heavy foreign debt[864].

Turkey adopted the Swiss Civil Code in 1926, which means that the government adapted its domestic legislation on property rights to a benchmark country of the West. The Central Bank of the Republic of Turkey was created in 1930 and encouraged economic development. However, the huge debt inherited from the Ottoman Empire, the lack of capital and the global economic crisis obliged policy makers to follow protectionist policies during the 1930s. There were two opposing factions in government proposing different economic models:

- A planned economy, as in the Soviet Union[865]. Countries following this model were able to achieve industrialization rapidly. Moreover, the then ongoing world economic crisis had a minor impact on these countries. Thus, according to this view, the best economic policy for Turkey was a statist model based on intensive and permanent state intervention and monitoring. Prime Minister Ismet Inonu supported this view;

---

[863] Eroglu, N. (2007), p. 65

[864] Weiker, W. (1973), pp. 59-61

[865] Vural (2008), p. 96

- A "mixed" economy, where state invested in infrastructure and industry through SOEs and a partially planned economy[866]. This model considered the market economy as the basic framework and that state intervention was to be temporary. Minister of Economy Celal Bayar supported this type of framework, considerably more moderate than the first.

President Kemal Ataturk preferred the second view. The government policy was defined as promoting agricultural production through private initiative. State monopolies were allowed only in the case of public interest. Nevertheless, the state planned to withdraw such intervention as soon as the private sector had become efficient through the needed technology and capital accumulation[867].

2. Had the second policy achieved its target, i.e., the needed capital accumulation?

According to Ataturk's original plan, savings and internal capital accumulation would lead to reduced state presence in the economy. But this never occurred in the following decades. On the contrary, the state presence increased after the 1960s through an intensive import substitution industrialization policy and SOEs-led development plans. Capital accumulation was never realized because the politically managed economy led to inefficiencies. The "Making Farmers Landowner Law" of 1945 remained in effect until 1973 but was ineffectual. During almost three decades only 0.7 percent of total land distributed was obtained through expropriation, of which only one-third through expropriation of private property[868], which shows that the government was unwilling to take on major landowners. In the meantime, Turkish agriculture remained inefficient, absorbing state support in the form of tax exemptions, support buying and subsidized credits. These subsidies became a way for politicians to assure the rural poor's votes[869]. Not only was capital accumulation not achieved due to inefficiencies in the semi-planned economy, but as we observed in Chapter 2, inefficiencies also led to budget deficits, which were in turn financed through Central Bank resources. Food prices had to be kept artificially low to favor the low-income urban population, which in turn

866 Vural (2008), p. 98

867 Ibid.

868 Demirel, Z. and Gulsever, F. Z. (2007), p. 14

869 Together with overemployment in SOEs aimed at keeping the unemployment rate artificially low.

distorted prices and discouraged private initiative. We observed that the Central Bank of the Republic of Turkey was established to encourage economic development in 1930, but printing money to finance subsidized credits in the agricultural sector, to cover SOEs' losses and budget deficits impeded the Central Bank from performing its functions. Excessive money creation led to persistent instability and not to economic development. High and persistent inflation rates from the early 1970s to the early 2000s showed this.

Conclusion

Secure property rights is a major component of a sound development policy as Turkish experience shows. Kemal Ataturk, by adopting the Swiss Civil Code in 1926, showed the determination of Turkey to integrate itself into the Western Civil law system. Consequently, Turkey invested in land registry and cadastre to create a legal basis for secure property rights, but never took the next step to reduce vast feudal land holdings or even sell-off its own state-owned lands.

I emphasize that development policies need to include secure property rights. However, Turkey while adopting the "Washington Consensus" principles during the 1980s and the 1990s, neglected the 10th principle, which was precisely in this area.

Let me now examine the rest of the story, i.e., the reforms achieved after 1980, which will lead us to reflect on the impact of the EU process on this issue. We observed in chapters 2 and 3 that the "Washington Consensus" principles introduced during the 1980s changed the whole structure of the economy, giving priority to the private initiative as a development policy.

4.2.3.2. Reforms of the Cadastre from the 1980s to the 2010s

Introduction

The Turkish Cadastre had the mandate[870] to determine the boundaries and legal conditions of privately owned land to create cadastral maps and establish a title deed registration system[871]. We observed in the previous section that Law No. 3'402 in 1985 incorporated cadastral laws and regulations into one law[872] of which major aims were:

---

[870] according to the Turkish Civil Code adopted from Swiss Civil Code

[871] Kokturk, E. (2002), p. 1

[872] Aydin, C. C. (2008), p. 6972

- True determination of rightful owners;
- Registering immovable properties in a title deed register;
- Introducing cadastral maps.

It is essential to look at the technical aspects of this process in order to judge whether property rights were adequately secured in Turkey[873]. In this section, I will discuss the degree of progress achieved since the 1980s, the decade during which Turkey adopted the "Washington Consensus" principles and I will discuss efforts to introduce technologically updated methods meeting EU requirements in the particular case of agricultural property.

Technical process

Two major periods characterize the Turkish land registry:

1. Textual period[874]: This is the expression of the cadastral information with words and numbers, i.e., "there is a road to the north and a river to the south". This sort of cadastre was used when there was no adequate information, techniques or qualified personnel for elaborating data;
2. Linear period[875]: The cadastre gained technical perspective with the introduction of arithmetic and geometric methods. While "classical", "graphical", and "photogrammetric" methods were traditionally used, these are not to be considered adequate to determine property boundaries with the necessary accuracy. Integration of computer technology allowed the use of "electronic tachometry" as an effective tool[876] from 1985 onwards. This method is used in "digital" cadastral records allowing also to introduce coordinates in digital format, which was absent in traditional methods[877].

Cadastre information in Turkey is traditionally defined in two-dimensional (2D) forms[878]. New technologies allow producing three-dimensional (3D) cadastral data, in particular in digital cadastre projects with a high degree of

---

873 Kokturk, E. (2002), p. 2

874 Demir, O. and Cete, M. (2004), p. 389

875 Demir, O. and Coruhlu, Y. E. (2008), p. 5563

876 Ibid., p. 5564

877 Ibid., p. 5561

878 Aydin, C. C. (2008), p. 6976

accuracy[879]. Cadastral databases with 3D coordinates are needed in particular in urban areas where complex engineering projects use underground spaces[880]. Law No. 3'402 of 1985, mentioned at the beginning of this section, aimed to produce 3D cadastral databases, including thus underground spaces, leading to determine their legal status in Turkey[881]. The following year another project[882] aimed to digitalize the land registry and cadastral data in order to create the basis for a modern cadastral information system[883]. Unfortunately, this project was not completed, leaving unresolved problems caused by insufficient cadastral data. Policy makers launched another project in the early 1990s (the "Land Registry and Cadastre Information System"), whose goal was again to introduce computer technology to establish a country-wide complete land information system[884]. Nevertheless, its implementation began only after the February 2001 currency crisis[885]. The "National Program for the Adoption of the Acquis" in March 2001[886] emphasized this project[887].

In the meantime, a rival project sponsored by the World Bank, was the "Agricultural Reform Implementation Project" introduced after the February 2001 currency crisis with the objective to:

- Replace partially state-owned cooperatives with farmer-led business companies[888];
- Introduce a "Direct Income Support" system[889], which aimed both to disengage government from politically managed subsidized credits to

---

[879] Demir, O. and Coruhlu, Y. E. (2008), p. 5560

[880] Aydin, C. C. (2008), p. 6973

[881] Ibid., p. 6972

[882] Mapping Cadastre Reform Project of 1986 (Cete, M., Palancioglu, H. M., Geymen, A. and Alkan, M. (2010), p. 626)

[883] Cete, M., Palancioglu, H. M., Geymen, A. and Alkan, M. (2010), p. 626

[884] Aydin, C. C. (2008), p. 6975

[885] Cete, M., Palancioglu, H. M., Geymen, A. and Alkan, M. (2010), p. 626

[886] I mentioned this Program in section 4.1.3.

[887] Yalcin, G., Yildirim, O. and Bakici, S. (2008), p. 2

[888] Aerni, P. (2007), p. 434

[889] This is a GATT obligation dating from the Uruguay Round in 1994.

farmers[890] and to partly compensate farmers' potential losses during the process of elimination of these subsidies[891].

While I showed in Chapter 3 how subsidies had become a major cause of deficits and financial instability in Turkey, it is worth noting that the World Bank-led project was implemented with the goal of preparing the Turkish economy for eventual EU membership, with the "Direct Income Support" system seen as an initial phase of agricultural reforms leading to the adoption of the EU's Common Agricultural Policy[892]. The implementation of the "Direct Income Support" system required complete land records, leading to the introduction of the "National Registry of Farmers" in 2001, based on the cadastral information (titles) declared by farmers[893]. A major problem arose as old cadastre maps were unable to produce accurate records. All this shows that reforms introducing a digitalized land registry system were essential[894]. It is not surprising that other problems were encountered also during this process, ranging from lack of qualified staff to inadequacy of the software[895] and lack of a clear definition of property rights to space above and beneath the surface, due to legal gaps. To note that in urban areas complex constructions such as underground tube stations, underpasses, and underground arcades created disputes over unregistered land[896].

The Turkish Civil Code recognized both of the following aspects[897]:

- Ownership for all space above and below the surface of the plot;
- Rights of an easement under and above spaces while registration of title deeds is in process[898].

---

[890] Inan, H. I., Cete, M. (2006), p. 3

[891] Aerni, P. (2007), p. 434

[892] Inan, H. I., Cete, M. (2006), p. 1

[893] Ibid., p. 1

[894] Cete, M., Palancioglu, H. M., Geymen, A. and Alkan, M. (2010), p. 627

[895] Ibid., pp. 631, 632

[896] Ayazli, I. E., Batuk, F. and Stoter, J. (2008), p. 942

[897] Aydin, C. C. (2008), p. 6980

[898] The following example will give an idea regarding the size of potential problems. In 2006, during the excavation for constructing a new building in Istanbul, workers penetrated the security wall of the Metro. The only reason was the lack of an accurate map of Istanbul's underground construction (Aydin, C. C. (2008), pp. 6977-6981).

Confusion emerged when the latter was not accurately registered. The government launched additional projects in the late 2000s, this time aiming to adapt Turkish reforms specifically to meet EU standards. The EU Directive establishing the "Infrastructure for Spatial Information in the European Community (INSPIRE)" was published in 2007 and aimed to ensure compatibility of spatial data amongst the EU member states[899]. Turkey for her part launched the "Project for National Geographic Information System Infrastructure" in an attempt to introduce the INSPIRE Directive. Many inter-institutional meetings held in 2008 aimed to examine the way to put this project into practice. Modernization in public administration was to be undertaken through some sub-projects[900], such as the Continuously Operating Reference Stations (CORS-TR). This project targeted the substitution of old-fashioned techniques and methods with a nation-wide single, fast, and efficient system in three-dimensional form, where all data was to be coordinates[901], by using information based on satellites[902].

Conclusion: I introduced in section 2.1, under "Critics of the Washington Consensus", the view of Hernando de Soto who emphasized the impact of secure property rights on additional wealth creation. I discussed in the "introduction" of section 4.2.3 again the arguments of the same author pointing out the importance of institutional framework on property rights in generating capital. Then, I examined the situation in Turkey from the 1920s to 2010s. I summarize my conclusions as follows:

I examined in Chapter 2 that Turkey began to introduce the "Washington Consensus" principles in 1980 and I emphasized that the first nine of them were introduced during the two decades. The 10th one, on property rights, was neglected. I added an additional 11th principle to the "Washington Consensus", identifying it with a de-politicized institutional framework. While the 11th principle provided benefits in the second half of the 2000s as I will examine in Chapter 5, the 10th principle, i.e., reforms on property rights, is still an ongoing reform process in the 2010s. I argue thus that reforms on cadastre leading to a digitalized environment will further contribute to generating additional production, especially in urban areas. This will be, in De Soto's terms[903], capital

---

899 INSPIRE-European Commission official website

900 Yalcin, G., Erkek, B., Bakici, S. and Sahin, N. (2009), p. 1

901 Yalcin, G., Yildirim, O., Bakici, S. (2008), p. 17

902 Kisa, A. and Bakici, S. (2011), p. 3

903 De Soto, H. (2000), p. 56

created through a secure property system, which was hidden in people's assets and that "can produce the non-inflationary money with which to finance and generate additional production". This reinforces my argument: During the 1980s and 1990s, instability was persistent in Turkey also because only the first nine principles of the "Washington Consensus" were adapted to Turkey's conditions.

I conclude that Turkey made a great effort to conduct a vast and complex reform agenda in the area of establishing secure title deeds to real estate property. Despite delays, it has made significant progress in adopting EU standards[904]. While Turkey does still not possess a 3D cadastre structure up to EU standards, corners of cadastral parcels started to be surveyed in 3D in 2004 and covered 99 percent of the whole cadastral area by 2009[905]. Table 4.20 shows the proportion of the cadastral area over the total. To note that old cadastre maps still compose a major technical problem. These works, though still insufficient, show an important effort in the right direction towards the accurate records required by the "Direct Income Support" system within the EU Common Agricultural Policy.

Table 4.20: Statistics of Turkish Cadastral Data

Type of Area	km^2	percentage
Forest	202'208	26.0
Pasture	96'000	12.3
Cadastral Area (rural)	440'000	56.6
Cadastral Area (urban)	40'000	5.1
Total	778'000	100.0

Source: Bank, E. and Mataraci, O. (2004), p. 3

The General Directorate of Land Registry and Cadastre is a major institution in the area of land registration. The projects I examined in this section are to be evaluated within the context of institutional reforms aiming to adopt EU standards. The ongoing projects by the early 2010s will provide benefits not only by enabling overloaded Turkish Courts to access accurate land registry and cadastre data rapidly[906], but also will contribute to enhancing prosperity which

---

904 Yalcin, G., Erkek, B., Bakici, S. and Sahin, N. (2009), p. 8

905 Doner, F., Demir, O. and Biyik, C. (2011), p. 1

906 Cete, M., Palancioglu, H. M., Geymen, A. and Alkan, M. (2010), p. 631

can be achieved and maintained only when property rights are accurately designed and guaranteed[907].

I argue that while an examination of improvements in urban and rural areas can be a subject for future research, substantial reforms in the real estate market can have a significant impact on social welfare, especially if financial market reforms develop a proper market for mortgage finance.

Let me now examine first the demand for real estate changes over decades, what was the supply and politics behind. Then, I will discuss the attempt of the government to discover the potential hidden in real estate assets in the late 2000s: The mortgage market.

4.2.3.3. Migration from rural to urban areas and politics behind

Industrialization had a significant impact on migratory flows from rural to urban areas. The majority of migrants came from farm communities in order to find employment in the big cities[908]. Unfortunately, industrialization occurred more slowly than the rate of urbanization and governments failed to supply housing units to meet the increasing demand. Thus, the newcomers increased both the proportion of low-income groups and of unemployed people in the cities and their housing needs created major slum dwellings.

Table 4.21 shows that by the early 2000s, 2'200'000 illegal dwellings housed around 12 million people. More than 20 percent of the urban population lived in inadequate housing conditions at the beginning of the 21st century. These slums were constructed spontaneously and, in a *de facto* manner, had formed "squatter towns" surrounding cities[909]. The growing number of urban poor created a new interest group in the Turkish political system.

---

[907] Ayazli, I. E., Batuk, F. and Stoter, J. (2008), p. 944

[908] Uzun, B., Cete, M. and Palancioglu, H. M. (2010), p. 205

[909] Ibid.

Table 4.21: Urbanization rate versus illegal slum settlements from the 1950s to 2000s

Years	Urbanization Rate %	Nb. squatter settlements
1955	22	50'000
1960	25	240'000
1965	30	430'000
1970	33	600'000
1980	45	1'150'000
1990	51	1'750'000
1995	55	2'000'000
2002	62	2'200'000

Source: Uzun, B., Cete, M. and Palancioglu, H.M. (2010), p. 205

While the whole picture shows that from a legal point of view, Turkey experienced a persistent violation of property rights with public land being used without any permission, the socio-economic transformation that involved large masses living in these conditions obliged governments in responding. I used the term "respond" because there had never been, until the 2000s, a concrete and uniform policy to solve the housing problem of migrant people. To note that the relationship between the material interests of squatters and their voting behavior increased competition among political parties[910]. In fact, the cozy patron-client relationship in Turkish politics began to change and became more competitive. In a broad setting, while the Democratic Party (DP), founded in 1946, represented the "rural people" or "periphery", the Republican People's Party (CHP) represented the "bureaucratic center" or the "state", aiming mainly to take position against a wide range of extremist threats from communism to Islamic fundamentalism. Concerns about material interest were naturally a predominant factor influencing the voting behavior of the "periphery". However, although squatters voted for DP in the 1965 general elections, the DP government enacted the Slum Law No. 775 the following year to demolish these illegal settlements and to prevent the construction of new ones[911]. Nevertheless, this law was not implemented due to socio-economic pressures. Gradually the approach of politicians changed over time in favor of legalization of these settlements. Squatter groups voted for CHP, in the 1973 elections, because CHP leader Bulent Ecevit promised to issue land deeds to all squatter settlements built before the end of 1973[912]. However, this policy encouraged new amnesty expectations. By the 1970s, the oldest slums became

---

910 Ozler, S. I. (2000), pp. 42, 43

911 Uzun, B., Cete, M. and Palancioglu, H. M. (2010), p. 205

912 Ozler, S. I. (2000), pp. 44, 45

proper towns and suburbs, with shopping centers and rented accommodation available[913].

In the 1980s, while Prime Minister Turgut Ozal encouraged deregulating financial markets by introducing the "Washingon Consensus" principles, he also enacted amnesty laws (No. 2'805 and 2'981 in 1983 and 1984, respectively) to legalize illegal settlements[914]. Through the process of legalization, secure property titles were delivered to squatters. Additional amnesty laws were issued in 1986, 1987 and 1988[915]. Nevertheless, the overall problem of squatter settlements remained unresolved. The transformation of the slums into normal suburbs progressed much further during the 1980s as many shopping centers, offices and business spaces were built on the legalized real estate. Thus, amnesty laws facilitated occupation of more public lands with the expectation of new amnesties, transforming the whole mechanism into a profitable business[916].

It is worth mentioning at this stage a new political cycle in Turkish politics, which increased the popularity of pro-Islamist leaders in representing the "periphery". While during the 1980s and the 1990s, the Motherland Party (ANAP) and the True Path Party (DYP) received the "periphery"' support, as the DP had during the 1950s, worsening macroeconomic conditions by the late 1980s increased the popularity of the pro-Islamist party, which addressed the immediate needs of the urban poor[917]. Ozler (2000) found a positive relationship between the urban squatter constituencies and the pro-Islamist RP's increasing votes during the 1990s[918]. While from 1973 to the early 1990s the pro-Islamist party obtained 7 to 12 percent of votes at the national level, it reached 19.1 percent of votes in local elections held after the February 1994 financial crisis in March, closely behind ANAP and DYP, which obtained 21.1 and 21.5 percent of votes, respectively. The victory of the pro-Islamist party was also significant because the mayors of Istanbul and Ankara, Turkey's two largest cities, inhabitants of which composed around 20 percent of the country's population, were elected from the pro-Islamist Welfare Party (RP). Moreover, during the general elections held in December 1995, the RP increased its share

---

913 Gokgur, P. (2010), p. 121

914 Uzun, B., Cete, M. and Palancioglu, H. M. (2010), pp. 205, 206

915 Ataov, A. and Osmay, S. (2007), p. 66

916 Uzun, B., Cete, M. and Palancioglu, H. M. (2010), p. 206

917 Ozler, S. I. (2000), pp. 45, 54

918 Ibid., p. 47

of the vote at the national level to 21.3 percent. While the anti-secular ideology of the RP was a threat to the basic values of the Republic, the issue of fundamentalist Islam was not the main reason behind the increase in the RP's votes. Rather, efficiently delivered services at the micro level addressing the material needs of the urban poor was much more relevant[919]. Nevertheless, this did not prevent both the military and the judiciary from intervening. On 28th February 1997 the armed forces sent a memorandum to Prime Minister Necmettin Erbakan, leader of the RP, demanding his resignation. The following year, the Constitutional Court suppressed the RP. Recep Tayyip Erdogan, mayor of Istanbul from the RP after the March 1994 local elections, who in a speech in November 1994 had stated that their aim is to introduce "shari'a" or Islamic Law[920], was put in prison in 1999, for having insulted national values of Turkey[921]. Freed four months later, his style still contradicted basic values of the Republic.

Despite all of this, Recep Tayyip Erdogan founded a political party (AKP) after the 2001 currency crisis and succeeded in winning the general elections held in November 2002. The new government launched a project in 2003 to find a solution to the squatter settlements problem with a completely new approach aiming to upgrade illegal settlements and to improve socio-economic conditions. The government established a new public entity affiliated with the Prime Ministry: The Governmental Mass Housing Administration (TOKI)[922]. The model envisaged, in the first stage, moving the slum owners[923] to temporary housing, where rents were paid for by the local administration, then demolishing illegal settlements and constructing new housing units in the same or in different areas. The model gave the possibility for people in need to buy only one residential unit each with long-term mortgages, where the amount to be paid would be the difference between the newly constructed unit and the old slum value. This approach discouraged slum trading activities for commercial purposes and addressed the housing needs of the urban poor.

To conclude, the migratory flows to urban areas starting in the 1950s accelerated in subsequent decades, transforming an economic problem into a serious social phenomenon, where politicians faced increasingly complicated

---

919 Ozler, S. I. (2000), p. 53

920 Baykal, A. (2009), p. 4

921 Demiralp, S. and Eisenstadt, T. A. (2006), p. 1

922 Uzun, B., Cete, M. and Palancioglu, H. M. (2010), pp. 206-209

923 owners of slums which gained a legal status, despite inadequate housing conditions

issues. Neither demolishing the slums nor amnesty laws provided an adequate solution, because while the first one neglected the social dimension of the question, the second created "incentive" by encouraging public land occupation for extra-profit seeking individuals or holdings, in an expectation of new amnesty laws. Finally, a comprehensive approach was launched in 2003 addressing both the social and economic dimensions of the question, providing adequate housing units for urban poor, while at the same time preventing speculative slum trading. This approach should be considered an important step in protecting property rights as it designated a path to purchase an adequate housing unit for people in need, while also clarifying the line between private and public property.

4.2.3.4. Mortgage market in Turkey

Introduction

We noted in section 4.2.3.1 that land ownership, in eastern provinces as in the central regions of Turkey, was traditionally not registered and even when it was, it was not accurate[924]. Thus, land had never been a legally well-documented asset, impeding farmers from using property as collateral or accessing credit markets. In De Soto's terms[925], farmers were not able to discover the potential of their assets. While adopting the Swiss Civil Code in 1926 was a significant step forward in importing Western rules, this was adapted to the conditions of Turkey and the outcome diverged greatly from that of the Western world, as the implementation of Swiss Civil Code had never secured an accurate land registry at the local level. I showed in Chapter 4 that state aid in agriculture had always been an aspect contradicting EU standards, a situation that continues to this day to some degree.

The following quote from "Mystery of Capital" where Hernando de Soto takes the city of Cairo as an example, shows how capital can efficiently be used to increase its own utility[926]:

> "Mortgages and accountable addresses to generate additional wealth are unavailable even to those people in Cairo who would probably strike you as quite rich. Outside Cairo, some of the

[924] Odekon, M. (2005), p. 99

[925] De Soto, H. (2000), p. 56

[926] Ibid., p. 13

> poorest of the poor live in a district of old tombs called "the city of the dead". But almost all of Cairo is a city of the dead – of dead capital, of assets that cannot be used to their fullest. The institutions that give life to capital – that allow you to secure the interests of third parties with your work and assets – do not exist here.

I argue that, despite all, Turkey has made a big effort, not only in improving the land registry but also on a topic related with the land registry: The mortgage market.

Reform in mortgages

Credit markets in Turkey have traditionally been weak due to lack of demand and an under-developed legal framework. Regarding the housing market, I discussed in the previous section that urbanization had accelerated by the 1950s[927] and migration from rural areas to big cities created significant socio-economic problems. While initially only state banks provided housing loans from the 1970s onwards, private commercial banks also began offering mortgages. By the end of the year 2000, 23 percent of the population was settled in Istanbul and 44 percent of the total urban population lived in cities with populations of more than 1 million inhabitants[928]. Nevertheless, a range of factors from a weak legal and financial system to macroeconomic instability impeded the development of a mortgage market.

The most important factor in pricing a mortgage is forecasting annual compound interest rates[929]. I showed in chapters 2 and 3 that high inflation rates from the early 1970s to the early 2000s led to high and volatile interest rates. Under these conditions, long-term credit markets could not develop.

Nevertheless, we will observe in Chapter 5 that macroeconomic parameters began to match the EU standards in the years 2004-2005. This improvement also had an impact on the housing loans/GDP ratio. We observe in Fig. 4.6 a substantial increase from 2004 onwards.

---

[927] Karakas, C. and Ozsan, O. (2005), p. 37

[928] Ibid.

[929] Chinloy, P. (1989), p. 21

Fig. 4.6: Increasing Housing Loans in Turkey from 1998 to 2007, in percentage

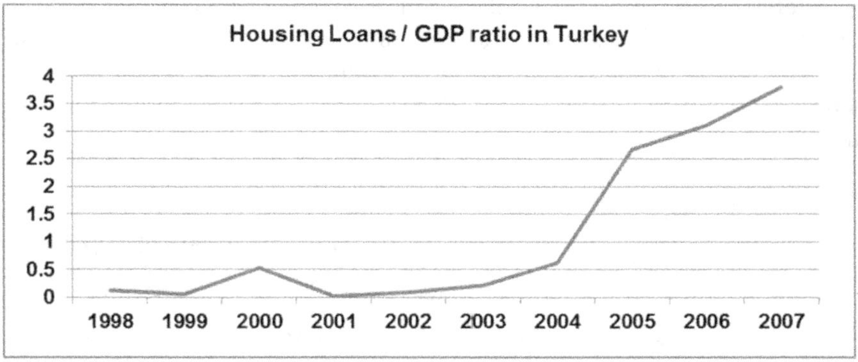

Source: Turkish Bankers' Association, CBRT official websites

Moreover, the government enacted a new law on mortgages in March 2007, which unified several items in related laws[930]. This law enabled non-bank institutions, i.e., leasing companies and consumer finance companies, in addition to banks, to lend money to households at both fixed and variable interest rates for purchasing houses[931]. It also allowed mortgage securitization, transferring risk from banks to other parties willing to bear it, increasing thereby the funds available for mortgages[932]. The same law also made possible the establishment of mortgage finance companies that could act as intermediaries in the securitization process. Nevertheless, the market depended on reforms in the land registry and cadastre because only good titles would allow securitization at low-interest rates[933]. Ibrahim Turhan[934] argued that the inefficient registration mechanism of real estate in Turkey represented a major obstacle for the development of mortgage securitization[935].

---

930 Erdogdu, G. P., (2010), p. 109

931 Ibid.

932 Turhan, I. (2008), p. 3

933 Ibid., p. 4

934 Ibrahim Turhan, one of the four vice-governors of the Turkish Central Bank, was appointed as the President of the Borsa Istanbul (BIST) in January 2012 (Today's Zaman, 2nd January 2012). He left this position in February 2015 as he joined the AKP and elected as deputy from Izmir.

935 Turhan, I. (2008), p. 4

Concerning the social impact of the 2007 Law on Mortgages, to note that at the interest rate levels of the late 2000s, only individuals with high incomes (the top 10 percent in Turkey) can benefit from mortgage credit[936]. A Turkish Central Bank study provides the following estimate regarding the relationship between the level of interest rates in 2008 and the size of the mortgage market in Turkey[937]:

> "When the payment capacity of households related to housing credits for various interest rates and maturities is analyzed, it is found that the number of households who can use housing credits is only 1.8 million. If monthly interest rates, which is about 1.5 percent (in 2008) diminishes to 0.5 percent and the maturity, which is about 7 years (in 2008) extends to 30 years, this figure would increase to 9 million."

A comparison with advanced and emerging economies of the world in Fig. 4.7 shows that despite all the progress in the housing market, Turkey's mortgage market was still quite far from that of advanced countries in 2009. A decline in interest rates would improve Turkey's place in this figure. Nevertheless, given the 2008 financial crisis generated by housing bubbles in the U.S., U.K., and Spain, further research can question whether the regulatory framework in Turkey is adequate to prevent an unexpected bubble in the housing sector.

---

936 Turhan, I. (2008), p. 5

937 Ibid.

Fig. 4.7: Comparing mortgage debt with a sample of countries, in percentage of GDP

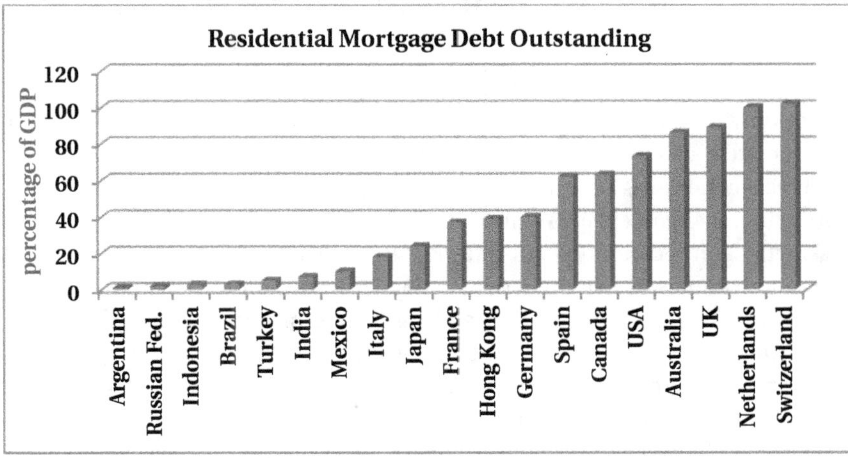

Source: Financial Stability Board (2011), p. 6, World Bank 2009 data except for Saudi Arabia (2007 data), Russia and Indonesia (2008 data)

What do we learn from all this?

I showed in chapters 2 and 3 that Turkey adopted the first nine principles of the "Washington Consensus" during the 1980s and 1990s, neglecting the 10th one, on property rights. We observed in the previous section that land registry and cadastre were traditionally inaccurate and far from international standards. While improving macroeconomic variables from 2004 onwards allowed lower interest rates, thus increasing the ratio of housing loans to GDP, the use of mortgages had been limited when compared with advanced economies. I introduced in this section Ibrahim Turan's view that the development of a modern mortgage securitization also depends on the digitalization of the land registry, which will improve the financing options of banks and non-bank institutions[938]. Moreover, the hoped-for further decline in interest rates will surely allow lower mortgage rates, allowing a higher percentage of households to benefit from the mortgage market in purchasing houses. This story highlights the impact of institutional reforms on financial stability.

---

[938] Turhan, I. (2008), p. 5

Conclusion

1. In this chapter, I examined institutional transformation in the Turkish economy that attempted to adapt the EU regulations to local conditions. I introduced also political and historical aspects, which aimed to shed light on local conditions and traditions. I emphasized in section 1.6 that, "being a functioning market economy" requires first of all, according to the Copenhagen (economic) sub-criteria, "the existence of a broad consensus about essentials of economic policy" and "macroeconomic stability". This is what my 3rd research question addressed. We observed that institutional transformation enabled the CBRT to gain its independence at gradually increasing degrees from 2001 to 2006, which in turn allowed the interest rates to play, in words of Ludwig von Mises, a "coordinating role" between savings and investments and meeting the two Copenhagen (economic) sub-criteria mentioned above. Moreover, the banking sector regained its intermediation function in the economy between the real and financial sector, thanks also to the creation of Banking Regulatory and Supervisory Agency;

2. I also examined other reforms contributing to a "functioning market": The adoption of the EU-inspired rules to create a competitive regulatory framework and to eliminate administrative obstacles, aiming both to encourage privatizations and to attract FDI, important elements for the development of financial markets. Finally, I overviewed the situation of property rights as examples of meeting EU requirements. Turkey opened its economy to global markets during the 1980s and the 1990s. Nevertheless, Turkish households were not able, again in De Soto's terms, "to discover the potential in assets" they could leverage over a long time horizon and thus be in a position "to produce the non-inflationary money to finance and generate additional production". While the major reason behind the absence of a developed credit markets in Turkey was high-interest rate levels due to macroeconomic instability, I argue that also the lack of secure property rights was an additional factor contributing to uncertainty, right up to the present day.

Chapter 5

Post-2002 Economic Performance

Introduction

This chapter aims to investigate the last research question of the study:

> "Was the "institutional migration" successful? If not, why was it not successful? Is it possible that "import" of Western pro-market formal institutions, i.e., an independent central bank or free financial markets, was not compatible with Turkish traditions and caused chaos rather than successful transition? Or perhaps it did go rather well?"

According to the Capital Asset Pricing Model (CAPM), investors expect a higher return when the riskiness of their assets increases. We have already seen how "opacity" could be measured as equivalent to a substantial increase in corporate tax rates. Investors also demand a risk premium when they compare investment opportunities across countries with different risk profiles. This shows up as an interest rate differential on global financial markets. I shall examine in this section risk exposure versus interest rates in Turkey and in a sample of EU countries. Variations in interest rate differentials for sovereign debt across economies will serve to show how international markets priced Turkey's sovereign risk exposure. While FDI flows are an important indicator that Turkey had succeeded in improving its institutional framework, let me now examine, in this chapter, two other indicators, which also confirm this positive trend in the second half of the 2000s: Credit Ratings and Credit Default Swaps (CDSs).

I overview, in section 5.1, Turkey's sovereign risk exposure through both rating agencies and macroeconomic data. Credit rating agencies[939] regularly carry out sovereign risk rating exercises[940], which are forward-looking assessments of a sovereign's capacity to honor its obligations[941]. They include analysts' predictions of future performance. They claim that financial transactions frequently imply information asymmetries between investors and lenders and that the role of rating agencies is to assemble and process information in an attempt to fill the gap[942]. Credit ratings are important for this study for a variety of reasons[943]:

- First, they influence interest rates at which countries can obtain credit in international financial markets. The higher their rating is, the lower the interest rate they can obtain;
- Second, they affect risk perception of international investors, thus influencing their decisions;
- Finally, institutional investors are sometimes contractually restricted on the degree of risk they can assume, i.e., they cannot invest in assets rated below a prescribed rating.

Macroeconomic performance has a significant weight in their evaluation. Therefore, I will first observe macro improvements in the post-institutional reform period in Turkey. Then, I will compare the latter with a sample of EU countries to illustrate that Turkey stood above EU countries' average for two major benchmark macro parameters in the late-2000s (the public debt and budget balance). I will further proceed with a comparison of the credit rating of Turkey and a sample of EU countries, which will allow us to observe that, although Turkey obtained the lowest ratings of the group, there was a marked improvement in the second half of the 2000s.

Next, I will examine in section 5.2. Credit Default Swaps, which have become an important alternative measure of sovereign credit risk. I will

---

[939] The principal international official and private credit risk rating agencies are Moody's, Standard & Poor's (S & P) and Fitch Ratings.

[940] Canuto, O., Fonseca, P., and de Sà Porto, C. (2004), p. 4

[941] From a rating perspective a sovereign issuer is the government that *de facto* exercises primary authority over a recognized jurisdiction. Central banks and other public policy institutions are agents of the sovereign (Fitch Ratings (2010a), p. 1).

[942] Canuto, O., Fonseca, P., and de Sà Porto, C, (2004), p. 4

[943] Hammer, P.L., Kogan, A., and Lejeune, M. A. (2007), p. 2

compare CDS spreads of Turkey and those of my sample. Improved macroeconomic data, together with credit ratings and CDS spreads will show a significant change in sovereign ratings due to Turkey's regulatory and institutional reforms. This result will also confirm the impact of reforms on privatizations and FDI flows that I examined in the previous chapter.

5.1. Credit Ratings

Sovereign credit risk diverges conceptually from that of country risk, though both are highly related[944]. The latter refers to the risk associated with doing business in a particular country, which can include a variety of factors ranging from the situation of property rights and tax as well as legal regimes leading to uncertainty in operating environment[945]. On the other hand, sovereign credit ratings are more concerned with the risk of a sovereign government defaulting on its debt obligations[946]. Rating agencies base their sovereign credit risk analysis on qualitative and quantitative examination in an attempt to capture the willingness as well as the capacity of a sovereign to repay[947]. One of the major rating agencies, Fitch Ratings, considers the following factors in determining its sovereign ratings[948]: Macroeconomic performance and

944 Fitch Ratings (2010a), p. 1

945 Ibid.

946 Ibid.

947 Ibid.

948 Ibid., p. 5

prospects[949], structural features of the economy that render it more or less vulnerable to "shocks"[950], public finances[951] and external finances[952].

Are rating assignments reliable? Why do we use them?

Credit rating agencies have performed badly. For example, the "investment grade" rating assigned to Thailand, Republic of Korea and Indonesia on the eve of the 1997 East Asian currency crisis did not reflect the risk of investing in these governments' securities[953]. It is important to note that ratings do not aim to indicate when a default will occur or whether a sovereign debtor will be involved in a balance-of-payments crisis. They suggest, nevertheless, that a sovereign rated "investment grade" will be more able to manage crises episodes than sovereign borrowers rated "speculative grade"[954]. Attempts to correct their failures led the agencies, after the 1997 East Asian currency crisis, to observe external liabilities of the private financial sector, in particular, those with a short-term horizon and contingent liabilities of public sector more carefully. Nevertheless, the agencies performed poorly again during the 2008 crisis, this

---

949 Macro volatility reduces savings and investment, affects negatively development of the financial sector and long-term business decision-making. Fitch uses the standard deviation in GDP, CPI and Real Effective Exchange Rate as proxy for macro volatility. The longer the period of low and moderate inflation (i.e., less than 10 per cent) and stable growth, the greater will be confidence, leading to greater resilience to shocks, instead of chronic inflation and cyclical GDP. Another quantitative factor is the ratio of foreign currency to total deposits, or the dollarization ratio. Moreover, sustainability of macroeconomic policies is carefully observed in particular in the case of pegged exchange rate regimes. Additionally, the trend of key macro indicators from balance-of-payments to the level of international reserves plays a significant role (Fitch Ratings (2010a), p. 7).

950 Fitch Ratings uses the United Nations Human Development Index and the World Bank's "Ease of Doing Business" survey and "Governance Indicators" to examine the business environment, human capital and the overall level of governance. Other factors from political risk to regulatory framework of the banking sector also play an important role (Fitch Ratings (2010a), p. 8).

951 These include the structure and sustainability of public debt, contingent liabilities of the government as well as fiscal policy (Fitch Ratings (2010a), pp. 11, 12).

952 These cover the Balance-of-Payments, the main component carefully observed being the current account balance. The sustainability of international trade balances is of particular concern, i.e., large current account deficits can potentially lead to macroeconomic instability when they are financed by volatile capital flows (Fitch Ratings (2010a), pp. 13, 14).

953 Canuto, O., Fonseca, P., and de Sà Porto, C., (2004), p. 9

954 Ibid., p. 10

time in a private sector-led failure[955]. While rating agencies do not publish their models, the interest from an academic perspective is that if they do not change the model, at least one can see how the model performs over time. However, comparisons between countries are not reliable and I can state that credit rating agencies are always running, *grosso modo*, at least six months behind the real world. On the other hand, CDS and interest rate spreads provide real-time data to market participants.

Let me present now Turkish macroeconomic data for the 2000s, using a new series introduced to fit EU standards[956] in line with the "Accession Partnership"[957], which declared priorities in the field of statistics[958]. Accordingly, the Turkish government in the "National Program for the Adoption of the Acquis Communautaire" (March 2001) declared as follows[959]:

> "All accounting records will be realized according to the principles and standards of European System of Accounts (ESA) 95 and data systems will produce data in accordance with these principles".

---

[955] For example, they failed to provide reliable information to markets on Lehman Brother's financial situation before its default.

[956] Turkish national accounts were traditionally recorded on the basis of the OECD 1968 System of National Accounts. Moreover, there was lack of coordination among several public institutions producing statistical information. In fact, statistical data on identical objects were produced by different institutions with different definitions and methodologies, which caused comparability problems and a waste of resources. Thus, the Turkish Statistical Institute (TURKSTAT) was not able to produce reliable data (Demir, O. and Toprak, O. (2004), pp. 4, 5).

[957] A document prepared by the European Commission as a formal procedure of a candidacy.

[958] For short-term priorities it included: "Adopting a strategy for the further development of statistics, in particular demographic and social statistics, regional statistics, business statistics, external trade and agricultural statistics, bringing the business register up to EU standards. [....]Revising the National Accounts methodology for the implementation of European System of Accounts (ESA) 95 and ensuring adequate training of staff and improving the administrative capacity". For the long-term, it emphasized the need for "Adopting EU compatible statistical methodologies and practices, in particular as regards GDP estimates, harmonized consumer price indices, short-term indicators, social statistics, business register and balance-of-payments, aligning macroeconomic statistics further with the statistical *acquis*" (State Planning Organization (2003), p. 16).

[959] Republic of Turkey (2001), p. 286

TURKSTAT published the new figures during the same month and included a revision of the GDP series for the period 1998-2006 in current and constant prices[960]. Adopting EU statistical requirements has ensured that Turkish statistics are now comparable with those of other countries. Thus, the revised national accounts represent a major improvement in the measurement of economic activity and in harmonization with international standards. During the revision process, statistical institutions such as EUROSTAT and the IMF provided technical assistance and conducted training programs.

Based on these improvements in the field of statistics, in the next section, I begin by examining two Maastricht criteria considered as major EU membership obligations: Public debt stock and budget balance. The EU definition of General government nominal Turkish debt stock[961] based on the methodology defined in ESA 95 will also allow me to compare the Turkish public debt with a sample of EU countries.

5.1.1. Macroeconomic improvements and comparison with a sample of EU countries

Figure 5.1 shows that the EU-defined General government nominal public debt stock in Turkey followed a declining trend after the 2001 currency crisis, meeting the Maastricht criteria of 60 percent of GDP, by the year 2004.

960 Turkish Statistical Institute (2009), p. 1

961 General government consists of the central government, regional and local administrations, extra-budgetary funds, social security institutions (including Unemployment Insurance Fund). General government nominal debt stock consistent with the EU standards is calculated by adding general government gross (domestic and external) debt stock and the adjustment items (Undersecretariat of Treasury, Public Debt Management Report, (2009), pp. 28, 29).

Fig. 5.1: Turkish public debt stock/GDP ratio and Maastricht criteria, in percentage of GDP

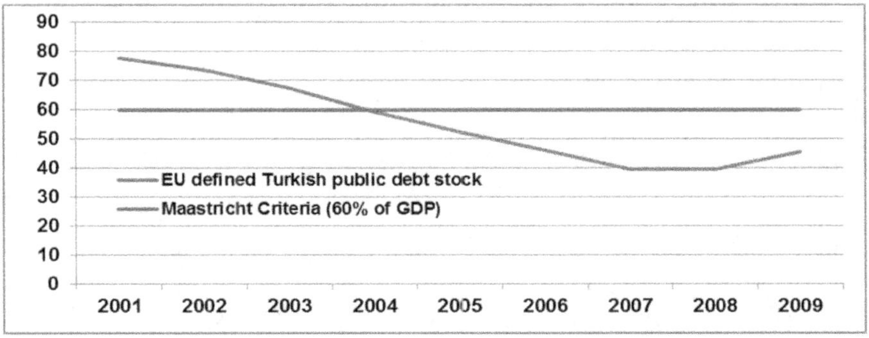

Source: Undersecretariat of Treasury, Public Debt Management Reports 2008, 2009, 2010

Similarly, in Figure 5.2 we observe that high budget deficits were reduced to sustainable levels by the year 2005, meeting Maastricht threshold of 3 percent budget deficit/GDP ratio[962].

---

962 The following article and protocol of the Treaty on the Functioning of the EU introduce thresholds for budget deficits and public debt:

"Art. 126: 1) Member States shall avoid excessive government deficits. 2) [....] The reference values are specified in the Protocol on the excessive deficit procedure annexed to the Treaties." (Official Journal of the European Union (2012a), pp. 99, 100);

"Protocol No. 12, Art. 1: The reference values referred in Article 126 (2) of the Treaty on the Functioning of the European Union are 3 percent for the ratio of the planned or actual government deficit to gross domestic product at market prices and 60 percent for the ratio of government debt to gross domestic product at market prices." (Official Journal of the European Union (2012a), p. 279).

Fig. 5.2: Turkish Budget Balance and Maastricht Criteria, in percentage of GDP

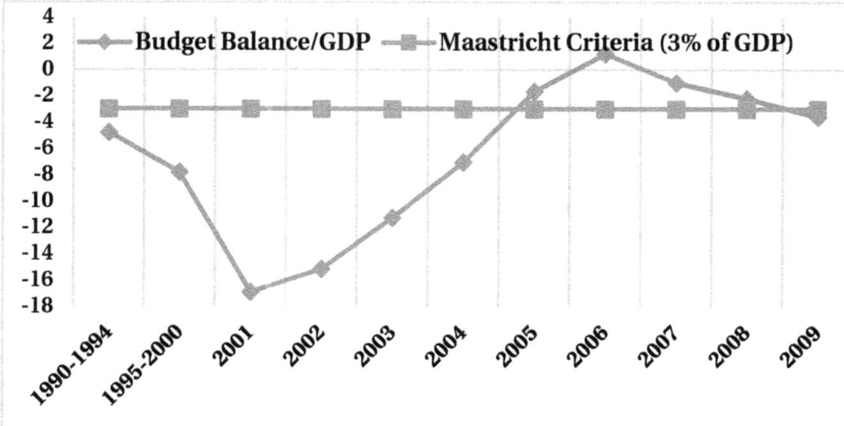

Source: State Planning Organization

Table 5.1 shows that Turkey has achieved a lower public debt/GDP ratio when compared with the average of EU-27 countries and the 16 countries in the Euro area in the second half of the 2000s. This result is important as public debt had become a serious problem for the entire economy during the 1980s and 1990s. A relatively balanced budget in Table 5.2 shows that the economy's borrowing requirement was significantly reduced also presenting a better performance when compared with EU-27 countries and 16 countries of the Euro area for all the years from 2005 to 2009, except for the year 2007.

Table 5.1: Public Debt/GDP ratio, in percentage

	2005	2006	2007	2008	2009
EU-27	62.7	61.4	58.8	61.6	73.6
Euro area (16)	70.1	68.3	66.0	69.4	78.7
Portugal	63.6	64.7	63.6	66.3	76.8
Ireland	27.6	24.9	25.0	43.9	64.0
Italy	105.8	106.5	103.5	106.1	115.8
Greece	100.0	97.8	95.7	99.2	115.1
Spain	43.0	39.6	36.2	39.7	53.2
The Czech Rep.	29.7	29.4	29.0	30.0	35.4
Hungary	61.8	65.6	65.9	72.9	78.3
Poland	47.1	47.7	45.0	47.2	51.0
Belgium	92.1	88.1	84.2	89.8	96.7
France	66.4	63.7	63.8	67.5	77.6
U.K.	42.2	43.5	44.7	52.0	68.1
Germany	68.0	67.6	65.0	66.0	73.2
Austria	63.9	62.2	59.5	62.6	66.5
Netherlands	51.8	47.4	45.5	58.2	60.9
Finland	41.8	39.7	35.2	34.2	44.0
Sweden	51.0	45.7	40.8	38.3	42.3
Denmark	37.1	32.1	27.4	34.2	41.6
Turkey	52.3	46.1	39.4	39.5	45.5

Source: Public Debt Management Report (2010), pp. 3, 32

Table 5.2: Budget balance/GDP ratio, in percentage

	2005	2006	2007	2008	2009
EU-27	2.4	-1.4	-0.8	-2.3	-6.8
Euro area (16)	2.5	-1.3	-0.6	-2.0	-6.3
Portugal	6.1	-3.9	-2.6	-2.8	-9.4
Ireland	1.7	3.0	0.1	-7.3	-14.3
Italy	-4.3	-3.3	-1.5	-2.7	-5.3
Greece	-5.2	-3.6	-5.1	-7.7	-13.6
Spain	1.0	2.0	1.9	-4.1	-11.2
The Czech Rep.	-3.6	-2.6	-0.7	-2.7	- 5.9
Hungary	-7.9	-9.3	-5.0	-3.8	-4.0
Poland	-4.1	-3.6	-1.9	-3.7	-7.1
Belgium	-2.7	0.3	-0.2	-1.2	-6.0
France	-2.9	-2.3	-2.7	-3.3	-7.5
U.K.	-3.4	-2.7	-2.8	-4.9	-11.5
Germany	-3.3	-1.6	0.2	0.0	-3.3
Austria	-1.6	-1.5	-0.4	-0.4	3.4
Netherlands	-0.3	0.5	0.2	0.7	-5.3
Finland	2.8	4.0	5.2	4.2	-2.2
Sweden	2.3	2.5	3.8	2.5	-0.5
Denmark	5.2	5.2	4.8	3.4	-2.7
Turkey	-0.6	1.2	-1.0	-2.2	-3.6

Source: Public Debt Management Report (2010), pp. 32, 34

Table 5.3 illustrates other key macro indicators during the 2000s. Considering the period from 2002 to 2007, thus excluding exogenous factors, i.e., the impact of the 2008-2009 global recession on the Turkish economy, three aspects warrant development:

- The economy experienced a high GDP growth rate, i.e., an annual average GDP growth rate of over 6 percent from 2002 to 2007;
- Around 10 percent or less inflation rates starting by the year 2004;
- Finally, the SOE borrowing requirement ratio, an important component of budget deficits during the 1980s and 1990s, vanished (a negative mark indicating a surplus). This was achieved thanks to the reforms aiming at increasing efficiency of the SOEs and the accelerated privatization process (Figure 5.3).

Table 5.3: Turkey – Key macroeconomic indicators

	(1) GDP	(2) Infl. aver.	(3) Infl. end-y.	(4) TL/$ aver.	(5) CA/ GDP	(6) Budget Balance	(7) Primary Budget	(8) PSBR/ GDP	(9) SOE borr. req.
2000	6.8	54.9	39.0	0.6	-3.7	-7.9	4.4	8.9	-
2001	-5.7	54.4	68.5	1.2	1.9	-11.9	5.2	12.1	-
2002	6.2	45.0	29.7	1.5	-0.3	-11.5	3.3	10.0	-0.8
2003	5.3	25.3	18.4	1.5	-2.5	-8.8	4.1	7.3	-0.6
2004	9.4	10.6	9.4	1.4	-3.7	-5.2	4.9	3.6	-0.4
2005	8.4	8.2	7.7	1.3	-4.6	-1.1	6.0	-0.3	-0.1
2006	6.9	9.6	9.7	1.4	-6.1	-0.6	5.5	-1.9	-0.5
2007	4.7	8.8	8.4	1.3	-5.9	-1.6	4.2	0.1	-0.1
2008	0.7	10.4	10.1	1.3	-5.7	-1.8	3.5	1.6	-0.02
2009	-4.8	6.3	6.5	1.5	-2.3	-5.5	0.1	5.1	-0.4
2010	9.2	8.6	6.4	1.5	-6.6	-3.6	0.8	3.3	-0.3

Source: General Directorate of Budget and Fiscal Control, Ministry of Finance

1. GDP, at constant 1998 prices, annual percentage change;
2. Consumer Price Index (CPI), annual average percentage change;
3. CPI annual percentage change based on end-year values;
4. TL/USD FX nominal rate annual average;
5. Current Account Balance/GDP ratio, annual percentage change;
6. Ratio Budget Balance/GDP, annual percentage change;
7. Ratio Primary Budget Balance/GDP (excluding interest payments), annual percentage change;
8. Public Sector Borrowing Requirement/GDP ratio, in percentage;
9. State-Owned Enterprises borrowing requirement/GDP ratio, in percentage.

Fig. 5.3: Privatization implementations 1999-2010, in million USD

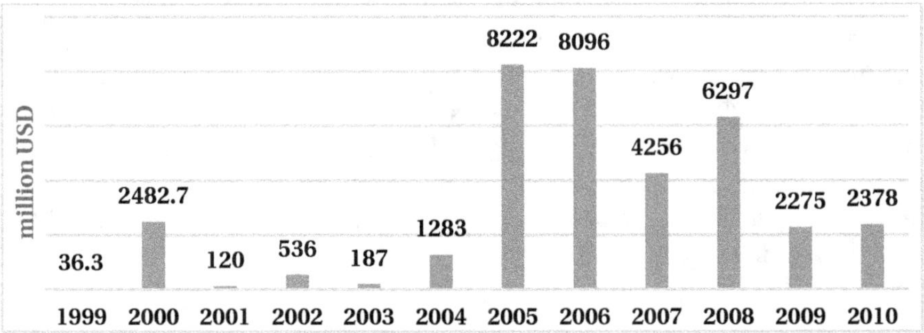

Source: Office of the Turkish Prime Minister, Privatization Administration, official website

5.1.2. Rating assignments: Turkey versus a sample of EU countries

I discussed factors taken into account by rating agencies in evaluating sovereign credit risk and presented the macroeconomic data for Turkey in the previous sections. Let me now examine ratings for Turkey and compare them with those of a sample of EU countries.

The most relevant distinction from a sovereign credit perspective is the share of public debt issued in local or foreign currencies. The market in which it is issued is an additional factor that can result in differences in ratings assigned to debt instruments in the same currency[963]. Table 5.4 provides information regarding changes from 1994 to 2010 in foreign versus local currency ratings[964] of the sovereign debt of Turkey and Greece. To note, in the case of Turkey, the following up and downgrades caused by particular events:

- 10th April 2000: Upgrade to "Rating Watch Positive", due to the increased confidence and improving macro parameters in the initial phase of the IMF Stabilization Program. Two weeks later, on 27th April 2000 "Long-term Foreign Currency" rating was upgraded as well;
- 22nd February 2001 (the day of speculative attack to currency triggering the financial crisis): Downgrade to "Rating Watch Negative" and "Local Currency Rating" downgraded from BB to B+;
- "Positive Outlook" rating given on 6th December 2005, following the opening of EU accession talks with Turkey, on 3rd October 2005.

In terms of inter-country comparisons, it is possible to observe that while Turkey gained a "BB-" for the long-term "Foreign Currency" rating on 27th April 2000, thanks to the implementation of the IMF Stabilization Program, it was downgraded to "B+" after the February 2001 currency crisis, on 2nd April 2001, and maintained a "B+", "B" or "B-" for almost four years, only regaining "BB-" by 13th January 2005, and "BB+" by 3rd December 2009. Turkey never compared favorably with Greece in these ratings. While the grades for long-term foreign currency debt given to Greece, from 1995 to April 2010, ranged from "BBB (-)" to "A+", despite its huge debt burden, Turkey never achieved better than "BB (-)" or "BB (+)" in the same period.

---

963 Fitch Ratings (2010b), p. 3

964 Annex 5 provides further information regarding the ratings assignments.

Table 5.4: Credit Rating Assignments – Turkey and Greece

TURKEY	Foreign Currency Rating			Local currency rating	
Date	**Long-term**	**Short-term**	**Outlook/Watch**	**Long-term**	**Outlook/Watch**
3 Dec 2009	BB+	B	stable	BB+	stable
27 Oct 2009	BB-	B	positive	BB	positive
12 Dec 2007	BB-	B	stable	BB	stable
9 May 2007	BB-	B	stable	BB-	stable
6 Dec 2005	BB-	B	positive	BB-	positive
13 Jan 2005	BB-	B	stable	BB-	stable
25 Aug 2004	B+	B	positive	B+	positive
9 Feb 2004	B+	B	stable	B+	stable
25Sep 2003	B	B	positive	B	positive
6 Aug 2003	B-	B	positive	B-	positive
25 Mar 2003	B-	B	negative	B-	negative
5 Feb 2002	B	B	stable	B	stable
2 Aug 2001	B	B	negative	B-	negative
2 Apr 2001	B+	B	negative	B	negative
22 Feb 2001	BB-	B	negative	B+	negative
21 Sep 2000	BB-	B	stable	BB	stable
27 Apr 2000	BB-	B	-	BB	-
10 Apr 2000	B+	B	positive	-	positive
20 Dec 1996	B+	B	-	-	-
29 Jul 1996	BB-	B	negative	-	negative
26 Oct 1995	BB-	B	-	-	-
26 Sep 1995	BB-	-	-	-	-
10 Aug 1994	B	-	-	-	-

GREECE	Foreign Currency Rating			Local currency rating	
Date	**Long-term**	**Short-term**	**Outlook/Watch**	**Long-term**	**Outlook/Watch**
9 Apr 2010	BBB-	F2	negative	BBB-	negative
8 Dec 2009	BBB+	F2	negative	BBB+	negative
22 Oct 2009	A-	F1	negative	A-	negative
12 May 2009	A	F1	negative	A	negative
20 Oct 2008	A	F1	stable	A	stable
5 Mar 2007	A	F1	positive	A	positive
16 Dec 2004	A	F1	stable	A	stable
28 Sep 2004	A+	F1	negative	A+	negative
20 Oct 2003	A+	F1	stable	A+	stable
23 Oct 2002	A	F1	positive	A	positive
20 Jun 2001	A	F1	stable	A	stable
21Sep 2000	A-	F1	stable	A-	stable
27 Jul 2000	A-	F1	-	A-	-
13 Mar 2000	BBB+	F2	positive	A-	positive
25 Oct 1999	BBB+	F2	-	A-	-
10 Aug 1999	BBB	F3	positive	-	positive
4 Jun 1997	BBB	F3	-	-	-
13 Nov 1995	BBB-	F3	-	-	-

Source: Fitch Ratings

In relative terms, while Turkey went from mostly negative to a positive "outlook/watch", over this period, Greece went the other way.

Similarly, Table 5.5 compares Turkey's ratings with those of Portugal and Spain. While Portugal, despite a "Negative Outlook" due to the 2008-2009 global recession, maintained its "Long-term Foreign Currency" ratings in the A category, Spain was rated as the strongest economy in the sample.

Table 5.5: Credit Rating Assignments – Spain and Portugal

PORTUGAL	**Foreign Currency Rating**			**Local currency rating**	
Date	**Long-term**	**Short-term**	**Outlook/Watch**	**Long-term**	**Outlook/Watch**
24 Mar 2010	AA-	F1+	negative	AA-	negative
3 Sep 2009	AA	F1+	negative	AA	negative
1 May 2007	AA	F1+	stable	AA	stable
29 Jun 2005	AA	F1+	negative	AA	negative
21 Sep 2000	AA	F1+	stable	AA	stable
14 Jul 1998	AA	F1+	-	AA	-
4 Jun 1998	AA	F1+	-	AAA	-
26 Oct 1995	AA-	F1+	-	AAA	-
10 Aug 1994	AA-	-	-	-	-

SPAIN	**Foreign Currency Rating**			**Local currency rating**	
Date	**Long-term**	**Short-term**	**Outlook/Watch**	**Long-term**	**Outlook/Watch**
28 May 2010	AA+	F1+	stable	AA+	stable
10 Dec 2003	AAA	F1+	stable	AAA	stable
21 Sep 2000	AA+	F1+	stable	AA+	stable
1 Sep 1999	AA+	F1+	-	AA+	-
14 Jul 1998	AA	F1+	-	AA	-
26 Oct 1995	AA	F1+	-	AAA	-
10 Aug 1994	AA	-	-	-	-

Source: Fitch Ratings

Table 5.6 compares Turkey with another sample of countries that joined the EU during the 2000s. To note that the lowest rating that the Czech Republic, Hungary, and Poland obtained during the 2000s was "BBB", a grade that has never been assigned to Turkey.

Table 5.6: Credit Rating Assignments – Hungary, the Czech Republic and Poland

HUNGARY	Foreign Currency Rating			Local currency rating	
Date	**Long-term**	**Short-term**	**Outlook/Watch**	**Long-term**	**Outlook/Watch**
2 Mar 2009	BBB	F3	negative	BBB+	negative
9 Nov 2008	BBB	F3	stable	BBB+	stable
15 Oct 2008	BBB+	F2	negative	A-	negative
5 Nov 2007	BBB+	F2	stable	A-	stable
20 Sep 2006	BBB+	F2	negative	A-	negative
6 Dec 2005	BBB+	F2	stable	A-	stable
12 Jan 2005	A-	F2	negative	A	stable
15 Jul 2003	A-	F2	negative	A+	negative
30 Nov 2000	A-	F2	stable	A+	stable
21 Sep 2000	BBB+	F2	positive	A	positive
29 Oct 1999	BBB+	F2	-	A	-
2 Jul 1998	BBB	F3	-	A	-
24 Jun 1997	BBB	F3	-	A-	-
23 May 1997	BBB-	F3	positive	BBB+	positive
25 Apr 1996	BBB-	F3	-	BBB+	-

CZECH R.	Foreign Currency Rating			Local currency rating	
Date	**Long-term**	**Short-term**	**Outlook/Watch**	**Long-term**	**Outlook/Watch**
4 Jun 2010	A+	F1	positive	AA-	positive
4 Mar 2008	A+	F1	stable	AA-	stable
26 Aug 2005	A	F1	stable	A+	stable
20 Jun 2003	A-	F2	stable	A	stable
28 Mar 2001	BBB+	F2	stable	A	stable
21 Sep 2000	BBB+	F2	stable	A+	stable
22 Dec 1998	BBB+	F2	-	A+	-
24 Nov 1997	BBB+	F2	-	AA-	-
26 Oct 1995	A-	F1	-	-	-
10 Aug 1995	A-	-	-	-	-

POLAND	Foreign Currency Rating			Local currency rating	
Date	**Long-term**	**Short-term**	**Outlook/Watch**	**Long-term**	**Outlook/Watch**
18 Jan 2007	A-	F2	stable	A	stable
23 Mar 2005	BBB+	F2	positive	A	stable
6 May 2004	BBB+	F2	stable	A	stable
4 Nov 2003	BBB+	F2	positive	A+	stable
21 Sep 2000	BBB+	F2	stable	A+	stable
19 Nov 1998	BBB+	F2	-	A+	-
7 Jun 1996	BBB	F3	-	A-	-
29 Apr 1996	BB+	B	positive	-	positive
26 Oct 1995	BB+	B	-	-	-

Source: Fitch Ratings

To conclude, Turkey's ratings improved after 2005, despite the fact that Fitch ratings for Turkey were still lower than our sample of EU countries.

Let me now examine in the next section, another indicator, which reflects market participants' sentiment regarding sovereign default risk: the Credit Default Swaps.

5.1.3. Credit Default Swap data as an alternative market-based evaluation

In Figure 5.4, it is straightforward to observe a decline in the CDS spreads from 2004 to 2006. A comparison of Turkish CDS spreads with the same sample makes evident the negative impact of the 2008-2009 global recession for Turkey as for other countries. However, the figure shows also that Turkish CDS spreads were lower than those of Greece, Portugal, and Spain by the 2nd and 3rd quarters of 2010, which means that markets attributed lower probability of default to Turkish sovereign debt than others in the sample – quite a different picture when compared with scores assigned by credit rating agencies.

Fig. 5.4: Comparing CDS spreads, in basis points (bps): Turkey, Greece, Portugal and Spain, 17th May 2004 - 30th September 2010[965]

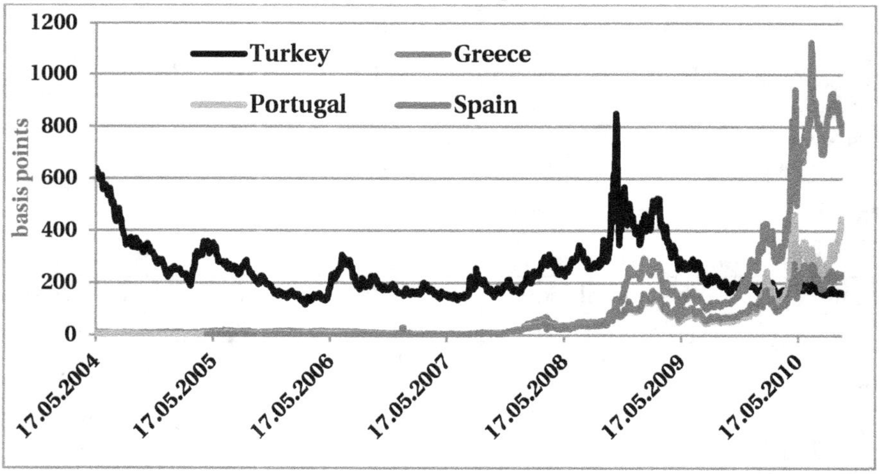

Source: Datastream, Thompson Reuters

[965] To note that spreads in the figure corresponded to 627 bps on 17th May 2004 for Turkey, and to 159.6, 775.3, 408.8 and 230.7 bps on 30th September 2010 for Turkey, Greece, Portugal and Spain, respectively.

Nevertheless, a sudden movement, in particular of the Greek spreads in 2010 in the figure above is to be analyzed under the European sovereign debt problem, which is not a theme of this study. The governments of Greece, Spain, and Portugal voluntarily entered the European Monetary Union, thus they renounced their ability to borrow in a currency they can control[966]. This means that in case of a capital outflow these governments would not be able to borrow from their central bank as the art.123 of the Treaty on the Functioning of the EU does not allow such an operation and they would default on their obligations[967]. Thus, in case of a loss of confidence of global investors, a self-fulfilling attack[968] may lead the country into default[969]. The EU governments adopting the Euro as their currency, have fallen into the position of emerging market issuers increasing their sovereign default risk exposure[970]. In fact, the situation of Greece in the figure above is similar to that of Argentina in 2000 when it would have to default on its sovereign dollar bonds[971]. In an attempt to avoid the bias due to the increased sovereign default risk of Eurozone economies in figure 5.4, let me now consider another sample including three EU countries which have not yet adopted the Euro, and thus have kept control over the currency in which they issue debt[972] (Hungary, Poland, the Czech Republic) and other three countries beyond the European continent (Brazil, South Africa, Australia).

In any case, a similar observation is valid when I compare Turkey with Hungary, Poland, and the Czech Republic. In fact, while Turkish CDS spreads were higher than the others from 2004 until 2008, Turkish spreads converged to others during the global recession, becoming only slightly higher than Poland and the Czech Republic but lower than Hungary (Fig. 5.5).

---

[966] De Grauwe, P. (2011), p. 18

[967] Kopf, C. (2011), p. 4

[968] I discussed dynamics behind self-fulfilling speculative attacks in section 3.2.2, in the context of Second Generation Currency Crisis models.

[969] De Grauwe, P. (2011), p. 18

[970] Ibid., p. 10

[971] Kopf, C. (2011), p. 4

[972] De Grauwe, P. (2011), p. 2

Fig. 5.5: Comparing CDS spreads, in basis points: Turkey, Hungary, Poland and the Czech Republic, 17th May 2004 - 30th September 2010[973]

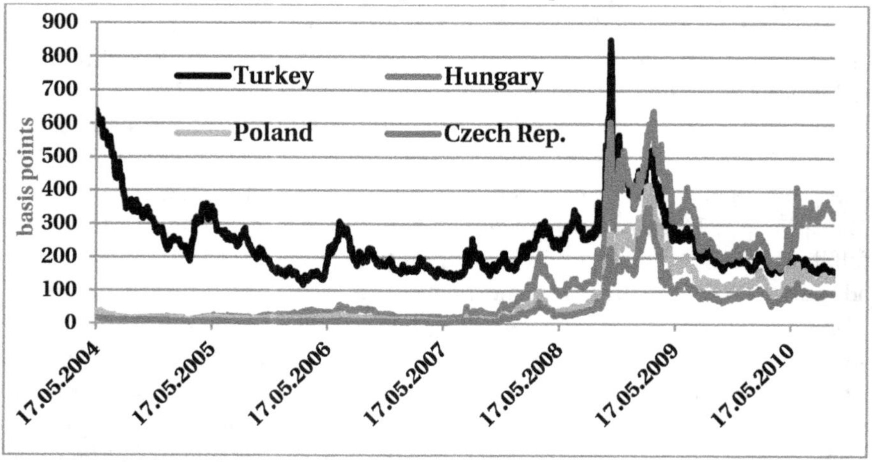

Source: Datastream, Thompson Reuters

Finally, the figure 5.6 shows again a convergence of spreads, in particular, those of Turkey and South Africa by the year 2010. To note that while the difference between Turkish and Australian spreads was 631.8 basis points on 17th May 2004, it was only 85.3 basis points 6 years later.

---

[973] To note that spreads in the figure corresponded to 627 bps on 17th May 2004 for Turkey, and to 159.6, 320.6, 136.2 and 93.4 bps on 30th September 2010 for Turkey, Hungary, Poland and the Czech Republic, respectively.

Fig. 5.6: Comparing CDS spreads, in basis points: Turkey, Brazil, South Africa and Australia, 17th May 2004 - 30th September 2010[974]

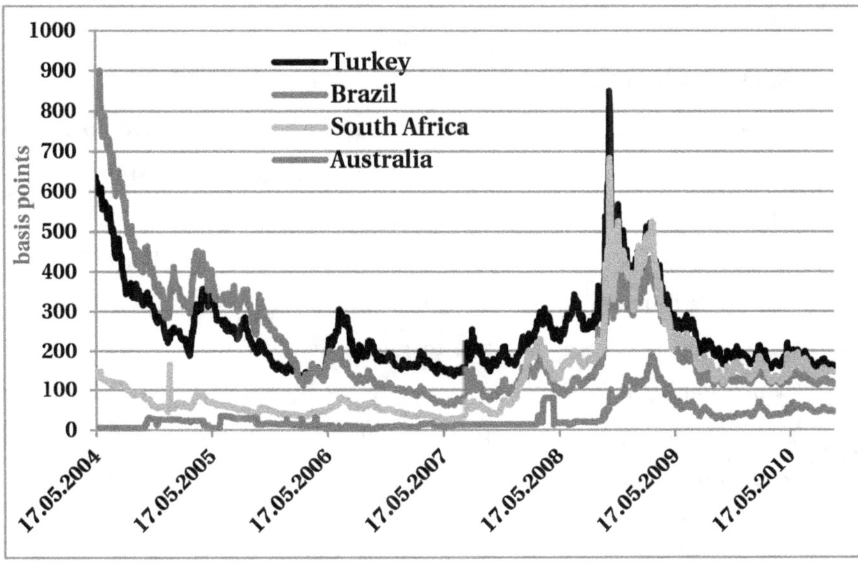

Source: Datastream, Thompson Reuters

The shift in Turkish spreads in May 2006 in these figures is due to a decline in risk appetite of global investors, which led to a capital outflow. I will discuss this aspect in the next section (5.3).

To note that while rating agencies have a standard methodology for allocating ratings, the CDS spreads are based on markets' instantaneous perception of the sovereign probability of default, that is to say, without any pre-established or homogeneous methodology. Additionally, investors can trade either for hedging or for speculative purposes. Thus, while an investor holding Turkish government securities can buy a CDS contract on Turkish sovereign debt in an attempt to hedge credit risk inherent in the bonds she holds, another investor can trade a CDS contract without any prior exposure to credit risk associated with the underlying asset, thus expecting to gain from her unhedged credit risk position. While my aim is not to analyze the factors behind the divergence between credit ratings and CDS spreads, I draw attention to the

974 To note that spreads in the figure corresponded to 627 bps on 17th May 2004 for Turkey, lower only than the spreads of Brazil, and to 159.6, 114.8, 144.3 and 46.0 bps on 30th September 2010 for Turkey, Brazil, South Africa and Australia, respectively. The latter is the economy with the lowest spreads in the sample in the time frame considered.

possible reasons for their existence. The following quotations from Friedrich Hayek's "Use of Knowledge in Society" will enlarge our perspective[975]:

> "The peculiar character of the problem of a rational economic order is determined precisely by the fact that the knowledge of the circumstances of which we must make use never exists in concentrated or integrated form but solely as the dispersed bits of incomplete and frequently contradictory knowledge which all the separate individuals possess. The economic problem of society is thus not merely a problem of how to allocate "given" resources - if "given" is taken to mean given to a single mind which deliberately solves the problem set by these "data". It is rather a problem of how to secure the best use of resources known to any of the members of society, for ends whose relative importance only these individuals know. Or, to put it briefly, it is a problem of utilization of knowledge which is not given to anyone in its totality."

Friedrich Hayek then emphasizes the "relative importance of different kinds of knowledge" as follows[976]:

> "It may be admitted that, as far as scientific knowledge is concerned, a body of suitably chosen experts may be in the best position to command all the best knowledge available-though this is of course merely shifting the difficulty to the problem of selecting the experts. [....]
>
> Today it is almost heresy to suggest that scientific knowledge is not the sum of all knowledge. But a little reflection will show that there is beyond question a body of very important but

[975] Hayek, F. A. (1945), pp. 519, 520

[976] Ibid., p. 522

> unorganized knowledge which cannot be possibly called scientific in the sense of knowledge of general rules: the knowledge of the particular circumstances of time and place. It is with respect to this that practically every individual has some advantage over all others because he possesses unique information of which beneficial use might be made, but of which use can be made only if the decisions depending on it are left to him or are made with his active co-operation. [....]
>
> The shipper who earns his earns his living from using otherwise empty or half-filled journeys of tramp-steamers, or the real estate agent whose whole knowledge is almost exclusively one of temporary opportunities, or the arbitrageur who gains from local differences of commodity prices, are all performing eminently useful functions based on special knowledge of circumstances of the fleeting moment not known to others.

To note that the "use of knowledge" in Hayek's sense will be effective in CDS spreads depending whether investors use CDS contract for hedging or speculative purposes. Let me consider both of the cases:

1. Hedging: A risk adverse investor will use a CDS contract to hedge her position, for example, on a sovereign bond. This does not mean that she possesses private information on particular circumstances, but her aim is to be protected against an unexpected outcome. To note in this case there is an underlying asset;

2. Speculation: A risk loving investor aiming to bear risk or possessing private information on particular circumstances can take an unhedged position, without thus an underlying asset[977]. This is the case, for example, of an investor who "buys protection" without owning a commensurate amount of debt instrument of the referenced borrower[978]. This is called as having a "naked" CDS where the investor expects to make a profit based on her

---

[977] Undersecretariat of Treasury (2011), p. 60

[978] Duffie, D. (2010), p. 56

private information or knowledge. Thus, this kind of transaction can provide a source of information to third parties on the credibility of the reference entities[979].

While CDS spreads can provide information regarding credit risk of reference entities, they can also have an impact on the stability of the financial system itself. For example, banks might wish to transfer their risks to unregulated hedge funds[980]. Moreover, the CDS is an over-the-counter contract, thus, in the absence of clearing house arrangements, unexpected events can lead to a high-level systemic risk[981]. For example, the US government bailed out the American International Group, Inc. (AIG) in September 2008. If AIG had gone bankrupt this could have led to financial instability as many institutions had sold CDS protection on AIG[982]. The global recession initiated in 2008 led to a long-lasting debate, which culminated with the European Parliament and Council, introducing on 18th October 2011, a general ban on "naked" sovereign CDSs[983]. I discussed in section 3.2.3.2 the impact of short selling restrictions on efficient pricing. In a similar way, this ban on "naked" CDS transactions can impede information and knowledge to be fully reflected in CDS contracts. The Regulation (No. 236) on short selling and certain aspects of credit default swaps entered into force on 25th March 2012 and started to apply from 1st November 2012[984]. Nevertheless, it exempts market makers from the prohibition on entering into a "naked" sovereign CDS transaction[985]. To note that 87.2 percent of the CDS trading activity comes from the top 15 dealers, which act as market makers (like for example the JP Morgan)[986]. Thus, it is likely that markets continue to use the CDS spreads as an indicator of sovereign credit risk also after 1st November 2012.

In the light of the quotations above, I can now compare strong and weak aspects of rating agencies and CDS spreads in an attempt to explore potential factors leading to diverging results:

---

979 Undersecretariat of Treasury (2011), p. 59

980 Ibid.

981 Ibid.

982 Ibid., p. 60

983 Europolitics official website

984 Official Journal of the European Union (2012b), p. 24

985 Ibid., p. 4

986 Delatte, A. L. (2012), VOX website

1. Credit rating assignments

Rating agencies gather all published macroeconomic data, including political events. Nevertheless, only a few experts' knowledge is used in the final assessment.

Result: Agencies are always late in providing reliable information.

2. CDS spreads

Market participants use CDS contracts with or without an underlying asset based not only on published data but also on informal "Hayekian" knowledge through specific, local and unpublished information.

Result: All available knowledge (i.e., formal, informal, published, unpublished) is brought to bear on the problem. Information contained in prices is always up-to-date and in real time, gathers all available information and is a much more reliable guide than credit rating agencies.

It is worth to note the study of Shen, C. H. and Huang, A. Y. (2010), who worked on 31 countries' sovereign CDS data from January 2001 to February 2010 to investigate the relationship between credit ratings and sovereign CDS spreads[987]. They found a long-term interdependence and short-term convergence between credit rating assignments and CDS spreads and argued that fund managers and bondholders should consider CDS data as the primary benchmark for credit quality[988].

What is the relevant aspect in this discussion for this study?

It is important for me to note that both agency credit ratings and markets' perception of default risk for Turkey improved considerably in the late 2000s. I argue that a major reason behind this progress was the implementation of structural regulatory and institutional reforms discussed earlier.

Having discussed the methodology of Fitch Ratings, I now turn to defining a CDS contract and attempt to model the CDS market. I will also illustrate the relationship between these spreads and the probability of sovereign default using the Turkish example.

---

[987] Shen, C. H. and Huang, A. Y. (2010), p. 15

[988] Ibid., p. 16

5.2. Credit Default Swaps (CDSs)

The CDS is an insurance contract with payoffs contingent on the realization of a negative credit event, such as the default of a reference entity[989] like a treasury bond. It provides protection against credit risk in exchange for periodic premium payments[990].

Fig. 5.7: Basics of CDSs

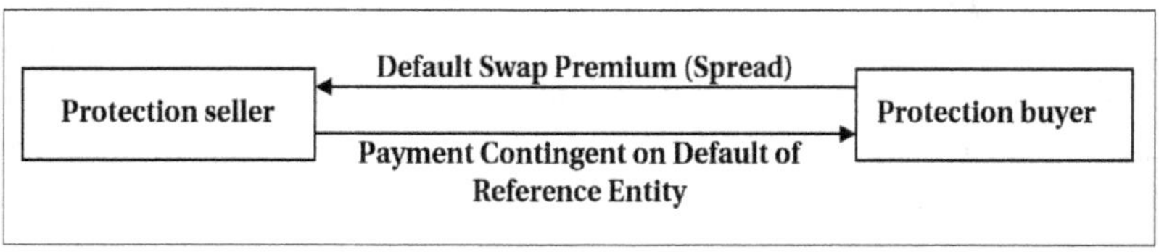

Source: O'Kane, D. and Turnbull, S. (2004), p. 2

CDS "spreads" are the variable insurance premium as a percentage of the notional value of the underlying asset[991] paid quarterly to the "protection seller". Quotation is made in basis points (bps) per annum of the contract's notional amount[992]. For instance, a Turkish 5-year sovereign CDS spread of 600 bps in figures 5.4 and 5.5 on 25th May 2004, means that for a notional amount of USD 1 million, the default swap premium to be paid to the protection seller was USD 60'000 per annum or USD 15'000 per quarter.

The first CDS transaction appeared when JP Morgan transferred credit risk exposure to the European Bank for Reconstruction and Development (EBRD), on a USD 4.8 billion loan to Exxon[993]. Thus, JP Morgan was engaged to pay a periodic fee to EBRD until the expiration of the contract. In case of a negative

---

989 Chan-Lau, J. A. (2003), p. 3

990 Ibid., p. 5

991 International Swaps and Derivatives Association (ISDA) define the "Net Notional Value" as follows: "The sum of the net protection bought by net buyers (or net protection sold by net sellers)". Net notional positions represent the maximum possible net funds transfers between net sellers of protection and net buyers of protection that could be required upon the occurrence of a credit event relating to particular reference entities (actual net funds transfers are dependent on the recovery rate for the underlying bonds or other debt instruments) (ISDA official website).

992 Beck, R. (2004), p. 11

993 Tang, D. Y. and Yan, H. (2011), p. 5

event, i.e., Exxon's default, the EBRD was to cover the JP Morgan's loss. In this case, JP Morgan is the protection buyer and EBRD is the protection seller. Exxon is the reference entity. The notional amount of the contract is USD 4.8 billion[994].

What was the motivation of JP Morgan in introducing a CDS deal with EBRD?

In line with the Basel Committee on Banking Supervision framework, JP Morgan was motivated to use CDSs in order to reduce regulatory capital. Selling the credit risk to EBRD through a CDS transaction allowed JP Morgan to provide a loan to Exxon, increasing its profits.

While the reference entity may be a corporate private firm or a sovereign government, in line with the purpose of this study, I will consider only sovereign CDSs. We will observe that the CDS price is a function of the probability of default of the issuer and of the expected recovery value in case of default[995]. Two approaches are used in modeling and pricing a CDS contract: "Structural" and "reduced-form"[996]. I discuss them briefly, as my aim is to show the way CDS spreads can be used in estimating the sovereign default risk.

1. "Structural" approach to modeling the CDS market (Contingent Claim Analysis)

Robert Merton (1973)[997] introduced the structural approach in quantitative modeling of credit risk, where default occurs when the asset value of the firm is inferior to what the firm owes to its debtors[998]. It is also called "contingent claims analysis"[999] because liabilities are claims on current or future assets. Since pricing dynamics behind corporate CDS contracts and sovereign CDS contracts are the same[1000] I can, in line with the purpose of my study, state the following: This approach implicitly assumes that market participants' views

---

994 Ibid.

995 Chan-Lau, J. A. (2003), p. 3

996 O'Kane, D. and Turnbull, S. (2004), p. 5

997 Merton, R. (1973), pp. 449-455

998 Capuano, C. et al. (2009), p. 4

999 Benos, A. and Papanastasopoulos, G. (2005), p. 1

1000 Pan, J. and Singleton, K. J. (2007), p. 8

include forward-looking information about the future economic prospects of the sovereign[1001]. This does not mean that the markets' view on sovereign default risk is always correct, but that the CDS spreads reflect the best available collective forecast of the market participants' expectations[1002] concerning, for instance, the level of reserves and "debt sustainability". While "reserves adequacy" can be defined as the ratio of foreign currency reserves to total public and private short-term foreign currency debt[1003], "debt sustainability" is a more complex concept incorporating also current perception and judgment of investors whether the sovereign will be able to pay back its debt in the future. According to the "structural" approach to CDS modeling, sovereign default risk is driven by three main elements interacting with each other[1004]: The value of "sovereign assets", "asset volatility" and "leverage"[1005]. Nevertheless, in line with the scope of the book, I use the second approach, the "reduced-form", as it gives me the possibility to transform, through simple equations, the CDS spreads into market participants' view related sovereign default probability.

2. The "reduced-form" approach to estimating the sovereign default risk from CDS spreads

Jarrow, R. A. and Turnbull, S. M. (1995) proposed an exogenous model for the "hazard rate", where the latter is defined as the likelihood of the firm defaulting over the next period[1006]. While the "structural models" I examined in the previous section estimated the default threshold by looking at the intertemporal consistency between assets and liabilities, here in the "reduced-

---

[1001] Gapen, M. T., Gray, D. F., Li, C. H. and Xiao, Y. (2008), p. 115

[1002] Ibid.

[1003] Ibid., p. 111

[1004] Gapen, M. T., Gray, D. F., Li, C. H. and Xiao, Y. (2005), p. 6

[1005] "Sovereign asset value" is defined as the combined market value of all sovereign assets, which depend on the country's future prospects and policy decisions. Due to uncertain future prospects, "asset volatility" is associated with uncertainty of future "sovereign asset value". "Leverage" measures the size of the sovereign's contractual liabilities that the sovereign is obligated to pay (Ibid.).

[1006] Madan, D. and Unal, H. (1999), p. 1, Giesecke, K. (2003), p. 15

form" approach the credit event follows a "Poisson Process"[1007] and occurs randomly.

In pricing a CDS contract with the "reduced form" approach, we observe two opposing legs[1008]: The present value of the fixed periodic premium payments (premium leg) is set equal to the expected present value of the loss in the event of default before the maturity of the contract (contingent or default leg). Thus, on the "premium leg" side, the protection buyer periodically pays a stream of discounted, fixed cash flows, whereas, on the "contingent leg" side, the protection seller makes one payment only if the reference credit defaults[1009]. The amount of the contingent payment is the notional value of the CDS contract multiplied by (1-R), where R is the recovery rate as a percentage of the notional value of the insured asset.

O'Kane, D. and Turnbull, S. (2004) used the Jarrow, R. A. and Turnbull, S. M. (1995) model to find implied probabilities of default from CDS spreads. For simplicity, they assumed that "hazard rate" is deterministic, which also implies that it is independent of interest rates and recovery rates[1010]. I use here a Deutsche Bank research paper, which proposes a further simplification, using the so-called "credit triangle", where the only unknown is the recovery rate[1011] and I calculate the sovereign probability of default in Turkey and in a sample of EU countries from CDS spreads. During an interview I conducted on 8th December 2010, Dominique O'Kane[1012] also suggested using this "credit triangle" relationship, arguing that it gives a very accurate approximation as

---

1007 Jarrow, R. A. and Turnbull, S. M. (1995) introduce a Poisson Process as follows: They assume that default occurs at some time T with a probability defined as $PD[\mathrm{T} < t+dt/T \geq t] = \lambda(t)dt$. This equation represents the probability of a default (PD) occurring within the time interval $[t, t+dt]$ which is conditional on surviving to time *t*. Within this framework, default is modeled in a one-period setting in which the entity survives with probability $q = 1-\lambda(t)d(t)$ or defaults and obtains a recovery value R with probability $(p) = \lambda(t)d(t)$ (O'Kane, D. and Turnbull, S. (2004), p. 5).

1008 Whetten, M., Adelson, M., and Van Bemmeler, M., (2004), p. 7

1009 Ibid.

1010 O'Kane, D. and Turnbull, S. (2004), p. 5

1011 Beck, R. (2004), p. 12

1012 Dominique O'Kane, one of the authors of paper O'Kane, D. and Turnbull, S. (2004), was a Lehman Brothers expert in "Fixed Income Quantitative Credit Research".

long as the CDS curve is flat or close to flat[1013]. I now briefly explain this relationship as follows: Let us consider a 5-year CDS contract and assume that the total premium is paid up-front. The protection buyer expects to pay the CDS spread S (or premium). His expected payoff is:

$$(1-R)*PD$$

where PD is the annualized sovereign probability of default and R is the expected recovery rate. When two parties agree on a CDS trade, the CDS spread is set so that the value of the swap transaction is zero[1014], that is to say:

$$S = (1-R)/PD$$

where S is the annualized CDS spread. To obtain the probability of default I assume a value for the recovery rate and take the annualized CDS spread value from the market as given. Based on the relationship:

$$PD=S/(1-R)$$

and assuming a recovery rate of 20 percent (a widely used percentage in financial markets), I obtain the implied probability of default rates from the CDS spreads[1015].

The figures below illustrate the probability of default of the Turkish government and of a sample of EU and non-EU countries that I derived from CDS spreads using a recovery rate of 20 percent, from 1st October 2009 to 30th September 2010. Figure 5.8 compares Turkish sovereign probability of default with that of Greece, Portugal, and Spain. To note that while in October and November 2009, markets perceived Turkish sovereign default risk to be higher than the others in the sample, they reversed their assessment by December 2009 and January 2010. Turkey was perceived as the lowest risky economy in this group from June 2010 onwards.

[1013] For accurate results, also in the case of non-flat CDS curve, Dominique O'Kane suggested the model that I provide in Annex 6. This is widely used in fixed income quantitative research, with a discount rate and some probability factors, where a "bootstrap methodology" is also necessary.

[1014] Beck, R. (2004), p. 12

[1015] Ibid.

Fig. 5.8: Comparing Market implied Sovereign Probability of Defaults from CDS Spreads: Turkey, Greece, Portugal, Spain, 1st October 2009 - 30th September 2010, in percentage[1016]

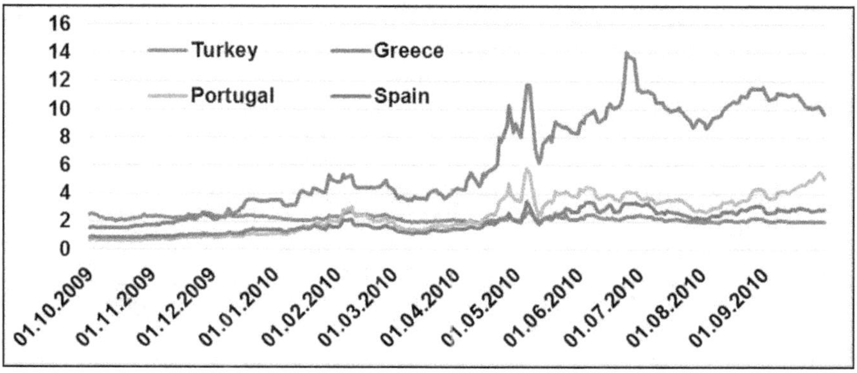

Source: CDS spreads obtained from Datastream, Thompson Reuters. Own calculations in deriving the probability of default from spreads.

As in the previous section 5.1.3, let me consider now three EU countries that have not adopted the Euro yet, in order to eliminate the additional sovereign risk exposure of Eurozone economies due to issuing debt in a currency over which they have no control: Poland, Hungary, and the Czech Republic. Similarly, we observe in figure 5.9 that markets perceived Turkey as less risky than Hungary during the period under consideration, while rating agencies took the opposite view.

1016 To note that sovereign probability of default in the figure corresponded to 2.0, 9.7, 5.1 and 2.9 percent on 30th September 2010, for Turkey, Greece, Portugal and Spain, respectively.

Fig. 5.9: Comparing Market implied Sovereign Probability of Default from CDS Spreads: Turkey, Hungary, Poland, the Czech Rep., 1st October 2009 - 30th September 2010, in percentage[1017]

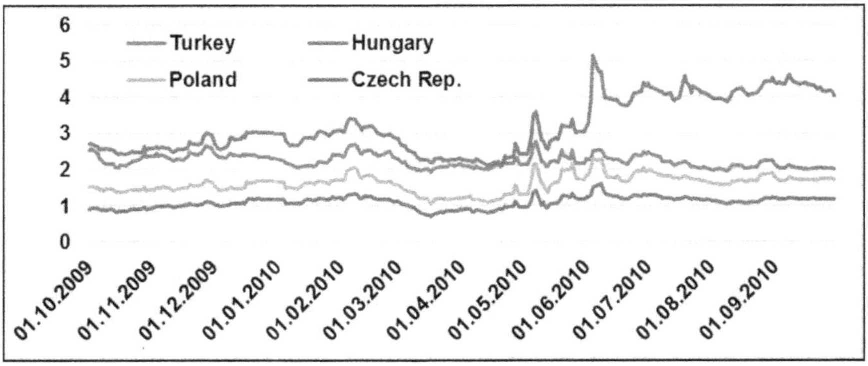

Source: CDS spreads obtained from Datastream, Thompson Reuters. Own calculations in deriving the probability of default from spreads.

Finally, I compare Turkey with another sample of countries composed of, this time, economies issuing three major currencies of the world: the U.K., Switzerland, and Japan[1018]. While the U.K. is a benchmark EU member beyond the Eurozone, Switzerland and Japan are two low-risk economies of the world, despite the fact that the latter presents chronic macroeconomic problems ranging from deflationary pressure to high public debt. Calculating the average value of daily data in figure 5.10, to note that markets attributed 0.6 percent probability of default to Switzerland, 0.9 percent to both the U.K. and Japan and 2.2 percent to Turkey from 1st October 2009 to 30th September 2010. Although Turkey is the economy with the highest risk exposure in the sample, it should be taken into account the fact that Turkish CSD spreads on 17th May 2004 (Fig. 5.4) were 627 basis points, equivalent to 8 percent probability of default, much further from the benchmark economies in the sample, i.e., it has fallen by a factor of 8/2.2 since then.

[1017] To note that sovereign probability of default in the figure corresponded to 2.0, 4.0, 1.7 and 1.2 percent on 30th September 2010 for Turkey, Hungary, Poland and the Czech Republic, respectively.

[1018] The British pound sterling, the Swiss franc and the Japanese yen, together with the US dollar and the Euro compose the highest proportion of outstanding securities in global markets and form a significant part of global debt issuance (Eichengreen, B., Hausmann, R. and Panizza, U. (2002), p. 3).

Fig. 5.10: Comparing Market implied Sovereign Probability of Defaults from CDS Spreads: Turkey, U.K., Switzerland, Japan, 1st October 2009 - 30th September 2010, in percentage[1019]

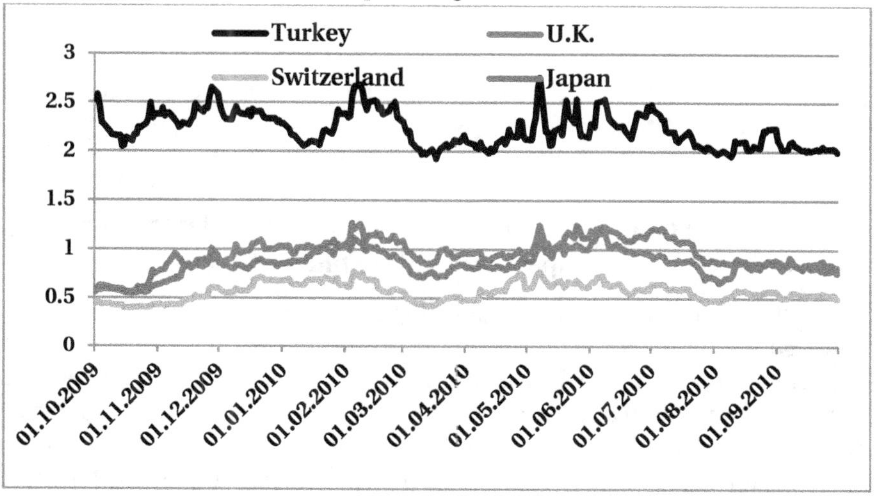

Source: CDS spreads obtained from Datastream, Thompson Reuters. Own calculations in deriving the probability of default from spreads.

Concluding remarks

1. What is my aim in discussing the CDS pricing models?

CDS pricing models are useful in illustrating the relationship between the CDS spreads and the sovereign probability of default. While I provided pricing formulas widely used in fixed income quantitative research, I took simplifying assumptions and calculated the sovereign probability of default in Turkey and in a sample of EU countries. I provide, in Annex 6, a method widely used by market professionals in computing and calculating implied sovereign probabilities of default, which can be useful for future research on some specific aspects. My aim here is to demonstrate that the CDS spreads incorporate sovereign default probability perception of market participants, which reflects the market participants' view that I examined in Second

---

1019 To note that sovereign probability of default in the figure corresponded to 2.0, 0.8, 0.5 and 0.8 percent on 30th September 2010 for Turkey, the U.K., Switzerland and Japan, respectively.

Generation models in section 3.2.2. Thus, I argue that regulatory and institutional improvements, or my 11th element of the "Washington Consensus", had a significant impact in declining Turkish CDS spreads or markets' perception of a lower sovereign probability of default. In any case, this is one of the explanatory variables as other factors ranging from decreasing public debt (section 5.1.1 fig 5.1) to the EU membership process itself would have had an impact on decreasing level of risk perception of global investors, thus on the level of the CDS spreads.

2. Why is the relationship between CDS spreads and interest rates important for this study?

It is well known that investors demand higher interest rates for higher risk. We observed in figures 5.8 and 5.9 that from the fourth quarter of 2009 to the third quarter of 2010, markets perceived the Turkish sovereign probability of default as being lower than many EU economies. However, nominal interest rates in Turkey were higher than in many EU countries and caused short-term capital flows to Turkey. The result was the familiar dynamic behind so many financial crises in emerging markets: An overvalued currency leading to a possibly unsustainable current account deficit. The latter can generate higher risk if the economy enters into unsustainable current account deficit dynamics.

5.3. Adopting EU-inspired standards and emerging problems

Introduction

I showed in chapters 2 and 3 that Turkey suffered from high and chronic inflation from the early 1970s to early 2000s, the major cause of which was excessive money creation in order to finance government budget deficits. The establishment of a bond market in 1986 constituted a first attempt to address this problem by encouraging the financing of deficits by selling bonds to the public rather than money creation by the Central Bank. A standard proposition in macroeconomics states that a central bank aiming to make domestic government debt more attractive increases real interest rates which leads to real appreciation of the currency[1020]. However, as we observed in Chapter 3 (fig. 3.4) the increase in the real interest rate can also signal to markets that the probability of default on debt increases, creating the opposite effect making domestic debt less attractive and leading to a real depreciation. We also examined through Second Generation models (SGMs) that in the case of fully liberalized capital markets, when public debt reaches unsustainable levels, a shift in market sentiment can lead the economy to "multiple equilibria" even when there is no deterioration in macroeconomic fundamentals. The consequent "self-fulfilling" mood of markets can lead to a speculative attack. Thus, under these circumstances an inflation targeting monetary policy can have perverse effects: An increase in interest rates can thus lead, paradoxically to a further increase in inflation. This means that fiscal policy and not monetary policy is the right instrument to decrease excessively high inflation levels[1021].

Turkish policy makers were aware, during the 1990s, that interest rates on public debt were excessively high. However, attempts to lower rates led to two major crises: I showed in section 3.3.1 that the government policy in 1993 to lower interest rates on domestic debt through laws, without taking into consideration market expectations, led to a capital flight triggering the 1994 financial crisis. This resulted in an increase in both interest rates and inflation. The 2001 currency crisis occurred during an IMF-led stabilization program[1022], which aimed at and succeeded in lowering the inflation rate, despite the fact that it could not prevent a serious financial crisis, again due to a shift in market sentiment that I explained through Second and Third Generation models. One of the lessons to be learned from these Turkish crises is that under highly unstable domestic economic circumstances, priority should be given to fiscal policy to restore public finances and to radical structural reforms. This means that structural reforms and a fiscal policy targeting sustainable public debt levels must be achieved before implementing an inflation targeting monetary policy. A major concern in this regard was the need for a solid banking system able to react properly to the central bank's policy signals[1023]. We also observed that policy makers achieved significant progress in April and May 2001 both in providing a legal basis for the Turkish Central Bank's independence and in restructuring the banking sector[1024]. The Central Bank preferred to introduce

---

[1020] Blanchard, O. (2004), p. 2

[1021] Ibid.

[1022] Section 3.3.2.3

[1023] Ersel, H. and Ozatay, F. (2008), p. 10

[1024] Section 4.1

an "implicit" inflation targeting regime from 2002 to 2005 before switching to a "full-fledged" inflation targeting policy in 2006. The major reason behind the delay in implementing the latter was to observe the impact of structural reforms, in particular, achievement of sustainable public debt levels. Figures 5.1 and 5.2 in section 5.1.1 showed that public debt and budget balance met Maastricht criteria by the years 2004 and 2005, respectively.

We also note a significant structural innovation introduced during the 2000s. The Capital Markets Board established the Turkish Derivatives Exchange (TURKDEX) in July 2002, which became operational in February 2005[1025]. The creation of a financial derivatives market is an important step in introducing international best practices in risk management, where hedgers and speculators can trade to share risks. The volume at the TURKDEX gradually increased, reaching 38.4 percent of GDP in 2010 (Fig. 5.11).

Fig. 5.11: Turkish Derivatives Exchange – Yearly Trading Volume, in percentage of GDP

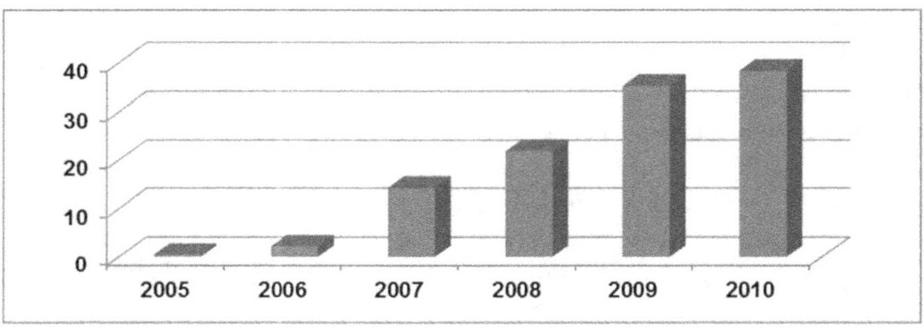

Source: Turkish Derivatives Exchange (TURKDEX) official website

Nevertheless, the economy encountered several problems while adapting international standards to the Turkish context. Let me investigate two important issues: The consequences of the inflation targeting policy from 2002 onwards, i.e., a worsening current account balance and the impact of the Turkish Central Bank's behavior on the derivatives market in 2006.

[1025] Budak, A. and Cikot, O. (2011), p. 55

1. Inflation Targeting policy and consequent problems

The Turkish Central Bank introduced an "implicit" inflation targeting policy from 2002 to 2005[1026]. During the year 2004, the CPI inflation rates were reduced to single-digit figures and starting by January 2006, the Central Bank initiated a "full-fledged" inflation targeting policy[1027]. Figure 5.12 shows a high level of interest rates when compared with the inflation rate during the 2000s, which was the necessary risk premium offered to bondholders. To note that these two rates converged by the beginning of 2010 making the risk premium disappear. On the other hand, figures 5.13 and 5.14 lay bare the relationship between the appreciating currency and current account deficits due to capital inflows. In addition to inflation targeting policy, there was another reason behind capital inflows: Negotiations with the EU impressed foreign markets. Market participants were prepared to bet that Turkey was going to succeed. Appreciating currency, nevertheless, led to a worsening current account balance.

Fig. 5.12: Inflation Targeting: comparing interest rates versus inflation rate, in percentage

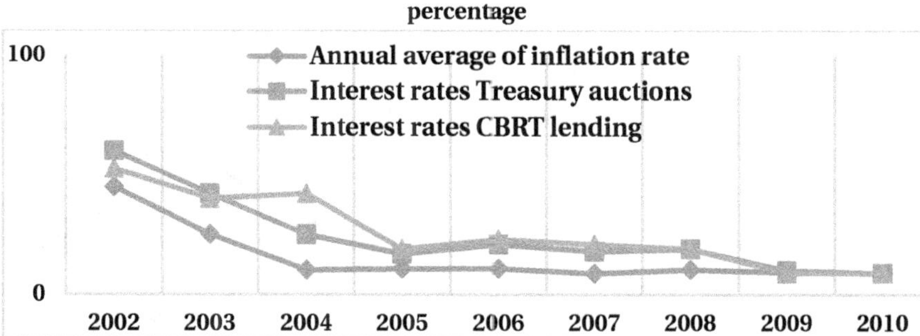

Source: Turkish Central Bank, State Planning Organization, General Directorate of Budget and Fiscal Control, Turkish Ministry of Finance. Interest rates Treasury Auctions level and the CBRT lending rate were 60 percent and 52.5 percent respectively in 2002, much higher than the average inflation rate, 44.8 percent, during the same year.

[1026] Premature initial conditions could have undermined the credibility of the Turkish Central Bank. The solution was to adopt a transition period during which communication, transparency and institutional framework would be enhanced gradually (Kara, H. (2006), p. 10). I discussed the difference between "implicit" and "full-fledged" inflation targeting policies in section 4.1.3.

[1027] Kara, H. (2006), p. 13

Fig. 5.13: Inflation Targeting: appreciating Real Effective Exchange Rate (REER)

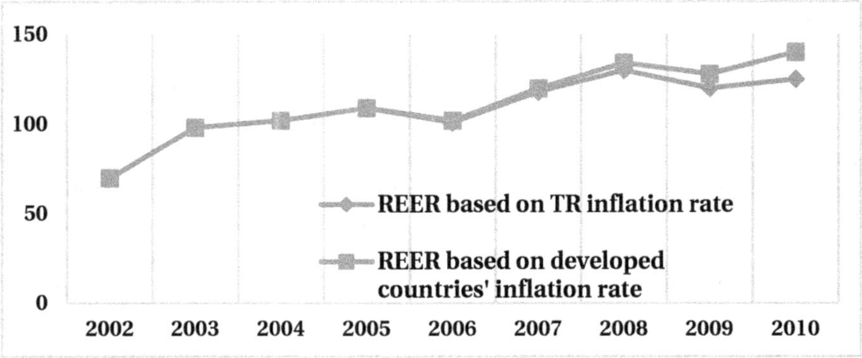

Source: Turkish Central Bank. The vertical axis represents the index value.

Fig. 5.14: Inflation Targeting: worsening Current Account deficits, in percentage of GDP

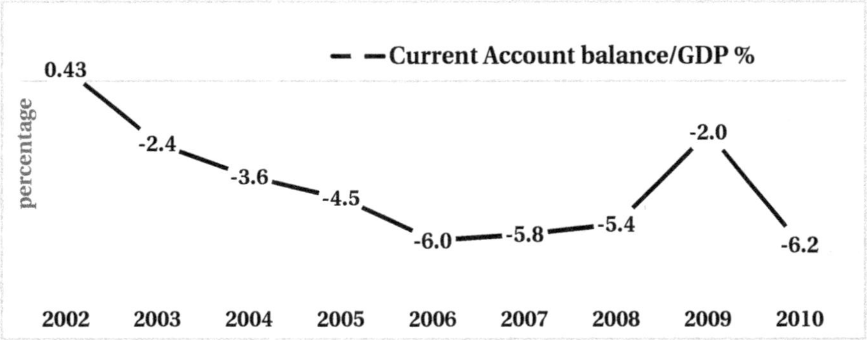

Source: General Directorate of Budget and Fiscal Control, Turkish Ministry of Finance

Briefly, one of the causes of the appreciating currency was the (implicit) inflation targeting policy. In fact, short-term interest rates, a major instrument of the Turkish Central Bank to achieve price stability, were higher than those of advanced economies while, as we saw in the previous section, the sovereign default risk was lower, directing capital flows to Turkey. Let me show this differential as follows: An investor preferring to eliminate sovereign default risk related to a government bonds portfolio can buy a CDS contract on that investment. In case of default, it will be the CDS seller who will cover the loss. The differential between government bond yields and CDS spreads will represent a yield excluding sovereign default risk. I called this yield the "sovereign default risk-free" yield on Turkish government bonds.

I calculated the "sovereign default risk-free" yield of Turkish government bonds from 2004 to 2010. The graph in the middle in Fig. 5.15 is the yield that an investor would obtain if she held a Turkish government bond together with a CDS contract on these bonds.

Fig. 5.15: Turkish Government Bond Yield excluding the Sovereign Default Risk, 17th May 2004 - 30th September 2010, in percentage

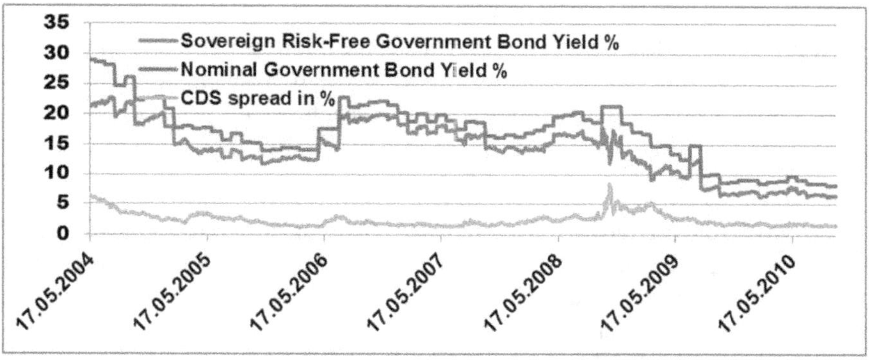

Source: Undersecretariat of Treasury, Datastream, Thompson Reuters; Nominal Government Bond Yield, the upper curve, is the annual compound average interest rate in Treasury auctions.

Based on Fig. 5.15, I show in Table 5.7 the maximum and minimum values of "sovereign default risk-free" Turkish government bonds yields, in pre- and post-global recession periods. To note that even the minimum values[1028] diverged considerably from the interest rates in economies where borrowing cost is low (Table 5.8).

Table 5.7 shows that in the pre-recession period the lowest "sovereign default risk-free" yield was 11.7 percent, high even when compared with interest rate levels of less than 1 percent in Japan for the same period (Table 5.8), whereas during the 2008-2009 global recession, the lowest Turkish "sovereign default risk-free" yield fell to 6.2 percent. This value, though low for Turkey, was still considerably higher than interest rates in Japan, which was equal or lower than 0.5 percent over this period.

1028 The yields between the minimum and maximum provide an additional profit for bondholders.

Table 5.7: "Sovereign default risk-free" Turkish government bond yields' min-max values in pre- and post-2008/2009 global recession, in percentage

Period	Max.	Min.
17th May 2004 - 17th May 2008	22.8 (19th July 2004)	11.7 (7th Nov. 2005)
18th May 2008 - 30th Sept 2010	17.8 (3rd Oct. 2008)	6.2 (8th Febr. 2008)

Source: Own observations of "Sovereign default risk-free" rate from Turkish government bond yields' and CDS spreads, data from the Undersecretariat of Treasury, Datastream, Thompson Reuters

A preliminary discussion on "currency carry trade" is necessary in order to shed light on the way speculators' positions can have an impact on key variables of macroeconomic interest, i.e., the exchange rate.

Currency carry trades

I start with an overview of the profitable nature of uncovered interest parity (UIP)[1029]. Let me consider currencies such as the Japanese yen and the Turkish lira. The UIP hypothesis states that the interest rate differential equals expected rate of change in the exchange rate[1030]:

$$i_{YEN} - i_{TL} = [E(S_{t+1}) - S_t] / S_t$$

where i_{YEN} and i_{TL} are interest rates in Japan and in Turkey respectively, and the right-hand side of the equation represents the expected rate of change in the exchange rate between the two currencies.

The equation above means that if interest rates in Turkey are higher than those in Japan, the Turkish lira is expected to depreciate by approximately the same percentage. In other words, it states that gains due to interest rate differentials are offset by the loss in the high-yielding currency. Nevertheless, a variety of empirical studies show that the UIP is regularly violated[1031], which means that in many cases the high-yielding currency tends to appreciate, allowing super profit from "currency carry trades". To note that the latter had

---

[1029] Gubler, M. (2011), pp. 1, 2

[1030] Cheol, S. E. and Resnick, B. (2000), p. 106

[1031] For a literature survey on potential carry trade strategies see, for example, Gubler, M. (2011), pp. 1-4.

become, since the mid-1990s, one of the major currency trading strategies of Turkish banks[1032].

A "currency carry trade" involves borrowing money in low-interest rate currencies and investing simultaneously in high-interest rate currencies[1033]. Low-interest rate currencies such as Japanese yen or Swiss franc are called "funding" currencies, whereas, high-yielding currencies are called "target" currencies[1034]. Among the latter are considered as the typical ones, for example, the Australian dollar, the South African rand, the Brazilian real and the Turkish lira. This strategy is profitable as long as gains from interest rate differentials are not offset by exchange rate movements, i.e., the UIP is not expected to hold[1035]. Thus, the main risk for a carry trade investor is sudden exchange rate changes. That is why carry trades tend to take place when exchange rate volatility is low[1036].

To note in Table 5.8 that the major funding currencies, Japanese yen and the USD, were attractive due to quantitative easing policies followed by their central banks, whereas rates in Switzerland were traditionally low as the latter was perceived as a secure place to invest. On the other hand, Table 5.9 shows interest rates in Turkey and Brazil, which were leading "target" currencies due to their high-interest-rate levels.

An example will make clear the way currency carry trades can be profitable. Let me consider an investor borrowing funds in yen at 0.1 percent in 2005 and simultaneously investing in Turkish government bonds yielding 16.3 percent (Table 5.9 column 3). Nevertheless, our investor would like to transfer sovereign credit risk exposure related to Turkish government bonds to a "protection seller". She buys a CDS contract on Turkish sovereign of which average spread during the year 2005 was 246 basis points, or 2.46 percent (Table 5.9, column 4). Thus, this "currency carry trade" operation allows her to make a sovereign default risk-free profit of 13.5 percent (Table 5.9, column 5), which is a high profit with a cost close to zero, or 0.1 percent, as long as Turkish lira does not depreciate, i.e., the UIP does not hold. This had been the case for several years as we observe in figure 5.13, which means that our investor was able to make an

---

1032 Li, M. (2011), p. 72

1033 Galati, G., Health, A. and McGuire, P. (2007), p. 28

1034 Gubler, M. (2011), p. 1

1035 Ibid.

1036 Cucuru, S., Vega, C. and Hoek, J. (2010), p. 437

additional profit due to currency appreciation. How long would this opportunity last? Nobody knew this. But it was clear that an unexpected negative event would trigger a reversal, leading to catastrophic capital outflows.

Carry trades are mostly used by large financial institutions like hedge funds[1037]. The use of leverage makes these positions more sensitive to changes in exchange and interest rates and increases the likelihood of gains with zero capital[1038]. Nevertheless, this also increases risk exposure, as the impact of a sudden reversal will be higher and can threaten financial stability[1039]. I discussed market expectations-led self-fulfilling cycles in Chapter 3 in sections on Second Generation models and hedge funds (3.2.2 and 3.2.3.1). While efforts in exploiting profits from carry trades may help to equilibrate rates of return[1040], a sudden reversal may also launch "herd behavior" due to global deleveraging and repositioning of portfolio investments across international financial markets.

[1037] Galati, G., Health, A. and McGuire, P. (2007), p. 30

[1038] Li, M. (2011), p. 73

[1039] Galati, G., Health, A. and McGuire, P. (2007), p. 27

[1040] Cucuru, S., Vega, C. and Hoek, J. (2010), p. 437

Table 5.8: Funding currencies in carry trade

	Japanese yen			Swiss franc			USD		
	mm (1)	disc (2)	bond (3)	mm (4)	disc (5)	bond (6)	mm (7)	disc (8)	bond (9)
1996	0.5	0.5	0.4	1.5	1.0	1.7	5.3	5.3	5.0
1997	0.5	0.5	0.4	1.0	1.0	1.4	5.5	5.5	5.1
1998	0.4	0.5	0.2	0.9	1.0	1.3	5.4	4.8	4.8
1999	0.1	0.5	0.4	1.1	0.5	1.2	5.0	5.5	4.7
2000	0.1	0.5	0.2	3.5	4.0	2.9	6.2	6.5	5.8
2001	0.1	0.1	-	1.7	2.3	2.7	3.9	1.8	3.5
2002	-	0.1	-	0.4	1.3	0.9	1.7	1.3	1.6
2003	-	0.1	-	0.1	0.8	0.2	1.1	1.0	1.0
2004	-	0.1	-	0.6	1.3	0.4	1.4	2.3	1.4
2005	-	0.1	-	0.6	1.5	0.7	3.2	4.3	3.2
2006	0.1	0.4	0.4	1.9	2.5	1.4	5.0	5.3	4.7
2007	0.5	0.8	0.6	2.0	3.3	2.2	5.0	4.3	4.4
2008	0.5	0.3	0.4	-	1.0	1.3	1.9	0.1	1.5
2009	0.1	0.3	0.1	0.1	0.8	-	0.2	0.1	0.2
2010	0.1	0.3	0.1	-	0.8	-	0.2	0.1	0.1

Source: Turkish Statistical Institute (TUIK) official website, where "mm" stands for "money market", "disc." for "discount rate", and "bond" for annual government bond yields

Table 5.9: Target currencies in carry trade

	Turkish lira					Brazilian real				
	mm (1)	disc. (2)	bond (3)	cds (4)	b-cds (5)	mm (6)	disc (7)	bond (8)	cds (9)	b-cds (10)
1996	-	50	134.2	-	-	27.5	-	25.7	-	-
1997	-	67	124.5	-	-	25.0	-	24.8	-	-
1998	-	67	115.5	-	-	29.5	-	28.6	-	-
1999	-	60	109.6	-	-	26.3	19.0	26.4	-	-
2000	-	60	36.2	-	-	17.6	15.8	18.5	-	-
2001	-	60	99.6	-	-	17.5	19.0	20.1	-	-
2002	51.0	55	62.7	-	-	19.1	25.0	19.4	-	-
2003	31.0	43	46.0	-	-	23.4	16.5	22.1	-	-
2004	22.0	38	**24.7**	**3.95**	**19.96**	16.2	17.8	17.1	5.34	11.2
2005	17.5	23	**16.3**	**2.46**	**13.51**	19.1	18.0	18.8	3.27	15.0
2006	22.5	27	**18.1**	**1.86**	**15.94**	15.3	13.3	14.4	1.42	12.8
2007	20.0	25	**18.4**	**1.70**	**16.42**	12.0	11.3	11.5	0.90	10.5
2008	17.5	25	**19.2**	**3.17**	**15.54**	12.4	13.8	13.7	1.88	11.6
2009	9.0	15	**11.6**	**2.82**	**8.54**	10.1	8.8	9.7	2.11	7.4
2010	9.0	14	**8.1**	**1.75**	**6.24**	9.8	10.8	10.9	1.27	9.5

Source: Turkish Statistical Institute (TUIK) official website, where "mm" stands for "money market", "disc." for "discount rate", "bond" for annual government bond yields, and "b-cds" represents sovereign default risk-free rate. The latter are our calculations from government bond yields and cds spreads.

Relationship between carry trades and monetary policies

Moreover, excessive capital inflows can potentially raise inflationary pressure in the "target" currency economy[1041]. If the central bank of the latter follows an inflation targeting policy, this can lead to an increase in interest rates, attracting capital and appreciating the currency further reinforcing the boom phase of the cycle[1042]. Once the carry trade bubble is reversed, however, the depreciation will be larger as well.

To note that the Turkish Central Bank followed inflation targeting policy from 2002 onwards (implicit inflation targeting until 2005 and full-fledged from 2006 on). While it is difficult to estimate whether "currency carry trades" created additional inflation in this period, I can nevertheless argue that one of the reasons behind high-interest rates in Turkey (Table 5.9) was the inflation targeting policy.

1041 Hassan, S. and Smith, S. (2011), p. 20

1042 Ibid.

Current account deficits

We observed in figure 5.13 the appreciating currency mainly due to carry trades-led capital inflows and in figure 5.14 the worsening current account deficits due to real appreciation. Figure 5.16 shows that there was a co-movement between short-term capital inflows and current account deficits. The following national income identities will be useful to show the changing trend in the Turkish economy in the second half of the 2000s[1043]:

$$Y = (C + S + T) \tag{1}$$

where *Y* represent the domestic income or *GDP*, *C* represents consumption, *S* represent savings and *T* represents taxes. This means that all domestic income feeds consumption, taxes and/or becomes savings. On the other hand, *GDP* must arise also from the following equation[1044]:

$$Y = (C + I + G) + (NX + NFI) \tag{2}$$

where *I* represents investment, *G* represents government spending, *NX* and *NFI* represent net exports and net factor income from abroad respectively, of which the sum defines the current account balance, i.e., $NX+NFI=CA$[1045]. Combining equations (1) and (2) I obtain the following equation[1046]:

$$(S - I) = (G - T) + CA \tag{3}$$

I examined in chapters 2 and 3 that a major problem in Turkey during the 1980s and 1990s was on $(G - T)$, i.e., high and persistent budget deficits, which were financed through government bonds leading to unsustainable public debt dynamics. I showed in section 5.1.1 that in the mid-2000s the budget deficits and public debt were reduced to a level lower than the EU-27 countries' average. Thus, assuming the $(G - T)$ in the equation (3) in equilibrium (or close to equilibrium) after institutional reforms, the rest will provide insight on figure 5.16 as follows:

$$(S - I) = CA \tag{4}$$

1043 Zengin, A. (1997), p. 221

1044 Bagnai, A. (2004), p. 5, Corsetti, G. and Muller, G. J. (2006), p. 4

1045 Bagnai, A. (2004), p. 4

1046 Zengin, A. (1997), p. 222

That is to say, an excess of savings over national investment leads to current account surplus. To note that when investments exceed savings, the difference must be financed through foreign capital[1047]. In other words, current account deficits increase the need for capital inflows[1048].

We observed in figure 5.13 that an appreciating currency in Turkey made foreign goods attractive and thus accelerated imports, leading to current account deficits (Fig. 5.14), which in turn were financed through foreign capital (Fig. 5.16). The conventional way of looking at a CA deficit is to ask "how is it financed?" Short-term capital flows and FDI breakdown in figure 5.16 provide us this information, where we observe that the FDI flows reached historically record levels, contributing to a stable macroeconomic environment.

Conclusion

I conclude that while the inflation targeting policy in the Eurozone can provide results close to expectations, divergence from expectations can occur in an emerging economy like Turkey, where the local currency is more sensitive to speculative movements compared to a major currency like Euro. Thus, widening current account deficits can potentially be a major risk factor generated due to an inflation targeting monetary policy. Nevertheless, the way they are financed is important. In the case of Turkey, increasing FDI flows contributed to stable growth. Figure 5.16 highlights FDI inflows in the second half of the 2000s, attracted by the improved institutional and regulatory environment as described in section 4.2.2. This was significant progress as compared to previous episodes.

[1047] Bagnai, A. (2004), p. 5

[1048] Ibid.

Fig. 5.16: Turkey - FDI, Short-term Portfolio Investment and Current Account Balance from 2000 to 2010, in percentage of GDP

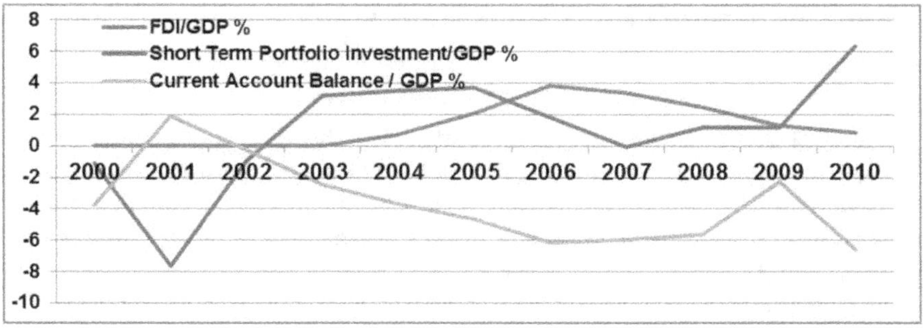

Source: State Planning Organization and Central Bank of the Republic of Turkey. The figure makes evident both the short-term portfolio investment outflow and the consequent current account surplus after the February 2001 financial crisis as well as the high and persistent current account deficits level after 2004 due to capital inflows (both short-term portfolio investment and FDI).

Let us observe, in the next section, one of the consequences of leveraged currency carry trade positions. In fact, the declining risk appetite of global investors in May 2006 caused capital outflows leading to turbulence in Turkish financial markets. I will further discuss how the Central Bank reacted and why this undermined its independent status.

1. The Turkish derivatives exchange and the Central Bank's behavior: Why is interaction important?

My aim is to show that despite significant progress achieved in introducing the Turkish Central Bank's independence and establishing a market where risks can be shared, the behavior of the Central Bank can undermine both its independence and the market pricing of derivative products. One such event occurred in 2006 and a crisis was only narrowly avoided.

In May 2006, the declining risk appetite of global investors caused them to revise their portfolio, resulting in a capital flight from Turkey. Figures 5.13 and 5.14 illustrated the relationship between an appreciating currency and a worsening current account balance up to 2006, the latter being perceived in global markets as a signal of increasing risk exposure. A wide proportion of the private sector, in particular banks, was again involved in interest rate carry trades and again chose not to hedge the FX risk (fig. 5.17). In the event of no Central Bank intervention, the unhedged FX positions in the private sector would have led to a series of bankruptcies, which in previous times led interest groups to expect a Central Bank bailout. However, this time Central Bank, in June 2006, both increased interest rates and intervened in the FX market buying up Turkish lira and selling USD, signaling its determination to stick to its inflation target and the implicit exchange rate, even at the cost of inflicting a recession on the economy.

This event shows not only that the Central Bank acted quickly and decisively, but also that the Turkish derivatives market was not properly used. While in the short-term, private sector bankruptcies could have proved disruptive, because depreciating currency made the cost of carry trades higher than the profit it would provide, if the Central Bank had signalled to the markets that it would not intervene in case of an unexpected FX movement, players would have been more careful, i.e., they would not take excessively unhedged positions. They would have begun, for example, to use FX futures contracts to hedge their positions, increasing also liquidity in the derivatives market. In fact, we can see the Derivatives Exchange really took off after 2006: Banks had learned their lessons (see fig. 5.11).

Fig. 5.17: Private sector short-term foreign debt, in million USD

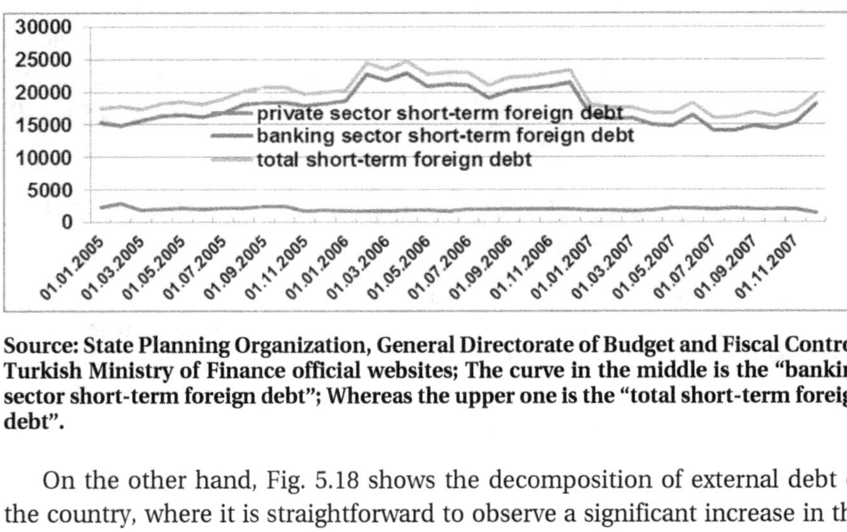

Source: State Planning Organization, General Directorate of Budget and Fiscal Control, Turkish Ministry of Finance official websites; The curve in the middle is the "banking sector short-term foreign debt"; Whereas the upper one is the "total short-term foreign debt".

On the other hand, Fig. 5.18 shows the decomposition of external debt of the country, where it is straightforward to observe a significant increase in the private sector (short and long-term) debt by the year 2004.

Fig. 5.18: External debt of Turkey from 2002 to 2010, in percentage of GDP

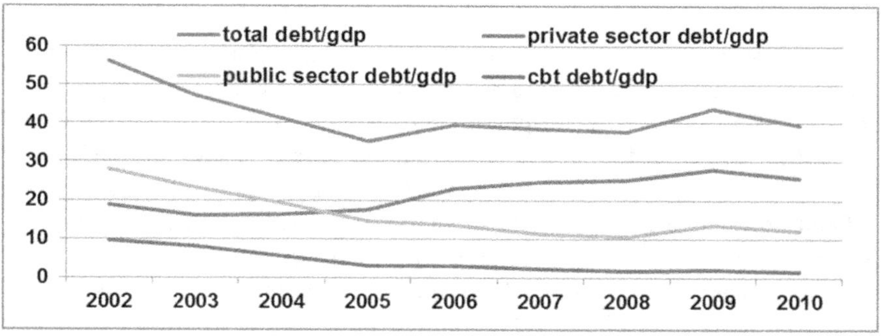

Source: Turkish Statistical Institute official website; While the upper curve is the total debt/gdp, the one below, increasing from 2004 to 2009, is the private sector debt/gdp; Whereas, the cbt/gdp stands at the lowest level in the figure.

Concluding remarks

We saw in Chapter 2 that moral hazard lay behind Thailand's 1997 currency crisis (implicit government guarantees for banks bearing unhedged positions). We saw again in Chapter 3 that moral hazard lay behind Turkey's 1994 financial crisis (100 percent government guarantee in the event of bank defaults).

I maintain in Chapter 5 that the Turkish Central Bank was once again creating moral hazard by adopting policies to save the banking sector from its own follies. The logic was again: "If the loan is repaid, I win, if the borrower defaults, the taxpayer loses"[1049]. The Central Bank's intervention in 2006 was perceived as an implicit FX rate guarantee.

To conclude, we observe that the derivatives market was newly created and the Turkish Central Bank had only recently gained its independence. Thus, adopting EU standards represented only a first step. Turkish operators remained unfamiliar with the hedging possibilities of derivatives markets and still preferred to rely on the Central Bank's implicit bailout guarantees. Nevertheless, there was a growing enthusiasm for hedging FX bets from 2006 onwards, as the figure 5.11 showed the increasing volume in the Turkish derivatives market. This means that the use of risk management tools increased over time, leading to a gradual change of customs. We observed in chapters 2 and 3 that economic agents in Turkey traditionally took unhedged positions,

---

[1049] See section 2.1.1 for a more in-depth look at the case of Thailand, on the eve of the 1997 East Asian currency crisis.

whereas, adaptation of risk management culture to local circumstances allowed, though slowly, an increase in the size of hedged positions.

Conclusion 1: The Turkish economy had traditionally been based on agricultural production, far from risk management culture, where subsidized credits led the Central Bank to act as a state body that intervened in the event of difficulties. While reforms in institutional framework in the second half of the 2000s achieved significant progress in the Central Bank's independence, it was difficult to change the expectations of market players, which appeared as unwritten customs or norms "forcing" the Central Bank to intervene in the event of excessive risk taking. Nevertheless, to note that this was only a transition period. The increasing volume in the Turkish derivative exchange market from 2006 onwards shows a progressive adoption of risk management culture, finally allowing the Central Bank to act as an "independent" agency.

Conclusion 2: Let me consider three sub-periods from the 1989 capital account liberalization to 2010 in order to observe major shifts in key macroeconomic indicators. The first period covers the 1994 financial crisis, while the second includes not only the 2001 financial crisis but also the completion of regulatory framework changes from 1999 to 2002. Finally, the period from 2004 to 2010, reveals the impact of the structural regulatory changes on selected macro parameters. While the second period makes evident the worsening trend by the first three parameters, to note in the third period that the level of public sector borrowing requirement (PSBR) and budget deficit were reduced to sustainable levels, while the current account deficit increased showing rising private capital inflows. Moreover, higher unemployment levels in the third period are disappointing, allowing me to argue that the inflation targeting policy had been quite powerless in lowering the unemployment rates in Turkey. Table 5.10 makes these shifts evident.

Table 5.10: Comparison of PSBR, budget and current account deficit and unemployment levels in pre- and post-regulatory reforms, in percentage of GDP

	1989-1995	1996-2003	2004-2010
PSBR/GDP	7.76	9.94	1.66
Budget Deficit /GDP	4.36	9.38	2.78
CA Deficit/GDP	0.59	0.87	4.98
Unemployment rate	8.34	7.96	11.25

Source: State Planning Organization, General Directorate of Budget and Fiscal Control, Turkish Ministry of Finance official websites

Conclusion 3: The current account deficits reached 9.9 percent of GDP in 2011[1050], marking a new record level (figure 5.19). While this shift increased the risk exposure of the whole economy, let me reconsider this aspect under sustainability of current account deficits discussed in section 2.1.1, where I introduced some authors' views that current account deficits exceeding a certain threshold are not sustainable, i.e., levels higher than 4 or 5 percent of GDP or higher than 80 percent of GDP growth[1051]. Nevertheless, I also argued that the asset allocation perspective depending on expected return and perceived risk by investors is more realistic (see equations in section 2.1.1). In fact, a persistent current account deficit requires foreign exchange to clear it. This means that as long as global investors are willing to invest in Turkey, current account deficits can be sustainable. It is sufficient to observe the sovereign CDS spreads to have an idea about market sentiments.

While 9.9 percent of GDP is "excessive" according to authors that I mentioned above, it seems that it has not been "excessive" for global investors by the early 2012 thanks to the achievement of EU-inspired structural reforms (or my 11th Washington Consensus principle). I do not mean that a 9.9 percent current account deficit is not a risk factor, but I argue that if this were the case before the achievement of structural reforms, i.e., during the 1990s, the likelihood of a capital outflow would have been higher. Nevertheless, this is a potentially risky situation as the Fig. 5.16 shows the decreasing size of FDI flows due also to the global recession that initiated in 2008. This aspect allows me to suggest, in the next section, some aspects on current account deficits to be investigated for future research.

Suggestions for future research

Table 5.10 also shows that Turkey had financed its growth through budget deficits until the early 2000s and through current account deficits afterwards. GDP growth and current account balance seem in fact to be interdependent as fig. 5.19 shows a co-movement. This also means that Turkey's economic growth largely depends on foreign capital inflows due to its low level of savings[1052]. To note in figure 5.19 that excluding exogenous factors like the 2008-2009 global recession, Turkey succeeded to achieve a stable growth for a long time after the EU-inspired structural reforms. Nevertheless, to improve current account

---

1050 General Directorate of Budget and Fiscal Control, Turkish Ministry of Finance

1051 Dornbusch (2001), Milesi-Ferretti, G. M. and Razin, A. (1996) and Calvo G. and Vegh, G. (1999), respectively.

1052 International Investors Association (2011), p. 9

imbalances policy makers should implement structural reforms ranging from increasing the level of savings to producing domestically the intermediate goods needed to export final consumption goods[1053], exploring alternative energy sources[1054] and others measures that further research can explore. As long as policy makers will be delayed at implementing structural reforms to reduce current account deficits, they will be obliged to target lower growth rates, which in turn will not contribute to generating additional employment, making high unemployment rates persistent. The shift in unemployment rates in Table 5.10 from around 8 percent until the early 2000s to over 11 percent afterwards reinforces the need for development-oriented policies.

Fig. 5.19: Co-movement between GDP growth and current account/GDP ratio from 1979 to 2011, in percentage

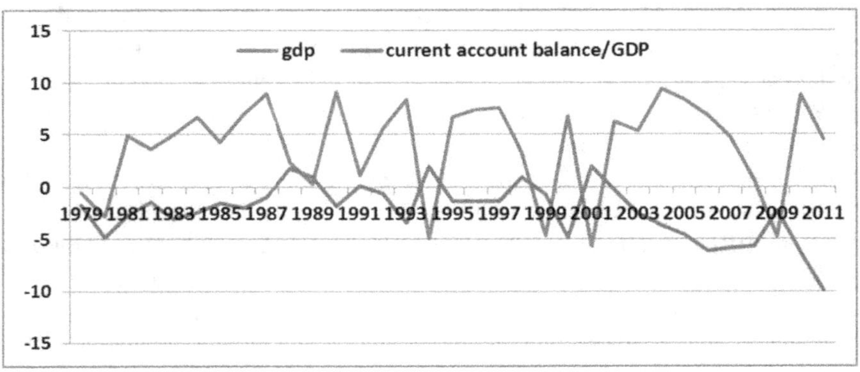

Source: Turkish Statistical Institute (TUIK) official website

Discussion 1: Would the problems emphasized in section 5.3 have a significant impact on the economy when compared with the unstable period from 1980 to 2002?

In order to investigate this aspect, let me first overview what was the role of political processes in implementing structural reforms? Had the achievement of the latter made the economy more resistant to turbulences or adverse

---

1053 as in many cases Turkey has first to import intermediate goods in order to export final consumption goods.

1054 Turkey has to import crude oil, which is an additional factor increasing current account deficits, independent from real changes in exchange rates.

movements? This is a preliminary discussion, which will lead us later in section 6.2.4, to answer the last research question:

> "Was the "institutional migration" successful? If not, why was it not? Is it possible that "import" of Western pro-market formal institutions, i.e., an independent central bank or free financial markets, was not compatible with Turkish traditions and caused chaos rather than successful transition? Or perhaps it did go rather well?"

Let us look at three major phases:

1. **1980-1991**: We observed in Chapter 2 that this was the period of single-party governments where the military had an influence at different degrees. Although the same single-party ANAP was democratically elected from 1983 to 1991, it was the objective of the armed forces to monitor the situation in the event of problems;

2. **1991-2002**: During the 1990s, the old political leaders were again active on the political scene. We observe nine coalition and minority governments formed from 1991 to 2002. I explained at the end of the section on privatizations (4.2.1) the reason why a complete agreement among coalition partners is important in achieving the implementation of reforms within the context of game theory. Political instability was one of the major reasons behind the incomplete reform process;

3. **2002-2011**: The split within the pro-Islamist RP led Recep Tayyip Erdogan to found the AKP in 2001. This was a survivor of previous pro-Islamist parties suppressed several times by the armed forces during the 1990s. The political parties present during the 1990s also participated in the 2002-2011 period, but electors preferred the AKP, which formed three single-party governments[1055]. One of the major differences, when compared with the single-party governments of the 1980s, is that while Turgut Ozal governed with military support, the pro-Islamist party leader Recep Tayyip Erdogan was elected in spite of opposition of the armed forces. While the AKP took advantage of the EU process to invalidate the presence of the military in political life, this process also gave priority to the implementation of

---

[1055] In 2002, 2007 and 2011, respectively.

structural reforms introduced by the 57th Bulent Ecevit coalition government after the 2001 crisis. We observed in section 4.1.3 that immediately after the crisis Kemal Dervis took the position of Minister of Economy and the CBRT gained independent status two months later, in April. The pro-Islamist single-party governments formed by November 2002 implemented the same program introduced in the aftermath of the 2001 currency crisis. What was this program? This was surprisingly the structural reforms that the 1999 IMF Stabilization Program broadly suggested[1056] (see section 3.3.2.3):

> "Our structural reform program aims at making sustainable over the medium-term the fiscal adjustment lowering the burden of interest payments on public sector debt, improving transparency and economic efficiency and reducing the contingent liabilities of the public sector. All these are essential to create an environment where high growth rates could be sustained in a low inflation environment."

To conclude, the creation of IRAs, in particular of the one in the banking sector and the CBRT independence were significant reforms that, combined with political stability due to pro-Islamist single-party governments, which in turn accelerated the EU full membership process, allowed a successful implementation of structural reforms. This allows me to argue that the problems discussed in section 5.3 are important to a minor degree when compared with the chaotic circumstances of the period 1980-2002. Turkey stands, by the mid-2000s, as an economy able to face any turbulence or shock, thanks to its effectively operational EU-inspired institutions. Thus, although Turkish economy presents difficulties due to its customs and traditions and also due to the inflation targeting monetary policy, there is a significant progress in introducing the EU standards when compared with the period from 1980 to 2002.

[1056] IMF (1999), "Letter of Intent" dated 9th December 1999, section 38

Discussion 2: Has the inflation targeting framework contributed to creating employment?

I argued in the previous paragraph that the problems discussed in section 5.3 are important to a minor degree, which does not mean that they are unimportant or that we present the inflation targeting monetary policy as the adequate one for the Turkish economy. Such framework gives priority to stabilization rather than to development. It thus implicitly assumes that the achievement of stable circumstances would automatically lead economic growth and employment generation[1057].

Nevertheless, while this policy contributed to the achievement of stable growth rates in Turkey, it has not contributed to lower the level of unemployment rates, in contrary the latter increased after the adoption of inflation-focused monetary policy as we observe a shift in average unemployment rates from 7.9 percent to 11.1 percent respectively, from period 1989-2001 to period 2002-2010 (Fig. 5.20). Thus, the creation of employment has not been an automatic consequence of stabilization-focused central bank monetary policy in the Turkish case, although central bank "independence" avoided any inappropriate pressure from governments to fund fiscal deficits, contributing thus to the achievement of stable circumstances. In other words, the jobless nature of growth was one of the major consequences of the inflation-focused policy from 2002 onwards, as appreciating local currency allowed the rise of current account deficits, in turn contributing to employment generation in economies Turkey imported from, and to lowering domestic inflation thanks also to relatively cheap imports.

This study covered the period until 2010, but I included in the figure below also 2011 data, as current account deficits reached by this year an ever seen historical record hitting USD 74 billion, corresponding to 9.9 percent of GDP.

[1057] Epstein, G. (2007), p. 1

Fig. 5.20: Impact of inflation targeting monetary policy on unemployment, GDP and current account balance

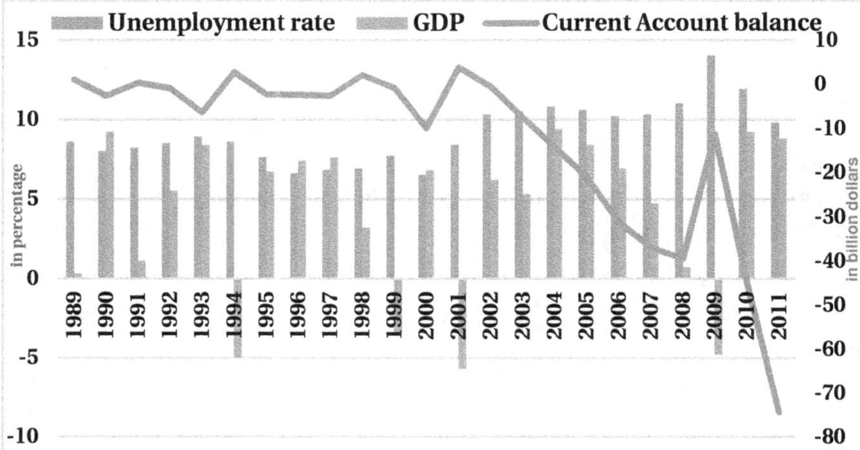

Source: Unemployment rate and GDP (left axis in percentage), data from Turkish Statistical Institute (2013), pp. 126, 127, 705; GDP by expenditures approach at 1998 prices; Current Account balance in billion dollars (right axis), data from CBRT website, Balance of Payments (BPM6) Analytic Presentation, p. 11.

Non-linear relationship between inflation and growth: What should be the adequate monetary policy for the Turkish economy?

Since the adoption of the "full-fledged" inflation targeting monetary policy in 2006, the CBRT has targeted 5 percent or lower CPI inflation rate[1058]. Although it has generally not even achieved values close to this target, it has mainly used one policy instrument, the short-term interest rates, the level of the latter had also an impact on unemployment rates. Further research can investigate whether this 5 percent inflation target has also been compatible with creating employment. Several studies have found that very high and low inflation rates cannot contribute to growth due to threshold effects. It is important to explore the rate range which would contribute to growth in country-specific circumstances. While Bruno, M. and Easterly, W. (1998) argued that inflation rates over 40 percent are detrimental to a positive growth path[1059], other studies

[1058] Except for the years 2009, 2010 and 2011 during which targets were 7.5, 6.5 and 5.5, respectively. The target was 4 percent for the years 2007 and 2008. It achieved the target only in years 2009 and 2010.

[1059] This is one of the key conclusions of Bruno, M. and Easterly, W. (1998) who examined the relationship between inflation and growth for 127 countries between 1960 and 1992.

sustained that negative effects of inflation would occur somewhere below a 20 percent threshold. For instance, Pollin, R. and Zhu, A. (2005)[1060] found that every percentage of inflation contributes to between 0.1-0.15 percent of GDP growth up to a 15-18 percent threshold, i.e., beyond this threshold inflation restrains economic growth; Whereas Anwar, S. and Islam, I. (2011) found a threshold level at 11-17 percent[1061]. To note that despite the use of sophisticated techniques to capture the impact of non-linearities in the growth-inflation relationship, there is no a clear evidence in support of a policy goal of maintaining an inflation target at 5 percent.

Moreover, the Preamble of the Obligations of Members under IMF's Article of Agreement IV does not specify any quantitative target. It notes that "..each member state should endeavor to direct its economic and financial policies toward the objective of fostering orderly economic growth with reasonable price stability, with due regard to its circumstances."[1062] In other words, it does not identify a universally applicable 5 percent inflation target, as due regard should be given to country-specific circumstances through a case by case study. Also to note that Olivier Blanchard, IMF's former Economic Counsellor, has been a major critique to the theoretical basis of the inflation-focused monetary policy arguing that the 2007-2008 global recession exposed flaws in the pre-crisis macroeconomic policy framework. He advanced that presenting stable and low inflation as the primary mandate of central banks and the fiscal policy playing a secondary role was to be revised and that policy makers should consider many targets and use more instruments[1063].

Regarding the preferences of the rich and the poor towards anti-inflationary and anti-unemployment policy, Jayadev, A. (2006) used a cross-country survey data. He found that those in the top quintile of income distribution are more likely to perceive unemployment as a less serious problem than inflation. Whereas, those in the lowest quintile are more likely to have the opposite view.

[1060] They considered a data set of 80 countries between 1961 and 2000 (Pollin, R. and Zhu, A. (2005), pp. 9, 11).

[1061] For further cross-country and country-level threshold studies, see Anwar, S. and Islam, I. (2011), pp. 7-9. On the other hand, Khan, M. and Senhadji, A. (2001) used conditional least squares technique and found that the threshold level above which inflation significantly slows growth is 11-12 percent for developing countries; Whereas, Burdekin, R., Denzau, A., Keil, M., Sitthiyot, T., and Willett, T. (2004), utilized spline estimation techniques and found a threshold level of 3 percent for developing countries.

[1062] IMF (2006a), p. 8

[1063] Blanchard, O., Dell'Ariccia, G. and Mauro, P. (2010), pp. 3, 16.

Further research can thus explore whether the Turkish monetary authorities have investigated such a relationship between growth and inflation in Turkey, also in line with different segments of income distribution in the country. Moreover, it is also important to explore whether they used the knowledge on threshold effect in an attempt to estimate the ideal growth rate, which would create more employment "with reasonable price stability".

As alternatives to inflation targeting monetary policy, Epstein, G. (2007) proposes a real targeting approach, where a target is linked to the real aspects of the economy, i.e., to the unemployment rate, GDP growth, investment and the real exchange rate. This approach is likely to be more developmentally relevant. An example of real targeting is employment targeting, where the central bank, in collaboration with the government, would estimate a target range for employment growth taking into account a moderate inflation target. This would change the attitude of the central bank, allowing it to study also the relationship between monetary policy and employment growth. In case the CBRT should adopt an employment targeting policy with an inflation constraint, it would need more instruments in addition to short-term interest rates[1064].

To summarize, while "independence" of the CBRT achieved in April 2001 eliminated inappropriate political pressures to fund fiscal deficits in Turkey, it has also meant a relative lack of coordination between monetary and fiscal policies, which have not contributed to additional employment creation. Further research can also explore how the Turkish Central Bank can effectively collaborate with political institutions in order to reach different challenges, including employment generation, allowing to fulfill its stabilization function while contributing to the development[1065], as the design of multiple targets needs to be structured in line with historical and country-specific factors[1066].

[1064] These may range from various credit allocation mechanisms to capital management techniques (Epstein, G. (2007), pp. 13-15).

[1065] Epstein, G. (2015), p. 12

[1066] Bhattacharyya, N. (2012), p. 8

Chapter 6
Conclusion

6.1. Introduction

This study has focused on the adaptation of Turkey's financial market regulations to EU requirements. I examined a variety of problems on different levels, allowing me to draw lessons from this transition process.

In the beginning of the book, I emphasized that Turkey's objective of full membership to the European Economic Community was explicitly formulated in the Ankara Agreement signed in 1963. Nevertheless, the economic policies that Turkey followed at that time were inconsistent with this major goal. While the Western world was identified with a functioning free-market economy, Turkish policy makers in the early 1960s intensified public ownership-led development plans, where Import Substitution Industrialization was maintained as a guiding star. Thus, the full membership argument appeared as an ideal without any concrete policy aiming to achieve it. The balance-of-payments crisis of the late 1970s and early 1980s was a severe shock to the economy. This led policy makers to introduce private initiative-led development plans and Turkey thus set out on the long road of deregulating its financial markets.

My research spans 30 years from which many lessons can be drawn and many questions asked, in particular:

> "How effective can EU financial market regulations be in the Turkish context?"
> "How appropriate is a de-politicized institutional framework for re-conceptualizing economic management in the Turkish cultural environment?"
> "Are there general lessons to be learned concerning the deregulation of financial markets in emerging market economies like Turkey?"

The statist economic policies followed by Turkey were clearly inconsistent with its goal of a full EU membership, but could policies aiming to dismantle the state's presence in the economy lead automatically to a functioning free-market economy? This led me to investigate the following **research questions**:

> "Do deregulation of financial markets and elimination of exchange controls on capital movements create conditions for stable growth?"
>
> "What is the role of institutions, culture, and tradition? What is the appropriate regulatory framework for an emerging market economy like Turkey?"
>
> "What is the role of monetary stability and the attitude of the central bank? How do central bank policies affect the vulnerability of an economy? Is its independence important?"
>
> "Was the "institutional migration" successful? If not, why was it not? Is it possible that "import" of Western pro-market formal institutions, i.e., an independent central bank or free financial markets, was not compatible with Turkish traditions and caused chaos rather than successful transition? Or perhaps it did go rather well?"

I began the book with the "Washington Consensus" principles in Chapter 2. This was the list of prescriptions that Turkey started to introduce in 1980. I first examined Thailand, another emerging market economy where these prescriptions were followed, leading to high growth rates and inflation rates of less than 6 percent until the onset of the East Asian currency crisis, in 1997. This episode provided useful insight because Turkey experienced similar dynamics during the deregulation of its financial markets, in particular on the eve of the 2001 currency crisis. While high GDP growth and reduced inflation were seen as a success, banks' extremely risky policies together with governments' implicit bailout guarantees made the whole economy unstable. The lack of an adequate institutional and regulatory framework was evident in both cases. In this chapter, while section 2.1 introduced the "Washington Consensus" principles and overviewed the case of Thailand, section 2.2 examined its implementation in Turkey during the 1980s.

Then, the theoretical framework that I introduced in Chapter 3 allowed me to emphasize the following points:

- First, "business cycle theory" provided an insight into the "coordinating role" of interest rates and therefore the importance of central bank behavior. Moreover, this framework allowed me to introduce concepts such as "loss of confidence" and "herd behavior", showing that market expectations-led cyclical capital movements were not a new phenomenon. It had also been a destabilizing factor during the 1930s. In addition to Austrian School's approach, Hyman Minsky's view provided me elements that I encountered in deregulated Turkish markets (in addition to those in Thailand): a tendency to underestimate financial risks at the beginning of a cycle, feeding a boom, resulting in a highly leveraged situation where increasing risk perception made the economy unstable leading to collapse. I then introduced the Mundell-Fleming framework to emphasize the fact that central bank behavior is crucially important not only regarding the interest rate movements but also in relation with the exchange rate regime chosen. The "impossible trinity" concept can provide insight on the likelihood of some unexpected events, i.e., currency crises;
- Secondly, I introduced the "three generation currency crisis models" of which the first is a restructured version of the Mundell-Fleming model, emphasizing that in the presence of a fixed FX rate regime and liberalized capital account, a central bank's monetary policy is ineffective. In addition, the "second" and "third" generation models introduced the importance of market expectations, which could cause a "herd behavior" and trigger a currency crisis.

Thus, chapters 2 and 3, composed of Washington Consensus" principles and the theoretical framework, are crucially important for my analysis because they introduced basic elements necessary for analyzing the Turkish case, where it is possible to observe that during the deregulation process, policy makers introduced the first nine "Washington Consensus" principles (the last one on the protection of property rights was neglected). I examined the impact of these prescriptions. I noted that there was no attempt to create a competitive environment, i.e., financial markets were only "deregulated". I use the latter term to mean "dismantling the state presence in the economic management without any effort to create competitive forces in markets". It is worth noting that these reforms were necessary and ranged from freeing interest rates to lifting capital controls and restrictions on foreign trade. Nevertheless, they were insufficient, as they did not introduce any substantial institutional and regulatory framework change aiming to create competitive forces in markets or in protecting property rights. Moreover, the fragile banking sector based on a weak institutional framework together with a central bank under political interference were serious obstacles for the functioning of financial markets. I thus defined an 11th element in the introductory section that, in my view, was essential, namely, the establishment of independent regulatory agencies and a functioning competition policy. I argued that the absence of my 11th element to "Washington Consensus" increased the likelihood of the 1994 and 2001 crises.

In chapters 2 and 3, I examined the implementation of these first nine "Washington Consensus" principles in three phases:

- The "first phase" covered the period from the initiation of the deregulation process in 1980 to 1988, during which important reforms included freeing interest and exchange rates, introducing export-led growth and the first attempts of the Turkish Central Bank in controlling the growth of money supply in the economy. An analysis of its balance sheet served to show that this important institution functioned previously as a state agency charged to create high-powered money for the Treasury to cover the government's budgetary needs. Thus, I emphasized that a substantial reform in this area was needed to address the root causes of problems in the Turkish economy;
- The "second phase" covered the period between 1989, the year of complete capital account liberalization, and 1994, the year of the financial crisis. The dynamics behind the 1994 crisis showed that not only were the efforts to implement the first nine "Washington Consensus" principles insufficient but also neglecting the expectations of global markets was a policy error. Markets penalized inconsistent policies because high sovereign default risk in the presence of a weak institutional framework required an interest rate level that was unsustainable for the Turkish economy. The collapse was inevitable;
- The "third phase" covered the period between 1995, the year of achievement of the Customs Union, and the currency crisis of 2001. After the 1994 financial crisis, policy makers attempted to approach European standards by introducing the Customs Union agreement with the EU in 1995. While I emphasized that this was an important psychological step for an eventual full membership and although it was instrumental in creating an independent competition agency in 1997, I argued that priority should instead have been given to improvements in the banking regulatory framework, which was completely neglected. I examined, in this section, not only the Customs Union agreement but also the weaknesses in the banking sector and the dynamics behind the banking sector related currency crisis of 2001. I used the Mundell-Fleming framework to examine dynamics behind both the 1994 and 2001 crises and the "second" and "third" generation models for a detailed analysis of the 2001 crisis.

In Chapter 4, I introduced the 11th element of the "Washington Consensus", which I consider crucially important for the functioning of markets: The EU-inspired institutional and regulatory framework to promote competition. While section 4.1 examined the Central Bank Independence and the creation of independent regulatory agencies, section 4.2 focused on regulatory reforms on privatizations, FDI and property rights.

More precisely, section 4.1.1 introduced the Central Bank Independence and inflation targeting monetary policy as an EU requirement. Section 4.1.2 attempted to define the concept of central bank independence and discussed proxies that can be used to measure its degree of independence and transparency. Section 4.1.3 examined reforms aiming towards leading the CBRT to become an independent institution. Section 4.1.4 focused on the creation of IRAs in Turkey and argued that while the Competition Agency became operational in 1997, the Capital Market Board gained a de-politicized status in 1999 and more importantly, the independent regulatory agency created in the banking sector became operational in 2000. These agencies, in particular, the one in the banking sector, started to function effectively only after the 2001 currency crisis. It showed that the 2001 crisis also served to motivate policy makers to implement a comprehensive de-politicized regulatory system. The latter was effectively achieved specifically in the banking sector. Moreover, the Central Bank gained the independent status and efforts were made to reduce distorted prices in the agricultural sector. The impact of these reforms was to become evident a few years later.

Section 4.2 focused on privatizations, FDI and property rights. That is to say, sections 4.2.1 and 4.2.2 showed the record-breaking high privatization revenues and FDI flows from 2004-2005 onwards, achieved thanks to improvements in both the legal framework and administrative procedures, which were a serious obstacle for resident and non-resident investors. I argued that a significant increase in FDI flows also showed that Turkey was perceived in global markets as a reasonably secure economy worth investing in over the long-term, which had not been the case before, as FDI flows were traditionally at very low levels. In section 4.2.3, I overviewed the property rights situation in Turkey, which is the 10th prescription of the "Washington Consensus" neglected in Turkey during the 1980s and the 1990s.

In Chapter 5, I examined the post-2002 economic performance. I focused, in sections 5.1 and 5.2, on a variety of market indicators ranging from macro variables to the Fitch Rating Agency's assignments and CDS spreads. Finally, in section 5.3, I discussed some problems that arose in the late 2000s.

6.2. Conclusions about research questions and hypotheses

In this section, I will reconsider my research questions and hypotheses and summarize the conclusions drawn in Chapter 5. I will also discuss my agreement or disagreement with the authors introduced in Chapter 2.

6.2.1. Do deregulation of financial markets and elimination of exchange controls on capital movements create conditions for stable growth?

In Chapter 2, I introduced the "Washington Consensus" principles[1067] and examined the way these principles were introduced in the Turkish case. In an attempt to answer this research question, it is worth highlighting the perspective of the "Washington Consensus" on interest rates. In section 2.1, point "4)" we observed that:

> "The "Washington Consensus" agreed that two main principles should guide the level of interest rates. First, interest rates needed to be market-determined to avoid misallocation of resources. Second, positive real interest rates were necessary to discourage capital flight, to encourage savings and to make capital accumulation more likely."

We noted in Table 3.8 (section 3.3.2.2) that the differential between compound interest rates and inflation rates in Turkey from 1991 to 2001 was high (except for the year 2000 during which the IMF Stabilization program had an impact on their level). Why? One of the major reasons was the lack of an adequate institutional and regulatory framework, in particular in the banking sector, which created uncertainty. Thus, investors were reluctant to hold Turkish assets and the economy was obliged to offer higher interest rates to discourage a capital flight. But higher interest rates increased both the debt

---

1067 Williamson, J. (1990), pp. 1, 3, 4, 5

burden and the sovereign default risk perception. It is worth making two observations regarding the banking sector:

- State-owned banks: We observed in section 3.3.2.2 that state-owned banks had been providing subsidized credit to the agricultural sector. The Turkish economy was traditionally based on agriculture and employment in this sector, therefore, made up a large percentage. Subsidized credits provided to farmers had become a major reason behind budget deficits and price controls distorted the markets;

- Private banks: Free capital movements made it possible to obtain low-cost credit abroad and invest in high-yielding government securities. We observed in chapters 2 and 3 that private commercial banks replaced the Central Bank during the 1990s in allowing the Treasury to cover deficits. Nevertheless, poor risk management practices and inadequate monitoring allowed private banks to bear unhedged positions, making the private banking sector fragile.

Thus, introducing the first nine "Washington Consensus" principles led the Turkish economy into volatile growth conditions as the inadequate institutional and regulatory framework made investors request higher interest rates to compensate higher perceived risk. While this situation was unsustainable, leading to crises, their timing depended on market participants' expectations. I analyzed the dynamics behind these crises in Chapter 3 and showed that global investors' sentiment became crucially important.

Fig. 6.1 (section 6.4) shows that Turkey experienced unstable growth rates from complete liberalization of the capital account in 1989 to completion of regulatory reforms in 2002 and stable growth rates thereafter. This conducts me to argue that we can associate unstable growth rates with deregulated financial markets and elimination of exchange controls, in the absence of an adequate regulatory framework in Turkish financial markets. Nevertheless, to note that while Fig. 6.1 shows the presence of such a correlation, this does not necessarily imply causation. That is to say, while an adequate regulatory framework in financial markets can have an impact on stable growth rates from 2002 onwards, there might be other explanatory variables reinforcing growth stability, i.e., the EU full membership process itself. On the other hand, my first research question aimed to introduce only an initial conceptual investigation rather than trying to explore a direct causality. I explained in Chapter 1 that the Turkish economy had been highly regulated for many decades. I showed that, nevertheless, deregulation (including lifting FX controls) did not create conditions for a stable growth. And I continued to investigate what Turkey needed to achieve stable growth rates.

6.2.2. What is the role of institutions, culture, and tradition? What is the appropriate regulatory framework for an emerging market economy like Turkey?

I emphasized in the previous section that the lack of an adequate institutional and regulatory framework increased uncertainties. Investors become reluctant to keep their holdings when they are not convinced that they can obtain a competitive return, as the very low levels of FDI flows in Turkey until 2005 show. Thus, the economy was involved in short-term portfolio investment-led growth cycles during the 1990s, which required volatile interest rate levels in line with investors' sovereign default risk perceptions. Let us now reconsider the authors who criticized the "Washington Consensus" in section 2.1.1 and discuss whether their comments match my findings in the Turkish case.

Joseph Stiglitz was a major critic to "Washington Consensus". He was among those who emphasized that the "Washington Consensus" neglected the need for an institutional framework necessary to support effective markets and that the ultimate development objectives were compromised as a result. In his opinion, the basic problem underlying the economic theory of the "Washington Consensus" was the fact that it did not take dynamics of economic development and transition into account. Although it described the target, it was not able to provide the way to get there. In fact, macro stability, trade liberalization and low inflation were not sufficient to make markets work.

Conclusion 1: This book examined the impact of financial reforms on stability and development in Turkey. Evidence analyzed from chapter 2 to 5 lends support to Joseph Stiglitz's view, that while liberalized trade, macro stability, and low inflation are necessary factors for markets to work well, these were not sufficient to achieve the ultimate goal –the expected degree of economic development. However, my findings contradict Joseph Stiglitz's view with respect to social protection. I emphasize the importance of different institutions, in particular, those which promote de-politicization of the economy. In fact, in the light of the analysis in Chapters 3 and 4, any sort of social protection can only be an obstacle for "well-functioning" markets in an emerging market like Turkey's, where the middle class is small and the poor are very numerous. A social protection system like one finds in Europe would be premature in Turkey.

Dani Rodrik's critique also highlighted the need for an adequate institutional framework in developing countries [1068]. Moreover, he emphasized that protection of property rights and respect for the rule of law play a crucial role in economic development. He added ten more elements to the original "Washington Consensus" principles, which I enumerated in section 2.1.1[1069]. One of his suggestions deserves a particular mention: "An independent central bank following inflation targeting policy". While I argued in section 4.1 that the issue of the independence of the Turkish Central Bank was crucially important, I showed in section 5.3 that inflation targeting policy can potentially cause the domestic currency to appreciate, when short-term interest rates to fight inflation attract an excessive amount of foreign capital. Here the meaning of "excessive" is to be evaluated in the light of current account deficit sustainability that an overvalued currency can cause. Thus, while my study supports the views of Rodrik that central bank independence and inflation targeting are important reforms to be achieved, I argue that in the case of emerging economies like Turkey, an inflation targeting policy option is to be evaluated together with its impact on other macro variables, i.e., real exchange rates, the current account balance, investment, and employment.

Conclusion 1: This study supports Rodrik's approach regarding the need for protection of property rights and respect for the rule of law. Moreover, I examined and discussed in chapters 3, 4 and 5 why the Turkish Central Bank's independence was crucially important. However, I argue that while price stability is an important aspect in achieving macro stability, it is more suitable for an emerging economy like Turkey to achieve and to maintain overall macro stability and not to focus only on price stability[1070], to contribute to the creation of employment as well as to the promotion of economic development.

I discussed **Hernando de Soto's** view that the root cause of chronic underdevelopment is a weak legal protection of property rights. De Soto also argued that stable property rights have led the advanced nations to create capital and a functioning market economy[1071]. To note that this is the 10th prescription of the "Washington Consensus", unfortunately, neglected in Turkey during the deregulation process from the 1980s to 2000s. This study

---

[1068] Rodrik, D. (2006), pp. 977, 978

[1069] Under the title "Critics of "Washington Consensus" principles"

[1070] This is also the view of Prof. Zuhair Mikdashi during an interview held in the initial phase of this study.

[1071] De Soto, H. (2000), p. 10

lends support to Hernando de Soto's view that protection of property rights has an important function in private sector-led development. For this reason, I discussed in section 4.2.2.3 the role of industrial and intellectual property rights in attracting FDI flows. I emphasize that there is a close relationship in Turkey between improved regulatory framework, increased FDI flows and the demand for protection of industrial and intellectual property rights (see Fig. 4.5 for the increased demand for patent protection from 2005 onwards).

Conclusion 2: This book also endorses Hernando de Soto's approach on the need for a de-politicized institutional and regulatory framework in the economy, where independent supervisory bodies can introduce regulations based on economic incentives and with the objective of monitoring the rule of law.

Finally, I comment on **Douglass North**'s definition of institutions[1072]. The following quotes from Douglass North are essential for my study:

> "Institutions are rules of the game in society. They are humanly designed constraints that shape human interaction. In consequence, they structure incentives in human exchange[1073].
> Institutions reduce uncertainty, by providing a structure to everyday life. They are a guide to human interaction[1074].
> Institutions define and limit the set of choices of individuals[1075].
> Although formal rules may change overnight as the result of political and judicial decisions, informal constraints embodied in customs, traditions, and codes of conduct are much more impervious to deliberate policies. These cultural constraints not only connect the past with the present and future but provide us with a key to explaining the path of historical change[1076].

[1072] North, D. C., (1994), p. 360

[1073] North, D. C., (1996), p. 3

[1074] Ibid.

[1075] Ibid, p. 4

[1076] North, D. C., (2005), p. 1

> The structure of constraints we impose to order competition for resources shapes the way the game is played. Because various kinds of markets (political as well as economic) have different margins at which the competition can be played out, the consequence of the structure we impose will be to determine whether the competitive structure induces increasing economic efficiency or stagnation. Thus, well-developed property rights that encourage productivity will increase market efficiency. The evolving structure of political and economic markets is the key to explaining the performance[1077]."

This study aligns with these quotes from Douglass North not only because he emphasized the importance of protection of property rights but he highlighted another aspect which is useful for my analysis: The distinction between formal and informal constraints. While a political will can change institutions, informal rules can only change much more slowly. Thus, importing institutions from the EU does not necessarily imply a better economic performance. This is the essence of my study. Nevertheless, despite the most serious currency crisis of its history in 2001, Turkey stands with a relatively good performance in the early 2010s, not only among emerging economies but also when compared with some EU countries on certain measures, for instance, on public debt levels. Thus, the approach of Douglass North is crucial for this study, as my aim is to show how difficult –but also how successful– the institutional migration to Turkey was, as long as the central bank and the banking sector, in general, are concerned. This also allowed for an improvement in inflation rates leading to relatively stable circumstances.

Conclusion 3: Douglass North's approach constituted a milestone for this study. I examined in chapters 2 and 3 the way institutional migration was realized and I identified the root causes of instability in the absence of an adequate institutional framework. I addressed these shortcomings in Chapter 4 and developed my 11th prescription of "Washington Consensus" as a result.

To conclude, evidence examined in chapters from 2 to 5 lends support in particular to the views of Hernando de Soto and Douglass North. The definition of my 11th element of "Washington Consensus" is mainly based on these

---

1077 North, D. C., (2005), p. 2

thoughts, which in my opinion are essential for an understanding of the Turkish case. In Chapter 5, we observed that key macro variables became relatively stable after its implementation. The rate of inflation, for example, was reduced to less than 10 percent. While this is still not a low level when compared with the EU, it is important to note that it had never before been approached in Turkey. Before the 1970s, Turkey suffered from state-administrated prices suppressing inflation, and all data concerning the CPI would be highly suspect. The public debt and budget balance started to match Maastricht criteria by the years 2004 and 2005, respectively. In addition to macro variables, the rating assignments of Fitch Ratings and the CDS spreads confirm the positive impact of my 11th element on the Turkey's regulatory reforms. Nevertheless, I emphasize again that improvement in these indicators shows that institutional migration was successful as long as in particular instability in product markets is concerned, whereas high unemployment levels signal the need for more development-oriented policies.

6.2.3. What is the role of monetary stability and the attitude of the central bank? How do central bank policies affect the vulnerability of an economy? Is its independence important?

The set of factors in the initial conceptual framework of this study has become useful in explaining several phenomena behind the dynamics of Turkish financial markets. I elaborated concepts emphasized by Ludwig von Mises such as "coordinating role of interest rates" and "herd behavior". The latter was also a basic theme in the "third generation models", which I argued were an extension of the Mundell-Fleming model and I used them in examining Turkish crises episodes.

I reemphasize here another aspect that I introduced in the section on "first generation models": Speculators are liquidity providers. They bear risk and contribute to risk sharing. However, they will react in the event of inconsistent policies of authorities[1078]. At this stage, an important aspect of my study emerges: It is likely that a politicized economic management introduces inconsistent policies, i.e., excessive money creation to finance budget deficits. This was the case in Turkey for several decades, also during the deregulation process in the 1980s and 1990s. Thus, the reaction of global markets to

[1078] Section 3.2.1

inconsistent policies led to turbulence and crises. One of the major reasons behind this was the fact that the Turkish Central Bank was politically managed both to cover fiscal deficits and to bail out failing banks.

The Central Bank's independence is, therefore, a particularly important element for my study. I examined the Central Bank's balance sheet in section 2.2.1.1 and identified excessive money creation to match budget deficits as a root cause for chronic economic instability in Turkey. I emphasized that in the second half of the 1980s, a monetary policy addressed the need to control the size of its balance sheet. However, this goal was not achieved during the 1990s. While Central Bank resources were not used for budgetary needs after 1997, they were used in bailing out defaulting banks. Thanks to reforms introduced in the aftermath of the 2001 currency crisis, the CBRT not only gained independence from the government but also from the newly privatized and more market-aware private banking sector.

Nevertheless, I also emphasize that Central Bank Independence obliges this institution to implement an inflation-targeting monetary policy, which resulted quite powerless in lowering the unemployment rates in Turkey (Table 5.10 and Fig. 5.20)!

6.2.4. Was the "institutional migration" successful? If not, why was it not? Is it possible that "import" of Western pro-market formal institutions, i.e., an independent central bank or free financial markets, was not compatible with Turkish traditions and caused chaos rather than successful transition? Or perhaps it did go rather well?

After the discussion on political processes I introduced at the end of section 5.3, I will now investigate whether "the institutional migration was successful". I consider three phases separately:

1. **1980-1991:** There was a great effort to introduce the first nine prescriptions of the "Washington Consensus". Several institutional reforms were achieved as far as freeing interest and exchange rates, reducing restrictions on foreign trade, creating bonds and interbank markets were concerned. I also demonstrated that although privatizations and FDI attractiveness were major goals of the governments in the 1980s, limited changes and modifications in the legal framework have been achieved during this period. Thus, I state that institutions were imported from the West during the

1980s, but Turkish markets were not yet a secure place for investors. Consequently, in my opinion, institutional migration cannot be considered successful. I also emphasized in Chapter 2 that, while the complete capital account liberalization is an important reform, it mainly served to attract short-term capital flows, leading to volatile growth cycles. Why? Once again, because institutional migration was not successful. In fact, there was neither an independent central bank nor an adequate institutional framework supporting the banking sector;

2. **1991-2002**: While the Customs Union agreement with the EU was an important reform in the aftermath of the 1994 crisis, in my opinion, priority should have been given to the restructuring of the banking sector. Nevertheless, scandals in the banking sector originated from some politicians' relationship with organized crime leaders, in a period during which several banks failed, may also be a reason why reforms in the banking sector became subject to long delays. Despite the achievement of a Customs Union with the EU, I cannot state that the institutional migration was successful because neither the central bank nor the banking sector fulfilled their proper function in the economy. While the former created high-powered money for fiscal purposes or bailing out failing banks, the latter assumed unhedged positions in order to borrow low-cost abroad and invest in high-yielding government securities, instead of providing credit to the private sector. Thus, the institutional migration could not lead to the functioning of markets during this phase either: It was not successful. In my opinion, the 1994 and 2001 currency crises episodes, although followed different dynamics, were both rational reactions of the markets to inconsistent government policies;

3. **2002-2011:** A new era followed the February 2001 currency crisis. I examined in Chapter 4 the structural reforms, through which the banking sector gained its intermediation function in the economy and the Central Bank gained independent status. In addition to its legally recognized independent status, the Central Bank could also have an independent policy under the Mundell-Fleming framework as the exchange rate started floating[1079]. I examined in Chapter 4 the creation of independent regulatory agencies, which facilitated the creation of competitive forces in the markets. I discussed as an example the privatization of Turk Telekom, a major natural monopoly in the past. To note that, while the Bulent Ecevit coalition government introduced the reform process after the February 2001

[1079] I will discuss this aspect more in detail in the next section.

crisis[1080], the following single-party pro-Islamist AKP governments maintained the same economic policy. I can state that in this third phase the institutional migration achieved "substantial progress" for the first time since 1980. An example for this is a banking sector that aims to fulfill its function in the economy, i.e., intermediation between the real sector and the financial sector. In these conditions, while fiscal and monetary policies were conducted by separate institutions, the "coordinating role" of interest rates could emerge in terms of Ludwig Von Mises, as I discussed in section 3.1.2, whereas during the 1980s and the 1990s, interest rates served only to satisfy the risk appetite of global investors.

I stated above that institutional migration achieved "substantial progress". In fact, I cannot state that it was "completely" successful. I highlight a few major aspects:

1. Central bank bailouts (legal framework): Although the Turkish banking sector stands on a sound basis, thanks to comprehensive reforms, a Central Bank bailout in the case of a private bank default is still legally possible. While this is unlikely to occur in the circumstances of the 2010s, this scheme shows that the Turkish legal framework still presents significant caveats when compared with that of the EU[1081];

2. State aid: I examined in Chapter 4 that state aid in particular in agriculture had always been a major reason for distorted prices. I also argued that, while Turkish policy makers created a regulatory agency on state aid in 2010, this was still related to the ministry. Thus, another aspect far from the EU standards is the fact that a de-politicized institutional framework charged with monitoring state aids is still absent;

3. Inflation targeting framework: I emphasized at the end of Chapter 5 that the focus of this monetary policy is on stabilization rather than on development. It thus implicitly assumes that the achievement of stable circumstances would automatically lead to economic growth and the creation of employment. We observed that while stabilization was achieved

---

[1080] The 57th Bulent Ecevit coalition government that lasted from 28.05.1999 to 18.11.2002 (Annex 3)

[1081] During the European debt crisis that started by the late 2000s, several economies from Ireland to the U.K., bailed out defaulting banks. While the EU has not attempted to rule this as illegal, I argue that in the European debt crisis case we observe extraordinary circumstances, whereas the Turkish Central Bank had traditionally intervened as a matter of course!

after several decades[1082], the level of unemployment, a proxy for development, remained high and persistent over time also after the achievement of financial reforms (Chapter 5.3, Discussion 2). Moreover, this monetary policy can also be associated with destabilizing capital flows and outflows, cycles of over-valued exchange rates, current account imbalances and the need for short-term portfolio investment cycles. To note also that the Turkish Central Bank has never even approached the 5 percent inflation target. The latter has seemingly obliged the former in keeping monetary policy too tight, i.e., high-interest rates. In fact, abandoning inflation targeting framework would have lost the global investors' confidence, leading to capital flight and exchange rates instability as we observed in section 5.3. Under these conditions the central bank might have been locked into inflation targeting policy with possible negative implications on the rates of growth and unemployment;

4. The Turkish Central Bank "independence" achieved in April 2001 eliminated inappropriate political pressures to fund fiscal deficits in Turkey. Nevertheless, introducing multiple mandates for the central bank, including for instance an employment-targeting policy, will require a coordination between monetary and fiscal policies, undermining the central bank independence. Therefore, the way Turkish Central Bank can effectively collaborate with political institutions for development purposes needs to be investigated. Further research can thus explore the adequate institutional and governance structure for Turkey providing a solution out of this trade-off, as it is likely that the choice of central bank mandate is also a product of historical and country-specific factors;

5. I questioned, at the end of section 4.1[1083], whether the EU financial regulatory framework itself is adequate. I highlighted that even among EU members, an adoption of new regulatory changes can never be "complete". Thus, the adaptation of EU financial market regulations to Turkey is not an event but it is a process, which can never become "complete". Nevertheless, I can state that it accomplished "substantial progress" sufficient to have a significant impact on functioning of markets and stability in the third phase from 2002 to 2011. We are going to observe in the years ahead whether more development-oriented monetary policies will replace the inflation targeting framework in line with the overall goal of the international development guidelines.

[1082] i.e., less than 10 percent inflation rate, though far from the 5 percent target rate.

[1083] In the "Concluding Remarks", point 2.

6.3. Implications of the Mundell-Fleming (M-F) model

The Turkish Central Bank's role in the economy has been a central theme in my study. I examined its independence in the light of two respects:

1. Political: The CBRT had traditionally functioned under ministerial influence, with governments using its resources for their own deficits. It legally gained an independent status after the February 2001 currency crisis, in April of the same year;

2. Economic: I examined the Mundell-Fleming (M-F) model[1084], according to which in an economy open to global markets, the central bank's independence depends on the exchange rate regime chosen.

Table 6.1 provides a broad insight into the Turkish Central Bank's degree of independence, in both political and economic terms, in the periods before and after the financial and currency crises. While I considered it politically independent based on its legally recognized independent status in April 2001, I evaluated its economic independence under the Mundell-Fleming framework, in other words, according to the exchange rate regime chosen.

Table 6.1: Turkish Central Bank's independence scheme pre- and post-major crises

	Before the 1994 fin. crisis	**Before the 2001 curr. crisis**	**After April 2001**
Political	No	No	Yes
M-F model	Yes	No	Yes

Source: Table 3.3 and section 4.1.3

In this section, I discuss the views of major authors regarding the appropriate exchange rate regime in the context of the Mundell-Fleming model and express my opinion in the light of my analysis in chapters 2 and 3.

I start with **John Williamson**, the author of the "Washington Consensus". To note that, while the whole list aimed at opening towards global markets[1085], he

---

1084 I introduced the M-F framework in section 3.1.4 and I examined the 1994 and 2001 crises episodes in section 3.3.1 point 4 and section 3.3.2.3 point 8, respectively.

1085 In particular, the points 7 and 9 suggest free capital flows (see section 2.1)

supported an "intermediate" exchange rate regime[1086]. This implies that under the "Washington Consensus" framework, a central bank may pursue an independent monetary policy on occasion.

Conclusion 4: I do not agree with John Williamson's view on the choice of "intermediate" exchange rate regime, as this can undermine the central bank independence under the Mundell-Fleming framework. In line with the discussion I held in section 3.1.4, in the Turkish case, as the economy was completely open to global markets, the only exchange rate regime that could possibly result in effective CBRT monetary policy was the floating one. Monetary authorities can try "intermediate" combinations for a while, but these create unstable circumstances over the long-term.

We observed in Table 3.3 that an "intermediate" regime was the case for Turkey prior to February 2001 crisis, due to the IMF Stabilization Program signed in December 1999. Nevertheless, I examined the dynamics of the Turkish economy under this Stabilization Program[1087] and showed that the question was more complicated. The Stabilization Program prepared the ground for an "ineffective" Central Bank for the first 18 months. In fact, point (F) states that during the second 18 months, the exchange rate band would gradually widen, allowing a gradual shift from a monetary framework centered entirely on the FX rate to one that allows a greater flexibility in pursuing the inflation target. Although the exchange rate band was to begin widening by July 2001, the program collapsed well before, during the month of February.

The quote from Stanley Fisher (2002)[1088] I produced, in section 3.3.2.3 point 8, is significant for my analysis. He commented as follows:

> "These crises reinforced the conclusion that impossible trinity makes a softly pegged exchange rate non-viable when the capital account is open.
>
> [....]
>
> A country may succeed for some time in living with the impossible trinity particularly if the exchange rate is undervalued. But when the capital account is open, a pegged

---

[1086] Section 2.1, point 5

[1087] Section 3.3.2.3, point 8

[1088] Fisher, S. (2002), p. 3

exchange rate is crisis-prone, vulnerable to a speculative attack, possibly producing a second generation crisis, in which the measures necessary to defend the peg are not politically viable."

Conclusion 5: I agree with the view of Stanley Fisher, who argued that intermediate regimes are "crisis-prone". In fact, this is the implication of the Mundell-Fleming model. It is important for the legitimacy and real independence of the CBRT that the foreign exchange regime should be truly free. A freely floating exchange rate is not necessarily a volatile one. Quite the contrary, if properly managed, the macroeconomy will be stable and steady, in addition, the exchange rate will start a long and uninterrupted appreciation in relation to all other inferior currencies.

6.4. Role of institutions: the political crises of February 2001 and April 2007, lessons to be learned

We observed that a political crisis at a high-level meeting on 19th February 2001, caused a sudden capital flight triggering the currency crisis. I examined this crisis with "second and third generation models" explaining the importance of changing market expectations. At this stage, I ask the following question:

Question: A more serious political crisis occurred in April 2007 at the end of President Ahmet Necdet Sezer's mandate. The pro-Islamist Abdullah Gul's candidacy to this highest rank became subject to severe reactions both from the secularists and the generals. This led to a political shock on 27th April 2007 that was considerably more severe than the political crisis of 19th February 2001. However, the reaction of the markets was different: Although the stock market and the domestic currency lost value the day after, they rapidly stabilized[1089]. It did not lead to an economic shock at all. Why?

Answer: The major reason is that market confidence was not lost[1090] because, by 2007, the EU-inspired institutional and regulatory reforms had

---

1089 Bredenkamp, H., Joseffson, M. and Lindgren, C. J. (2007), p. 1

1090 Ibid.

already been largely achieved, mainly as far as the central bank and the banking sector are concerned.

Conclusion 6: The Fig. 6.1 shows that after 2002, Turkey started to have stable growth without sharp fluctuations. Although the time frame is short, I consider that the impact of our 11th element of the "Washington Consensus" on stability is evident[1091].

Fig. 6.1: Growth rate dynamics from 1989 to 2010, in percentage

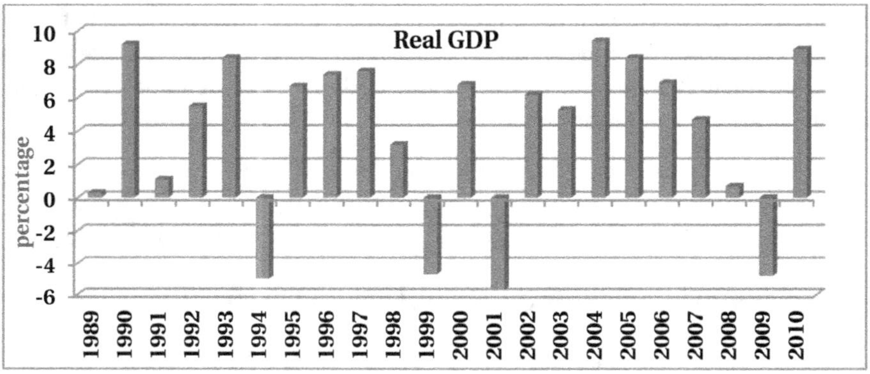

Source: State Planning Organization, General Directorate of Budget and Fiscal Control and Turkish Ministry of Finance. GDP by expenditures approach, annual growth rate based on 1987 prices from 1989 to 1999, based on 1998 prices from 2000 to 2010.

6.5. Concluding remarks and suggestions for further research

This is a fantastic story of a country where a variety of contradictions combined in different ways has led for long decades to socio-economic and political turbulences. While unsustainable coexistence of military influence, Islamic customs, secular rules and democratic principles in political life fed unstable circumstances, both state and market-led economic development approaches ended with failure until the beginning of the 21st century. Nevertheless, Turkey succeeded in becoming economically more stable by the mid-2000s, mainly thanks to institutional and regulatory reforms introduced first with the 1999

[1091] I do not consider the low growth in 2008 and negative growth in 2009, as this was caused by exogenous factors, i.e., the 2008-2009 global recession.

IMF Stabilization Program, during the 57th Bulent Ecevit coalition government, and later through the EU *acquis*[1092]. Nevertheless, at the same time, the jobless nature of growth emerged as a major problem.

I anticipated in Chapter 1.1 that my aim in this study is to explore the complex relationship between economic instability and structural reforms in Turkey and I investigated why the international development policies proposed to developing countries have not always been successful. I highlight here a couple of major aspects:

1. Stanley Fisher, the then Deputy Director of the IMF was a major critique to the theoretical basis of the 1999 Turkey-IMF Stabilization Programme, after the occurrence of the February 2001 crisis, arguing that adopting an intermediate exchange rate regime when the capital account is open makes the central bank ineffective and the economy crisis-prone[1093]. We observed that the consequent February 2001 currency crisis in itself accelerated the implementation of institutional and regulatory reforms during the same Bulent Ecevit coalition government. In May 2001, the Bulent Ecevit government, in the Letter of Intent addressed to the IMF, emphasized that priority was to be given to fiscal discipline[1094]. Later, the pro-Islamist single-party AKP governments fulfilled the IMF-imposed fiscal discipline and continued these reforms from 2002 onwards, one of them being the inflation-targeting monetary policy, which, while allowing the achievement of stabilization, has not substantially contributed to economic development as the high and persistent unemployment rates have shown;
2. Olivier Blanchard, IMF's former Economic Counsellor, has been a major critique to the conceptual framework of the inflation-targeting framework after the 2007-2008 global recession, arguing that one target (inflation), one instrument (short-term interest rates) rule is to be replaced by an attitude in favor of multiple targets, including development-oriented objectives and multiple instruments, though this would undermine the degree of central

[1092] I emphasized during the book that structural reforms were first introduced into the agenda with the December 1999 IMF Stabilization Program (section 3.3.2.3 and section 3.3.2.3 "discussion" point 11) and later through the *Acquis Communautaire* (Chapter 4). I also noted that while the 1999 IMF Stabilization Program was agreed on 9th December, Turkey became an official candidate for full EU membership in the following days, i.e., on 10th and 11th December. The presence of a double external anchor played significant and complementary roles, recommending both the same institutional and regulatory reforms (Annex 1).

[1093] We discussed this aspect in section 3.3.2.3, "discussion" point 8.

[1094] We discussed this aspect in section 3.3.2.3 "discussion" point 12.

bank independence. It seems that the trade-off between the degree of central bank independence and the design of multiple targets needs to be restructured in line with historical and country-specific factors[1095].

Turkey's overall sovereign risk profile is in a better shape by the early 2010s, not only among emerging markets but also when compared with several EU economies. For instance, while there was a fear in Eurozone economies like Italy and Spain by the first half of the 2010s which will be the next bank to be bailed out by the central bank, the Turkish banking sector of that era had become more solid. Similarly, risk perception of global markets has been lower when we compare Turkey with many EU economies.

This is an exciting story of an emerging market economy that succeeded to put an end to its chronic economic instability. Nevertheless, this was achieved at the cost of jobless growth, failing thus to fulfill the overall goal of international development policies. Therefore, priority for 21st century Turkey should not be focusing exclusively on inflation but implementing in particular development-oriented policies, i.e., targeting also unemployment levels, with reasonable price stability. While growth is needed for the creation of employment, the main challenge for Turkish policy makers now should be to use policy instruments to prevent global capital flows-led growth and boom-bust cycles. In addition, it is crucially important to achieve structural reforms to reduce and hopefully avoid current account deficits. Otherwise, policy makers will be obliged to keep growth rates low, in order to restrain current account deficits, failing, therefore, the developmental purpose of the monetary policy. In such a case, Turkey might face a different type of crisis, not explained in this book in the years ahead, led by persistent jobless low growth levels.

On the other hand, by the year 2016, Turkey has also been exposed to security related concerns from the South-Eastern region. For instance, the refugee flows (accessing the country) from the Syrian border does not contribute to the achievement of Turkish development objectives.

To note that development is a human rights issue. Every human being has the right to development. Kofi Annan, former Secretary General of the United Nations launched in 2005 the Alliance of Civilizations initiative, co-sponsored by prime ministers of Spain and Turkey, which "affirms a broad consensus across nations, cultures and religions that all societies are bound together in their humanity and interdependent in their quest for stability, prosperity and

---

[1095] We discussed this aspect in section 5.3, "discussion" point 2.

peaceful co-existence"[1096]. He further stated that "we will not enjoy security without development, we will not enjoy development without security, and we will not enjoy either without respect for human rights. [....] Not only are development, security and human rights all imperative, they also reinforce each other."[1097]. The Human Rights Council[1098] meets regularly at the Human Rights and Alliance of Civilizations Chamber at the European headquarters of the United Nations in Geneva.

Turkey is "a real bridge between East and West"[1099]. It also strives for stability in the Middle East as it stands as a natural leader both in political and economic terms. The Alliance of Civilizations project has been for long years a major sponsor of the Turkish government to promote full membership as the EU integration process offers unprecedented challenges and opportunities for both sides in terms of economic and political gains. Nevertheless, while the project itself promotes universality of human rights and mutual respect among different cultures, probably the pro-Islamist AKP has promoted this project also for other reasons. The ongoing adoption of both institutions from the West and of the Islamic lifestyle from the Arabic world since the late 2000s, signals unsustainable social dynamics in the long-term as political Islam contradicts secular basis of the Republic of Turkey[1100]. Moreover, it seems that the Arab Spring associated with a variety of social movements in different countries – Algeria, Tunisia, Egypt, Yemen, Bahrain, Iraq, Libya, Jordan, and Syria– sees Turkey as a model for the benefit of political Islam in respective Arab countries. Would the Alliance of Civilization project be able to embrace these contradictory elements? Or is it a way to make a pro-Islamist lifestyle in Turkey more acceptable?

As a matter of conclusion, the multidimensional nature of development process obliges us to reflect on recent humanitarian emergencies in the region. Several security concerns have arisen by the year 2016, from suicide bombers and ethnic terrorism to a US-based Islamic preacher Fethullah Gulen, a rival

---

1096 United Nations Alliance of Civilizations (2006), p. 5

1097 United Nations General Assembly (2005), pp. 5, 6

1098 Human Rights Council is a major inter-governmental body within the United Nations system responsible for strengthening the promotion and protection of human rights around the world. It was established in 2006, replacing the former Commission of Human Rights.

1099 As commented by Pope Benedict 16th, during his visit to Turkey, in November 2006.

1100 The Atlantic website, 11th December 2012

Islamic group to AKP, who led a *coup* through the armed forces, put Turkish policy makers to a serious test. My book is not subject to humanitarian aspects of development. Thus, here I only emphasize that further research can explore whether Turkish foreign policy will be capable of managing several serious security problems, among others those the refugee flows can generate, which will also have an impact on security and development in the country. For instance, Turkey allowed the access of many refugees from Syria without an identity card or passport, i.e., persons having declared only verbally their origins and names were registered at the border as a "Syrian refugee", since civil war conditions in this country present a real human tragedy. Nevertheless, Turkish policy makers decided also to grant them citizenship, without any humanitarian obligation or international pressure, although the normal procedure to become a Turkish citizen requires among others a judicial extract of the candidate. This means that under the circumstances of the Middle Eastern region, anybody from a criminal or terrorist organization can verbally declare himself at the Turkish border as a Syrian refugee without any official document and later potentially become a Turkish citizen. This is only one of the examples that can create serious security problems in Turkey in the years, decades ahead. It is also to be explored whether the pro-Islamist AKP aims to grant citizenship for humanitarian reasons or to increase its vote potential in the next general elections to be held in 2019.

My study examined the period from 1980 to 2010 (with some flashbacks to earlier times when appropriate) and mainly focused on the adaptation of EU financial market regulations in an attempt to explore the impact of monetary policies on stability and development. The EU integration is an ongoing process and, of course, I cannot state that I covered all of the problems, although I focused on some major ones. On the other hand, many other problems may arise at different degrees in the years ahead, depending on the conditions of the global economy and both the Turkish and Middle-Eastern regional circumstances. I would like to suggest a few aspects for further research as my study is to be considered only an investigation focused on the initial phase of this transition process:

1. I emphasized that Turkey had suffered from high and persistent inflation for several decades. In addition, governments' inappropriate pressures on CBRT to fund fiscal deficits only expanded and accelerated these unstable circumstances. Then, the IMF-led inflation-focused monetary policies, which was reinforced through the *EU-Acquis* adaptation process, allowed a relative stabilization of general price levels, i.e., from high inflation rates to less than 10 percent levels. Nevertheless, while stabilization of prices is important, high and persistent unemployment rates showed that monetary policies pursued have not had a significant impact on the creation of

employment. Further research can investigate the effect of non-linearities in the growth-inflation relationship (Chapter 5.3, Discussion 2) in an attempt to explore the threshold level for the Turkish case, which will, in turn, allow estimation of the ideal growth rate range that can generate more employment "with reasonable price stability". Moreover, I used only the unemployment rate as a proxy for development. Further research can make use of other proxies from inequality of income distribution, women's literacy and employment rates to life expectancy and infant mortality as well as others, to explore the degree of economic development in Turkey. On the other hand, Turkey has never been a current account deficits-prone economy. To note in figure 6.2 that current account balance improved in a period of crisis or turbulences (i.e., after the 2001 financial crisis and the 2009 global recession). Deficits reached in 2011 a historical record with 73 billion dollars (Fig. 6.2), corresponding to 9.9 percent of GDP. Then, policy makers' aim has been to keep the level of GDP lower in order to restrain current account deficits. Of course, lower GDP levels did not contribute to generating more employment, quite the contrary! Further research can explore how structural reforms can be implemented to reduce current account deficits and what will be their cost for the economy with an overall objective to reduce high and persistent unemployment rates. It is possible to observe in Fig. 6.2 the current account balance and unemployment rates together with growth through data from 1999 to 2015, in an attempt to provide a forward-looking perspective about the trend after the adoption of an inflation-targeting framework, from 2002 to the most recent period.

Fig. 6.2: Impact of Inflation-Targeting framework on key macro indicators

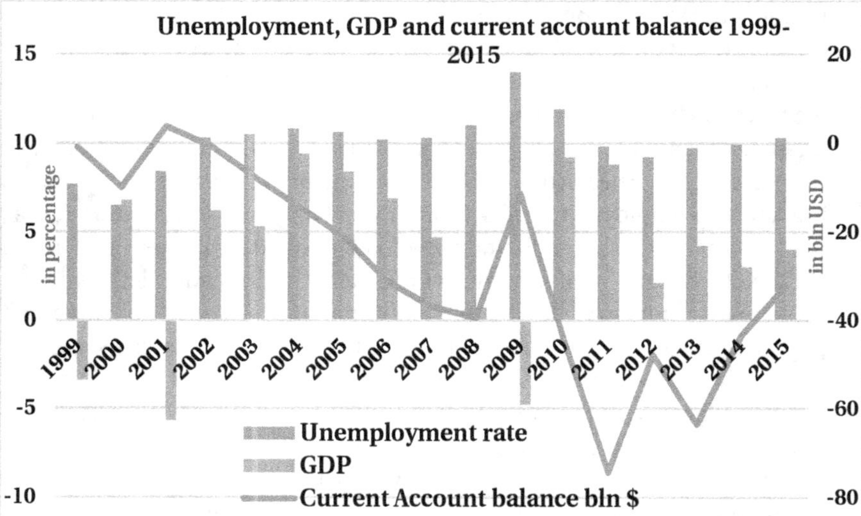

Source: Unemployment rate and GDP (left axis in percentage), data from Turkish Statistical Institute (2013), pp. 126, 127, 705, GDP by expenditures approach at 1998 prices; Current Account balance in billion dollars (right axis), data from CBRT website, Balance of Payments (BPM6) Analytic Presentation, p. 11.

2. I discussed in section 4.2.3 the property rights situation in Turkey, where I emphasized the importance of newly created mortgages market in Turkey. While I argued that structural institutional reforms made Turkey a well-performing emerging economy of the world by the late 2000s, it is worth also to investigate its eventual weaknesses. In my opinion, one of the reasons why the 2008 sub-prime crisis did not hit the Turkish economy is probably because of the absence of well-developed credit markets in Turkey. During the 1980s and the 1990s, economic agents in Turkey took unhedged positions only on interest rate carry trades bearing exchange rate risk, probably because there was not a developed mortgage market. The section 4.2.3 can be further developed under several other aspects that were not directly related to this study. For example, what is the relationship between interest rate levels and low-medium income segments of Turkish society benefiting from mortgages? Would lower interest rates make the solving of housing problems more likely or would it create a housing bubble? What lessons can Turkey draw from the sub-prime crisis regarding the regulatory framework in order to prevent excessive risk taking or to avoid an eventual bubble in the housing market?

3. The central bank independence has been a major focus theme of this study. I analyzed this issue both under the Mundell-Fleming framework and the

political circumstances. I emphasized that one of the main reasons why Turkey stood as a brilliant emerging economy by the early 2010s is its independent status. Nevertheless, the EU integration process leads to the full membership ideal, which will inevitably undermine the CBRT independence under the M-F framework, i.e., adopting fixed exchange rates. Under this perspective, it seems that the ongoing EU full membership process might be more beneficial for Turkey than the full membership ideal itself. In fact, an independent central bank can introduce, under the M-F framework, *ad-hoc* measures, for example, when unexpected global or local events create turbulence or when the local currency is too strong making the economy less competitive. Nevertheless, its intervention can become ineffective at different degrees when its independence is undermined. Moreover, the public debt related problems in several EU economies by the early 2010s showed that some of the economies in the Union needed specific intervention tailored to their domestic needs. Thus, further research could investigate the following trade-off: Is it appropriate for Turkey to adopt the Eurozone currency if and when it joins the Union or is it more suitable opting for other alternatives allowing the CBRT independence? Such a study may give different results depending on the time frame considered. Nevertheless, it would be a useful investigation, as it would be based on an approach aiming to adapt Western institutions to local circumstances and not to imitate or copy them. On the other hand, by the year 2016, there are serious doubts whether the Eurozone can be sustainable over time and whether Turkey can join the EU after, among others, the occurrence of increasingly chaotic circumstances in Syria.

Despite all, the EU process continues, though policy makers, both in Turkey and in the EU, are aware of the fact that Turkey will not join the EU in the short/medium term (or never). Nevertheless, both parts behave as if it will join since the process itself seems mutually convenient. In fact, it may allow changes in rules and regulations in benefit of some interest groups, a major one being the political Islam in Turkey, which has continuously been reinforced since the beginning of the EU full membership process up to these days. It is also beneficial for the EU as Turkey is a strategic partner playing a crucial role in the Middle East.

Nevertheless, the use of EU-inspired democratic principles also for ramification of political Islam in the country not only contradicts the spirit of democratic rules themselves but is not beneficial neither for Turkey nor for the EU itself in the long term, regardless of any kind of membership or partnership the EU can explore with Turkey over time!

Annex 1

A Guide to Transition in Turkey

1854: First foreign debt of Ottoman Empire

Ottoman Administration applied for a foreign loan for the first time in its history. The aim was to cover both domestic debt repayments and additional military expenditures due to the Crimean War from 1853 to 1856, during which Ottomans were allied with England and France against Russia[1101];

1875: Ottoman Sovereign Debt Default

Ottoman Empire declared moratorium as the total debt repayments scheduled for that year amounted to 120 percent of the annual budget revenue;

1881: Foreign control on Ottoman accounts and financial stability

Financial stability was achieved through the establishment of the Ottoman Public Debt Administration, which controlled a large proportion of state revenues. For the first time in its history, the Ottoman Empire was subject to a form of foreign control;

1923 (17th February - 4th March): Izmir Economic Congress

Kemal Ataturk-led team discussed during the Izmir Economic Congress appropriate economic policies for Turkey to reach the level of contemporary civilizations. The aim broadly was to adopt a Western framework for economic development. There was agreement on promoting private initiative but also preventing monopolistic tendencies. Foreign capital was allowed as long as it contributed to economic development and it respected Turkish laws[1102];

1101 First loans were provided from Rothschilds and Dent, Palmers and Co. of London (Saygili, A. T. (2009), pp. 154, 157).

1102 Eroglu, N. (2007), p. 65

1923 (24th July): Lausanne Treaty

Through the Lausanne Treaty, the Allies recognized full independence and the young Republic inherited heavy foreign debt from the Ottoman period, where articles from 46 to 57 provided repayment scheme[1103];

1923 (29th October): Proclamation of the Republic

Kemal Ataturk founded the Republic of Turkey, a secular parliamentary democracy. CHP (Republican People's Party)-led single-party system lasted until the creation of Democratic Party in 1946;

1926: Adopting Swiss Civil Code

Kemal Ataturk's aim was to bring the country to the level of contemporary civilizations. The new Republic adopted the Swiss Civil Code;

1930s: Protectionist policies were institutionalized

The Central Bank was established in 1930 and protectionist policies were institutionalized through Five-Year Industrial Plans (1933) and the creation of state-owned enterprises (SOEs). The statist principle was included into the Constitution as a milestone of the Republic (1937);

1938 (10th November): President Kemal Ataturk passed away

The founder of the Republic of Turkey passed away, Ismet Inonu had become President;

1940s-1950s: Foreign policy-strategic partner of the West[1104]

Although Turkey signed a military agreement with Britain and France, it remained neutral during WWII. However, it became involved in world affairs during this period. In fact, it joined the IMF in 1944, the United Nations in 1945, the OECD in 1948, the Council of Europe in 1949, GATT in 1950, NATO in 1952 and applied for Associate Membership of the European Economic Community (EEC) in 1959;

[1103] Ozcelik, O. and Tuncer, G. (2005), p. 256

[1104] Cetinsaya, G. (2007), p. 11

1940s-1950s: Domestic political structure-Transition to multi-party system

The CHP-led single-party system ended with the foundation of Adnan Menderes's Democratic Party (DP) in 1946. This was the initial phase of multi-party politics. The DP won the 1950 general elections and introduced a liberal economic policy in line with post-WWII trends in the West;

1954: End of Ottoman Debt Repayment

Ottoman foreign debt from 1854, inherited through the Lausanne Treaty (1923) was entirely reimbursed 100 years later;

1958: The first IMF Stabilization Program[1105]

Worsening macroeconomic conditions obliged the Menderes government to ask for IMF assistance, which involved measures ranging from a major devaluation to import liberalization and increase in SOEs good prices. USD 400 million of foreign debt was consolidated. Nevertheless, there were serious disagreements on the implementation of the Program;

1959: Turkey applied for association to the European Economic Community (EEC)

This was the first application of Turkey for a future full membership to the EEC;

1960 (27th May): First military intervention[1106]

General Cemal Gursel led the first military *coup* intervening directly in Turkish politics. While the new Constitution of July 1961 introduced a wide range of civil liberties, together with social rights, the military institutionalized state presence in the economy more solidly through a strict Import Substitution Industrialization policy and Five-Year Development Plans. State Planning Organization was created as a constitutional body together with Constitutional Court. Ismet Inonu-led civilian government replaced military rule in November 1961;

1105 Ozdemir, H. (2000), p. 174

1106 Burak, B. (2011), p. 150

1961-1970: IMF Stand-by agreements

During this period, the Turkish government annually signed Stand-by agreements with the IMF, the duration of which varied from 9 to 12 months;

1963 (September): Signature of the Association Agreement with the EEC[1107]

While Greece signed an association agreement in 1961, Turkey signed the same (the so-called Ankara Agreement) two years later, which aimed at establishing a customs union between Turkey and the EEC. This would have eventually led to full membership;

1963 (December): Initial phase of Cyprus conflict[1108]

A constitutional crisis following the Greek Cypriots' amendment proposal provoked inter-communal battles. The partnership Republic formed in 1960 was interrupted and the United Nations Security Council agreed in March 1964 (Resolution 186) to create a UN peacekeeping force;

1970 (23rd November): Initiation of Transitional Phase in Ankara Agreement[1109]

The second (transitional) phase of the Ankara Agreement began with the signature of the Additional Protocol including the regulations on Customs Union. This phase sought to finalize a customs union between parties, which took effect on 1st January 1996;

1971 (12th March): Second military intervention

Politics moved towards an ideological debate in the end-1960s. Worsening macroeconomic conditions and civil violence caused social turbulence. The military intervened in politics with a memorandum, appointing a new prime minister who ruled until May 1972. Amendments to the Constitution restricted civil rights[1110];

[1107] General Secretariat for EU Affairs, website

[1108] Wenzke, C. and Lindley, D. (2008), pp. 7, 8

[1109] General Secretariat for EU Affairs, website

[1110] Burak, B. (2011), p. 151

1971 (1st September): The EEC unilaterally abolished customs duties

The Additional Protocol's commercial adjudications took effect with the "Temporary Agreement". The EEC abolished customs duties and quantity restrictions unilaterally, which were applied to industry products imported from Turkey (apart from textile products);

1973 (1st January): Turkey introduced the first reduction of customs duties

The Additional Protocol signed on 23rd November 1970, took effect in 1973. Turkey introduced the First Reduction of Customs Duties and Harmonization of Consolidated Liberation List (EEC Customs Union Tariff);

1973 Oil crisis[1111]

The increase in international oil prices in 1973 had a significant impact on the Turkish economy. This was the initial phase of an economic cycle, which led to unsustainable current account deficit dynamics in the late-1970s;

1974 (20th July): Turkish military intervention in Cyprus[1112]

The Cyprus conflict that emerged in 1963 culminated with Turkish military intervention, as a response to a potential Greek military *coup* in Cyprus aiming to unite the island with Greece. In the aftermath of the military operation, the US arms embargo and European economic sanctions further reduced the funding options of the Turkish economy[1113];

1976 (30th June): EEC canceled customs duties to agricultural products imported from Turkey

The Association Council decided to cancel the customs duties applied to nearly all agricultural products in Turkey[1114], which lasted until 1987;

[1111] Kopits, G. (1987), p. 2

[1112] Uslu, N. (2003), p. 115

[1113] Ahmad, F. (1993), p. 176

[1114] 1/80 Association Council Decision

1976 (19th September): Turkey introduced the second reduction of customs duties

Turkey introduced the Second Reduction of Customs Duties and Harmonization of Consolidated Liberation List as an obligation of the Additional Protocol signed on 23rd November 1970;

1978 (11th October): Turkey suspended obligations under EEC Customs' Union tariff[1115]

Reduction of customs duties on 1st January 1973 and 19th September 1976 increased progressively the current account deficits up to 1978[1116]. Turkey claimed, during the 4th Five-Year Development Plan, to suspend the obligations under the EEC Customs' Union tariff;

1978-1979: IMF Stand-by agreements

A variety of factors, ranging from the 1973 oil crisis and the 1974 military intervention in Cyprus to inefficiencies due to import substitution industrialization-based protectionism, involved the Turkish economy in a balance-of-payments crisis in the late 1970s. While no Stand-by agreement was signed from 1971 to 1977, the IMF assistance became necessary[1117];

1980 (24th January): Introducing IMF/Washington Consensus-led deregulation process

The first modern IMF Stabilization Program based on the "Washington Consensus", during the 43rd Demirel government, symbolized the end of a traditionally public investment-led development policies era by dismantling state presence in the economy. This date marked the initiation of a deregulation process, transforming the whole economic approach from inward-looking to an outward-oriented;

1115 General Secretariat for EU Affairs, website

1116 State Planning Organization (1979), pp. 69-71

1117 Table 2.4

1980 (July): Liberalization of interest rates on loans and deposits

For the first time in Turkish history, ceilings were lifted to avoid misallocation of resources, in line with "Washington Consensus" principle no. 4[1118];

1980 (12th September): Third Military Takeover

Unstable coalition and minority governments throughout the decade, together with worsening macroeconomic conditions after 1978, provoked social disorder leading to another armed forces' intervention. While the military takeover of 1960 increased state presence in the economy, this time generals favored the implementation of the "Washington Consensus" principles, a private initiative-led development. The new Constitution of 1982 restricted civil and political rights. Military rule lasted until the general elections held in November 1983. However, political parties of the pre-1980 period were excluded and their leaders regained their political rights only in 1987. Relations with the European Economic Community were suspended until 16th September 1986;

1981 (April): Floating exchange rate regime

A managed floating regime replaced the traditional complex multiple fixed exchange rate regime. In this way, Turkey aimed to introduce a competitive exchange rate regime in line with the "Washington Consensus" principle no. 5. Nevertheless, a flexible regime was chosen, contrary to John Williamson's suggestion, i.e., an intermediate one. Turkish lira was still not convertible by this date;

1982: Bankers' crisis

The government bailed out five small banks and reintroduced ministerial control on interest rates. Thus, the "Washington Consensus" principle no. 4 was invalidated and would remain so until 1988. This crisis signaled the weakness of regulatory framework in the banking sector;

1983: Establishing Capital Market Board (CMB) and Savings Deposit Insurance Fund (SDIF)

CMB was established as a ministerial body, whereas SDIF worked under the auspices of the CBRT and aimed to prevent liquidity problems in the banking sector. This first attempt to improve regulatory framework as a response to the

---

1118 Section 2.1

previous year's bankers' crisis had not been effective. In fact, these bodies were politically managed;

1983 (November): End of military rule, election of civilian government

The democratically elected, militarily backed single-party ANAP government aimed to accelerate financial market regulatory changes, which ranged, until 1986, from trade and external financial liberalization, lifting quantitative restrictions on import regime and partial capital account liberalization, to reestablishing a new capital adequacy ratio for banks, creation of a government securities market, opening of Istanbul Stock Exchange, designation of a monetary policy and the beginning of Open Market Operations by the CBRT;

1986-1987: Some improvements in foreign relations and domestic politics[1119]

Relations with the European Economic Community, which had been suspended with the 12th September 1980 military intervention, restarted on 16th September 1986 and Turkey applied for a full membership on 14th April 1987, based on article 237 of the Rome Treaty, article 98 of the European Coal and Steel Community and article 205 of the EURATOM. On 21st December 1987, Turkey began to re-implement the obligations, which were suspended on 11th October 1978;

In domestic politics, a referendum held on 6th September 1987 invalidated the ban on old politicians, which had been introduced by generals through the 12th September 1980, military intervention. A majority of 50.1 percent allowed the return of old political leaders to policy making. Suleyman Demirel and Bulent Ecevit had again become key political figures during the 1990s. While this was an important step for democracy, we note that coalition and minority governments from 1991 to 2002 also led to political instability;

1989 (March): Institutional reform limiting CBRT's money creation capability[1120]

An accord signed between the Treasury and the CBRT aimed to reduce the size of credits to the public sector. This was an important institutional arrangement

---

[1119] General Secretariat for EU Affairs, website

[1120] Bayazitoglu, Y., Ersel, H. and Ozturk, E. (1991), p. 11

to limit excessive money creation. Nevertheless, Short-term Cash Advance Facility to the Treasury continued until 1997;

1989 (August): Complete Capital Account Liberalization and convertibility of currency

Lifting all restrictions on capital movements allowed complete integration with global markets. The Turkish lira became convertible in April 1990. This reform is to be evaluated together with the flexible exchange rate regime introduced in 1981. Under the Mundell-Fleming framework, the CBRT could follow an independent monetary policy. Nevertheless, it was still under ministerial control, i.e., Short-term Cash Advance Facility continued until 1997 and it bailed out banks in the late 1990s;

1989 (November): Parliament elected Prime Minister Turgut Ozal as President

Turgut Ozal was a key political figure introducing the "Washington Consensus" principles on 24th January 1980, during the 43rd Suleyman Demirel government. He succeeded to form single-party governments after the 1983 and 1987 general elections. To note that Turgut Ozal started to lose his popularity due to worsening economic conditions in 1987. He was elected as President of Republic in November 1989 and he appointed Yildirim Akbulut and Mesut Yilmaz, unpopular figures from ANAP, as prime ministers in 1989 and 1991, respectively. ANAP was losing its reputation as a major political formation;

1991: Negative impact of Gulf Crisis on Turkish economy

In addition to deteriorating macro indicators (i.e., budget deficits, PSBR and interest rate levels from 1988 to 1991, see Table 3.1), the conflict in the region adversely affected the Turkish economy, i.e., GDP fell from 9.2 in 1990 to 1.1 in 1991 (Table 2.3);

1991 (November): Old politicians on the political scene: the 49th Suleyman Demirel government

After the election of Turgut Ozal as President, ANAP had lost its reputation as a major political party. Suleyman Demirel, a key political figure of the 1960s and 1970s, regained his political rights thanks to the 1987 referendum and formed the first of the nine coalition governments to be composed during the 1990s;

1991-1993: CBRT creating increasingly more high-powered money

To note that the creation of bonds market allowed reducing the size of CBRT resources in financing deficits from 1985 to 1990 (Fig. 2.5). Nevertheless, higher interest rates due to higher sovereign credit risk perception of investors led the governments to again use the CBRT Short-term Cash Advance Facility more intensively from 1991 to 1993. Both of these tools in financing deficits were unsustainable;

1993 (April): President Turgut Ozal passed away

The death of President Ozal had a significant impact on Turkish political life. The Parliament elected Prime Minister Suleyman Demirel as President, who in turn appointed Tansu Ciller as Prime Minister. To note that the latter was an economist without any previous political experience;

1994 (February): Government funding crisis

Tansu Ciller government's major policy had been to reduce interest rates. While the level had been unsustainable, there was a policy flaw. Under the M-F framework, flexible exchange rates and free capital movements allowed the CBRT to follow an independent monetary policy. However, the government intervened with a law to reduce the level of interest rates, causing the CBRT governor to resign. This was also against the will of market forces leading to capital outflow and to a major crisis. The interbank interest rates rose to over 400 percent (Fig. 3.7);

1994 (March): Local elections, surprising victory of pro-Islamist party RP

While the pro-Islamist party had obtained from 7 to 12 percent of votes in elections during the previous two decades, in local elections held on 27th March 1994, Islamists obtained 19.1 percent of votes. This record was only a couple of points behind the votes of major liberal-wing parties ANAP and DYP. Moreover, Istanbul and Ankara mayors, the largest cities of the country, were elected from the RP. Recep Tayyip Erdogan, elected as mayor of Istanbul, would later go on to become the key political figure after 2002, as leader of the pro-Islamist AKP and prime minister;

1994 (April-July): Stabilization Program

This program also included 100 percent guarantee on bank deposits to increase the credibility of the financial system. However, this only created moral hazard as banks assumed more risk, which led to banking sector-led currency crisis 7 years later. Once again "Washington Consensus" principles were on the agenda, including privatization of SOEs, but an EU-inspired regulatory framework in the banking sector was still absent. Efforts for privatizations were ineffective, despite good intentions, due to an inadequate regulatory framework and unstable coalition governments. While Turkey had signed Stand-by agreements with the IMF frequently from 1961 to 1984, no agreement was signed after this date. In July 1994, a new Stand-by agreement supported the government's reform program;

1994 (December): Adopting the EU-inspired Competition Law

The Parliament adopted the EU Competition Law in preparation for the impending application of Customs Union with the EU: a first step in adopting the vast "acquis". While from 1980 to 1994 financial markets were only "deregulated" without any regulation aiming to create competitive conditions in markets, the Competition Law approved in 1994 launched the initial phase of "liberalization". I use the latter term in the sense of deregulated markets where, while state presence is minimized, creation of de-politicized regulatory bodies play a role in enhancing efficiency and contributing to the "functioning" of markets;

1995 (December): Pro-Islamist RP obtained the highest votes in general elections

A wide range of factors, from lack of confidence in political leaders of the center because of worsening macroeconomic conditions culminating with the 1994 financial crisis to the efficiency of pro-Islamist mayors in delivering services and addressing the material needs of the urban poor, was influential in pro-Islamist RP's success;

1996 (1st January): Customs Union entered into force[1121]

This was the finalization of a target established in December 1963 with the signature of Ankara Agreement and also the end of the second or "Transitional Phase" of the same agreement, which started on 23rd November 1970;

1997 (28th February): Military intervention

Generals obliged the pro-Islamist RP-led government to resign and allowed another civilian government to take power. To note that, though this was not a

---

[1121] General Secretariat for EU Affairs, website

complete military intervention, the new civilian government was not democratically elected;

1997: CBRT's Short-term Cash Advance Facility to Treasury was forbidden

Monetization of deficits had always been a major reason behind economic instability in Turkey. The CBRT was not allowed to provide liquidity to cover budget deficits after 1997. This seemed as an important effort in de-politicizing the Central Bank behavior. Nevertheless, the latter bailed out several defaulting banks from 1998 to 2000;

1997-1998: Exogenous factors on the economy

A variety of external factors, from East Asian currency crises in 1997 to Russian debt crisis and collapse of LTCM in 1998, decreased risk appetite of global investors and caused capital outflow from emerging markets including Turkey;

1997-1998: Relations with the EU[1122]

At the Summit of Heads of State on 13th December 1997 in Luxembourg, convened by the EU, Turkey took place in the context of enlargement though it was not mentioned yet as a candidate state. On 3rd March 1998, the European Commission announced a document titled "European Strategy of Turkey" relating to improving relations between Turkey and the EU. On 4th November 1998, the European Commission published the first "Regular Progress Report for Turkey", representing the opinion of the Commission in light of criteria for membership. These reports have been annually published after this date;

1998: IMF Staff Monitoring Program, two banks' default

Worsening macro indicators led the government to ask assistance from the IMF. Disinflation, reduced budget deficits and structural reforms were on the agenda. The Program succeeded in lowering inflation rate in the short-term. Nevertheless, unhedged FX positions of banks increased from 81 percent of shareholders equity in 1997 to 123 percent in 1998. Two banks defaulted;

[1122] General Secretariat for EU Affairs", website

1999 (28th May): Bulent Ecevit formed a coalition government

Following the general elections, Bulent Ecevit, leader of DSP, formed the 57th government with coalition partners MHP (far right) and ANAP (center right);

1999 (17th August): Natural disaster hitting the economy

The earthquake in Northwestern Turkey in a densely populated region caused the death of nearly 20'000 people and hit the economy with an estimated cost equivalent to 7 percent of GDP[1123];

1999 (30th November): Relations with the IMF and EU positively influenced the rating assignments

Moody's changed Turkey's outlook for foreign currency bonds and bank deposits from stable to positive. Major factors behind this upgrade were expectations regarding a new agreement with the IMF and improving relations with the EU;

1999 (9th December): IMF Stand-by agreement

This agreement introduced a soft peg and restricted the CBRT behavior. The latter was also ineffective under the Mundell-Fleming framework as the economy was exposed to global market flows. The Program succeeded in reducing exchange rate volatility together with the level of interest and inflation rates in the short-term;

1999 (10th-11th December): Official candidature for EU membership

During the Helsinki Summit held on this date, Turkey became an official candidate for full EU membership;

1999-2000: Pending fragile situation in financing deficits

A new banking law, introduced in June 1999, aimed to restructure the banking regulatory framework and created the Banking Regulation and Supervision Agency (BRSA) as an independent regulatory body, which became operational in August 2000. Nevertheless, the overall deficits financing mechanism was already close to collapse. Budget deficits reached a record high with 11.9 percent and 10.9 percent of GDP in 1999 and 2000, respectively (Table 3.8). In

---

1123 This is an estimate including indirect socio-economic costs (Erdik, M. (2000), p. 1).

addition, the two state banks' losses amounted to 13 percent of GDP in 1999. While the CBRT was not allowed to monetize deficits after 1997, government securities, of which major holders were private commercial banks, were used for this purpose. However, the latter was making money through interest rate carry trades in global markets, of which unhedged FX positions reached 362 percent and 212 percent of shareholders equity in 1999 and 2000, respectively (Table 3.9). During these two years the CBRT bailed out 19 banks (Table 3.4);

2000 (4th July): Establishing General Secretariat for EU Affairs

Law No. 4'587 saw the establishment of the General Secretariat for EU Affairs affiliated with the Prime Ministry;

2000 (August): Banking Regulation and Supervision Agency became operational

At the end of August, the newly created IRA in the banking sector became operational. However, it was too late to prevent a banking sector-led currency crisis in February 2001, as during the following months global markets had priced excessive credit risk of Demirbank and of other banks. Lack of confidence created volatility;

2000 (November): Liquidity crisis

Demirbank's highly risky position became publicly known and caused a liquidity crisis in November 2000. The CBRT intervened to defend the crawling peg, violating the 1999 IMF Program. The situation was under control in short time, thanks to an additional IMF loan of USD 7.5 billion, equivalent to Demirbank's bailout cost;

2001 (19th February): Currency crisis

The 1999 IMF Program restricted any CBRT intervention, which was also ineffective under the Mundell-Fleming framework. Thus, global markets were the only liquidity providers. Nevertheless, excessively high deficits and increasing sovereign default risk perception of global investors, due to failing banking sector, created fragile circumstances. A political dispute at a high-level meeting triggered capital outflow and led to a major currency crisis. The currency was floated, which also meant that the CBRT could follow an independent monetary policy under the Mundell-Fleming framework;

2001 (March): Launching the post-crisis reform process

The World Bank Vice-Chairman Kemal Dervis left his position to take the post of Minister of Economy and the government adopted a package of financial and economic reforms on 2nd March. The Council of EU formally approved the Accession Partnership on 8th March. The government adopted its "National Program for the Adoption of the *Acquis*" on 19th March, which implied a wide range of economic and financial reforms;

24th March saw the publication of the Council Decision of 8th March 2001, titled "Principles, Priorities, Intermediate Objectives and Conditions Contained in the Accession partnership with the Republic of Turkey" (No. 2001/235/EC), and "Decision on National Program of Turkey for the Adoption of the *Acquis*", in the Official Journal of European Community (No. 24'352)[1124];

2001 (April): Central Bank Independence

A new law established the full autonomy of the CBRT. That is to say, this central institution in economic policymaking gained a de-politicized framework, a significant effort in EU full membership process. The law introduced a transition period to an inflation targeting regime, which lasted from 2002 to 2005;

2001 (August): Pro-Islamist party AKP in the scene

The split within the pro-Islamist RP, led Recep Tayyip Erdogan to found the AKP;

2001-2002: State Aid in agriculture

The government launched privatization for public monopolies in tobacco and sugar sectors and founded two IRAs in these sectors. Nevertheless, it seemed to be difficult to prevent state aid in agriculture, a major aspect contradicting the EU standards. The state aid agency was finally created in 2010, but it was affiliated to Ministry;

1124 General Secretariat for EU Affairs, website

2002 (July): Establishing the Turkish Derivatives Exchange (TURKDEX)

A financial derivatives market allowing economic agents to share risks was created, although it only became operational three years later;

2002 (November): Pro-Islamist party AKP won general elections

This had been the initial phase of political stability as AKP formed single-party governments also following the 2007 and 2011 general elections;

2003 (19th April): Creation of the EU Harmonization Committee[1125]

This committee aimed to examine conformity of draft bills submitted to the Parliament with the "Acquis Communautaire";

2003 (17th June): FDI Law

New FDI Law, in line with the "Acquis Communautaire" went into effect;

2003: Establishment of the Governmental Mass Housing Administration (TOKI)

The government established the TOKI as a new public entity affiliated with the Prime Ministry and introduced a comprehensive approach addressing both social and economic dimensions of housing problems of society, allowing thus adequate housing units for the urban poor;

2004: Modernizing Industrial and Intellectual Property Rights (IIPRs)

Improvements in legal framework, together with twinning projects launched in collaboration with EU countries from 2004 onwards, aimed to address the gap in respect of IIPRs;

2004 (April): Referenda in Cyprus for reunification of the Island, failure of "Annan Plan"

The United Nations Secretary General Kofi Annan compiled in 2002 the most comprehensive proposal since 1974 for a solution in Cyprus[1126]. The so-called

[1125] Grand National Assembly of Turkey, website

[1126] Arslan, K. and Guven, H. (2007), p. 5

"Annan Plan" launched a new series of negotiations between the two parties under the UN auspices, proposing a unified Cyprus before 1st May 2004, the deadline for the Greek part's adhesion to the EU. The UN, the EU and the US strongly supported the "Annan Plan". The referenda were laid down to both sides simultaneously in April 2004. While Turkish Cypriots accepted with 69.4 percent, the Greek part rejected with 75.8 percent;

2004-2005: Turkey matched the Maastricht parameters while privatization receipts reached record levels

Turkey matched the Maastricht thresholds (i.e., public debt to GDP ratio 60 percent and budget deficits to GDP ratio 3 percent) and these indicators performed better than the EU-27 average in the second half of the 2000s, during which privatization receipts also reached record levels;

2005 (February): The Turkish Derivatives Exchange (TURKDEX)

The derivatives market created in 2002 became operational by this date. It allowed economic agents to share risks on currencies, commodities and interest rates;

2005 (3rd June): Ali Babacan, Chief negotiator of Turkey[1127]

The government appointed Ali Babacan, state minister, as the Chief negotiator of Turkey in the EU accession negotiations;

2005 (September): Additional Protocol extending the Customs Union to the Republic of Cyprus

The failure of "Annan Plan" also implied that Turkey has a legal obligation to extend the 1996 Customs Union with the EU to the new member states, i.e., the Republic of Cyprus. Turkey signed the "Additional Protocol" calling for the reopening of Turkish ports to the Greek Cypriots-led Republic of Cyprus. Nevertheless, Turkey argued that it will not apply the protocol as long as the Greek Cypriots veto the approval of direct trade between Turkish part of the island and the EU member states[1128];

[1127] General Secretariat for EU Affairs, website

[1128] Kyris, G. (2010), p. 104

2005: New Turkish lira

Six zeros were deleted from Turkish lira which was renamed the "New Turkish Lira". This monetary reform not only aimed to have a psychological impact but it signaled, in particular, the initial phase of a new era, where markets could have confidence in the overall economic management;

2005 (3rd October): Initiation of negotiations with the EU for a full membership[1129]

The EU Council of Ministers decided to open accession negotiations with Turkey. During the same month the "screening process", the first stage of accession negotiations, began. The main purpose of this was to examine the ability of Turkey in adopting the "Acquis Communautaire" categorized into 35 chapters. The screening process terminated in October 2006;

2006 (January): Full-fledged inflation targeting policy

The aim of the CBRT in introducing a transition period to inflation targeting policy from 2002 to 2005 was to observe the impact of structural reforms on macro indicators. Relatively stable parameters allowed credibility of monetary policy. It was time to introduce a full-fledged inflation targeting policy;

2006 (20th January): Turkey's proposal for a solution to Cyprus problem

If both parties accepted the "Annan Plan", the Turkish Cypriots would also have become EU citizens by 1st May 2004, the first Muslim community in the EU. This, in turn, would have a positive impact on the EU-Turkey relations. The failure of the Plan became a major problem, as Turkey had not recognized the Greek part of Cyprus. In early 2006, Turkey proposed an agreement based on Turkish Cypriots' integration within the Customs Union in return for Turkey fulfilling its own obligations to the Greek part of the island. Nevertheless, the latter required additional measures including demilitarization and territorial adjustments, further increasing the degree of complexity of Cyprus issue[1130];

[1129] General Secretariat for EU Affairs, website

[1130] Kaymak, E. (2006), p. 13

2006 (11th December): The pending Cyprus question and its impact on EU-Turkey relations

The EU General Affairs Council stated that eight chapters shall not be opened until confirming the commitments relating to Additional Protocol of Turkey. This meant that the chronic problem between Turkey and Greece dating from the 1960s had been transformed into a problem between Turkey and the EU, though the true place to settle international disagreements had been the United Nations auspices;

2007: Negotiations reopened on several chapters but not on Cyprus issue[1131]

Negotiations were opened on the chapter of Policies of Enterprises and Industry on 29th March 2007, on Financial Control and Statistics on 26th June and on Health and Consumer Protection and on Trans-European Transport on 19th December. The government declared the Harmonization Package of Turkey to *EU Acquis* on 27th April;

2007 (March): New Law on Mortgages

Decreasing level of interest rates allowed the government to introduce a new law on mortgages aiming to enable large masses in Turkey to purchase housing units. Though in the early 2010s, low-income segments of the society are still unable to benefit from mortgages, it is expected that a lower level of interest rates will have a significant impact on this market;

2007 (27th April): Political crisis before the elections for the post of President

At the end of President Ahmet Necdet Sezer's mandate, the pro-Islamist Abdullah Gul's candidacy became subject to severe reactions both from secularists and the military. This led to a political shock more severe than the one occurred on 19th February 2001. Nevertheless, its impact on the economy was insignificant, as market confidence was not lost thanks to structural reforms achieved between 2000 and 2005;

[1131] General Secretariat for EU Affairs, website

2008: Further chapters were opened while the one on Cyprus was still pending

Chapters on Company Law and Intellectual Property Law were opened on 12th June 2008, and those on Free Movement of Capital and Information Society and Media were opened on 18th December;

2009 (10th January): Egemen Bagis, Chief negotiator of Turkey

The government appointed Egemen Bagis, Minister of EU Affairs as the Chief Negotiator of Turkey in full membership negotiations;

2009 (30th July): Chapter on Taxation opened

2010: State-Aid Agency established

The Turkish government established a state-aid agency affiliated with the Ministry. Thus, it was failed to meet EU requirements, which requested an independent body.

Annex 2

Hedge Funds

Definition

Although there is no an official or universally accepted definition of hedge funds, the U.S. President's Working Group on Financial Markets[1132] defined in the aftermath of the Long Term Capital Management (LTCM) event as "a pooled investment vehicle that is privately organized, administered by professional investment managers and not widely available to the public"[1133]. This definition distinguishes this category of funds from public investment companies but not from venture capital companies, private equity funds, and real estate funds. Moreover, it does not specify many of the special features of hedge funds, which intensively use financial derivatives, leverage, and short selling. Although it is true that other financial institutions like banks or investment companies can also make use of these instruments, the key distinguishing feature then lies in the fact that, while they can bear highly risky positions, they are not subject to any restriction on the type of instruments or strategies they can use. In other words, hedge funds are not constrained by regulation as other funds are[1134]. Alternatively, a European Central Bank research paper describes as follows[1135]: "A hedge fund is an unregulated or loosely regulated fund which can freely use various active investment strategies to achieve positive absolute returns. Typically, the fees of fund managers are related to the performance of the fund in question and managers often commit their own money."

Hedge fund managers have monetary incentives to beat the benchmark[1136]. Thus, they may be involved in investment strategies where priority is given to short-term expectations of an investment process, rather than its long-term

---

[1132] US President's Working Group on Financial Markets is composed of representatives of the U.S. Department of Treasury, Board of Governments of Federal Reserve System, Securities and Exchange Commission and Commodity Futures Trading Commission.

[1133] US President's Working Group on Financial Markets (1999), p. 1

[1134] Garbaravicius, T. and Dierick, F. (2005), p. 7

[1135] Ibid., p. 5

[1136] Basak, S. and Makarov, D. (2009), pp. 1, 30

economic fundamentals. On the other hand, investors may have very low level of information regarding the investment process, the risks associated with the fund and the skills or ability of the fund manager. Thus, hedge funds can bear higher risk when compared with other funds and, at the same time, involve investors in a high degree of asymmetric information. However, the lack of transparency and a large number of possible market and trading strategy combinations make it difficult to discover the correct set of pricing factors[1137]inducing to model uncertainty. Nevertheless, I will focus here on a major aspect differentiating hedge funds from another type of funds. While, for instance, mutual funds develop strategies to eliminate "alpha" through diversification within the CAPM framework, hedge funds' aim is to create a positive "alpha".

Hedge Fund pricing

Let us have a look at the risk-return relationship of hedge funds, which will give an idea about their risk exposure. The most basic performance measurement model is the Jensen's Alpha[1138], which is based on classical Capital Asset Pricing Method (CAPM). The skill of a fund manager is generally associated with an estimate of its "alpha"[1139]:

$$R_{it} - R_{ft} = \alpha_i + \beta_i (R_{mt} - R_{ft}) + \varepsilon_{it}$$

where R_{it}= the return on fund i in month t (with t=-1, -2, ..., -T);

R_{ft} = the risk-free return;

α_i= Jensen's alpha, used as a performance measure relative to the market portfolio (intercept of the regression);

β_i= an efficient estimate of *systematic* risk (slope of the regression), which measures sensitivity of individual asset to market movements;

R_{mt} = the return on the market portfolio;

1137 Vrontos et al. (2008), p. 741

1138 Jensen, M. C. (1967), p. 8

1139 Ibid.

ε_{it} = an error term.

In simple terms, "alpha" is equal to the differential between the actual return and expected return[1140]. It represents the average incremental rate of return on a portfolio per unit of time due to the manager's ability to forecast. If the fund manager has the ability to forecast security prices, "alpha" will be positive. To note that "random selection", say buy and hold policy, can be expected to yield a zero "alpha"[1141]. Sharpe W. F. (1991) demonstrated that an average investor cannot outperform the market average, and will actually underperform the average when transaction costs are taken into account. He argued this aspect as follows[1142]:

> "To repeat: properly measured, the average actively managed dollar must underperform the average passively managed dollar, net of costs. Empirical analyses that appear to refute this principal are guilty of improper measurement."

However, several researchers, i.e., Harri, A. and Brorsen B. W. (2004), demonstrated that some hedge funds showed persistently higher returns than others. The existence of performance persistence, thus of a "positive alpha" over time, is also consistent with the hypothesis that hedge fund managers can exploit market inefficiencies[1143].

CAPM is a single factor model and it is extended in literature to a multifactor framework, i.e., Fama and French (1993), to enable the model to capture other factors. However, classical, linear performance measurement models cannot sufficiently capture the dynamic trading strategies in the different asset classes and markets, for which the Asset Class Factor Model (ACFM) seems more suitable[1144]. The basic equation of the ACFM takes the following form[1145]:

[1140] Jensen, M. C. (1967), p. 9

[1141] Ibid., p. 8

[1142] Sharpe, W. F. (1991), p. 9

[1143] Harri, A. and Brorsen B. W. (2004), pp. 1, 19

[1144] Eling, M. and Faust, R. (2010), p. 3

[1145] Sharpe, W. F. (1992), p. 7

$$R_{it} = \alpha_i + \sum_{i=1}^{N} b_i F_{i,t} + \varepsilon_{it}$$

where $F_{i,t}$ is the value of factor i at time t;

b_i is the sensitivity of R_i to factors F_i;

ε_{it} is the non-factor component of return R_i, uncorrelated with N factors (or idiosyncratic noise) .

An asset class factor model will then be able to expose, not only the skill of the manager measured by "alpha", but also his "style", measured by $\sum_{i=1}^{N} b_i F_{i,t}$.

To summarize, investing in hedge funds is mainly an attempt to purchase "alpha" which is a manager's skill in identifying market inefficiency and exploiting it[1146], exposing investment to risks of a different nature.

Eling and Faust (2010)[1147] analyzed returns of 566 hedge funds and 1'542 mutual funds, all active in emerging markets, for the period from 1995 to 2008. Their results show that hedge fund returns and "alphas" are much higher than those of mutual funds. While some hedge funds outperform traditional benchmarks, most of the mutual funds tend to underperform. Moreover, they note that in bad or neutral market environments, hedge funds outperform mutual funds while generating the same returns in good environments. Overall, their analysis indicates that emerging market hedge funds perform better than their traditional competitors, i.e., mutual funds.

The size and impact of hedge funds

It is difficult to obtain an accurate estimation of the size of hedge funds industry due to the fact that they are not obliged to disclose all information about their activities[1148]. During the 1990s, the number of hedge fund firms seems to have

---

[1146] Lhabitant, F. S. (2007), p. 509

[1147] Eling, M. and Faust, R. (2010), p. 2

[1148] Estimates on the number and total capital managed are based on information voluntarily provided by them and varies from one source to the other. In 1968, a U.S. Securities and Exchange Commission survey identified 140 funds operating by that time. It is estimated that, as of mid-1998, there were between 2'500 and 3'500 hedge funds with managed capital approximately from USD 200 billion to USD 300 billion (US President's Working Group on Financial Markets (1999), p. 1).

shifted from around 2'000 in 1996 to 10'000 in 2007. To note that the size of capital managed by hedge funds was much lower than pension funds and mutual funds. However, to consider that through the use of leverage, hedge funds can potentially increase their impact on markets by a factor of several times their managed capital size.

Annex 3

Governments formed in Turkey from 1961 to 2011

The Turkish Republic was founded on 29th October 1923. CHP (Republican People's Party), the unique political formation in the Parliament governed for more than two decades. The transition to the multi-party period in the late 1940s allowed the newly founded DP (Democratic Party) to come to power on 22nd May 1950. The latter succeeded to form single-party governments until the first military intervention occurred on 27th May 1960. Table A-3.1 provides a chronological account of governments from 1960 to 1980.

Table A-3.1: Governments formed between two military interventions (1960 and 1980)

Nb.	Prime Minister	Wing	Government	Parties in coalition	Date
24	*Gursel*	-	*miltary*	-	*30.05.1960*
25	*Gursel*	-	*military*	-	*05.01.1961*
26	**Inonu (CHP)**	**center-left**	**coalition**	**AP**	**20.11.1961**
27	Inonu (CHP)	center-left	coalition	CGP,YTP, independents	25.06.1962
28	Inonu (CHP)[1149]	center-left	coalition	independents	25.12.1963
29	Urguplu (indep.)		coalition	AP, YTP, CGP	20.02.1965
30	**Demirel (AP)**	**center-right**	**single-party**	-	**27.10.1965**
31	**Demirel (AP)[1150]**	**center-right**	**single-party**	-	**03.11.1969**
32	Demirel (AP)[1151]	center-right	single-party	-	06.03.1970

1149 Prime Minister Ismet Inonu resigned because the Parliament refused the budget.

1150 Prime Minister Suleyman Demirel resigned because his 41 ministers voted against the budget, hence it was rejected.

1151 Prime Minister Suleyman Demirel resigned following the military intervention (memorandum), on 12.03.1971.

33	*Erim (indep.)*[1152]	-	*military*	-	*26.03.1971*
34	*Erim (indep.)*[1153]	-	*military*	-	*11.12.1971*
35	Melen	-	coalition	AP, CHP, CGP	22.05.1972
36	Talu[1154]	-	coalition	AP, CGP, independents	15.04.1973
37	**Ecevit (CHP)**[1155]	**center-left**	**coalition**	**MSP**	**26.01.1974**
38	Irmak[1156]		coalition	CGP	17.11.1974
39	Demirel (AP)	center-right	coalition	MSP, MHP, CGP	31.03.1975
40	**Ecevit (CHP)**[1157]	**center-left**	**minority gvt**		**21.06.1977**
41	Demirel (AP)	center-right	coalition	MSP, MHP	21.07.1977
42	Ecevit (CHP)	center-left	coalition	CGP	05.01.1978
43	Demirel (AP)[1158]	center-right	minority gvt	-	12.11.1979
44	*Ulusu*[1159]	-	*military*	-	*20.09.1980*

Source: Grand National Assembly of Turkey (GNAT)[1160]

Notes to Table A-3.1: "Nb." in the first column corresponds to the number of government since the foundation of the Republic on 23rd October 1923;

1152 This was an over-party (neutral) government after the 1971 military intervention. Prime Minister Nihat Erim resigned following the resignation of his 11 ministers.

1153 Prime Minister Nihat Erim resigned because of health problems.

1154 General elections were held in October 1973. The President of Republic appointed Bulent Ecevit (the first party) to form a government. He did not succeed. Hence, Suleyman Demirel and later Naim Talu were appointed. They did not achieve an agreement either.

1155 Finally, Bulent Ecevit led a coalition government, but it lasted less than 10 months.

1156 Sadi Irmak formed a minority government consisting of four deputies from the CHP. All other members of the Cabinet were appointed from outside the Parliament. Prime Minister resigned since the Government could not obtain a vote of confidence.

1157 The minority Government could not obtain a vote of confidence.

1158 Prime Minister Suleyman Demirel governed until the military coup of 12.09.1980.

1159 Bulent Ulusu was a member of the armed forces and was appointed by General Kenan Evren, the head of the National Security Council, which approved the Government.

1160 GNAT and Inter-Parliamentary Union (IPU) websites

Regarding the acronyms major political parties during these two decades were:

AP=Justice Party (center-right), the continuation of the ex-Democratic Party; CHP=Republican People's Party (center-left); MSP=National Salvation Party (pro-Islamist); MHP= Nationalist Action Party (far-right)[1161].

The rest of the political parties having minor weight in Parliament were:

CKMP=Republican Peasant Nation Party; YTP=New Turkey Party and CGP= Republican Reliance Party.

The governments **in bold** were formed following the general elections, whereas those *in italics* were appointed by the military, both in Table A-3.1 and Table A-3.2.

To note that the "Washington Consensus" principles started to be adopted during the Suleyman Demirel-led 43rd government on 24th January 1980 and these were backed by the Bulent Ulusu-led 44th (military) government. Generals withdrew in late 1983 allowing thus the general elections held on 6th November 1983. Table A-3.2 shows civilian governments formed from 1983 to 2011.

[1161] MHP was founded by Alpaslan Turkes, military officer leader during the 1960 military takeover.

Table A-3.2: Governments formed from 1983 to 2011

Nb.	Prime Minister	Wing	Government	Parties in coalition	Date
45	**Ozal (ANAP)**	**center-right**	**single-party**	-	**13.12.1983**
46	**Ozal (ANAP)**	**center-right**	**single-party**	-	**21.12.1987**
47	Akbulut (ANAP)	center-right	single-party	-	09.11.1989
48	Yilmaz (ANAP)	center-right	single party	-	23.06.1991
49	**Demirel (DYP)**	**center-right**	**coalition**	**SODEP**	**21.11.1991**
50	Ciller (DYP)	center-right	coalition	SODEP	25.06.1993
51	Ciller[1162] (DYP)	center-right	minority	-	05.10.1995
52	Ciller (DYP)	center-right	coalition	CHP	30.10.1995
53	**Yilmaz (ANAP)[1163]**	**center-right**	**coalition**	**DYP**	**06.03.1996**
54	Erbakan (RP)	pro-Islamist	coalition	DYP	28.06.1996
55	Yilmaz (ANAP)	center-right	coalition	DSP, DTP[1164], independents	30.06.1997
56	Ecevit (DSP)	center-left	minority	-	11.01.1999
57	**Ecevit (DSP)**	**center-left**	**coalition**	**MHP, ANAP**	**28.05.1999**
58	**Gul (AKP)**	**pro-Islamist**	**single-party**	-	**18.11.2002**
59	Erdogan (AKP)	pro-Islamist	single-party	-	14.03.2003
60	**Erdogan (AKP)**	**pro-Islamist**	**single-party**	-	**29.08.2007**
61	**Erdogan (AKP)**	**pro-Islamist**	**single-party**	-	**06.07.2011**

Source: Grand National Assembly of Turkey (GNAT)[1165]

[1162] Tansu Ciller composed a minority government, which failed to obtain a vote of confidence in the Parliament.

[1163] Mesut Yilmaz succeeded to compose a coalition government following the general elections held on 24th December 1995, which lasted less than four months.

[1164] DTP was founded by some members of DYP (led by Husamettin Cindoruk) who reacted to the coalition of the party with pro-Islamist RP.

Notes to Table A-3.2: Acronyms of major political parties during these two decades: ANAP=Motherland Party (center-right); DYP=True Path Party (center-right, the continuation of the ex-AP); RP=Welfare Party (pro-Islamist, the continuation of the ex-MSP); AKP=Justice and Development Party (pro-Islamist, the continuation of the ex-RP); SODEP=Social Democratic Party (center-left); DSP=Democratic Left Party (center-left) and DTP=Democratic Turkey Party (center-right).

1165 GNAT and Inter Parliamentary Union (IPU) websites

Annex 4

Supervising Privatized Natural Monopolies

The pricing methodologies discussed in this section consider circumstances once privatization is implemented. Since each method presents different advantages and disadvantages, the regulator should attempt to choose the best method for specific country conditions. While in Turkey, inefficiencies in state monopolies were due to arbitrary pricing schemes under political considerations, lacking a rational pricing model and subsidizing losses, which fostered budget deficits, the regulatory reforms introduced the "Price Caps" method, an EU-inspired incentive mechanism[1166].

The way natural monopolies are regulated involves a "principal-agent" problem[1167]. The principal (regulator) strives to establish a mechanism such that the goals of the agent (firm) become consistent with his own, hence "incentive compatible". This aspect also implies that the agent, who has more information than the principal on the cost function, would report correct information about its cost structure. In such an ideal case, the regulator might be able to determine optimal prices. In other words, the invisible hand in competitive markets will be replaced by the regulators' "incentive compatible" mechanism. On the other hand, if the regulators' pricing method does not provide incentives to correctly report the cost structure, the regulator will not be able to achieve optimal prices.

Let us overview the logic behind price regulation and incentive mechanisms:

1166 Price Caps are used in the United Kingdom, Malaysia, Mexico, Peru and Argentina and Turkey, whereas, the Rate of Return (ROR) method is mainly used in the United States (Ian, A. and Timothy, I. (1996), p. 1).

1167 Linhart, P. B., Radner, R. and Sinden, F. W. (1983), pp. 6-8

Marginal Cost (MC) Pricing

Regulators cannot set prices with MC because monopolist firms incur fixed costs up-front[1168]. Hence, fixing prices with MC will result in a loss for the firm and staying in business will require public subsidies. In other words, MC pricing is politically undesirable because of its association with subsidization. Moreover, the regulator may not be able to ascertain the cost and demand curves of the firm[1169]. To note that informational asymmetry between the principal (regulator) and the agent (firm) impedes the optimal outcome: The firm has an incentive to report a higher marginal cost and has no incentive to produce efficiently because in any case, it receives a subsidy from the regulator.

Average Cost Pricing

Here the price is raised above the marginal cost until the profit is zero, corresponding to the average cost. However, economies of scale and scope will lead the monopoly to create a multi-output situation, where many different price combinations will result in a zero profit. For example, for a utility selling electricity and gas, the price of either the latter or the former can be raised sufficiently to break-even, while keeping the other at marginal cost. Or the prices of both can be raised above their marginal costs. The pertinent question is: Which combination, among the infinite number of pricing possibilities, maximizes social welfare? Ramsey (1927) developed a method to address this question in the context of optimal taxation[1170]. "Ramsey Pricing" (or "Inverse Elasticity Rule") maximizes total surplus while allowing the firm to break-even. However, it charges higher prices where demand is less elastic, introducing fairness issues. Customers with relatively inelastic demand could be viewed as those for whom the service is more necessary (i.e., demand for medical care for low-income households). Hence, optimal pricing under the Ramsey method could come into conflict with socially equitable policies.

Rate of Return (ROR) Regulation[1171]

This method allows the regulated firm a "fair" return on its investment in capital, determining a maximum threshold for acquired profits. The ROR

[1168] Deporter B. (1999), p. 506

[1169] Currier, K. M. (2004), pp. 49, 50

[1170] Ramsey, F. P. (1927), pp. 47, 48

[1171] Train, K. (1991), pp. 20-22

method is defined as revenues minus costs for non-capital inputs, divided by the level of capital investment. This rate must be no greater than the "fair" rate of return announced *ex-ante* by the regulator. Consequently, the excess profits are the difference between the firm's revenues and its cost for all inputs, including capital. The following example will make this concept clear:

If the firm borrowed its capital, excess profits are those it earns after making the interest payments on the borrowed capital. If the fair return is announced as 5 percent and the price of capital is 3 percent, then the firm is allowed to earn no more than 2 percent of invested capital. If it uses its own capital, it should consider the opportunity cost of capital, which is the return that it could obtain by lending. In such a case, the excess profits are those earned minus the interest it would have obtained by lending capital[1172].

Averch, H. and Johnson, L. L. (1962) investigated the effects of ROR regulation on the behavior of the firm, arguing that it leads firms to inefficiencies[1173]. In fact, the firm can increase its profits by expanding its capital base, incentivising the overuse of capital[1174]. To note then that the ROR regulatory procedure does not encourage the firm to choose socially optimal outcomes. Train, K. E. (1991) discusses other methods similar to the ROR regulation, where profits are allowed to rise with output, sales and costs.[1175]

Price Caps

The main idea behind the price cap restriction is to stimulate competitive behavior. This approach, first developed in the United Kingdom in the 1980s as the regulatory framework for the country's newly privatized enterprises[1176], was designed to provide firms with stronger incentives to improve their productive efficiency. It was introduced as an alternative to the ROR regulatory rule[1177] to overcome inefficiencies due to lack of incentives. Firms adopting price cap

---

[1172] Train, K. (1991), p. 34

[1173] Averch, H. and Johnson, L. L. (1962), p. 1068

[1174] Train, K. E. (1991), p. 40

[1175] For a detailed description see Train, K. E. (1991), pp. 69-76

[1176] Jamison, M. A. (2005), p. 3

[1177] King, S. P. (1997), p. 46

regulations were motivated to lower their costs, which were then transformed into profits for a certain period of time[1178].

For example[1179], let me assume that the regulator sets an expected reduction in costs X = 2 percent, and I=PPI at 8 percent to reflect the input price increases. This means that the price change will be capped at 6 percent per year, throughout the review period. If the firm can achieve higher cost reduction, say 5 percent instead of 2 percent, such a differential in the reduction of the cost will be transformed into profit until the next review period[1180]. Hence, firms have the incentive to operate efficiently by adopting cost minimizing production techniques. In the opposite case, where unexpected increased costs are experienced, the firm will be involved in a loss. Periodic reviews of the caps will ensure that firms will neither keep making large profits nor lose money[1181]. Normally, at the end of each review period, the regulator adjusts prices. Hence, in case of higher reduction of costs achieved by the firm, the consumer will obtain lower prices starting at the end of the review period. As consequence, the firm's motivation to reduce costs also depends on the frequency of the review period: Price caps that are too frequently reviewed will tend to promote wasteful behavior similar to that of ROR regulation[1182]. Less frequent reviews give potential to the creation of surplus through increased efficiency, which it then passes to the consumer at the end of the review period.

1178 King, S. P. (1997), p. 48

1179 Aybar, C. B., Guney, E. S. and Suel, H. (1998), p. 36

1180 In the United Kingdom, price caps were typically reviewed every five years (Ian, A. and Timothy, I. (1996), p. 1).

1181 Aybar, C. B., Guney, E. S. and Suel, H. (1998), p. 36

1182 King, S. P. (1997), p. 49

Annex 5

Methodology of Rating Agencies

Fitch Ratings long-term rating scales[1183]

Ratings assignments from AAA to BBB correspond to "investment grade" and from BB to D to "speculative grade". More precisely, they are identified with the following features:

AAA: Highest credit quality; AA: Very high credit quality; A: High credit quality; BBB: Good credit quality; BB: Speculative; B: Highly speculative; CCC: Substantial credit risk; CC: Very high levels of credit risk; C: Exceptionally high levels of credit risk; D: Default

Fitch Ratings short-term rating scales (corresponding to a maximum 13 months)[1184]

F1: Highest short-term credit quality; F2: Good short-term credit quality; F3: Fair short-term credit quality: B: Speculative short-term credit quality; C: High short-term default risk; RD: Restricted default; D: Default

---

[1183] Fitch Ratings (2010a), pp. 9, 10

[1184] Ibid., p. 18

Table A-5.1: Rating Correspondence Table

Long-term rating	Short-term rating
AAA	F1+
AA+	F1+
AA	F1+
AA-	F1+
A+	F1 or F1+
A	F2 or F1
A-	F2 or F1+
BBB+	F2
BBB	F3 or F2
BBB-	F3 or F2
BB+	B
BB	B
BB-	B
B+	B
B	B
B-	B
CCC	C
CC	C
C	C
RD/D	RD/D

Source: Fitch Ratings (2010a), p. 20

Rating Watch[1185]

"Rating Watches" indicate that there is a heightened probability of a rating change and indicate the likely direction of such a change. A "positive" watch indicates a potential upgrade, a "negative" watch indicates a potential

---

1185 Fitch Ratings (2010a), p. 48

downgrade, and an "evolving" indicates that ratings may be raised, lowered or affirmed. Nevertheless, ratings that are not in the *Rating Watch* can be raised or lowered without being placed on the *Rating Watch*, if circumstances require such an action. A *Rating Watch* is typically event-driven.

Rating Outlook

"Rating Outlooks" indicate the direction a rating is likely to move over a one to two-year period. They reflect financial trends that have not yet reached the level that would trigger a rating action. "Positive" or "Negative" rating outlooks do not imply that a rating change is inevitable. Similarly, ratings with "Stable" outlooks can be raised or lowered without a prior revision of the outlook, if circumstances warrant such an action. When the fundamental trend has strong, conflicting elements of both positive and negative, the *Rating Outlook* may be described as "Evolving".

Annex 6

Calculating the probability of default from CDS Spreads

The relationship between the CDS spreads and the probability of default – the real world case[1186]:

A CDS contract involves two cash-flow streams: A fixed leg and a contingent leg. The CDS spread, which is the premium paid by protection buyer to protection seller, maintains the value of swap transaction zero. That is to say:

$$\text{PV fixed leg} = \text{PV contingent leg} \tag{1}$$

Let me start with the "fixed leg". The periodic premium payment is calculated as follows: On each payment date, the annual CDS premium *S* is multiplied by *d*, the accrual days[1187] between payment days. For example, let us consider the CDS premium quoted at 600 basis points on 25th May 2004[1188] and assume that payments are made quarterly, the periodic payment is:

$$d_i S = 0.25 * (600) = 150\, bps \tag{2}$$

To note that this payment is to be made when the reference credit has not defaulted by the payment date. Thus, I have to take into account the "survival probability" or the probability that the reference credit has not defaulted by the payment date. For example, if the "survival probability" of the reference credit in the first quarter is 80 percent, the expected payment three months later is:

$$q(t_i) d_i S = 0.80 * 0.25 * (600) = 120\, bps \tag{3}$$

where $q(t)$ is the "survival probability" three months later (at time t). Then, introducing the discount factor $D(t)$, I obtain the present value for this payment. Their sum gives the following:

1186 Whetten, M., Adelson, M., and Van Bemmeler, M., (2004), pp. 7, 8

1187 expressed in a fraction of one year

1188 See section 5.1.3, figures 5.4 and 5.5

$$\sum_{i=1}^{N} D(t_i)q(t_i)Sd_i \tag{4}$$

There is, nevertheless, another component of the "fixed leg". Let us consider, the accrued premium paid until the time of default. Let us assume that default occurs at the middle of the interval between consecutive payment days. Thus, when the reference entity defaults between two payment days t_{i-1} and t_i, the accrued payment amounts to:

$$Sd_i/2$$

(5)

Here it is important to note that the reference credit survived through payment date t_{i-1}, but NOT to the next payment date t_i. This probability is given by:

$$q(t_{i-1}) - q(t_i) \tag{6}$$

Consequently, for this particular interval, the expected accrued premium payment is:

$$[q(t_{i-1}) - q(t_i)]S\frac{d_i}{2} \tag{7}$$

Thus, the present value of all expected accrued payments is given by:

$$\sum_{i=1}^{N} D(t_i)[q(t_{i-1}) - q(t_i)]S\frac{d_i}{2} \tag{8}$$

Adding the two components of the fixed leg, the (4) and the (7), we obtain the "present value of the fixed leg":

$$\sum_{i=1}^{N} D(t_i)q(t_i)Sd_i + \sum_{i=1}^{N} D(t_i)[q(t_{i-1}) - q(t_i)]S\frac{d_i}{2} \tag{9}$$

Now, let us compute the "contingent leg". Let us assume again that the reference entity defaults between the two payment dates t_{i-1} and t_i.

The protection buyer will receive the contingent payment of *(1-R)*, which is made only if the reference credit defaults with probability $(q(t_{i-1}) - q(t_i))$. This means that credit survived through payment date t_{i-1} but NOT to next payment date t_i.

Discounting each expected payment and summing over the term of a contract, I obtain the present value of the contingent leg:

$$(1-R)\sum_{i=1}^{N} D(t_i)[q(t_{i-1}) - q(t_i)] \tag{10}$$

Equalizing the PV of "fixed leg" with that of the "contingent leg" I obtain the following equation:

$$\sum_{i=1}^{N} D(t_i)q(t_i)Sd_i + \sum_{i=1}^{N} D(t_i)[q(t_{i-1}) - q(t_i)]S\frac{d_i}{2} = \\ = (1-R)\sum_{i=1}^{N} D(t_i)[q(t_{i-1}) - q(t_i)] \tag{11}$$

From this equation, I obtain the values of the "credit default swap spread" (*S*) as follows:

$$S = \frac{(1-R)\sum_{i=1}^{N} D(t_i)[q(t_{i-1}) - q(t_i)]}{\sum_{i=1}^{N} D(t_i)q(t_i)d_i + \sum_{i=1}^{N} D(t_i)[q(t_{i-1}) - q(t_i)]\frac{d_i}{2}} \tag{12}$$

To note that there is a direct relationship between the CDS spreads quoted in markets and the implied survival probabilities[1189]. However, this stage does still not allow me to extract the "survival probabilities" and the related probabilities of default. Let us consider the example of 5-year CDS spread *S*, quoted at 600 basis points on 25th May 2004.

1189 O'Kane, D. and Turnbull, S. (2004), p. 11

$$0.06 = \frac{(1-R)\sum_{i=1}^{N} D(t_i)(q_{i-1} - q_i)}{\sum_{i=1}^{N} D(t_i)q(t_i)d_i + \sum_{i=1}^{N} D(t_i)(q_{i-1} - q_i)\frac{d_i}{2}} \quad (13)$$

In this equation, I know or assume:

- *R*: recovery rate, i.e., 20 percent (a widely used percentage in financial markets);
- D: I can calculate all the Libor discount factors from the Libor discount curve;
- d: I define accrual days as quarterly payments.

The only unknowns are survival probabilities (*q*), to estimate which I need to make simplifying assumptions. Thus, I assume that the term structure of survival probabilities is a piecewise flat function of maturity time because given only one data point, it is not possible to extract more than one piece of information about the term structure[1190]. To construct the latter, I need to use the "bootstrapping methodology", which starts with taking the shortest maturity contract to calculate the first survival probability[1191]. While the survival probability *q* of the reference credit with a time profile is:

$$(q)t_i \quad (14)$$

where, i=1,..,N,

the relationship between survival probability and the probability of default (*PD*) is broad[1192]:

q=1-PD (15)

Thus, this framework allows me to estimate probabilities of default from the CDS spreads quoted in markets[1193].

1190 O'Kane, D. and Turnbull, S. (2004), p. 12

1191 Ibid., p. 13

1192 Korner, K. (2011), p. 5

1193 Chan-Lau, J.A. (2003), p. 11

Bibliography

Papers

ACEMOGLU, D., JOHNSON, S. and ROBINSON, J. A. (2001), "The Colonial Origins of Comparative Development: An Empirical Investigation", *American Economic Review,* Vol. 91(5), pp. 1369-1401

ADES, A. and DI TELLA, R. (1999), "Rents, Competition and Corruption", *American Economic Review,* Vol. 89(4), pp. 982-993

AERNI, P. (2007), "Agriculture in Turkey – Structural Change, Sustainability and EU-Compatibility", *International Journal of Agricultural Resources, Governance and Ecology,* Vol. 6 (4, 5), pp. 429-439

AGARWAL, V. and NAIK, N. Y. (2000), "Performance Evaluation of Hedge Funds with Option-based and Buy-and-Hold Strategies", *unpublished paper,* pp. 1-50

AKSOY, A. S. (1994), "State-Owned Enterprises in Turkey: A General Overview", *Public Management Journal,* Vol. 27 (2), pp. 1-21

ALAWODE, A., and AL SADEK, M. (2008), "What is Financial Stability", *Central Bank of Bahrain Financial Stability Paper Series,* No.1, pp. 1-22

ALESINA, A. (1988), "Macroeconomics and Politics", *NBER Macroeconomics Annual,* No. 3, pp. 13-52

ALESINA, A., COHEN. G. and ROUBINI, N. (1991), "Macroeconomics Policies and Elections in OECD Democracies", *Economics and Politics,* Vol. 4, pp. 1-30

ALESINA, A. and ROUBINI, N. (1992), "Political Cycles: Evidence from OECD Economies", *Review of Economic Studies,* Vol. 59, pp. 663-668

ALTINKEMER, M. (1992), "A Note on the Turkish Convertibility of the Turkish Lira", *Central Bank of the Republic of Turkey Research Department Discussion Papers,* No. 9211, pp. 1-3

ALTIPARMAK, A. (2002), "Development of Private Sector during the Statist Period in Turkey", *unpublished paper,* pp. 1-25

ALPER, E. (2001), "The Turkish Liquidity Crisis of 2000: What Went Wrong..?", *Russian and East European Finance and Trade,* Vol. 37(6), pp. 51-71

ANWAR, S. and ISLAM, I. (2011), "Should Developing Countries Target Low, Single Digit Inflation to Promote Growth and Employment?", *ILO Employment Working Paper No. 87,* pp. 1-25

ARAT, K. (2003), "Optimum Exchange Rate Regime Choice in Turkey and Examination of Exchange Rate Impact on Prices" (in Turkish), *unpublished paper,* pp. 1- 118

ARIAS, G. (2003), "Currency Crises: What We Know and What We Still Need to Know", *Centre d'Economie et de Finance International (CEFI) Working Paper,* No. 13, pp. 1-73

ARCHICK, K. and KIM, J. (2008), "European Union Enlargement", *Congressional Research Service Report,* No. 21344, pp. 1-6

ARSLAN, K. and GUVEN, H. (2007), "International Law in Cyprus Problem", *Presented at the September, 2007 Ankara 38th International Congress of Asian and North African Studies, ICANAS 38,* pp. 1-10

ATALAY, B. (2002), "Nets of Iron: Foreign Influence on Railway Technology Development in Turkey (1850-1955)", *unpublished paper,* pp. 1-107

ATAOV, A. and OSMAY, S. (2007), "A Methodological Approach to Urban Transformation in Turkey" (in Turkish), *METU JFA,* Vol. 24 (2), pp. 57-82

ATIYAS, I. (2009), "Recent Privatization Experience of Turkey – A Reappraisal", *unpublished paper,* pp. 5-6

ATIYAS, I. and DOGAN, P. (2009), "The Political Economy of Liberalization of Fixed Line Telecommunications in Turkey", *Regulatory Policy Program Paper,* No. 1, pp. 1-23

ATIYAS, I. and EMIL, F. (2005), "Political Economy of Governance Failures, Crises and Opportunities for Reform", *unpublished paper,* pp. 1-39

ATIYAS, I. and ERSEL, H. (1992), "The Impact of Financial Reform: the Turkish Experience", *Industry and Energy Department Working Paper, Industry Series Paper,* No. 65, pp. 1-42

AVERCH, H. and JOHNSON, L. L. (1962), "Behavior of the Firm under Regulatory Constraint", *The American Economic Review,* Vol. 52(2), pp. 1052-1069

AYAZLI, I. E., BATUK, F. and STOTER, J. (2008), "Three Dimensional Property Right Problems and Suggestions for Turkey", *The International Archives of the Photogrammetry, Remote Sensing and Spatial information Sciences,* Vol. 37, pp. 941-944

AYBAR, C. B., GUNEY, E. S. and SUEL, H. (1998), "Privatization and Regulation in Turkish Telecommunications, A Preliminary Assessment", *unpublished paper,* pp. 2-54

AYDIN, C. C. (2008), "Usage of Underground Space for 3D Cadastre Purposes and Related Problems in Turkey", *Journal Sensors,* Vol. 8(11), pp. 6972-6983

AYYILDIZ, E. (2005), "The SOE Transfer's Proportion in Consolidated Budget Transfers, 1994-2005" (in Turkish), *Research Report,* pp. 35, 36

BADE, R. and PARKIN, M. (1980), "Central Bank Laws and Monetary Policy", *Working Paper Department of Economics,* University of Western Ontario, pp. 1-36

BAGNAI, A. (2004), "Structural Breaks and the Twin Deficits Hypothesis", *unpublished paper,* pp. 1-30

BARDADIOGLU, N. and CETINKAYA, M. (2007), "Sequencing in Telecommunications Reform: A Review of EU and Turkish Experience", *unpublished paper,* pp. 1-15

BARNES, P. (2010), “Minsky’s Financial Instability Hypothesis: Information Asymmetry and Accounting Information. An Addendum: The Financial Crisis of 2007-09 in the U.K.”, *unpublished paper,* pp. 1-19

BASAK, S. and MAKAROV, D. (2009), “Strategic Asset Allocation in Money Management”, *Working Paper Series London Business School and Centre for Economic Policy Research,* pp. 1-30

BAYAZITOGLU, Y., ERSEL, H. and OZTURK, E. (1991), “Financial Market Reforms between 1980 and 1990”, *the Central Bank of the Republic of Turkey Research Department Discussion Papers,* No. 9102, pp. 1-18

BAYKAL, A. (2009), “Recep Tayyip Erdogan”, *House of Commons, Library,* pp. 1-12

BAYTAL, Y. (2007), “Economic Policies during the Democrat Party Period” (in Turkish), *Journal of Ataturk Path,* No. 40, pp. 545-567

BECK, R. (2004), “The CDS Market: A Primer”, *Deutsche Bank Research,* pp. 1-14

BENOS, A. and PAPANASTASOPOULOS, G. (2005), “Extending the Merton Model: A Hybrid Approach to Assessing Credit Quality”, *unpublished paper,* pp. 1-34

BERBEN, R. P., BERK, J. M., NITITHANPRAPAS, E., SANGSUPHANS, K., PUAPAN, P. and SODSRIWIBOON, P. (2002), "Requirements for Successful Currency Regimes: the Dutch and Thai Experiences", *De Nederlandsche Bank, Occasional Studies,* Vol. 1(1), pp. 36, 37

BHATTACHARYYA, N. (2012), “Monetary Policy and Employment in Developing Asia”, *ILO Asia- Pacific Working Paper Series,* pp. 1-28

BLANCHARD, O. (2004), “Fiscal Dominance and Inflation Targeting: Lessons from Brazil”, *NBER Working Paper Series,* No. 10389, pp. 1-46

BLANCHARD, O., Dell’Ariccia, G. and Mauro, P. (2010), “Rethinking Macroeconomic Policy”, *IMF Staff Position Note/10/3,* pp. 1-19

BLINDER, A. S. and SOLOW, R. M. (1972), “Does Fiscal Policy Matter?”, *Econometric Research Memorandum,* No. 144, pp. 1-23

BLISS and DI TELLA (1997), “Does Competition Kill Corruption?”, *Journal of Political Economy,* Vol. 105(5), pp. 1001-1018

BOHL, M. T. and REITZ, S. (2000), “The Influence of Positive Feedback Trading on Return Auto-correlation: Evidence for the German Stock Market”, *unpublished paper,* pp.1-18

BORENSZTEIN et al. (1999), "Anticipating Balance of Payment Crises-The Role of Early Warning Systems", *IMF Occasional Paper,* No.186, pp. 1-30

BOULANGER, P., FERRARI, E., MICHAKEL, J. and VINYES, C. (2013), “Analysis of the Impact of Croatia’s Accession to the EU on the Agri-Food Sectors – A Focus on Trade and Agricultural Policies”, European Commission, JRC Scientific and Policy Reports, pp. 1-45

BREDENKAMP, H., JOSEFFSON, M. and LINDGREN, C. J. (2007), “Turkey’s Renaissance: from Banking Crisis to Economic Revival”, *unpublished paper,* pp. 1-12

BREUER, P. (2000), “Measuring Off-Balance Sheet Leverage”, *IMF Working Paper,* No. 202, pp. 1-37

BRUNO, M. and EASTERLY, W. (1998), “Inflation Crisis and Long-run Growth”, *Journal of Monetary Economics, Vol. 41,* pp. 3-26

BUBULA, A. and OTKER-ROBE, I. (2002), “The Evolution of Exchange Rate Regimes since 1990: Evidence from De Facto Policies”, *IMF Working Paper,* No. 155, pp. 1-44

BUBULA, A. and OTKER, I. (2003), “Are Pegged and Intermediate Exchange Rate Regimes more Crisis-Prone?”, *IMF Working Paper,* No. 223, pp. 1-20

BUCHHEIT, L. C. and GULATI, G. M. (2009), “Responsible Sovereign Lending and Borrowing”, *unpublished UNCTAD paper,* pp. 1-35

BURAK, B. (2011), “The Role of the Military in Turkish Politics: to Guard Whom and from What?”, *European Journal of Economic and Political Studies,* Vol. 4(1), pp. 1-27

BURDEKIN, R., DENZAU, A., KEIL, M., SITTHIYOT, T., and WILLETT, T. (2004), “When Does Inflation Hurt Economic Growth? Different Nonlinearities for Different Economies,” *Journal of Macroeconomics, 26*, pp. 519-532

BURNSIDE, C., EICHENBAUM, M. and REBELO, S. (2001), "Prospective Deficits and the Asian Currency Crisis", *Journal of Political Economy*, Vol. 109(6), pp. 1155-1198

BUSSIERE, M. and MULDER, C. (1999), "External Vulnerability in Emerging Market Economies: How High Liquidity Can Offset Weak Fundamentals and the Effects of Contagion", *IMF Working Paper Series*, No. 88, pp. 1-41

CADOT, O. (1987), “Corruption as a Gamble”, *Journal of Public Economics*, Vol. 33, pp. 223-244

CAGLA, H., AKKUS, S., CIVCIK, E. and OZUGUR, I. (2011), “Konya Example of Cadastre Renovation Work in Turkey”, *Paper prepared for the 18-22 May 2011 Marrakech FIG Working Week*, pp. 1-11

CAKIR, E. A. (2002), “Turkey’s Adoption of the Acquis Communautaire: an Undervalued Acquaintance”, *unpublished paper*, pp. 328-345

CALVO, G. (1996), “Varieties of Capital Market Crises”, *unpublished paper*, pp. 1-22

CALVO, G. and VEGH, C. (1999), “Inflation Stabilization and BOP Crises in Developing Countries”, *NBER Working Paper*, No. 6925, pp. 1-91

CANDEMIR, H. B. (1994), “External Debt and Internal Transfer Problem, the Case of Turkey: 1980-1990”, *Central Bank of the Republic of Turkey Discussion Paper*, No. 9404, pp. 99-160

CANUTO, O., FONSECA, P., and DE SA PORTO, C, (2004), “Macroeconomics and Sovereign Risk Ratings”, *unpublished paper*, pp. 1-36

CAPORALE, T. (1993), “Knut Wicksell: Real Business Cycle Theorist”, *Scottish Journal of Political Economy*, Vol. 40(4), pp. 466-471

CAPUANO, C., CHAN-LAU, J., GASHA, G., MEDEIROS, C., SANTOS, A. and SOUTO, M. (2009), "Recent Advances in Credit Risk Modeling", *IMF Working Paper Series,* No. 162, pp. 1-32

CARUANA, J. (2011), "Why Central Bank Balance Sheets Matter", *Speech at the Bank of Thailand-BIS Conference held in Thailand on December 11th 2011,* pp. 1-10

CELASUN, O. (1997), "The 1994 Currency Crisis in Turkey", *World Bank Policy Research Working Paper,* No. 1913, pp. 1-30

CETE, M., PALANCIOGLU, H. M., GEYMEN, A. and ALKAN, M. (2010), "The Turkish Cadastral Information System and Lessons Learned", *Academic Journals, Scientific Research and Essays,* Vol. 5(7), pp. 625-633

CHANDLER, D. (2012), "Development as Freedom? From Colonialism to Countering Climate Change", *Development Dialogue, The End of the Development-Security Nexus?,* pp. 115-129

CHAN-LAU, J. A. (2003), "Anticipating Credit events Using Credit Default Swaps, with an Application to Sovereign Debt Crises", *IMF Working Paper,* No.106, pp. 3-18

CHINLOY, P. (1989), "The Option Structure of a Mortgage Contract", *Journal of Housing Research,* Vol. 2(1), pp. 21-38

COLE, H. R. and KEHOE, T. J. (2000), "Self-fulfilling Debt Crises", *Journal of International Economics,* Vol. 41, pp. 309-30

CORSETTI, G. and MULLER, G. J. (2006), "Twin Deficits: Squaring Theory, Evidence and Common Sense", *Economic Policy,* Vol. 1(48), pp. 597-638

CORSETTI, G., PESENTI, P. and ROUBINI, N. (2001), "The Role of Large Players in Currency Crises", *NBER Working Paper,* No. 8303, pp. 1-52

CROWE, C. and MEADE, E. E., (2007), "The Evolution of Central Bank Governance around the World", *Journal of Economic Perspectives*", Vol. 21(4), pp. 69-90

CUKIERMAN, A., WEBB, S. B. and NEYAPTI, B. (1992), "Measuring the Independence of Central Banks and Its Effect on Policy

Outcomes", *The World Bank Economic Review*, Vol. 6 (3), pp. 353-397

CURRIER, K. M. (2004), "Natural Monopoly Regulation in the Presence of Cost Misreporting", *Atlantic Economic Journal*, Vol. 32(2), pp. 49-61

DAVIS, E. (2003), "Towards a Typology for Systemic Financial Instability", *Financial Stability Review*, No. 2, pp. 1-17

DE GRAUWE, P. (2011), "The Governance of a Fragile Eurozone", *CEPS Working Document*, No. 346, pp. 1-25

DE KOCK, G. and GRILLI, V. (1993), "Fiscal Policies and the Choice of Exchange Rate Regime", *The Economic Journal*, No. 103, pp. 347-58

DEMIR, F. (2005), "Militarization of the Market and Rent-Seeking Coalitions in Turkey", *Development and Change*, Vol. 36(4), pp. 667-690

DEMIR, O. and CETE, M. (2004), "The Cadastre and Related Problems in Turkey", *Paper presented at 4-5 November 2004 Sofia International Symposium*, pp. 388-393

DEMIR, O. and CORUHLU, Y. (2008), "The Graphical Cadastre Problem in Turkey: The Case of Trabzon Province", *Sensors 8(9)*, pp. 5'560-5'575

DEMIR, O. and TOPRAK, O. (2004), "Turkish Statistical System: Current Situation and New Challenges", *Paper presented at the February 20th 2004 Bangkok Conference*, pp. 1-11

DEMIREL, Z. and GULSEVER, F. Z. (2007), "Land Reform and Practices in Turkey", *Paper presented at the May 25th 2007 Munich UNECE WPLA Workshop*, pp. 1-16

DEMIRALP, S. and EISENSTADT, T. A. (2006), "Prisoner Erdogan's Dilemma and the Origins of Moderate Islam in Turkey", *unpublished paper*, pp. 1-41

DENIZER, C. A., GULTEKIN, M. N. and GULTEKIN, N. B. (2000), "Distorted Incentives and Financial Development in Turkey",

Paper presented at the World Bank Conference on Financial Structure and Economic Development, pp. 1-29

DOGRUEL, F. and DOGRUEL, A. S. (2011), “Privatization and Regional Distribution of Manufacturing in Turkey”, *Turkish Economic Association, Discussion Papers,* No. 4, pp. 1-27

DONER, F., DEMIR, O. and BIYIK, C. (2011), “Need for Three-Dimensional Cadastre in Turkey”, *Paper Presented at the Marrakech FIG Working Week May 18th-22nd, 2011,* pp. 1-11

DORNBUSCH, R. (2001), “A Primer on Emerging Market Crisis”, *NBER Working Paper Series,* No. 8’326, pp. 1-14

DRAZEN, A. and MASSON, P. R. (1994), “Credibility of Policies versus Credibilities of Policy makers”, *Quarterly Journal of Economics,* Vol. 109, pp. 735-54

DRAZEN, A. (1999), "Political Contagion in Currency Crises", *NBER Working Paper Series* 7211, pp. 1-29

DUFFIE, D. (2010), “Is there a Case for Banning Short-Speculation in Sovereign Bond Markets?”, *Financial Stability Review,* No. 14, pp. 1-5

DUMITER, F. C. (2010), “Measuring Central Bank Independence and Inflation Targeting in Developed and Developing Countries”, Timisoara Journal of Economics, pp. 1-18

DUMITER, F. C. (2011), “Estimating the Impact of Central Bank Independence upon Macroeconomic Performance using a Panel Data Model”, *Romanian Journal of Economic Forecasting,* No. 4, pp. 106-128

EASTERLY, W. and LEVINE, R. (2002), “Tropics, Germs and Crops: How Endowments Influence Economic Development”, *NBER Working Paper,* No. 9106, pp. 1-35

ECTA (2009), “Regulatory Scorecard – Report on the Relative Effectiveness of the Regulatory Frameworks for Electronic Communications”, *unpublished paper,* pp. 1-116

EDWARDS, S. (2000), “Does the Current Account Matter?”, *NBER Working Paper Series,* No. 8275, pp. 1-69

EDWARDS, S. (2002), "Debt Relief and the Current Account: An Analysis of the HIPC Initiative", *World Economy*, Vol. 26(4), pp. 513-531

EDWARDS, S. and MONTIEL, P. (1989), "Devaluation Crises and the Macroeconomic Consequences of Postponed Adjustment in Developing Countries", *NBER Working Paper Series*, No. 2866, pp. 1-4

EICHENGREEN, B., HAUSMANN, R. and PANIZZA, U. (2002), "Original Sin: The Pain, the Mystery and the Road to Redemption, *Paper presented at a conference on Currency and Maturity Matchmaking: Redeeming Debt from Original Sin*, Inter-American Development Bank, pp. 1-78

EICHENGREEN, B., MATHIESON, D., CHADHA, B., JANSEN, A., KODRES, L. and SHARMA, S. (1998), "Hedge Funds and Financial Market Dynamics", *IMF Occasional Paper*, No. 166, pp. 1-22

EICHENGREEN, B., ROSE, A. K. and WYPLOSZ, C. (1995), "Exchange Market Mayhem: The Antecedents and Aftermath of Speculative Attacks", *Economic Policy*, Vol. 21(10), pp. 249-312

EIJFFINGER, S. C. W. and DE HAAN, J. (1996), "The Political Economy of Central Bank Independence", *Special Papers in International Economics*, No. 19, pp. 1-82

EIJFFINGER, S. C. W. and GERAATS, P. M. (2002), "How Transparent are Central Banks?", *CEPR Discussion Paper*, No. 3188, pp. 1-43

ELING, M. and FAUST, R. (2010), "The Performance of Hedge Funds and Mutual Funds in Emerging Markets", *Journal of Banking and Finance*, Vol. 34(8), pp. 1-16

EPSTEIN, G. (2007), "Central Banks, Inflation Targeting and Employment Creation", ILO Employment Analysis and Research Unit, *Economic and Labor Market Papers*, pp. 1-45

EPSTEIN, G. (2015), "Development Central Banking: A Review of Issues and Experiences", *ILO Employment Policy Department, Working Paper No. 182*, pp. 1-28

ERCAN, M. R. and ONIS, Z. (2000), "Politics within the State: Institutions and Dilemmas of Turkish Privatization in Comparative Perspective", *unpublished paper*, pp. 1-30

ERDIK, M. (2000), "Report on 1999 Kocaeli and Duzce (Turkey) Earthquakes", *unpublished paper*, pp. 1-39

ERDILEK, A. (2006), "A Historical Review of Turkey's Inward Foreign Direct Investment Environment and Policies from the Ottoman Empire to the Present", *unpublished paper*, pp. 4-19

ERDOGDU, G. P. (2010), "A Comparative Analysis of Entry to Home Ownership Profiles: Turkey and the Netherlands", *Middle East Technical University Journal of Faculty of Architecture*, Vol. 27(2), pp. 95-124

EROGLU, N. (2007), "Economic Policies during the Ataturk Period (1923-1938)", *Journal of the Faculty of Economic and Business Sciences*, Vol. 23(2), pp. 63-73

ERSEL, H. (1991), "Structural Adjustment: Turkey (1980-1990)", *Central Bank of the Republic of Turkey Research Department Discussion Papers*, No. 9107, pp. 1-13

ERSEL, H. and OZATAY, F. (2008), "Inflation Targeting in Turkey", *Economic Research Forum, Working Paper No. 445*, pp. 1-22

ERTUGRUL, A. and F. SELCUK (2001), "A Brief Account of the Turkish Economy: 1980-2000", *Russian and East European Finance and Trade*, Vol. 37(6), pp. 6-30

ESQUIVEL, G. and LARRAIN, F. (1998), "Explaining Currency Crises", *Harvard Institute for International Development Discussion Paper*, No. 666, pp. 1-42

FAMA, E. (1969), "Efficient Capital Markets: A Review of Theory and Empirical Work", *Journal of Finance*, Vol. 25(2), pp. 383-416

FERIDUN, M. (2004), "Turkish Financial Crisis of 2001: Did Politics Play any Role?", *Investment Management and Financial Innovations*, Vol. 1, pp. 41-49

FESTRE, A. (2006), “Knut Wicksell and Ludwig Von Mises on Money, Interest and Price Dynamics”, *Journal of the History of Economic Thought,* Vol. 28(3), pp. 333-355

FICICI, A. (2001), “Political Assessment of Turkish Privatization: A Critical Assessment”, *unpublished paper,* p. 1

FILHO, F. F. AND CONCEICAO, C. A. (2003), “The Concept of Uncertainty in Post-Keynesian Theory and in Institutional Economics: A Possible Conciliation?”, *Journal of Economic Issues,* Vol. 39, pp. 2-14

FINANCIAL STABILITY FORUM (2000), “Report of the Working Group on Highly Leveraged Institutions”, *Financial Stability Board Report,* pp. 1-155

FISHER, S. (1998), "The Asian Crisis: A View from the IMF", *Journal of International Financial Management and Accounting,* Vol. 9(2), pp. 167-176

FISHER, S. (2001), “Exchange Rate Regimes: Is the Bipolar View Correct?”, *Journal of Economic Perspectives,* Vol. 5(2), pp. 3-24

FISHER, S. (2002), “Financial Crises and Reform of the International Financial System”, *NBER Working Paper,* No. 9297, pp. 1-52

FLEMING, J. M. (1962), “Domestic Financial Policies under Fixed and under Floating Exchange Rates”, *IMF Staff Papers,* Vol. 9(3), pp. 369-379

FLOOD, R. and GARBER, P. M. (1984), “Collapsing Exchange-Rate Regimes: Some Linear Examples”, *Journal of International Economics,* Vol. 17 (1, 2), pp. 1-13

FLOOD, R., GARBER, P., KRAMER, C. (1996), “Collapsing Exchange Rate Regimes: Another Linear Example”, *Journal of International Economics,* Vol. 41, pp. 223-34

FLOOD, R. and MARION, N. (1994), “The Size and Timing of Devaluations in Capital-Controlled Developing Economies”, *NBER Working paper Series,* No. 4957, pp. 1-22

FLOOD, R. and MARION, N. (2000), "Self-fulfilling Risk Predictions: an Application to Speculative Attacks", *Journal of International Economics*, Vol. 50, pp. 245-268

FRANKEL, J. A. and ROSE, A. K. (1996), "Currency Crashes in Emerging Markets: An Empirical Treatment", *Journal of International Economics*, Vol. 41, pp. 351-66

FRENKEL, J. A. and RAZIN, A. (1987), "The Mundell-Fleming Model: A Quarter Century Later", *NBER Working Paper Series*, No. 2321, pp. 1-87

FRENKEL, R. and TAYLOR, L. (2006), "Real Exchange Rate, Monetary Policy and Employment", *DESA Working Paper*, No. 19, pp. 1-12

FUNG, W. and HSIED, D. A. (2000), "Measuring the Impact of Hedge Funds", *Journal of Empirical Finance*, Vol. 7, pp. 1-36

GALATI, G., HEALTH, A. and MCGUIRE, P. (2007), "Evidence of Carry Trade Activity", *BIS Quarterly Review September 2007*, pp. 1-15

GAPEN, M. T., GRAY, D. F., LI, C. H. and XIAO, Y. (2005), "Measuring and Analyzing Sovereign Risk with Contingent Claims", *IMF Working Paper*, Vol. 5(155), pp. 1-46

GAPEN, M. T., GRAY, D. F., LI, C. H. and XIAO, Y. (2008), "Measuring and Analyzing Sovereign Risk with Contingent Claims", *IMF Working Paper*, Vol. 55(1), pp. 109-146

GARBARAVICIUS, T. and DIERICK, F. (2005), "Hedge Funds and their Implications for Financial Stability", *European Central Bank Occasional Paper Series*, No. 37, pp. 1-73

GARRISON, R. W. (2004), "Overconsumption and Forced Saving in Mises-Hayek Theory of the Business Cycle", *History of Political Economy*, Vol. 30(2), pp. 323-348

GENCAY, R. and SELCUK, F. (2003), "Overnight Borrowing, Interest Rates and Extreme Value Theory", *Economic European Review (forthcoming)*, pp. 1-27

GOKGUR, P. (2010), "The Process of Transformation in the Squatting Fact: Examples of Sanayi and Yesilce Quarters in Istanbul", *Serbian Architectural Journal*, Issue 2, pp. 115-137

GOLDFAJN, I. and VALDES, R. (1997), "Capital Flows and Twin Crises: the Role of Liquidity", *IMF Working Paper,* No. 87, p. 5

GONEN, L. (2006), "Dynamics of Political Reform in Turkey", *Europa-Kolleg-Hamburg-Discussion Paper,* No. 1, pp. 1-37

GRILLI, V., MASCIANDRO, D. and TABELLINI, G. (1991), "Political and Monetary Institutions and Public Financial Policies in the Industrial Countries", *Economic Policy,* No. 13, pp. 341-392

GROS, D. (2004), "Financial Aspects of Central Bank Independence and Price Stability – The Case of Turkey", *EU-Turkey Working Papers,* No. 12, pp. 1-16

GRUENEWALD, S., WAGNER, A. F. and WEBER, R. H. (2009), "Short Selling Regulation after the Financial Crisis – First Principals Revisited", *Swiss Finance Institute Research Paper Series,* No. 09-28, pp. 1-12

GUBLER, M. (2011), "Carry Trade Activities: A Multivariate Threshold Model Analysis", *unpublished paper,* pp. 11-44

GUMUS, I. (2003), "Effects of Interest Rate Defense on Exchange Rates during the 1994 Crisis in Turkey", *The Central Bank of the Republic of Turkey, Research Department Working Paper Series,* No. 14, pp. 1-17

GUVEN, A. B. (2010), "The Feasibility of IFI-Led Institutional Reform: Four Turkish Experiments Compared", *Glodem Working Paper Series,* No. 2, pp. 1-33

HALL, R. E. and JONES, C. I. (1998), "Why Do Some Countries Produce So Much More Output per Worker than Others?", *NBER Working Paper Series No. 5812 (previous version under the title "The Productivity of Nations, (1996)"),* pp. 1-50

HARRI, A. and BRORSEN, B. W. (2004), "Performance Persistence and the Source of Returns for Hedge Funds", *Applied Financial Economics,* Vol. 5(2), pp. 1-19

HASSAN, S. and SMITH, S. (2011), "The Rand as a Carry Trade Target: Risk, Returns and Policy Implications", *South African Reserve Bank Working Paper,* No. 235, pp. 1-30

HERRERA, A. M. and OZBAY, P. (2005), "A Dynamic Model of Central Bank Intervention: Evidence from Turkey", *The Central Bank of the Republic of Turkey Research Department Working Paper,* No. 1, pp. 1-35

HERTIG, G. and LEE, R. (2003), "Four Predictions about the Future of EU Securities Regulation", *Forthcoming Journal of Comparative Studies,* pp. 1-24

HOLZNER, M. (2013), "Impact of Croatian EU Accession on Regional Trade Patterns", *The Vienna Institute for International Economic Studies, wiiw Policy Notes and reports, No. 10,* pp. 1-15

IAN, A. and TIMOTHY, I. (1996), "Public Policy for the Private Sector: Price Caps, Rate of Return Regulation and the Cost of Capital", *The World Bank Group Note No. 87,* pp. 1-4

IMF (2006a), "Article IV of the Fund's Articles of Agreement: An Overview of the Legal Framework", Prepared by Legal Department, pp. 1-22

INAN, H. I., CETE, M. (2006), "The Role of Cadastre in Agricultural Reform Applications of Turkey: Case Study of Trabzon Province", *Paper presented at the October 8-13th Munich 23rd FIG Conference,* pp. 1-9

INCI, I. (2010), "Distribution of Land Ownership When Ataturk Was Head of State", *Journal of Ataturk University Research Institute,* Vol. 44, pp. 345-359

ISLAM, R. and MONTENEGRO, C. (2002), "What Determines the Quality of Institutions?", *World Bank Policy Research,* Working Paper No. 2764, pp. 1-34

JAMISON, M. A. (2005), "Regulation: Price Cap and Revenue Cap", *unpublished paper,* pp. 1-17

JARROW, R. A. and TURNBULL, S. M. (1995), "Pricing Derivatives on Financial Securities Subject to Credit Risk", *Journal of Finance,* Vol. 1(1), pp. 53-85

JAYADEV, A. (2006), "Differing Preferences between anti-inflation and anti-unemployment Policy among the Rich and the Poor", Economic Letters, Elsevier, Vol. 91 (1), pp. 67-71

JEANNE, O. (1997), "Are Currency Crises Self-fulfilling? A Test", *Journal of International Economics,* No. 43, pp. 263-286

JEANNE, O. (2000), "Currency Crises: A Perspective on Recent Theoretical Developments", *Princeton University International Finance Section Special Papers in International Economics,* No. 20, pp. 1-41

JENSEN, M. C. (1967), "The Performance of Mutual Funds in the Period 1945-1964", *Journal of Finance,* Vol. 23(2), pp. 389-416

JOHNSON, S., MCMILLAN, J. and WOODRUFF, C. (2002), "Property Rights and Finance", *NBER Working Paper Series,* No. 8852, pp. 1-65

KAMINSKY, B. and NG, F. (2007), "Turkey's Evolving Trade Integration into Pan-European Markets", *The Journal of International Trade and Diplomacy,* Vol. 1(2), pp. 35-103

KAMINSKY, G. L. and REINHART, C. M. (1999), "The Twin Crises: The Causes of Banking and Balance-of-Payments Problems", *American Economic Review,* Vol. 89(3), pp. 473-500

KARA, A. H. (2006), "Turkish Experience with Implicit Inflation Targeting", *Central Bank of Turkey, Research and Monetary Department Working Paper,* No. 3, pp. 1-17

KARADAG, R. (2010), "Neoliberal Restructuring in Turkey: From State to Oligarchic Capitalism", *Max Plank Institute for Study of Societies Discussion Paper,* No. 7, pp. 5-32

KARAKAS, C. and OZSAN, O. (2005), "Turkey: Rapid Progress towards a Secondary Mortgage Market – Secondary Mortgage Market in Turkey", *Housing Finance International December 2005,* pp. 37-51

KARAMAN, F. N. and OZKALE, N. L. (2007), "Static Effects of the EU-Turkey Customs Union", *Conference paper presented at European*

Trade Study Group 8th annual Conference, University of Wien, pp. 1-18

KAYMAK, E. (2006), "Why the EU Catalyst Proved Insufficient to Solve the Cyprus Problem: The Politicization of European Values", *unpublished paper,* pp. 1-18

KHAN, M. and SENHADJI, A. (2001), "Threshold Effects in the Relationship Between Inflation and Growth," *IMF Staff Papers, 48:1,* pp. 1-21.

KIBRITCIOGLU, A. (2005), "Banking Sector Crisis and Related New Regulations in Turkey", *Economia Exterior,* Vol. 32, pp. 141-148

KING, S. P. (1997), "Access Pricing under Rate of Return Regulation", *Australian Economic Review,* Vol. 30(3), pp. 243-255

KISA, A. and BAKICI, S. (2011), "Spatial Data Infrastructure in Turkey and Projects", *Paper prepared for the FIG Working Week 18-22 May 2011, Bridging the Gap between Cultures, held in Marrakech,* pp. 1-9

KLEIN, M. W. and MARION, N. P. (1994), "Explaining the Duration of Exchange-Rate Pegs", *NBER Working Paper,* No.4651, pp. 1-21

KNACK, S. and KEEFER, P. (1995), "Institutions and Economic Performance: Cross Country Tests Using Alternative Institutional Measures", *Economics and Politics,* Vol. 7(3), pp. 207-223

KNACK, S. and KEEFER, P. (1995), "Institutions and Economic Performance: Cross-Country Tests Using Alternative Institutional Indicators", *MPRA Paper,* No. 23118, pp. 1-30

KOKTURK, E. (2002), "Conditions of Preparation of Cadastre of Turkey to Information System", *unpublished paper,* pp. 1-15

KOPF, C. (2011), "Restoring Financial Stability in the Euro Area, *CEPS Policy Brief,* pp. 1-26

KOPITS, G. (1987), "Structural Reform, Stabilization and Growth in Turkey", *IMF Occasional Paper, No. 52,* pp. 1-45

KORNER, K. (2011), "Sovereign Default Probabilities Online: Extracting Implied Default Probabilities from CDS Spreads", *Deutsche Bank Research Paper,* pp. 1-8

KOZLOVSKIS, K. (2011), "Analysis of Carry Trade Management Modifications in the Global Currency Market", *Economics and Management Paper Series,* No. 16, pp. 1142-1146

KRUGMAN, P. (1979), "A Model of Balance-of-Payments Crises", *Journal of Money, Credit and Banking,* Vol. 11(3), pp. 311-325

KRUGMAN, P. (1991), "History versus Expectations", *Quarterly Journal of Economics,* Vol. 108, pp. 535-542

KRUGMAN, P. (1998), "Currency Crises", *unpublished paper,* pp. 1-8

KRUGMAN, P. (2001), "Crises: The Next Generation?", *Paper prepared for Razin Conference Tel Aviv University,* pp. 1-27

KYRIS, G. (2010), "Turkey, Cyprus and the Turkish Cypriot Political Parties: The Ephemeral Catalyst of EU?", *Turkish Policy Quarterly,* Vol. 10(2), pp. 97-105

LA PORTA, R. et al. (1998), "The Quality of Government", *NBER Working Paper,* No. 6'727, pp. 1-44

LERNER, A. P. (1936), "The Symmetry between Import and Export Taxes", *Economica* Vol. 3 (11), pp. 306-313

LHABITANT, F. S. (2001), "Assessing Market Risk for Hedge Funds and Hedge Funds Portfolios", *Research Paper,* No. 24, pp. 1-35

LI, M. (2011), "An Evaluation of Exchange Rate Models by Carry Trade", *Journal of Economics and International Finance,* Vol. 3(2), pp. 72-87

LINHART, P. B., RADNER, R. and SINDEN, F. W. (1983), "A Sequential Principal-Agent Approach to Regulation", *Economic Discussion Paper,* No. 264, pp. 1-21

LIPSEY, R. G. and LANCASTER, K. (1956), "The General Theory of Second Best", *The Review of Economic Studies,* Vol. 24(1), pp. 11-32

MACKENZIE, D. (2003), “Long-Term Capital Management and the Sociology of Arbitrage”, *Economy and Society,* Vol. 32(3), pp. 349-380

MADAN, D. and UNAL, H. (1999), “A Two-Factor Hazard-Rate Model for Pricing Risky Debt and the Term Structure of Credit Spreads”, *Journal of Financial and Quantitative Analysis,* Vol. 35(1), pp. 1-32

MALISZEWSKI, W. S. (2000), “Central Bank Independence in Transition Economies”, *Economics of Transition,* Vol. 8(3), pp. 749-789

MASSON, P. (1998), "Contagion: Monsoonal Effects, Spillovers and Jumps between Multiple Equilibria", *IMF Working Paper Series,* No. 142, pp. 1-29

MCCALLUM, B. T. (1980), “Rational Expectations and Macroeconomic Stabilization Policy”, *Journal of Money, Credit and Banking,* Vol. 12(4), pp. 716-743

MERTON, R. (1973), “On the Pricing of Corporate Debt: the Risk Structure of Interest Rates”, *Journal of Finance,* Vol. 29(2), pp. 449-470

MILESI-FERRETTI, G. M. and RAZIN, A. (1996), “Current-Account Sustainability”, *Princeton Studies in International Finance,* No. 81, pp. 1-66

MILESI-FERRETTI, G. M. and Razin, A. (1998), “Current Account Reversals and Currency Crises, Empirical Regularities”, *IMF Working Paper Series,* No. 89, pp. 1-45

MISHKIN, F. S. (1996), “Understanding Financial Crises: A Developing Country Perspective”, *NBER Working Paper Series,* No. 5600, pp. 2-44

MISHKIN, F. S. (1999), “Global Financial Instability: Framework, Events, Issues, *Journal of Economic Perspectives,* Vol. 13(4), pp. 3-20

MUFTULER, B. M. (2004), “Turkey’s Accession to the European Union: Institutional and Security Challenges”, *Perceptions, Journal of International Affairs,* Vol. 9(3), pp. 29-43

MUMCU, A. and ZENGINOBUZ, U. (2001), "Competition Policy in Turkey"; *MPRA Paper,* No. 198, pp. 1-42

MUNDELL, R. A. (1960), "The Monetary Dynamics of International Adjustment under Fixed and Flexible Rates", *Quarterly Journal of Economics,* Vol. 74, pp. 227-257

MUNDELL, R. A. (1961b), "Flexible Exchange Rates and Employment Policy", *Canadian Journal of Economics and Political Science,* Vol. 27(4), pp. 509-517

MUNDELL, R. A. (1961c), "The International Disequilibrium System", *Kyklos-International Review for Social Sciences,* Vol. 14(2), pp. 154-172

MUNDELL, R. A. (1963), "Capital Mobility and Stabilization Policy under Fixed and Flexible Exchange Rates", *Canadian Journal of Economics and Political Science,* Vol. 29, pp. 475-485

MUNDELL, R. A. (1964), "A Reply: Capital Mobility and Size", *Canadian Journal of Economics and Political Science,* Vol. 30, pp. 421-431

NGUYEN, H. (2004), "Hedge Fund Behavior: an Ex-Post Analysis", *Paper prepared for the International Conference of the French Association of Finance,* pp. 1-25

NORDHAUS, W. D. (1990), "Alternative Approaches to the Political Business Cycle", *Cowles Foundation Paper,* No. 748, pp. 1-63

NORTH, D. C., (1994), "Economic Performance through Time", *The American Review,* Vol. 84(3), pp. 359-368

OBSTFELD, M. (1994), "The Logic of Currency Crises", *Cahiers Economiques et Monétaires,* Vol. 43, pp. 189-213

O'HEARN, D. (2009), "Amatya Sen's Development as Freedom: Ten Years Later", *Public Awareness, Spring 2009,* Issue 8, pp. 1-5

O'KANE, D. and TURNBULL, S. (2004), "Valuation of Credit Default Swaps", *Fixed Income Quantitative Credit Research Quarterly,* Vol. 2003-Q1/Q2, pp. 1-19

OLGUN, H. and TOGAN, S. (1989), "The Liberalization of International Trade in Turkey during the 1980s", *the Pakistan Development Review,* Vol. 28(4), pp. 949-960

ONDER, T. (2005), "Monetary Policy, Aims and Implementation in Turkey" (in Turkish), *unpublished paper,* pp. 325

ONDER, N. A. G. (2008), "CBRT Balance Sheet Size and its Relative Importance in Explaining Inflation, 1990-2007" (in Turkish), *unpublished paper,* pp. 1-30

ONIS, Z. (2004), "Turgut Ozal and His Economic Legacy: Turkish Neo-liberalism in Critical Perspective", *Middle Eastern Studies,* Vol. 40(4), pp. 113-134

ONIS, Z. and WEBB, S. B. (1992), "Political Economy of Policy Reform in Turkey in the 1980s", *World Bank Working Paper Series No. 1059,* pp. 1-66

OPPERS, S. A. (2002), "The Austrian Theory of Business Cycles: Old lesson for Modern Economic Policy?", *Working Paper,* No 2, pp. 3-12

OSMAN, A. (2000), "Planning and Implementing Monetary Policy in Turkey: an Exercise", *Journal of Economic Cooperation,* Vol. 21(3), pp. 1-25

OZATAY, F. (1997), "The 1994 Currency Crisis in Turkey", *Journal of Policy Reform,* Vol. 3(4), pp. 327-351

OZATAY, F and SAK, G. (2002), "The 2000-2001 Financial Crisis in Turkey", *unpublished paper prepared for Brookings Trade Forum 2002 on Currency Crises,* pp. 1-52

OZCAM, M. (2004), "Uluslararasi Para Fonu (IMF) ve Turkiye (The IMF and Turkey)", *Capital Market Board Research Department Paper,* pp. 1-14

OZCELIK, O. and TUNCER, G. (2005), "Economic Policies of Ataturk's Period", *Academia Social Sciences (ASOS) Index,* Vol. 9(1), pp. 1-14

OZLER, S. I. (2000), "Politics of the Gecekondu in Turkey: The Political Choices of the Urban Squatters in National Elections", *Turkish Studies,* Vol. 1(2), pp. 39-58

PAN, J. and SINGLETON, K. J. (2007), "Default and Recovery Implicit in the Term Structure of Sovereign CDS Spreads", *Journal of Finance,* Vol. 63(5), pp. 1-42

PATTON, M. J. (1999), "U.S. Advisory Aid to Turkey: the Hinnes-Kemmerer Mission, 1933-1934", *Working Paper,* MESV3-4, pp. 46-57

PAYNE, M. and LOSADA, C. (1999), "Institutions and Development in Latin America: An Approach Toward Quantitatively Describing Institutional Capacity in the Region", *unpublished paper,* pp. 1-50

POLLIN, R. and ZHU, A. (2005), "Inflation and Economic Growth: A Cross-Country Non-linear Analysis, Political Economy Research Institute (PERI), *Working Paper Series No. 109,* pp. 1-23

RAJAN, R. G. and ZINGALES, L. (2000), "Great Reversals: The Politics of Financial Development in the 20th Century", *NBER Working Paper,* No. 8178, pp. 1-55

RAMSEY, F. P. (1927), "A Contribution to the Theory of Taxation", *Economic Journal,* Vol. (37)145, pp. 47-61

REINHART, C. M. and ROGOFF K. S. (2002), "The Modern History of Exchange Rate Arrangements: A Reinterpretation", *NBER Working Paper,* No.8963, pp. 1-106

RODRIK, D. (2006), "Goodbye Washington Consensus, Hello Washington Confusion? A Review of the World Bank's Economic Growth of the 1990s: Learning from a Decade of Reform", *Journal of Economic Literature,* Vol. 44, pp. 973-987

RODRIK, D., SUBRAMANIAN, A. and TREBBI, F. (2002), "Institutions Rule: The Primacy of Institutions over Geography and Integration in Economic Development", *NBER Working Paper,* No. 9305, pp. 1-23

RODRIK, D. and VELASCO, A. (1999), "Short-Term Capital Flows", *NBER Working Paper*, No. 7364, pp. 1-44

SARGENT, T. J. and WALLACE, N. (1981), "Some Unpleasant Monetarist Arithmetic", *Federal Reserve Bank of Minneapolis Quarterly Review*, Vol. 5, pp. 1-17

SAXTON, J. (2002), "Why Currency Crises Happen?", *unpublished paper*, pp. 1-23

SAYGILI, A. T. (2009), "Impacts of Wrong Financial Decisions on Collapse of an Empire: The Ottoman Case", *African Journal of Business Management*, Vol. 3(4), pp. 151-159

SCHINASI, G. J. (2004), "Defining Financial Stability", *IMF Working Paper*, No. 187, pp. 3-17

SCHWARCZ, S. L. (2008), "Systemic Risk", *Duke Law School Legal Studies, Research Paper*, No. 163, pp. 194-247

SHARPE, W. F. (1991), "The Arithmetic of Active Management", *Financial Analyst's Journal*, Vol. 47(1), pp. 7-9

SHARPE, W. F. (1992), "Asset Allocation: Management Style and Performance Measurement", *Journal of Portfolio Management*, Winter 1992, pp. 7-19

SHEN, C. H. and HUANG, A. Y. (2010), "Sovereign Credit Default Swaps vs. Credit Ratings: Evidence from Error Correction Model", *unpublished paper*, pp. 1-30

SHEPPARD, P. (2008), "The Components of Central Bank Independence and Their Effects", *Undergraduate Economic Review*, Vol. 4(1), pp. 1-50

SIKLOS, P. L. (2008), "No Single Definition of Central Bank Independence is Right for All Countries", European Journal of Political Economy, Vol. 24, pp. 802-817

SINAPI, C. (2011), "Institutional Prerequisites of Financial Fragility within Minsky's Financial Instability Hypothesis: A Proposal in Terms of "Institutional Fragility", *Levy Economics Institute Working Paper Series*, No. 674, pp. 1-28

SISIK, Y. (2006), "Survey of the Implementation of Methodological Standards for Direct Investment (SIMSDI): Turkey' Experience in SIMSDI", *Balance of Payments Division, Statistics Department, Central Bank of Republic of Turkey,* p. 3

SORAL, H. B., ISCAN, T. B. and HEBB, G. (2005), "Fraud, Banking Crises and Regulatory Enforcement: Evidence from Micro-Level Transactions Data", *European Journal of Law and Economics,* Vol. 21(2), pp. 179-197

SOZER, A. (2005), "Turkey - EU Enlargement at a Crossroads: Turkey's Democratization in Light of its EU Candidate Status", *Paper Prepared for the 2004 Warsaw Conference on Enlargement and the Future of the EU,* pp. 1-25

STIGLITZ, J. (1998a), "Towards a New Paradigm for Development: Strategies, Policies and Processes", *Paper Presented at the Geneva Prebisch Lecture held at UNCTAD in October,* pp. 1-43

STIGLITZ, J. (1998b), "More Instruments and Broader Goals: Moving Toward the Post-Washington Consensus", *Paper Presented at the WIDER Annual Lecture at the World Institute for Development Economics Research in Helsinki,* pp. 1-34

STIGLITZ, J. (1999), "More Instruments and Broader Goals: Moving Toward the Post-Washington Consensus", *Revista de Economia Politica,* Vol. 19(1), pp. 94-118

STIGLITZ, J. (2002), "Whither Reform? Towards a New Agenda for Latin America, *CEPAL Review,* No. 80, pp. 1-58

STIGLITZ, J. (2004), "The Post Washington Consensus", *The Initiative for Policy Dialogue,* pp. 1-13

STRAUB, S. (2000), "Empirical Determinants of Good Institutions: Do We Know Anything?", *Inter-American Development Bank, Working Paper No. 423,* pp. 1-50

STROMQVIST, M. (2009), "Hedge Funds and Financial Crises", *Economic Review,* No. 1, pp. 87-104

STULEC, I, BAKOVIC and VUCKOVI, V. (2014), "Impact of Croatian EU Accession on its Foreign Trade and Customs System", *Ekonomski Vjesnik – Econviews*, pp. 381-392

SUMMERS, L. H. (2000), "International Financial Crises, Causes, Prevention and Cures", *American Economic Review,* Vol. 90(2), pp. 1-16

TANG, D. Y. and YAN, H. (2011), "What Moves CDS Spreads?", *unpublished paper,* pp, 1-47

TAYMAZ, E. and YILMAZ, K. (2007), "Productivity and Trade Orientation: Turkish Manufacturing Industry Before and After the Customs Union", *The Journal of International Trade and Diplomacy,* Vol. 1(1), pp. 127-154

THATCHER, M. and SWEET, A. S. (2002), "Theory and Practice of Delegation to Non-Majoritarian Institutions", *West European Politics,* Vol. 25(1), pp. 1-22

TREISMAN, D. (1998), "The Causes of Corruption: a Cross-National Study", *Journal of Public Economics,* Vol. 76(3), pp. 399-457

TURHAN, I. (2008), "Housing Sector in Turkey: Challenges and Opportunities", *Speech of the Central Bank of the Republic of Turkey Deputy Governor at the 17th Annual International Conference the Real Estate and Urban Economics Association,* pp. 1-7

TURKISH STATISTICAL INSTITUTE (2013), Statistical Indicators 1923-2008. Ankara: Turkish Statistical Institute Printing Division, 718 pp.

UNITED NATIONS ALLIANCE OF CIVILIZATIONS (2006), Report of High-level Group, pp. 1-63

UNITED NATIONS GENERAL ASSEMBLY (2005), "In larger freedom: towards development, security and human rights for all", *Report of the Secretary-General, Fifty-ninth session, A/59/2005,* pp. 1-62

UYGUR, E. (2001), "Turkey from Crisis to Crisis: Crises of November 2000 and February 2001 (in Turkish)", *Working Paper Series,* No.1, pp. 1-39

UZUN, B., CETE, M. and PALANCIOGLU, H. M. (2010), "Legalizing and Upgrading Illegal Settlements in Turkey", *Habitat International,* Vol. 34(2), pp. 204-209

VANICHVATANA, S. (2007), "Thailand Real Estate Market Cycles: Case Study of the 1997 Economic Crisis", *GH Bank Housing Journal,* Vol. 1(1), pp. 1-47

VELASCO, A. (1996), "Fixed Exchange Rates: Credibility, Flexibility and Multiplicity", *European Economic Review,* Vol. 40(3-5), pp. 1023-1035

VRONTOS, S. D., VRONTOS, I. D. and GIAMOURIDIS, D. (2008), "Hedge Fund Pricing and Model Uncertainty", *Journal of Banking and Finance,* Vol. 32(5), pp. 741-753

VOSS, J. and MURPHY, D. (2006), "European Union Twinning Project for Turkey: Towards Improving Investment Climate in Turkey: Comments on the YOIKK Reform Process", *Project Report,* pp. 1-272

VOYVODA, E. and YELDAN, E. (2005), "Turkish Macroeconomics under the IMF Program: Strangulation of the Twin-Targets, Lopsided Growth and Persistent Fragilities", *unpublished paper,* pp. 1-35

VURAL, I. Y. (2008), "Fiscal Policies of Ataturk's Period: from Liberal Economy to Mixed Economy" (in Turkish), *Dumlupinar University Journal of Social Sciences, No. 20,* pp. 1-38

WALTI, S. (2003), "Simple Models of Currency Crises", *unpublished paper,* pp. 1-16

WENZKE, C. and LINDLEY, D. (2008), "Dismantling the Cyprus Conspiracy: The US Role in the Cypriot Crisis of 1963, 1967 and 1974", *unpublished paper,* pp. 1-85

WHETTEN, M., ADELSON, M., and VAN BEMMELER, M., (2004), "Credit Default Swap Primer", *Nomura Fixed Income Research,* pp. 1-11

WILLIAMSON, J. (2000), "What Should the World Bank Think About the Washington Consensus?", *The World Bank Research Observer,* Vol. 15(2), pp. 251-264

WILLIAMSON, O. E. (2000), "New Institutional Economics: Taking Stock, Looking Ahead", *Journal of Economic Literature,* Vol. 38, pp. 596-601

WILLIAMSON, O.E. (1998), "Transaction Cost Economics: How it Works; Where it is Headed", *De Economist 146, No. 1,* pp 25-19

YALCIN, G., ERKEK, B., BAKICI, S. and SAHIN, N. (2009), "Through Spatial Data Infrastructure in Turkey", *Paper Prepared for the 3-8 May FIG Working Week 2009,* pp. 1-9

YALCIN, G., YILDIRIM, O. and BAKICI, S. (2008), "Map Related Projects in General Directorate of Land Registry and Cadastre in Turkey", *Paper Prepared for the 14-19 June FIG Working Week 2008,* pp. 1-16

YELDAN, E. (2003), "Behind the 2000/2001 Turkish Crisis: Stability, Credibility and Governance for Whom?, *unpublished paper,* pp. 1-15

YILMAZ, K. (2010), "Taking Stock: the Customs Union between Turkey and the EU Fifteen Years Later", *TUSIAD-Koç University Economic Research Forum Working Paper Series,* No.1023, pp. 1-20

YILMAZ, S. (2009), "Turkish Journalists as the "Chivalry" of Democracy: the Case of the Co-emergence of Democrat Party and Turkish Journalists' Association in 1946", *European Journal of Economic and Political Studies,* Vol. 2(2), pp. 1-16

ZENGIN, A. (1997), "The Twin Deficits Hypothesis (The Turkish Case)", *unpublished paper,* pp. 217-228

ZENGINOBUZ, U. (2008), "On Regulatory Agencies in Turkey and Their Independence", *Turkish Studies,* Vol. 9 (3), pp. 475-505

Texts

AMARTYA (1999), *Development as Freedom,* New York: Knopf, 366 pp.

ARTHUR T. and BOOTH, P. (2010), *Does Britain Need a Financial Regulator? Statutory Regulation, Private Regulation and Financial Markets.* London: The Institute of Economic Affairs, 164 pp.

ATIYAS, I. et al. (2005), *The Road Ahead for Turkey – Turkey Country Profile.* Cairo: Economic Research Forum, 172 pp.

BARTH. J. R., HALL, T. W., KURTZMAN, J., WEI, S. J. and YAGO, G. (2001), *The Opacity Index: Launching a New Measure of the Effects of Opacity on the Cost and Availability of Capital in Countries World-Wide.* London: PricewaterhouseCoopers, 58 pp.

BROWN, L. C. (2006), *Diplomacy in the Middle East–The International relations of Regional and Outside Powers.* London: Tauris, 367 pp.

BUDAK, A. and CIKOT, O. (2011), *The Handbook of the Turkish Capital Markets 2011.* Istanbul: TSPAKB Publication, No. 54, 76 pp.

CARBAUGH, R. J. (2011), *International Economics.* Ohio: South Western, 556 pp.

CHEOL, S. E. and RESNICK, B. (2000), *International Financial Management.* Boston: McGraw-Hill/Irwin, 536 pp.

CHERULINAM, F. (2006), *International Economics.* New Delhi: Tata McGraw-Hill, 691 pp.

COSAR, N. and BILDIRICI, M. (2010), *Turkish Economy, at the Light of Historical, Political and Social Developments, 1908-2008* (in Turkish). Bursa: Ekin Basin Yayin Dagitim, 801 pp.

CUKIERMAN, A. (1992), Central Bank Strategy, Credibility and Independence: Theory and Evidence, Cambridge, MA: The MIT Press, 496 pp.

DE SOTO, H. (1989), *The Other Path, the Invisible Revolution in the Third World.* London: Tauris, 271 pp.

DE SOTO, H. (2000), *The Mystery of Capital, Why Capitalism Triumphs in the West and Fails Everywhere Else.* London: Bantam Press, 243 pp.

FEIGENBAUM, H., HENIG, J. and HAMNETT, C. (2003), *Shrinking the State, the Political Underpinnings of Privatization.* Cambridge: Cambridge University Press, 192 pp.

GRABOWSKI, R., Self, S. and Shields, M.P. (2015), *Economic Development, A Regional, Institutional and Historical Approach, Routledge,* Taylor and Francis Group, London and New York, 276 pp.

HALE, W. (2000), *Turkish Foreign Policy, 1774-2000.* London: Frank Cass Publishers, 361 pp.

HAYEK, F. A. (1931), *Prices and Production.* London: Georges Routledge, 162 pp.

KANSU, A. (2006), *Exchange Rates Systems and Currency Crises* (in Turkish). Istanbul: Guncel Publishers, 232 pp.

KEPENEK, Y. and YENTURK, N. (2010), *Turkish Economy* (in Turkish). Istanbul: Remzi Kitabevi, 395 pp.

KEYNES, J. M. (1919), *The Economic Consequences of the Peace.* London: MacMillan St. Martin's Press, 191 pp.

KEYNES, J. M. (1930a), *A Treatise of Money, The Pure Theory of Money,* Vol. 5. London: Macmillan Press, 336 pp.

KEYNES, J. M. (1930b), *A Treatise of Money, The Pure Theory of Money,* Vol. 6. London: Macmillan Press, 390 pp.

KEYNES J. M. (1936), *The General Theory of Employment, Interest and Money.* London: Macmillan Press, 412 pp.

LHABITANT, F. S. (2007), *Handbook of Hedge Funds.* England: John Wiley and Sons, 637 pp.

MEADE, J. E. (1951), *The Theory of International Economic Policy: The Balance of Payments.* London: Oxford University Press, 432 pp.

MILLER, M. H. (1997), *Merton Miller on Derivatives.* New York: John Wiley and Sons, 226 pp.

MISES, L. V. (1934), *The Theory of Money and Credit.* London: Jonathan Cape, 541 pp.

MISES, L. V. (1949), *Human Action: A Treatise on Economics.* Chicago: Contemporary Books, 907 pp.

MUFTULER, M. (1997), *Europe in Change: Turkey's Relations with a Changing Europe.* Manchester: Manchester University Press, 133 pp.

NORTH, D. C. (1981), *Growth and Structural Change.* New York: Norton Press, 148 pp.

ODEKON, M. (2005), *The Costs of Economic Liberalization in Turkey.* New Jersey: Rosemont Publishing and Printing Corporation, 173 pp.

REICH, B. (1990), *Political Leaders of the Contemporary Middle East and North Africa, A Biographical Dictionary.* Connecticut: Greenwood Press, 570 pp.

SCHMUSCH, S. (2008), *Turkey's Trade Liberalization and its Accession to the European Union Customs Union,* Norderstedt Germany: Grin Verlag, 18 pp.

SOROS, G. (1994), *The Alchemy of Finance.* New York: John Wiley, 391 pp.

STELZER, I. M. (2001), *Lectures on Regulatory and Competition Policy.* London: Published by the Institute of Economic Affairs, 233 pp.

STIGLER, G. (1975), *The Citizen and the State: Essays on Regulation.* Chicago: University of Chicago Press, 224 pp.

TRAIN, K. E. (1991), *Optimal Regulation: The Economic Theory of the Natural Monopoly.* Cambridge: MIT Press, 352 pp.

UNAY, S. (2006), *Neoliberal Globalization and Institutional Reform: The Political Economy of Development Planning in Turkey.* New York: Nova Sciences Publishers, 221 pp.

WEIKER, W. (1973), *Political Tutelage and Democracy in Turkey.* Netherlands: E.J. Brill, 323 pp.

Articles in Texts

AHMAD, F. (1993), "Military Intervention, Institutional Restructuring and Ideological Politics, 1960-1971". In: Ahmad, F. (ed.). *The Making of Modern Turkey.* London, New York: Routledge, Taylor and Francis Group, pp. 148-180

ATAC, O. A. and AYDIN, N. (1990), "International Business Climate in Turkey". In: Kirpalani, V. H. (ed.). *International Business Handbook.* New York: Haworth Press Inc., pp. 539-574

ATIYAS, I. and DOGAN, P. (2010), "Glass Half Empty? Politics and Institutions in the Liberalization of the Fixed Line Telecommunications in Turkey". In: Cetin, T. and Yilmaz, F. (eds.). *Understanding the Process of Economic Change in Turkey: An Institutional Approach.* New York: Nova Science Publishers, pp. 261-283

CELASUN, M. (1994), "Trade and Industrialization in Turkey: Initial Conditions, Policy and Performance in the 1980s". In: HELLEINER, G. K. (ed.). *Trade Policy and Industrialization in Turbulent Times.* London: Routledge, pp. 453-481

CELASUN, M. and ARSLAN, I. (2001), "State-Owned Enterprises and Privatization in Turkey – Policy Performance and Reform Experience, 1985-1995". In: CELASUN, M. and ARSLAN, I. (eds.). *State-Owned Enterprises in the Middle-East and North Africa-Privatization Performance and Reform.* New York: Routledge, pp. 141-176

CETINSAYA, G. (2007), "A Tale of Two Centuries: Continuities in Turkish Foreign and Security Policy". In: GUNEY, N.A. (ed.). *Contentious Issues of Security and the Future of Turkey.* Hampshire: Ashgate, pp. 5-18

DEPORTER, B. (1999), "Regulation of Natural Monopoly". In: BOUCKAERT, B. and DE GEEST, G. (eds.), *Encyclopedia of Law and Economics,* Vol.3. Northampton, Mass: Edward Elgar, pp. 845-865

DIMAGGIO, P. and POWELL, W, (1991) "The Iron Cage Revisited: Institutional Isomorphism and Collective Rationality". In: POWELL, W and DIMAGGIO, P., (eds.). *New Institutionalism in Organizational Analysis.* Chicago: University of Chicago Press, pp. 63-81

DOLLAR, D. and DRIEMEIER, M. H. (2000), "Crisis, Adjustment and Reforms in Thailand's Industrial Firms". In: DEVARAJAN, S. (ed.). *The World Bank Research Observer,* Vol 15(1). Oxford: Oxford University Press, pp. 2-21

DUTZ, M., US, M. and YILMAZ, K. (2005), "Turkey's Foreign Direct Investment Challenges: Competition, the Rule of Law and EU Accession". In: Hoekman, B. M. and Togan, S. (eds.). *Turkey: Economic Reform and Accession to the European Union.* Washington: A co-publication of the World Bank and the Center for Economic Policy Research, pp. 261-294

EDWARDS, S. and SANTAELLA, J. (1993), "Devaluation Controversies in the Developing Countries: Lessons from the Bretton-Woods Era". In: BORDO, M. D. and EICHENGREEN, B. (ed.). *A Retrospective on the Bretton Woods System: Lessons for International Monetary Reform.* Chicago: University of Chicago Press, pp. 405-460

EVIN, A. O. (2006), "From Ozal to the Present Day". In: Mc Carthy, J. T. (ed.). *Federal Trust.* London: Tauris. 185 pp.

FINE, B. (1998), "Neither the Washington nor the Post-Washington Consensus: an Introduction". In: FINE, B., LAPAVITSAS, C. AND PINCUS, J. (eds.). *Development Policy in the Twenty-First Century, Beyond the Post-Washington Consensus.* London: Routledge, pp. 1-18

GIESECKE, K. (2003), "Credit Risk Modeling and Valuation: An Introduction". In: SHIMKO, D. (ed.). *Credit Risk: Models and Management,* Vol. 2. London: Riskbooks, pp. 487-524

GILARDI, F. (2008), "Delegation to Independent Regulatory Agencies: Credibility, Political Uncertainty and Veto Players". In: GILARDI, F. (ed.). *Delegation in the Regulatory State.* Massachusetts: Edward Elgar Publishing, pp. 28-54

GURAN, M. C. (2011), "The Political Economy of Privatization in Turkey: An Evaluation". In: CETIN, T. and OGUZ, F. (eds.). *The Political Economy of Regulation in Turkey.* New York: Springer, pp. 23-34

HAYEK, F. A. (1945), "Use of Knowledge in Society". In: HAYEK, F. A. (ed.). *Individualism and Economic Order.* Chicago: University of Chicago Press, pp. 77-91

KALAYCIOGLU, E. (2002), "The Motherland Party: The Challenge of Institutionalization in a Charismatic Leader Party". In: RUBBIN, B. and HEPER, M. (eds.). *Political Parties in Turkey.* London: Frank Cass Publishers, pp. 41-50

KAWAI, H. and URATA, S. (2003), "Competitiveness and Technology: an International Comparison". In: LALL, S. and URATA, S. (eds.). *Competitiveness FDI and Technological Activity in East Asia.* Massachusetts: Edward Elgar Publishing, pp. 57-79

LEIJONHUFVUD, A. (1997), "The Wicksellian Heritage". In: *Economic Notes,* Vol. 26(1), pp. 1-7

MAJONE, G. (1994), "The Rise of the Regulatory State in Europe". In: MULLER, W. C. and WRIGHT, V. (eds.). *The State in Western Europe, Retreat or Redefinition?.* London: Frank Cass Publishers, pp. 77-98

MASCIANDRO, D. and TABELLINI, G. (1988), Monetary Regimes and Fiscal Deficits: A Comparative Analysis". In: Cheng, H.S. (ed.). *Monetary Policy in Pacific Basin Countries.* Dordrecht: Kluwer Academic Publishers, pp. 1-44

MINSKY, H. P. (1992), "The Financial Instability Hypothesis". In: ARESTIS, P. and SAWYER, M. (eds.). *Handbook of Radical Political Economy.* Aldershot: Edward Elgar Publishing, pp. 1-8

ONIS, Z. (2002), "Post-War Development Performance of the Turkish Economy: A Political Economy Perspective". In: KOLLIAS, C. and GUNLUK-SENESEN, G. (eds.). *Greece and Turkey in the 21st Century: Conflict or Cooperation?* New York: Nova Science Publishers, pp. 1-33

OZDEMIR, H. (2000), "Turkish-American Relations toward 1960-Turkish Revolution". In: UZGEL, I., AKDEVELIOGLU, A. and YESILYURT, N. (eds.). *The Turkish Yearbook of International Relations,* Vol. 31. Ankara: Ankara University Press, pp. 159-181

PAZARBASIOGLU, C. (2005), "Accession to the European Union: Potential Impacts on the Turkish Banking Sector". In: HOEKMAN, B. M. and TOGAN, S. (eds.). *Turkey: Economic Reforms and Accession to the European Union.* Washington: World Bank and Center for Economic Policy Research Publication, pp. 161-185

USLU, N. (2003), "The Military Coup in Cyprus, the Turkish Military Intervention in the Island and the American Reaction (June-July 1974)". In: USLU, N. (ed.). *The Cyprus Question as an Issue of Turkish Foreign Policy and Turkish American Relations 1959-2003.* New York: Nova Science Publishers, pp. 115-138

WILLIAMSON, J. (1990), "What Washington Means by Policy Reform". In: WILLIAMSON, J. (ed.). *Latin American Adjustment: How Much Has Happened?* Washington D. C.: Peterson Institute for International Economics, pp. 1-12

ZURCHER, E. J. (2004), The Third Republic: Turkey since 1980". In: ZURCHER, E. J. (ed.). *Turkey.* London: Tauris Publication, pp. 278-337

Official Documents

BASEL COMMITTEE ON BANKING SUPERVISION (2000), "Banks' Interactions with Highly Leveraged Institutions: Implementation of the Basel Committee's Sound Practices Paper Basel Committee on Banking Supervision", *Working Group Paper,* pp. 1-11

BRSA (2002), "Banking Sector Restructuring Program", *Progress Report - V,* pp. 1-49

BRSA (2003), "Banking Sector Restructuring Program", *Progress Report - VI*, pp. 1-104

BRSA (2009), "Structural Developments in Banking", *Issue 4*, pp. 1-110

BRSA (2010), "From Crisis to Financial Stability (Turkish Experience), *Banking Regulation and Supervision Agency (BRSA) Working Paper, Revised Third Edition*, pp. 1-98

CENTRAL BANK OF THE REPUBLIC OF TURKEY (2002a), "Methodological Note on Money and Banking Statistics", pp. 1-12

CENTRAL BANK OF THE REPUBLIC OF TURKEY (2002b), *The Impact of Globalization on the Turkish Economy.* Ankara: Banknote Printing Plant Department, 113 pp.

CENTRAL BANK OF THE REPUBLIC OF TURKEY (2005), "General Framework of Inflation Targeting Regime and Monetary and Exchange Rate Policy for 2006", *CBRT Working Paper No. 45*, pp. 1-30

CENTRAL BANK OF THE REPUBLIC OF TURKEY (2007), "Financial Security and Stability-Measuring and Fostering the Progress of Societies: the OECD World Forum on Statistics, Knowledge and Policy", *the Istanbul Presentation of the Governor Durmus Yilmaz*, pp. 1-7

COMMISSION OF THE EUROPEAN COMMUNITIES (1998), "Regular Report on Turkey-Progress towards Accession", pp. 1-57

COMMISSION OF THE EUROPEAN COMMUNITIES (1999), "Regular Report on Turkey's Progress towards Accession", pp. 1-58

COMMISSION OF THE EUROPEAN COMMUNITIES (2000), "Regular Report on Turkey-Progress towards Accession", pp. 1-82

COMMISSION OF THE EUROPEAN COMMUNITIES (2001), "Regular Report on Turkey's Progress towards Accession", pp. 1-123

COMMISSION OF THE EUROPEAN COMMUNITIES (2002), "Regular Report on Turkey's Progress towards Accession", pp. 1-160

COMMISSION OF THE EUROPEAN COMMUNITIES (2003), "Regular Report on Turkey's Progress towards Accession", pp. 1-80

COMMISSION OF THE EUROPEAN COMMUNITIES (2004), "Regular Report on Turkey's Progress towards Accession", pp. 1-187

COMMISSION OF THE EUROPEAN COMMUNITIES (2005), "Regular Report on Turkey's Progress towards Accession", pp. 1-121

COMMISSION OF THE EUROPEAN COMMUNITIES (2006), "Regular Report on Turkey's Progress towards Accession", pp. 1-81

COMMISSION OF THE EUROPEAN COMMUNITIES (2008), "Regular Report on Turkey's Progress towards Accession", pp. 1-89

COMMISSION OF THE EUROPEAN COMMUNITIES (2009), "Institution Building in the Framework of European Union Policies Common Twinning Manual", pp. 1-120

COMMISSION OF THE EUROPEAN COMMUNITIES (2011), "Regular Report on Turkey's Progress towards Accession", pp. 1-116

COMMISSION OF THE EUROPEAN COMMUNITIES (2006), "Regulation (EC) No. 139/2004, Merger Procedure, Case No. 4'085, ARCELOR/OYAK/ERDEMIR", pp. 1-9

COMMISSION OF THE EUROPEAN COMMUNITIES (2000), *Glossary: Institutions, Policies and Enlargement of the European Union.* Luxembourg: Office for Official Publications of the European Communities, 79 pp.

COMPETITION AUTHORITY (1994), "Law on the Protection of Competition – Law No. 4'054", *Official Gazette No. 22140,* pp. 1-23

COUNCIL OF THE EUROPEN UNION (2003), pp. 1-65

EC-TURKEY ASSOCIATION COUNCIL (1995), "Decision of the EC-Turkey Association Council on Implementing the Final Phase of the Customs Union", pp. 1-61

EUROPEAN UNION (2006), "European Union, Consolidated Versions of the Treaty of European Union and of the Treaty Establishing the European Community", *Official Journal of the European Union*, pp. 1-331

FIAS (2001), "Administrative Barriers to Investment", pp. 1-219

FITCH RATINGS (2010a), "Definitions of Ratings and Other Forms of Opinion", pp. 1-51

FITCH RATINGS (2010b), "Sovereign Ratings Methodology", pp. 1-17

IMF (2002), *International Financial Statistics Yearbook, Vol. 54.* Washington D. C.: IMF Publication Services, 1077 pp.

IMF (2003), *External Debt Statistics-Guide for Compliers and Users,* Washington D. C.: IMF Publication Services, 309 pp.

IMF (2009), *Balance of Payments and International Investment Position Manual, Sixth Edition (BPM6),* Washington D. C.: IMF Publication Services, 371 pp.

IMF and OECD (2003), *Foreign Direct Investment Statistics, How Countries Measure FDI – 2001,* Washington D.C.: IMF Publication Services, 169 pp.

INTERNATIONAL INVESTORS ASSOCIATION (2011), "Current Account Deficits in Turkey: Macro and Micro Reasons and Suggested Solutions", *YASED Economic Research and Policies Working Group Report,* 44 pp.

LAW ON THE PROTECTION OF COMPETITION (1994). Ankara: Published in Official Gazzette No. 22'140, dated December 13th, 1994, 23 pp.

OECD (2001), *Economic Surveys – Turkey.* Paris: OECD Publications Service, 207 pp.

OECD (2008), *Benchmark Definition of Foreign Direct Investment, Fourth Edition,* Paris: OECD Publishing, 254 pp.

OECD (2008a), *Measuring Regulatory Quality, Policy Brief.* Paris: OECD Public Affairs Communications and Directorate, 8 pp.

OECD (2008b), *Introductory Handbook for Undertaking Regulatory Impact Analysis.* Paris: OECD-FIAS World Bank Group Publications, 27 pp.

OFFICIAL JOURNAL OF THE EUROPEAN UNION (2012a), "Consolidated Version of the Treaty on European Union and the Treaty on the Functioning of the European Union". In: *Information and Notices, C 326, Vol. 55,* pp. 1-390, *http://eur-lex.europa.eu/LexUriServ/LexUriServ.do?uri=OJ:C:2012:326:FULL:EN:PDF*

OFFICIAL JOURNAL OF THE EUROPEAN UNION (2012b), "Regulation No. 236 of the European Parliament and of the Council of 14 March 2012 on short selling and certain aspects of credit default swaps", http://eurlex.europa.eu/LexUriServ/LexUriServ.do?uri=OJ:L:2012:086:0001:0024:en:PDF, pp. 1-24

REPUBLIC OF TURKEY (1993), "Trade Policy Review Mechanism", *Government Report No. 2123,* pp. 1-214

REPUBLIC OF TURKEY (2001), "Turkish National Program for the Adoption of the *Acquis*", pp. 1-317

REPUBLIC OF TURKEY (2002), "Pre-Accession Economic Programme 2002", pp. 1-104

STATE PLANNING ORGANIZATION (1979), *Fourth Five-Year Development Program 1979-1983,* (in Turkish). Ankara: State Planning Organization Publication, No. 1664, 699 pp.

STATE PLANNING ORGANIZATION (2003), *Accession Partnership with Turkey.* Ankara: State Planning Organization Publication, pp. 1-26

TURKISH STATISTICAL INSTITUTE (2009), *Statistical Indicators 1923-2008.* Ankara: Turkish Statistical Institute Printing Division, 768 pp.

UNDERSECRETARIAT OF TREASURY (2009), "Public Debt Management Report 2009", 90 pp.

UNDESECRETARIAT OF TREASURY (2009a), "Investment Advisory Council for Turkey-Progress Report", pp. 1-108

UNDERSECRETARIAT OF TREASURY (2011), "Public Debt Management Report 2011", 90 pp.

US PRESIDENT'S WORKING GROUP ON FINANCIAL MARKETS (1999), "Hedge Funds, Leverage, and the Lessons of Long-Term Capital Management", pp. 1-42

WORLD BANK (2010), *Regulatory Quality Indicators.* Washington: World Bank Group, 50 pp.

Web Sites

BANK OF GREECE, *Statistical Indicators,* http://sdw.ecb.europa.eu/ (consulted on June 11th, 2011)

BANK OF THAILAND, *Data on debt, international reserves, budget balance, foreign liabilities of banking sector,* http://www2.bot.or.th/statistics/ReportPage.aspx?reportID=81&language=eng, (consulted on January, 12th, 2011)

CAPITAL MARKETS BOARD IN TURKEY, http://www.cmb.gov.tr/indexcont.aspx?action=showpage&menuid=0&pid=0&submenuheader=-1 (consulted on February 6th, 2011)

CENTRAL BANK OF TURKEY, *Price Stability – Law No. 4'651 of April 25th, 2001,* http://www.tcmb.gov.tr/yeni/ppyeni_eng/pricestability.html (consulted on January 8th, 2012)

EU BUSINESS. *Markets in Financial Instruments Directive* (2007), http://www.eubusiness.com/topics/finance/mifid-guide/ (consulted on August 27th, 2011)

EUROPEAN COMMISSION, http://ec.europa.eu/ enlargement/policy/conditions-membership/index_en.htm, (consulted on February 16th, 2013)

EUROPEAN COMMISSION, http://ec.europa.eu/ enlargement/policy/conditions-membership/chapters-of-the-acquis/index_en.htm, (consulted on February 18th, 2013)

EU HARMONIZATION COMMITTEE IN THE TURKISH PARLIAMENT, http://www.tbmm.gov.tr/komisyon/abuyum/index_eng.htm , (consulted on June 29th, 2011)

EUROPOLITICS, http://www.europolitics.Info/sectoral-policies/eu-agrees-permanent-ban-on-naked-cds-artb316036-1.html (consulted on 9th November 2011)

GENERAL DIRECTORATE OF BUDGET AND FISCAL CONTROL, http://www.bumko.gov.tr/TR/Genel/Default.aspx?F6E10F88924 33CFFAAF6AA849816B2EFCAC44E48D9FD67C0 (consulted on March 9th, 2012)

GENERAL SECRETARIAT FOR EU AFFAIRS, PRIME MINISTRY-REPUBLIC OF TURKEY, http://www.abgs.gov.tr/ index.php? p=117&l=2 (consulted on February 28th, 2011)

GRAND NATIONAL ASSEMBLY OF TURKEY, http://www.tbmm.gov.tr/ komisyon/abuyum/act_on.htm (consulted on 26th August 2011).

HURRIYET DAILY NEWS. March 15th, 2011, http:// www. Hurriyetdailynews.com/n.php?n=political-repression-lays-ground-for-economic-liberalization-2011-03-15 (consulted on November 19th, 2011)

IMF (1995), *Request by the Turkish government and Approval of six months' extension to the 1994 Stand-by Agreement,* http://www.imf.org/external/np/sec/nb/1995/nb9507.htm http://www.imf.org/external/np/sec/pr/1995/pr9526.htm (consulted on December 7th, 2011)

IMF STAFF MONITORING PROGRAM, *Memorandum of Economic Policies dated June 26th, 1998,* http://www.imf.org/external/ np/loi/062698.htm, (consulted on December 4th, 2011)

IMF (1999), *Strengthening the Banking System and Banking Regulation (Sections 1-64).* In: *Letter of Intent* dated 9th December 1999, submitted to the IMF, http://www.imf.org/external/np/loi/ 1999/120999.htm (consulted on March 11th, 2011)

IMF (2000), *Monetary and Exchange Rate Policies (Section 30).* In: *Letter of Intent* dated 18th December 2000, submitted to the IMF, http://www.imf.org/external/np/loi/2000/tur/03/index.htm (consulted on 10th August 2011)

IMF (2001), In: *Letter of Intent,* dated 3rd May 2001, submitted to the IMF, http://www.imf.org/external/np/loi/2001/tur/02/index.htm, (consulted on 7th January 2011)

INSPIRE – EUROPEAN COMMISSION, http://inspire.jrc.ec.europa.eu/ , (consulted on 22nd January 2012)

INTERNATIONAL CONSTITUTIONAL LAW, http://www.servat.unibe.ch/icl/info.html, (consulted on 30th August 2011)

INTER-PARLIAMENTARY UNION (IPU), http://www.ipu.org/english/home.htm, (consulted on 18th July 2012)

IS BANK (Turkiye Is Bankasi), *Investment Services, Treasury Bill and Government Bond,* http://www.isbank.com.tr/English/content/EN/Expatriate_Banking/Investment_Services/Treasury_Bill_and_Government_Bond-1042-413.aspx (consulted on 7th December 2011)

ISDA (INTERNATIONAL SWAPS AND DERIVATIVES ASSOCIATION), http://www.isdacdsmarketplace.com/exposures_and_activity/top_10_cds_positions, (consulted on 2nd September 2011)

MOODY'S, *Investors Service,* http://www.moodys.com/research/MOODYS-CHANGES-THE-OUTLOOK-ON-TURKEYS-COUNTRY-CEILINGS-TO-POSITIVE--PRM_19991130135437 (consulted on December 5th, 2011)

OFFICIAL JOURNAL OF THE EUROPEAN UNION, *Official Journal of the European Union (2006)* http://eur-lex.europa.eu/JOIndex.do (consulted on 9th March 2011)

REPUBLIC OF TURKEY, MINISTRY OF FOREIGN AFFAIRS, *Ankara Agreement,* http://www.abgs.gov.tr/index.php?p=117&l=2 (consulted on December 30th, 2011)

REPUBLIC OF TURKEY, MINISTRY OF FOREIGN AFFAIRS, Section 7. *The Luxembourg European Council and the Following Period, Turkey-EU Relations, Post-Helsinki Phase,* http://www.abgs.gov.tr/index.php?p=111&l=2 (consulted on January 7th, 2011)

SAVING DEPOSIT INSURANCE FUND IN TURKEY, http://www.tmsf.org.tr (consulted on February 6th, 2011)

STATE PLANNING ORGANIZATION OF TURKEY, *Official data*, State Planning Organization (consulted on February 1st, 2011)

THE ATLANTIC (December 11th, 2012), http://www.theatlantic.com/international/archive/2012/12/why-turkey-cant-be-a-model-for-the-future-of-the-arab-spring/266116/ (consulted on March 18th, 2013)

TODAY'S ZAMAN (26th November 2009), *Barriers to be Lifted on Foreign Firms in Public Procurement Tenders*,

http://www.todayszaman.com/news-194003-barriers-to-be-lifted-on-foreign-firms-in-public-procurement-tenders.html, (consulted on 19th August 2011)

TODAY'S ZAMAN (2nd January 2012), *New IMKB President assumes office*, http://www.todayszaman.com/newsDetail_getNewsById.action?newsId=267459, (consulted on 26th January 2012).

TURKISH COMPETITION AUTHORITY, http://www.rekabet.gov.tr/index.php?Lang=EN, (consulted on 18th July 2012)

TURKISH PATENT INSTITUTE, http://www.turkpatent.gov.tr/portal/default_en.jsp?sayfa=161&haber=925 (consulted on 31st August 2011)

TURKISH STATISTICAL INSTITUTE (TUIK), www.turkstat.gov.tr/Start.do;jsessionid=11HCYNpTnvj4QCCVQ2x7cmZ4pVgjDnK7hJz20w5xZFXKKnhxYJw6!-1351923751 , (consulted on 11th December 2016)

UNDERSECRETARIAT OF TREASURY (2003), *FDI Law No. 6'224*, http://www.treasury.gov.tr/irj/go/km/docs/documents/Treasury%20Web/Legislation/Foreign%20Direct%20Investment%20Legislation/About%20the%20New%20Foreign%20Direct%20Investment%20Law.pdf (consulted on 16th January 2012)

YOIKK, *European Union Twinning Project for Turkey*, http://www.yoikk.gov.tr/eng/yoikk/30 (consulted on 18th January 2011)

WORLD BANK, *Data from "indicators", "military expenditures",* http://data.worldbank.org/indicator/MS.MIL.XPND.GD.ZS/countries/1W?page=1&display=default (consulted on 26th December 2011)

WORLD TRADE ORGANIZATION, General Agreement on Tariffs and Trade 1994, http://www.wto.org/english/res_e/booksp_e/analytic_index_e/gatt1994_09_e.htm, (consulted on 29th November 2012)

Articles on online journals

CUCURU, S., VEGA, C. and HOEK, J. (2010), "Measuring Carry Trade Activity". In: *Irving Fischer Committee on Central Bank Statistics Bulletin No. 34, Initiatives to address data gaps revealed by the financial crisis,* No. 34, pp. 436-453. http://www.bis.org/ifc/publ/ifcb34.pdf (consulted on April 8th, 2012)

DELATTE, A. N. (2012), "The European Ban on Naked Sovereign Credit Default Swaps: A Fake Good Idea". In: *VOX/Research-based Policy Analysis and Commentary from Leading Economists,* http://www.voxeu.org/article/european-ban-naked-sovereign-credit-default-swaps-fake-good-idea

HAMMER, P. L., KOGAN, A., and LEJEUNE, M. A. (2007), "Reverse-Engineering Country Risk Ratings: A Combinatorial Non-Recursive Model". In: *Social Science Research Network,* 2007, pp. 1-30 *http://papers.ssrn.com/sol3/papers.cfm?abstract_id=975564* (consulted on 1st December 2013)

Index

www.ingramcontent.com/pod-product-compliance
Lightning Source LLC
LaVergne TN
LVHW010723210926
848485LV00007B/1432/J
* 9 7 8 1 6 2 2 7 3 1 6 8 8 *